THE ALBERNIS
1860–1922

THE ALBERNIS

1860-1922

Jan Peterson

1992

oolichan books

Lantzville, British Columbia

ISBN 0-88982-119-4   hardcover
ISBN 0-88982-118-6   paperbound

Canadian Cataloguing in Publication Data

Peterson, Jan, 1937-
   The Albernis, 1860-1922

   Includes bibliographical references and index.
   ISBN 0-88982-119-4 (bound). –
   ISBN 0-88982-118-6 (pbk.)

   1. Port Alberni (B.C.) – History. 2.
Alberni (B.C.) – History. I. Title.
FC3849.P56P48 1992   971.1′2   C92-091685-6
F1089.5.P56P48 1992

First printing October 1992
Second printing November 1992

Publication of this book has been financially assisted by The Canada Council and by the Province of British Columbia through the British Columbia Heritage Trust.

All the author's royalties from this book will be donated to the Alberni District historical Society.

Published by
Oolichan Books
Box 10, Lantzville
British Columbia, Canada V0R 2H0

Printed in Canada by
Morriss Printing Company Ltd.
Victoria, British Columbia

Acknowledgements

Over the past four years, the history of the Alberni Valley has been my constant companion since illness forced my early retirement as a journalist in 1987. A year later, unable to walk any distance and with little or no voice, I approached the Alberni District Historical Society Archives with the idea of researching the early history of the area. With their boundless enthusiasm and support, the Society Archival volunteers took me under their wing and pointed me in the right direction, and the result is between these pages.

Through my research I got to know many of the pioneer settlers, sharing their lives, their hopes, and their dreams in diaries, manuscripts, and other writings. I became so immersed in their stories that I felt happiness, sadness, optimism, and sometimes despair as I witnessed their struggle with life in what was then a remote part of Vancouver Island. The story of the Albernis could not have been told without them. Many of their descendants who continue to live in the Alberni Valley also made valuable contributions.

In this journey in history, I would be remiss if I did not mention several people who made the road a little easier. My special thanks to Dorrit MacLeod, who became my friend and travelling companion and a source of inspiration. Her knowledge of the area was a great asset in verifying names, locations, and events. My thanks also to Helen Ford, who carefully scrutinized the manuscript, and to my friend and fellow scribe, Rob Diotte, whose editorial expertise I valued and whose confidence in this project remained steadfast. Also my special thanks to the ADHS Archives workshop volunteers, who spend countless hours preserving, documenting, researching, and collecting community paper treasures. The contribution and support of Jean McIntosh and Lillian Weedmark of the Alberni Valley Museum cannot be overestimated. They totally believed in my ability to write this history. The staff of the Vancouver Island Regional Library, Port Alberni Branch, and the staff of both the provincial and national archives were also very helpful. I am especially grateful to Oolichan Books, who took a chance on an unknown author, and to editor Rhonda Bailey, who skillfully brought the book to publication.

My thanks to those I interviewed and consulted during the course of the research: Faye and Frank Flitton, Gilbert Renwick, Mrs. James E. Sidey, Tseshaht Chief Adam Shewish (now deceased), Opetchesaht Chief Hughie Watts, Harold E. Warren, Fred Bishop, Mary Wood, Lila McKenzie, Al West, Dr. Harry Webster, Joe Stanhope, Belle Sherwood, Lois Abbott, G. Smedley Andrews, Gus Jonasson, Kate Glover (Vancouver Fisheries Office), Simo Nurme (North Island College), Ms. Kieko (Japanese Consulate, Vancouver), Kathie Smith (B.C. Telephone), Kathy Minorgan (Archivist, Royal Bank of Canada, Montreal), George Wiley (Port Alberni City Clerk), Department of Fisheries, Port Alberni branch, Shirley Grad-Scrutton (B.C. Packers Ltd.).

My special thanks to my husband Ray, and children Karen, John, and Craig, who, knowing my physical limitations, were always there to offer help and encouragement.

Author's Note

Throughout this book I have used the word "Inlet" in reference to Alberni Inlet, except in direct quotations where "Alberni Canal" is used. The name was changed in 1931 to clarify that this was not a manmade waterway in the English sense of the word "canal." The ambiguity had led to some misunderstandings by ship captains who came prepared to pay a levy of canal-dues for their passage. I have also used the modern day spelling of Barkley Sound throughout the text, except in direct quotations where the old spelling "Barclay Sound" appears. Other spelling changes that should be noted are the names of the two Alberni Nootka tribes, which have changed over the years. The tribes now prefer to use the spelling "Tseshaht" and "Opetchesaht." There are different spellings of each used in direct quotations throughout the text.

CONTENTS

CHAPTER ONE

1860–1892

LAND OF THE NOOTKA

The Alberni Valley is located in the centre of Vancouver Island, at the head of the Alberni Inlet, forty-eight kilometres from the Pacific Ocean. The Beaufort Range on the north and the main Vancouver Island Range ring the valley below. Forests thick with Douglas fir, hemlock, and red and yellow cedar cover the mountains. Mount Arrowsmith, 1817 metres high, dominates the landscape. Two long, narrow lakes, Great Central Lake and Sproat Lake, lie to the west of the valley and feed into the Stamp and Sproat Rivers, which join to become the Somass River before entering into the head of the Alberni Inlet.

The valley is a hunting and fishing paradise. Salmon run in almost every stream that enters the Inlet. Elk, deer, black bear, mountain lions, wolves, raccoon, mink, and beaver roam the valley and surrounding mountains. Geese, ducks, and Trumpeter Swans use the Somass River delta as a favourite resting place.

Before the arrival of the white man, the Alberni Valley was home to two of the west coast Nootkan tribes, the Opetchesaht and the Tseshaht. The Opetchesaht, the original occupants, lived in the areas around Sproat and Great Central Lake, spending time in the island's interior hunting deer and elk. During the 19th century they participated in the seal and dogfish oil trade. Hunting excursions occasionally took them to the east coast of Vancouver Island where they made contact with their Coast Salish neighbours. It wasn't until the European settlement in 1860 that the tribes moved down to the Somass River and established their present village of Ahahswinis No. 1 on River Road.[1]

9

The Tseshaht, the largest of the two groups, lived in the Alberni Valley only during the fall and early winter, spending the rest of the year at sites along the Alberni Inlet and Barkley Sound, at Rainy Bay, Ecoole, Nettle Island, Keith Island, Dodd Island, and Effingham Island. Since there were no large salmon spawning rivers in their Barkley Sound territory, they moved to the lower Somass River where there was an abundance of fish.

There are many legends associated with both tribes, each handed down from one generation to another by word of mouth. Hereditary Chief of the Tseshaht, Adam Shewish, told of a time when there was a big flood all along the west coast "in Noah's time." He said, "The tribe retreated to a mountain where they stayed until the flood subsided. The Tseshaht mountain is where the whaling station is. Each tribe had its own place. Some got into canoes and drifted to Cape Flattery. This is the reason the tribes on the west coast and those in Washington State are able to communicate with language." On a wall in Chief Shewish's living room is a drawing of a thirteen generation family crest which was painted on the house front of his ancestral home on Effingham Island.

The west coast people lived a simple life concerned only with their territory and their immediate neighbours. It was a society in which all members of each social group were ranked in order, from top to bottom, with the highest ranking individuals being the leading chiefs.

Feasting was one of life's great pleasures. Along with the food came entertainment. The Potlatch, which means "to give," was one of the more spectacular aspects of their social life. Its prime purpose was to transfer a chief's privileges to his children. At various periods of their lives he gave a potlatch in a child's honour to announce that he or she was assuming a new name and new rights. Other reasons for the celebration were life milestones: birth, puberty, marriage, and death.[2]

In the Alberni Valley evidence was uncovered in the Shoemaker Dig (1982) which showed native people occupied the Alberni Valley for more than 4000 years. The advent of Nootkan culture was relatively recent.[3]

Gilbert M. Sproat, the Agent-General of British Columbia, described in his journal (1868), an old Opetchesaht hunter named Quicheenam, fifty-five years of age, who was "a most influential chief" and "with his whole family was accustomed to go every summer for the purpose of shooting elk and deer on a large rocky mountain. The hunter and his sons killed many elk and deer every season.

10

As the animals were too heavy to be removed any distance, they cut the flesh into long strips, which they dried in the smoke and carried in bags to their village." [4]

The Tseshaht have a legend that describes a tribe of women, occupying a village at the mouth of the Somass River, who transformed themselves into swans and flew off at the approach of the Tseshaht. "An Opetchesaht band member has stated that the Tseshaht acquired their Somass territory by moving in when the Opetchesaht men were away fighting the Comox and only the women and children were left in the area."[5]

Fishing for salmon has always been important to the Tseshaht. One of the band's favourite fishing locations was Macktush Creek, a few miles down the Inlet. Sometimes torches were used to attract fish when night fishing with harpoons.[6] By the end of November when the main spawning runs were over, the Tseshaht congregated at Lupsi Cupsi, the main winter village and present site of the MacMillan Bloedel Ltd. Alberni Pulp and Paper mill, at the mouth of the Somass River.

Sproat Lake was also popular for hunting and fishing. Temporary camps were established at the lake, at Faber Point, at Arbutus Island, and at the site of Klitsa Lodge. An island known to the tribes as Chauk, now recognized as Massacre Island, opposite Bishop's Landing, was used as a refuge. It later became a battleground. Dr. George Clutesi, a respected member of the Tseshaht band, told the story of Chauk Island. No exact date of the massacre is known.

The Opitchesaht made their summer home at Kleecoot, Sproat Lake. They were constantly harassed by bands from the East Coast of Vancouver Island, who crossed over the Beaufort Range for the purpose of conquering them and thereby obtaining their priceless hunting and fishing sites. Much of the warfare took place at Sproat Falls where the band lived during the salmon season. Hence the Chief thought it advisable to move his household to a safer place, the place chosen being Chauk. The belief that all the band moved to this island is erroneous.

After the Chief had moved his household to the island, the enemy learned of the Chief's new home. The enemy then straightway planned to launch a surprise attack on the island. One lonely night by the light of the moon, the Chief's household was rudely awakened and thrown into a turmoil, the enemy had reached the shores of the little island by means of crudely made rafts of driftwood picked up on the beach.

The small number of warriors on the island took up their arms and there ensured a bloody battle. The Opitchesahts were greatly outnumbered, their women and children were massacred, they could not spare one man to go for help, each man must fight to his last breath. "Do we not hold what advantageous position this small island affords?" said the Chief to spur his men on, "then fight!" he roared.

Stone axes clashed against tomahawks, bashed in skulls. The dead and the dying soon covered the island, the enemy were subsequently routed. They attempted a hasty retreat. The natives saw this and with bloodcurdling whoops and yells pressed the attack. The slowly moving heads in the moonlit waters made ideal targets for the warriors and very few of the swimming enemy reached home. Those few braves of Chauk who survived returned home, that is to the main reserve at Sproat Falls, to tell a very sorrowful tale. Thus the fishing and hunting areas in the district remain in the possession of the Opitchesahts.[7]

The Explorers

The west coast of Vancouver Island remained isolated and unknown on world maps until the 1770s. The Russians had reached this continent from Asia by 1741, establishing what is now Alaska. The British were advancing westward across North America. Spain, recognizing a threat to her claim of the whole western coast, set up at San Blas in Mexico a base of operations for an exploration northward.

In 1773 Spanish authorities instructed Spanish viceroy Antonio Bucareli in Mexico City to organize an expedition to the northwest coast. A ship was especially built for the expedition and was launched in October 1773. The frigate was christened the *Santiago*.

The *Santiago* was the largest ship ever to have been built in San Blas. The length on the main deck was over eighty-four feet; its width over twenty-six feet. The main topgallant mast was 102 feet above the water. It had two continuous decks, two partial decks above the second deck, a forecastle deck and a quarterdeck. The ship carried four bronze four-pounder cannons.

Under Juan Perez, the ship left San Blas in January 24, 1774, with ninety-five crew members. Two priests accompanied the expedition. They were Father Tomas de la Pena y Saravia and Father Juan Crespi. Both kept written accounts of the voyage. The crew sighted snow-covered peaks on July 18. Two days later the *Santiago* anchored near the Queen Charlotte Islands. At first the natives (Haidas) were hesitant at approaching the ship. Later they overcame their fears and exchanged beads for dried fish.

The next day twenty-one canoes appeared. More trading took place between the two groups.

Continuing on the expedition, the ship next anchored on August 8, offshore at the entrance to Nootka Sound. During the voyage a cross had been constructed with the hope of erecting it to signify formal possession of the area. The ship's launch was lowered with the cross and the two priests, who planned to conduct the official ceremony proclaiming the land for Spain. However, when a strong wind blew up and the *Santiago* appeared to be in danger, the launch returned to the ship.

During the ship's brief stay, the Hesquiat Indians came out in canoes, overcoming their fears to go aboard to exchange gifts of abalone shells and knives for otter skins. The Indians had sighted the *Santiago* far out at sea. As they had never seen anything remotely like it before, they at first thought it was a big bird. They watched it coming closer and closer.

Ka-koop-et, a Tseshaht Indian, the "Keeper of the Songs" known locally as Mr. Bill, told the Indian legend of the coming of the white man to local resident George Bird.

> The Indians saw far away at sea, an immense strange-shaped object which at first they took for a huge bird. They had never seen anything floating on the sea except canoes and whales. With eager eyes they all watched. Was it a huge bird with outstretched wings? It moved slowly nearer and nearer, yet it did not make use of its wings to fly as a gull does. No, it could not be a bird!
>
> The mystery grew along with a certain amount of fear in their minds. See, it looked like a floating lodge with immense sails. People seemed to be walking on it, walking on the roof of the house! They seemed to be strange-looking beings. In their small world people were all the same in appearance, and more or less of the same habits and ways of life.
>
> Shyly and cautiously they sent off a few canoes to investigate. Yes, there were real people on the strange creation, but how different from themselves, who all had black hair, dark eyes and copper coloured skins. They had no explanation. They exclaimed, "Mam-ath-ly tum tum," which, freely interpreted, is "wonderful mind." Since the coming of the White man, "Mam-ath-ly" is their name for him." The presentation of apt nicknames is a custom of the native people.[8]

The Spanish did not land, and the ship stayed only a few days. After an outbreak of scurvy among the crew, the *Santiago* returned to home base at San Blas.

Four years later Captain James Cook in the *Resolution*, on his third voyage of exploration, exchanged sea otter skins for knick-knacks. The lush brown pelts were worth more than their weight in gold, and the fate of the native cultures was sealed. Cook discovered a Sound which he named King George's but later changed to Nootka. The Indian village he named Friendly Cove. Cook was credited as being the first white man to set foot on Vancouver Island.

The flamboyant Captain John Meares, flying the Portuguese flag, made his first voyage to the northwest coast in 1787, his next in 1788 and 1789. Formerly a British officer and gentleman, Meares bought land at Friendly Cove from Chief Maquinna, erected some buildings, and set his Chinese craftsmen to work constructing a forty ton sloop named the *North West America*. It was launched in September 1788. He was followed by James Hannah, Charles Barkley, Nathaniel Portlock and George Dixon, John Hendrick and Robert Gray, then a multitude of others.

Spain, recognizing a threat to its Pacific empire by the encroachment of foreigners in what it considered Spanish territory, decided it must establish an outpost at Nootka Sound. In 1789 Esteban Jose Martinez was given the difficult job. Not only did he have to deal with the Nootkan Indians but also the persistent arrival of British, American, and Portuguese trading vessels. His measures included seizure of the *Ifigenia* flying Portuguese colours; the British frigate *Argonaut* and the *North West American*; and the American *Fair American*. However, it was the seizure of the British ships and imprisonment of the British sailors in Mexico that caused a serious international crisis between Spain and Britain. Meares, who partially owned the British ships, charged that Chief Maquinna had acknowledged British sovereignty during his previous visit. Britain threatened war against Spain.

Until this time the Nootkan Indians had been on good terms with the fur traders. They condemned Martinez for his heavy hand in dealing with the visitors. In one unfortunate incident during an argument, Chief Callicum was shot by a Spanish seaman. Martinez was ordered back to San Blas. The fort was abandoned.

In April of the following year Spain made a final attempt at securing another settlement at Nootka, this time under Fransisco de Eliza, a Navy lieutenant. He was accompanied by a small military force.[9] The officer in charge of the force, a lieutenant colonel, was Pedro de Alberni.

Pedro de Alberni was forty-five years of age when he led the Spanish Catalonian troops to Nootka. The Catalan Volunteers, as they were named, were formed in 1767 and were originally to be stationed in Havana, Cuba. But Spanish plans had changed; they were sent to New Spain instead. Their last great adventure was their assignment to the Pacific northwest, under the command of Pedro de Alberni, to establish the fort at Nootka.

Alberni was born January 30, 1747,[10] the son of Jaime de Alberni and Josefa Texedor, natives of Tortosa, Catalonia, Spain. He married Juana Velez of Tepic and they had one daughter. Between the years 1771 and 1788, he served in the garrisons at Guadalajara, in Jalisco, and Mesa Del Tonati, in Nayarit. In 1782 Alberni became commander of the volunteers when Agustin Callis died in Real Del Monte. He had held the rank of Lieutenant since March 1776. Alberni's career had been without lustre. This accidental rise in command in 1782 meant the discovery of an unusually talented man, as his future years would reveal.

Alberni left San Blas for Nootka on February 3, 1790, with eighty Catalonian Volunteers. Their mission was to guard Spanish vessels and re-establish a fort in what is now known as British Columbia. His particular assignment was that of Commandant of Arms and Governor of the Fort of Nootka, a position he held from 1790 to 1792. But it was in tasks incidental to his official duties that Alberni began to show his true worth, distinguishing himself through his own inventiveness.

An imaginative man, the Spanish officer developed good relations with the Indians of Vancouver Island who had before despised and lacked confidence in Spanish diplomacy. He carried out meteorological surveys which added useful information regarding Spanish activities in the area. He conducted agricultural experiments in the region, not only providing food supplements for all mariners who frequented the area, but adding to information on which food plants would grow in the northern climate. He made a study of the Nootkan language, helpful both to Alberni's contemporaries and to present day linguists.

Under Martinez, the Nootkans had suffered threats to one of their principal chiefs, Maquinna, who had been accused of robbery. Martinez had threatened to shoot him. Maquinna had been wronged. Alberni set out to befriend the chief. His plan was to have Maquinna praised and flattered through the native "grapevine." He would release comments about the chief to a Nootka commoner who unwittingly would pass the good word along to the unsuspecting Maquinna. Then all he had to do was sit and wait for Maquinna to hear the praise. Alberni also composed a jingle in the Nootkan dialect with a few of the Nootkan words he knew, praising Maquinna's greatness and friendship. Needless to say, Maquinna was impressed and a friendship was ignited. Alberni was given donations of fish and deer meat by the Nootkans.

Alberni's interest in the natives went beyond mere friendship. During his tour of duty he helped compile an eleven page word list consisting of 633 Nootkan words with their Spanish definitions. The final draft of the dictionary was completed and Alberni was credited with much of the field work.

He trained his soldiers to cultivate his gardens, personally digging trenches for irrigation and raising a number of chickens to supplement their diet. He noted that cabbage, garlic, and onions grew best in summer; lettuce and radishes in the fall; potatoes, beans, and peas grew in abundance, as did carrots and artichokes. He was unsuccessful in growing wheat and maize. The fort at Nootka was complete with livestock, two cows, one bull, and one calf; a goat, lamb, and twenty pigs; plus seventy chickens and four hundred chicks were raised. Alberni's agricultural experiments were given much notice and recognition. He was promoted to Lieutenant Colonel in the Spanish Army.

He was further honoured by Lieutenant Francisco de Eliza in 1791 by having the inlet "Alberni Canale" named after him. No record has been found of Alberni ever having visited the Alberni Valley at the head of the inlet, or ever having come up the inlet.

Even after Alberni left Nootka in 1792 the Indians continued to remember him although they had lost hope of ever seeing him again. He spent the next two years in Guadalajara with his family, continuing with his career as a soldier. Later he was sent to California where he became the highest ranking military figure at the close of the 18th century. He died of dropsy (congestive heart failure) at the age of fifty-seven on March 11, 1802, in Monterey.

Alberni left his mark in Sonora, California, and British Columbia. He had commanded troops in Sonora, Nootka, Nayarit, Guadalajara, Veracruz, San Francisco, Monterey, and Branciforte. Yet only two landmarks survive today to commemorate his presence – the inlet called "Alberni Inlet" and the town at its head called "Port Alberni."[11]

Captain George Vancouver described the Alberni area in his journal in 1792:

> To describe the beauties of this region will, on some future occasion, be a very grateful task to the pen of the skilful panegyrist. The serenity of the climate, the innumerable pleasing landscapes, and the abundant fertility that unassisted nature puts forth require only to be enriched by the industry of man with villages, mansions, cottages and other buildings, to render it the most lovely country that can be imagined, while the labours of the inhabitants would be amply rewarded in the bounties which nature seems ready to bestow on civilization.[12]

In 1795, Don Juan Francisco de la Bodega Y Quadra surrendered the outpost to the British. A few ships continued to come each year until the sea otter pelts had been almost depleted. The fort eventually reverted to the Nootkan Indians.

From about 1820 to 1875 there was little white contact, although in 1850 a brisk trade in dogfish oil developed in connection with the sawmill industry of the northwest. Two years later an epidemic of smallpox made heavy inroads into an already declining population.

Hudson's Bay Company

Vancouver Island remained relatively untouched by the outside world until the Hudson's Bay Company (HBC) arrived March 13, 1843, establishing itself at Fort Victoria. It's Chief Factor, James Douglas, accompanied by fifteen men aboard the *Beaver*, arrived at Victoria Harbour.

Douglas described the new headquarters on the island as, "a perfect 'Eden,' in the midst of the dreary wilderness of the North west coast . . . and so different is its general aspect, from the wooded, rugged regions around, that one might be pardoned for supposing it had dropped from the clouds into its present position."[13]

At this time the colonies of British North America were still scattered and separated, each with its own governor, administration, and customs houses, and each concerned with its own relations with Great Britain. The Oregon Treaty in 1843 had set the mainland boundary between American and British territory along the 49th parallel, with Britain keeping all of Vancouver Island. The British government, fearing an invasion by American settlers from Oregon, granted the island to the Hudson's Bay Company (HBC) in 1849. The company did not particularly want to colonize Vancouver Island but had little intention of letting anyone else have it.

The HBC was required to establish "settlements of resident colonists, emigrants from Our United Kingdom of Great Britain and Ireland, or from other of Our Dominions." It agreed to sell land to settlers at a fair price, but they had to purchase twenty acres at a time. "Land costs were set at one pound per acre."[14] Anyone wanting a larger spread had to bring out five single men or three married couples at his own expense. The regulations were designed to discourage squatters and land speculators and to attract gentlemen farmers.

By the end of five years "only seventy men, women and children had arrived and no more than five hundred acres had been settled."[15] All the sales of land, timber, and minerals went straight into the

Company's coffers. However, it was coal that proved to be a profitable venture and that brought the HBC to Nanaimo. Coal had already been discovered on the northeast coast, but it was a small seam. One day an elderly Nanaimo chief was in Fort Victoria having his gun repaired and noticed the coal used in the blacksmith's forge. He told the blacksmith there was plenty of the black rock where he lived. He was offered a bottle of rum and was not charged for the repairs.

A few months later he arrived back with his canoe filled with coal. Before long the coal rush was on and a major coal deposit outlined at Nanaimo. "Coal was mined at Nanaimo for most of the next century, first by the HBC and later by the Dunsmuir family. The pits employed three thousand miners at the height of their productivity."[16]

The British appointed Richard Blanshard, a thirty-two year old barrister, to govern the island colony. But James Douglas, who had no intention of sharing his authority with the newcomer, made life exceedingly difficult for the young lawyer. Eventually Blanshard returned home to England. Douglas was appointed Governor of Vancouver Island without having to give up his HBC post. The conflict of interest was obvious. Douglas went through the motions of trying to establish an elected assembly but made sure the HBC men held the balance of power.

Gold fever was in the air following the discovery of gold nuggets along the Thompson River, and a full-scale rush had begun. In 1858, it was estimated thirty thousand miners passed through the streets of Victoria.[17] The gold rush would forever leave its mark on Vancouver Island.

On August 2, 1858, British Columbia was declared a crown colony,[18] but Vancouver Island was not included. The HBC retained its exclusive trading license. Douglas was appointed Governor to head the new colony for a period of six years; he was ordered to sever his ties with the HBC and told to organize a Council with elections for an Assembly.

The site for the new capital of the colony was New Westminster – much to Douglas' dismay as he preferred Victoria. He governed by proclamation and kept the control of the government within his grasp, building roads and bridges, but still holding no election. Queen Victoria awarded him a knighthood in 1862. He became Sir James Douglas.

Douglas' Land Proclamation dated February 1859 put the price of all lands not intended for townsites at ten shillings per acre. In January 1861, the price was lowered to four shillings and twopence per acre. "A single man could have one hundred and fifty acres, and a married man, with a wife resident in the colony, could have two hundred acres. And for each of his children under eighteen years of age, an additional ten acres."[19]

By 1860 the population of Vancouver Island had spread upwards from Fort Victoria to Cowichan and Chemainus, Nanaimo and Saltspring. Two years later, the Crown took back all rights over Vancouver Island. The Hudson's Bay Company was reduced to the status of any other business enterprise. The first Legislative Council of the new government of British Columbia sat on January 22, 1864, under Sir James Douglas, the man who had guided the new frontier of Vancouver Island. However, Douglas did not last long; he resigned a few weeks later, retiring from public life.

Some of those gold-rush miners made their way north to Alberni. Rumours of gold in the area circulated. The strike was at Gold River, which later became known as China Creek. There were estimated to be about two hundred men place-mining on China Creek between the years 1860 and 1890,[20] but the amount of gold mined was nothing compared to the Cariboo gold strike. Some of the miners stayed on and became part of the new settlement of Alberni.

The small west coast village of Bamfield is named after William E. Banfield, a trader and colonial government agent in the Barkley Sound area, who in 1858 explored the Alberni region and felt the area would soon have rail service and would develop into an industrial centre. In a letter to the Colonial Secretary in February 1860, Banfield described the Alberni Valley as a

> large tract of beautiful country alternately plain and woodland, but the woodland is clear from underbrush and such. . . . by far the best tract of country on the Island.[21]

The mystery surrounding Banfield's death on October 20, 1862 has never been solved. He was reported to have accidentally drowned from a canoe when going out to meet a schooner for supplies, but the story emerged later that he had been killed by an Indian on shore. The Indian was tried for murder and acquitted due to lack of evidence, but when he returned to Barkley Sound he claimed that he had indeed killed Banfield.[22]

The HBC push was on to discover new trails across Vancouver Island, to establish friendly relations and open fur trading with the Nootkan Indians. A young Scottish man would lead the way to the Alberni Valley.

Adam Grant Horne, at twenty years of age, was a strapping Highlander, six feet and three inches tall, when he came to British Columbia aboard the sailing vessel *Tory* in 1851. The voyage had taken over four months, the vessel having come around Cape Horn. He was born at Edinburgh but raised at Kirkwall, in the Scottish Orkney Islands, the sixth child of eight.[23] When the Hudson's Bay Company opened its Nanaimo store in 1851, Horne was placed in charge and remained there until 1862 when the Company sold out its Nanaimo business.

In 1856, Horne was asked to find a trail across Vancouver Island. The request came from Roderick Finlayson, the Hudson's Bay Company Chief Factor at Fort Victoria. The trail, which Finlayson suspected the Indians used, was thought to start near Qualicum Creek, emerging somewhere at the head of Barkley Sound on the west coast. The mission was a dangerous one. Finlayson gave him one of the most famous HBC guides, a French-Canadian named Cote. Another French-Canadian acted as an interpreter. These and four other men – one an Iroquois named Tomo, who was considered an excellent guide, interpreter, and sharpshooter and had worked for the company around Nanaimo – made up the expedition. The Company engaged a number of Iroquois because of their great skill as canoe men. Governor Douglas considered Tomo his own personal servant.

Horne was instructed to land at Qualicum Creek and warned to beware of warlike natives. The Horne expedition left from Victoria in a Haida type canoe and called in at Salt Spring Island. They camped the first night at Newcastle Island near Nanaimo. The next morning they camped in a cove about one mile from Qualicum. Horne was awakened from a sound sleep by Tomo, who, with a finger on his lips, explained he had been watching a large fleet of northern canoes approaching the creek mouth. Thick columns of smoke arose from the creek area, pouring into the forest where they hid. Horne's party waited until they saw the first canoes pull out of the creek. As the Haidas hoisted makeshift sails on the great war canoes in the near-hurricane winds, a few stood in triumph holding a human head in their hands. Within hours they were gone.

The expedition worked its way slowly up the river seeing nothing yet of the Qualicum rancherie (an Indian village) but volumes of smoke. As they rounded a bend, they were sickened at the scene. The rancherie had been reduced to a heap of smoldering timber. To their horror they found naked bodies, headless and mutilated, lying in the clearing surrounding the rancherie. The only survivor, a woman, was found still clutching a bow and chanting a dirge in a low monotone. She was too weak to offer any resistance and between long gasps told the horrible story.

When the Haidas came up the river, the Qualicum tribe had been asleep, and more than half of them were killed as they slept. The Haidas, outnumbering the Qualicum, had killed all the grown men and women and taken away as slaves two young women, four little girls, and two small boys. The massacre had occurred because one of the northern warriors had been killed at Cape Mudge when he tried to carry off the daughter of one of the Euclataw chiefs. The Euclataws were too strong for the Haidas, but the Qualicums were a Euclataw sept (a division of the tribe) so the Haidas took their revenge on them. The old Indian woman died as Horne looked on.[24]

The expedition still had to find the trail across the island, and by going north and striking off through the bush in a southerly direction they felt they would come across the trail sooner or later. Four hours later they found a very rough trail and discovered one of the most beautiful lakes Horne had ever seen. (The lake was later named "Horne Lake." Captain Richards of the Royal Navy, in drawing up an official map of the area for the British Admiralty, named the lake for the first white man to set eyes on it.) Horne's expedition camped on the eastern shores. At daybreak they saw a beautiful yearling elk standing beside the lake. The elk was shot, providing meat for the return journey. The crossing took two days. They walked along a meandering trail, which took them to the foot of the Beaufort Range of mountains running along the centre of Vancouver Island.

They camped another night by a stream, and early the next day they started to climb over the range. At the top of the ridge there was a glorious view. The old Indian trail had a steep downward slope which made the going difficult because of their large packs. As they reached level ground near the water's edge they came upon a tribe of Indians who showed the greatest confusion and curiosity. None had seen a white man before.

The interpreter made himself understood to the natives and asked to be shown the chief's house. As they walked along, the natives crowded around, apparently trying to pilfer goods from their packs. When Horne confronted the chief, he told him his people were becoming troublesome and must behave. At a word from the chief all his men withdrew to a respectable distance.

Horne was familiar with most of the coast tribes. He immediately recognized these Indians as belonging to the Nootkan group. The men wore hats made from cedar fibres with the design woven in of a man in a canoe hunting whales. Also very common was the design of the Nootkan all-powerful one, Tootooch, the Thunder bird. On the beach were some canoes, most containing cedar fish spears. Horne gave the chief a message from (Chief Factor) Finlayson, inviting him and his band to bring furs and pelts to the company posts. Then he presented them with several blankets. The chief replied he would trade with the "Great Company." Many of the tribe had beaver and otter pelts and wanted knives and blankets. After trading, the expedition pitched camp several hundred yards away from the Indians.

As they were cooking supper a young Indian approached and spoke in the dialect used at Victoria. He was a Songhee from Sooke who wanted to return with the white men to Fort Victoria. The chief agreed to release the Songhee at a price of two blankets. However, the next morning when the young Songhee was escorted to the camp, the chief now demanded three blankets. Horne forcibly took the young Songhee and ordered his men on alert. They loaded their guns, ready for a speedy retreat. In a few moments they heard war cries from a hundred Indians. They came armed with clubs and spears. Before they got too close Horne fired a volley over their heads and the Indians ran into the bush. When Horne returned, Finlayson praised him for his good work.

The Fort Nanaimo Journal recorded: "Saturday, May 10, 1856, 2:30 p.m. Toma Ouatomy left here on an expedition across the Island, accompanied by three Indian men and one Indian woman. Mr. Horne also left with him with instructions not to proceed further than the high mountain beyond the large lake in the interior but if the interior tribes be peaceable he may proceed to Alberni Canal." His return was reported ten days later. In September of the same year, he led another expedition over the same route returning with quantities of furs and "accompanied by Indians of the tribe Seeshaad" (Tseshaht).

In January 1857 some new immigrants arrived in Nanaimo from Dudley, near Birmingham, England. Included was the Bate family, Mark, Lucy, and Elizabeth. Mark became Nanaimo's first mayor when the city incorporated in 1874. Elizabeth, then seventeen years of age, was attracted to the tall Scot. She and Horne were married two years later, on February 22, 1859. The wedding was witnessed by several prominent Nanaimo people, including Caroline and George Robinson, friends of the Bate family who had arrived on the same ship. Other witnesses included surgeon Dr. Alfred R. Benson, for whom the mountain behind Nanaimo is named, and Cornelius Bryant, Nanaimo's only schoolteacher. The Church of England ceremony was also witnessed by Elizabeth's sister Lucy and by brother Mark and his wife Sarah Ann.[25]

In 1868 the HBC sent Horne to operate a small store at Comox, where the first settlers had arrived only six years before. Horne and Elizabeth and their growing family lived there for ten years before moving back to Nanaimo. The couple had eleven children, but two girls and a boy died before their eighth birthdays. Large families were quite common in the nineteenth century.

Horne's granddaughter Carrie Brown Doney, of Seattle, wrote about an incident in her grandfather's colorful life that took place while he resided at Comox.

> One night there was a lot of noise at the gate of the fort. Grandfather went out to see what was wrong and there stood a huge Indian with an oatmeal sack in his hand. He said the Indians had all been fighting and the chief had been scalped and grandfather was to go sew the scalp on him. They were all very upset about this. Grandfather refused to do it at first, and tried to get rid of him. He had a medicine chest that he used for small wounds but he had never done anything like that before. The Indian persisted and grandfather was afraid he would stick a spear in him, so he went.
>
> The chief's hide was so tough that grandfather had to take his shoemaker's awl and make holes in his head and also through the scalp to sew it on. The old chief was so drunk that he could not feel a thing. Grandfather thought he would be dead by morning anyway, so he just sewed it on. But in the morning he was very much alive and lived to be an old man.[26]

One day, much later, when Doney's mother was married and living in Union Bay, an old Indian came to the house with a bucket of clams. He began talking to her mother in the kitchen and then suddenly lifted his hair up, and there were the scars where Horne had sewn on his scalp many years before. "Every stitch had grown together perfectly."[27]

Using the same route, Horne subsequently made yearly trips across the island to the Alberni Inlet to purchase sea-otter skins and furs from the Indians, who placed a canoe on Horne Lake for his convenience.[28] Adam Grant Horne was a respected man described by Captain John T. Walbran, commander of the Canadian ship Quadra, as "a man of fearless, daring disposition, whom the Indians seemed to admire as well as dread for his intrepidity."[29]

The *Nanaimo Free Press* reported Horne's death on August 10, 1901. His obituary read: "Pioneer of pioneers dies . . . his personality was a link between the first settlement and the living present."[30] Horne had been ailing for several years and was confined to his home. He served as alderman for the City of Nanaimo, councillor for North Ward, in 1886. He was buried in Nanaimo Cemetery along with other members of his family.

In October 1856, James Douglas sent Joseph Despard Pemberton, the Hudson's Bay Company surveyor, to explore the country between Qualicum and the Alberni Inlet. Pemberton crossed the island by the same route taken by Horne, exploring both the Inlet and Barkley Sound. The following year, he crossed the island again, this time venturing as far as Nitinat on the coast. Douglas now had a good idea of the vast wilderness of the Alberni Inlet.[31]

In 1859, Horne and Captain George Henry Richards crossed the island from Qualicum to Alberni via the Horne Lake trail. Richards had been commissioned in 1856 by the English government to survey and chart the waters along the coast of Vancouver Island. He was well known as a surveyor and Arctic explorer. After crossing Horne Lake his party climbed the western ridge and looked down on the Alberni Inlet. The ascent to the ridge was so steep Captain Richards was convinced it could never be used as a roadway. Another route would have to be found.

Two years later, Captain Richards instructed Lieutenant Richard Charles Mayne, R.N. to find out if a way existed across the island from Alberni to Nanaimo by a valley that seemed a more likely route than the one Richards had previously taken via Horne Lake. On April 29, 1861, Mayne started out from the top of the Alberni Inlet to find a route for a road to Nanaimo. The trip from Alberni took him seven days. Accompanying him were six Indians, needed as guides and packers, William E. Banfield, the Indian Agent at Barkley Sound, and one Royal Marine from H.M.S. *Hecate*.

The Indians' stock of winter provisions were almost used up, and they demanded that their wives be provided with food while they were gone. Mayne made arrangements with Captain Stamp, at the Anderson sawmill in Alberni, to look after the women's needs until the men returned from Nanaimo.

With these arrangements made, Mayne thought everything was now settled, but more trouble developed. First one Indian discovered he had no *scaarlux* (pants), and would be torn to pieces by the forest undergrowth. Another who declared he had no moccasins was given a pair of boots which he hung on his pack and then walked barefoot. Powder and balls had to be provided for their muskets, along with matches for everyone. After the Indians' demands were met, it still took all of Mayne's knowledge of the Chinook language, a mixture of English, Indian, and French, to get them to move. A few hundred yards along the trail, the leader decided his moccasins were improperly laced and his pack unbalanced. "So down he squats, the whole party following his example, and when you overtake them, you find them a few hundred yards from the starting-place, seated in a row, talking with the utmost animation and unconcern of the journey before them. Time, of course, they set no value on."[32] The group had covered less than three miles before camping for the night.

Mayne's difficulties did not end the first night. The journey ahead was through country the Indians had never travelled. They declared it to be impenetrable. But one old hunter, who supported Mayne, convinced the others to remain. They hadn't travelled far when one of the Indians complained of being ill and wanted to turn back. Mayne admitted the man was evidently ill, but he realized that if he let him go, the rest of the Indians would more than likely desert. Once again Mayne resorted to strong words in Chinook, branding him with being *carqua klootcluman*, "like a woman." Mayne finally dismissed the Indian with a note for Captain Stamp, in which he said that he was sorry he should have sent a woman instead of a man. When the note was read aloud, it had the desired effect of making the Indian ashamed. His companions laughed. The sick man shouldered his pack and completed the journey without another word of complaint.

They passed the Alberni Summit the next day, April 30th, and they came upon a beautiful stream running northward. Following it, they came across some herds of elk, one of which Mayne shot. Within fifteen minutes the Indians had reduced the elk to a skeleton. In another fifteen minutes everyone had made themselves moccasins from the hide. "The prime cuts, were cut into strips of meat five or six feet long, and four inches thick. These were sewn up in a piece of the elk's skin and slung on the chief Indian's pack."[33] After another hour, they rested under a huge tree.

Starting out again, they came across a small lake about three miles long, of which none of the Indians had any previous knowledge.[34] Mayne used his pocket-compass to locate Mount Arrowsmith. The Indians looked in awe at the instrument. One observant Indian posed the question, "If the compass showed me the way to Nanaimo, why did it not show me where the mountain was? I had to explain that the compass, being bound for Nanaimo, declined to trouble itself with any other consideration."[35]

Walking along the beach for half of the length of the lake, they came to a bluff, where they decided to camp for the night. The Indians built a raft rather than scramble over the almost inaccessible mountainside. The next morning they rafted down the lake and found another river running northward through the gorge, where a road could easily be constructed. They followed the river, then crossed the ridge down the north side, where they could see the Gulf of Georgia before them. This was May 1st, and from then until the afternoon of the 3rd, the group passed over land which Mayne described as "admirably adapted for settlement." They reached Nanaimo at 5:00 p.m.

The people in Nanaimo were surprised to see them and delighted to hear of the route they had travelled. When they were ready to start the return journey, on May 7, three of the Indians were suffering from swollen feet and had to be left behind, but Nanaimo Indians were willing to take their place. Mayne and his party arrived back in Alberni on May 12, 1861. The journey to Nanaimo and back had taken fourteen days.

Mayne reported to Governor James Douglas that roadbuilding across the island would be difficult but was possible. Douglas was disappointed. He had been "under the impression there was little to prevent a wagon road being built at once."[36]

Recalled to England in late 1861, Mayne was promoted to Commander and later Rear Admiral, R.N. Before he left he recommended the road from Nanaimo should go through the Nanoose Valley, then along the coast, with a branch to Cameron Lake and into Alberni.

In 1864, Commander Robert Brown of the Vancouver Island Exploring Expedition also travelled the route from Alberni to Qualicum. He suggested a fifteen mile trail connecting the east and west coasts could be easily constructed at an average expense of seventy-five dollars per mile. "This would form a transinsular road connecting the civilization of the east with the barbarism of the west coast; the coal miners of Nanaimo and the farmers of Comox, with the wild savage of Nootka, Klay-oquaht and the Barkley Sounds."[37]

Brown referred to the Horne Lake route being used by sailors and mill workers. "It is much travelled by run-away sailors and mill men from the Alberni sawmill. It can be travelled in from one-third to three days according to the facilities for finding canoes. There were several on Horne Lake but they were so convenient for running away sailors, that Capt. Stamp J.P. ordered them to be destroyed."[38]

After the explorations of Brown and Mayne, little was heard of this route for twenty-five years.

Anderson Sawmill

In 1859, Governor James Douglas received a letter from an English shipmaster, Captain Edward Stamp, expressing plans to establish a first-class sawmill in the Colony of Vancouver Island. Stamp, from Alnwick, Northumberland, England, was forty-five years of age. He had arrived on the Pacific Coast four years earlier to purchase lumber and spars on Puget Sound, where several mills were prospering from the California gold rush. After sailing the coast of Vancouver Island, Stamp was impressed by the great forests thick with fir and cedar. He returned to London, where he convinced two shipping companies, Thomas Bilbe & Company and James Thomson & Company, to back him in construction of a mill. The companies agreed, partly because they also built ships and feared the impending civil war in the United States would cut off their supplies of southern pine.

James Thomson & Co., was a private London firm run by a family named Anderson, who owned clipper ships working in the Australian trade. Later the Andersons would become one of the great shipping families of England with major interest in the Orient Line and the P. & O. Steamship Co.

Stamp said in his letter to Douglas that he would prefer to establish his mill on British soil, but prospects at Puget Sound were also favourable. Douglas was anxious to see such a promising industry established in the colony, however, he had no authority from London to take over the management of colonial lands. In spite of this, he and Stamp managed to come to an agreement. Douglas' decision was probably helped by the fact Stamp's backers were respected and wealthy merchants in England.

In a report dated October 24, 1859, the land and timber resources selected were reported by Agent William E. Banfield to W. A. G. Young, Colonial Secretary, to be "extensive and valuable." Stamp, representing the English company, received land grants in the Alberni area of "2000 acres for purposes of settlement and not more than 15,000 acres of timber limits."[39] The site chosen for the sawmill was an encampment of the Tseshaht "near a pretty point at one side of the bay where there was a beach shaded by young trees."[40]

27

The following year, June 29, 1860, the schooner *Meg Merrilies* landed nine workmen at the head of the Alberni Inlet. Next came the schooner *Woodpecker* with workmen and machinery for the new mill. Captain Stamp and Jeremiah (Jerry) Rogers, a New Brunswick logger, arrived on September 1st aboard the *Meg Merrilies*, skippered by Tom Pamphlet. Also accompanying them was Gilbert Malcolm Sproat, a representative for Thomson & Company in London, England. Sproat, from Scotland, was twenty-six years of age when he was sent to keep an eye on the shipbuilding company's interests.

Stamp and Sproat recognized the need to come to some understanding with the local Indians who lived on the land required for the settlement. Sproat described the encounter:

> Near a pretty point at one side of the bay, where there was a beach shaded by young trees, the summer encampment of a tribe of natives was to be seen. Our arrival caused a stir, and we saw their flambeaux of gunsticks flickering among the trees during the night.
>
> In the morning I sent a boat for the chief, and explained to him that his tribe must move their encampment, as we had bought all the surrounding land from the Queen of England, and wished to occupy the site of the village for a particular purpose. He replied that the land belonged to themselves, but that they were willing to sell it. The price not being excessive, I paid him what was asked – about twenty pounds' worth of goods – for the sake of peace, on condition that the whole people and buildings should be removed next day. But no movement was then made, and as an excuse it was stated that the children were sick.
>
> On the following day the encampment was in commotion; speeches were made, faces blackened, guns and pikes got out, and barricades formed. Outnumbered as we were, ten to one, by men armed with muskets, and our communications with the sea cut off by the impossibility of sailing steadily down the Alberni Inlet (the prevalent breeze blowing up it), there was some cause for alarm had the natives been resolute. But being provided, fortunately, in both vessels with cannon – of which the natives at that time were much afraid – they, after a little show of force on our side, saw that resistance would be inexpedient, and began to move from the spot.
>
> Two or three days afterwards, when the village had been moved to another place, not far distant, I visited the principal house at the new encampment, with a native interpreter.
>
> "Chief of the Seshahts," said I on entering, "are you well; are your women in health; are your children hearty; do your people get plenty of fish and fruits?"
>
> "Yes," answered the old man, "our families are well, our people have plenty of food; but how long this will last we know not. We see your ships, and hear things that make our hearts grow faint. They say that more King-George-men will soon be here, and will take our land, our firewood, our

fishing grounds; that we shall be placed on a little spot, and shall have to do everything according to the fancies of the King-George-men."

"Do you believe this?" I asked.

"We want your information," said the speaker.

"Then," answered I, "it is true that more King-George-men (Englishmen) are coming; they will soon be here; but your land will be bought at a fair price."

"We do not wish to sell our land nor our water; let your friends stay in their own country."

To which I rejoined: "My great chief, the high chief of the King-George-men, seeing that you do not work your land, orders that you shall sell it. It is of no use to you. The trees you do not need; you will fish and hunt as you do now, and collect firewood, planks for your houses, and cedar for your canoes. The white man will give you work, and buy your fish and oil."

"Ah, but we don't care to do as the white men wish."

"Whether or not," said I, "the white men will come. All your people know that they are your superiors; they make the things which you value. You cannot make muskets, blankets, or bread. The white men will teach your children to read printing, and to be like themselves."

"We do not want the white man. He steals what we have. We wish to live as we are."[41]

Sproat declared: "a civilized settlement was now formed almost immediately in their midst, and the natives stared at the buildings, wharves, steam engines, ploughs, oxen, horses, sheep, and pigs, which they had never seen before."[42] The first log house was built. Sproat described it as "a rather plain-looking hut . . . the kind of house that woodmen build with the axe alone."[43]

On July 9th, William E. Banfield, colonial agent, was called to the settlement. He was asked to come immediately as the nine workmen with Stamp were in danger. Seven hours later he arrived at the site. "The men were very frightened. Apparently the Tseshaht tribe had arrived where the whites were located. Their numbers, inquisitiveness and rude curiosity wishing to intrude into the white men's cabin, had brought some difficulty."[44] However, Banfield found the natives posed no danger to the settlers.

Stamp and Sproat purchased the land for about twenty pounds in goods, but the land transaction with the Indians troubled Sproat. He wrote in his journal of sitting around the fire with his men discussing the Indians' intentions, while the Indians, only a mile away, were no doubt doing the same thing. Sproat questioned who actually owned the land, as he had bought it from the government and he had also bought it from the Indians. Since the Indians did not recognize the colonial authority in Victoria and had sold the land only under the threat of a loaded cannon pointed at them, it was obvious to Sproat the land had been taken by force.[45] The American forestry workers who formed Sproat's party discussed the question with clarity, according to Sproat. They believed that the occupation was justifiable as the Indians had not occupied the land but had only used it to hunt, pick wild fruits, and cut a few trees to make canoes and houses. "Unless such a right were presumed to exist, there would be little progress in the world by means of colonization," they claimed.[46]

Sproat wrote in his journal:

> The particular circumstances which make the deliberate intrusion of a superior people into another country lawful or expedient are connected to some extent with the use which the Natives have made of the soil and with their general behaviour as a nation. The whole question of the right of any people to intrude upon another, and to dispossess them of their country, is one of those questions to which the answer practically is always the same, though differently given by many as a matter of speculative opinion.[47]

The Tseshaht were forced to give up their winter village of Nuupts'ikapis (Lupsi Cupsi) and move up the Somass River to the site of the present location of the reserve. Also, the all important winter ceremony site, at Tlukwatkuuwis (Wolf Ritual Beach) located midway between Tiipis and Nuupts'ikapis, was lost to the construction of the Anderson Company sawmill.[48]

In November Stamp was sworn in as Justice of the Peace. The following spring the new sawmill was in operation, with Jerry Rogers the head logger. "Captain Stamp's place has been named Alberni by the Survey," stated Victoria's newspaper, the *British Colonist*, on May 23, 1861. The new settlement now had an official name. The first shipment of lumber went to Victoria in early July.

> A first payment of four hundred pounds sterling was made in October, 1860, for the land acquired at Alberni by the Company, under the terms of the agreement with Douglas. However, no survey was made for many years and Sproat declared in 1864 that no government officer had ever visited the settlement.[49]

Logs for the mill were hauled by teams of oxen over skid roads which sloped down to the Alberni Inlet. After the fallers cut the tree down, a two-man team using a crosscut saw bucked it into lengths and then chained the lengths together. The logs were hooked up to the oxen and driven to the mill site. A man carrying a bucket of fish oil walked ahead splashing the skid logs with grease.

The market in Victoria in 1861 was strong; the *Meg Merrilies* made five trips loaded with lumber from Alberni. An office was established in Victoria to take care of purchasing supplies for the small settlement, and also to charter ships to carry cargoes of lumber. The Victoria business prospered, having arranged shiploads of spars for places around the world. Mayne described the sawmill settlement at Alberni.

> They (the mills) have been erected in a most solid fashion, and at a heavy outlay, by English labourers, and with English machinery. They contain two gangs of saws capable of cutting about 18,000 feet of lumber daily, and in the best way, as is proved by the high price obtained for it at Melbourne.
>
> Seventy white men are employed at and about the premises, so that the place has all the appearance of a flourishing little settlement. Two schooners and two steamers are also employed by the company here, the former trading with Victoria and bringing the necessary supplies to the place. One of the steamers, the *Diana*, a little tug, also trades to Victoria, and is used besides for towing vessels up to and away from the mills. The second steamer, the *Thames* has not yet reached the colony, but is on her way out from England.[50]

In August 1861, Alberni was made a Port of Entry, with Edward Stamp appointed the first Collector of Customs. The mill at Alberni had several advantages over similar mills in Puget Sound. Mayne pointed out one of its main points was its accessibility; Alberni's situation on the outside coast of the island allowed navigators to avoid the delay in journeying in and out of the Straits of Juan de Fuca and Admiralty Inlet, which sometimes took a week. Another consideration, which he said carried a lot of weight with skippers, was that there was no opportunity for men to desert at Alberni. Also there were no port charges, and Alberni was a Port of Entry, allowing vessels to sail directly to the mill.

To keep the small community in vegetables, Stamp established a farm on the far side of the Somass River, on the flatland at the river's mouth. This was named the Anderson Farm. The foreman was an American, his helper a Yorkshireman from England. Their duties included planting, harvesting, and guarding the vegetables.

The Indians, used to freely obtaining game, fish, and berries, developed a taste for the potato, and an unfortunate incident happened at the farm when some Indians helped themselves. Sproat described the incident in his journal:

> For several nights the foreman had been watching a field of potatoes which the Indians were plundering. They came in during the night and filled their canoes. By daylight they were gone. One night the foreman went out to watch the field and had taken his gun loaded with five hard peas, thinking he would frighten them by shooting the peas amongst them. He heard suspicious noises in the field and after firing a warning shot, fired another in the general direction. He was shocked to see the

Indian fall flat on the ground. Rushing back to the house, he yelled to his companion, "Jack, I've shot an Indian."[51]

The next morning the foreman informed Stamp, Sproat, and the mill workers of what had happened, and the body was taken to the settlement. Because the community feared retaliation, it was decided to place the foreman under arrest, hold a trial, and try to impress the Indians that justice would be done. A workman with surgeon's papers examined the body and produced a pea that he had found in the left lung, proving the cause of death.

Magistrate Malcolm Sproat appointed a jury of twelve loggers and mill hands to hear the evidence and render justice. These men believed that if they found the defendant guilty, the Indians would feel justified in retaliation. Sproat charged the jury, and they retired to consider their verdict. When they returned to the court, the magistrate asked, "What is your verdict?"

"We find the Siwash was worried by a dog," said the foreman.

The legal and moral responsibility troubled Sproat. He considered the verdict unacceptable. He dismissed the jury and asked them to return a verdict with something reasonably connected with the facts of the case. The jurymen returned with the finding, "We say he was killed by falling over a cliff." Sproat was astonished at the absurd verdict, considering the Indian had been found in a flat river bottom far from any cliff. He dismissed the jury and decided to return the verdict himself.

Sproat arrested the foreman and sent a constable with him on the company steamboat to Victoria, but he escaped from custody. The Indian was buried in the forest. He belonged to a distant tribe, but they were too much ashamed of the circumstances of his death to send for the body. Meanwhile, the settlement was on the defensive, waiting for a reaction from the Indians. Loggers took rifles to work, and plans were made to defend the mill and property.

The local Indians went about their usual routines rather pleased with the death of the Indian. They pointed to the body and said, "Now you see who steals your potatoes; our tribe does not." In his journal Sproat begged the reader to believe the trial as stated was not in the slightest degree exaggerated or distorted, but a statement of facts as they occurred.

The first wooden ship constructed on the shores of the Alberni Inlet in 1861 was the *Alberni*, an eighty-seven foot schooner weighing two hundred tons. The *Alberni* was built to replace the Anderson Company's schooner *Woodpecker*, which had brought the machinery for the mill to Alberni the previous year. A record of the *Alberni*'s construction came from Cyrus Sears, then Master of the *Pocahontas*, the ship chartered by Stamp that same year to carry spars to London. Sears met Stamp when the *Pocahontas* was anchored in the harbour at San Francisco; there he offered to charter the vessel. The port at Alberni was still unknown in shipping circles. Stamp furnished Sears with a chart.

On Tuesday, December 23, 1862, the *Alberni*, sailing under Captain Henderson, arrived in Victoria with 110,000 feet of lumber. Four months later, with a new captain, Master Anderson, at the helm, the *Alberni* transported thirty passengers and 100,000 feet of lumber for Anderson & Co. to Victoria. The trip had taken eighteen hours.

The *Pocahontas* arrived in Alberni in October 1861 and anchored in seven fathoms of water. Sears described the settlement at that time. "Alberni consisted of a store, a shipyard, a blacksmith shop, a saw-mill, lodging houses and a few other buildings of the plainest kind."[52]

The arrival of Sears' big ship caused some excitement among the Indian population as they came alongside to inspect it in their canoes. Sears reported: "They came on board and lying down they measured the length of the deck by their own length, from stern to stern. They then measured the outside length by their canoes. With exclamations of astonishment they pronounced her a 'hi you canoe'." (In Chinook *Hyas* means "very large.")[53]

This was a busy harbour in 1861-62; the American ship the *Visula* arrived to load a cargo for Valparaiso, followed by the American ship *Thomas A. Stone*, also to load for Valparaiso. The brigantine *Marcella* arrived to load for Callao, Peru. Sears also saw an English barque load cargo for Australia. After a severe winter, a total of fourteen vessels had loaded lumber and spars for various parts of the world.

Sears' cargo was large spars for the English and French navies. These spars were brought alongside the *Pocahontas* in rafts. They had been cut from "a large grove of towering trees located on the left bank of the creek which emptied into the sound about a mile or more from the so called village."[54]

One of the largest poles ever to be cut at the sawmill measured 253 feet in length. It was taken to England to be erected in Kew Gardens in 1862, the year of the International Exhibition in London. However, the pole lost thirty feet at the top when it was being unloaded into the Thames River. On this same shipment were sections of a tree 310 feet in length. The tree was estimated to be 350 years of age at the date of being cut down. With this flagpole and the sectional tree exhibits,

Anderson and Co. did their best to call the attention of European lumber buyers to the valuable characteristics of the Douglas fir, at that time a new competitor in the timber market.

In January 1862 there was an exceptionally severe freeze-up in Alberni. The temperature dipped to eight degrees below zero. The Inlet was frozen for ten miles and snow was four feet deep. Work at the mill was entirely suspended.[55] Other than the problems with the weather in the winter, everything seemed to be going well at the mill, that is, until Stamp had a disagreement with the Anderson Company and resigned.

"About this time our connection with Capt. Stamp became unsatisfactory and we altered the name of the firm to Anderson & Company and put Mr. Gilbert Malcolm Sproat, who had been in the London Office, in as manager," states correspondence from the P & O archives, now the descendant company.[56] The white newcomers had changed drastically the lives of the Indian people in the area. Sproat noted the change:

> I seemed all at once to perceive that a few sharp-witted young natives had become what I can only call offensively European, and that the mass of the Indians no longer visited the settlement in the former independent way, but lived listlessly in the villages, brooding seemingly over heavy thoughts. The fact was that the curiosity of the savage had been satisfied; his mind was confused and his faculties surprised and stunned by the presence of machinery, steam vessels, and the active labour of civilized men; he distrusted himself, his old habits and traditions, and shrank away despondent and discouraged.[57]

Sproat also noted the increase in mortality among the Indians.

Alberni was becoming an established community; in fact, the politicians in Victoria were considering giving the area political representation. On October 31, 1863, Dr. John Helmcken introduced an amendment to the Cowichan and Comox Representation Bill in Douglas' House of Assembly to give the district of Alberni provincial representation. "This said district to be 25 miles square, each side to be five miles long and the centre of the district to be at the forks of the Somass River."[58]

But Amor de Cosmos argued the cases of Alberni, Cowichan, and Comox were not the same. He stated: "The honourable member had not shown us that there were residents at Alberni qualified to vote; the land was all owned by gentlemen in England; if there were any residents there to vote he would, with pleasure, second the amendment."[59] A Mr. Street said he could not see that Alberni was entitled to a representative.

The following month Street, speaking on the amended clause, said he would oppose the amendment as he thought it would simply be granting a representative in Victoria to a commercial house. Dr. Tolmie proposed to enlarge the size of the district to twenty miles square instead of ten miles square, the centre part being "Observatory Rock" in "Stamp Harbour." The amendment carried and the bill passed.[60]

By 1863-64 all suitable trees on the timber reserve had been harvested. The lack of mechanization in the industry made all timber not adjacent to bodies of water inaccessible for commercial purposes. The Anderson Mill operated for about four years with little profit made by the company. Sproat blamed Stamp for having built the mill at Alberni rather than at Puget Sound, and for failing to lease enough timberland.

In a letter to the colonial secretary, Sproat complained, "there is no wood in the district to supply the wants of a large mill, and the business in fact is now being carried on simply from an unwillingness to wind it up until forced, but without yielding any profit and with the certainty of having to abandon the place at an early date after having sunk and lost fifty-thousand pounds sterling."[61]

On January 1, 1864, the Victoria newspaper the *British Colonist* reported the *Thames*, under Captain Henderson, had arrived with ninety-seven mill hands "to be paid off."

> Only one ship was loading there, and the mills have been reduced to one. A disturbance had nearly been occasioned through the remonstrance of some white men of the settlement against barbarism committed by the natives, who had killed and mutilated a slave woman. The Indians were incensed by the interference of the whites and drove the white men away with threats of violence. This caused apprehension and alarm, and the settlers armed themselves and were prepared for any sudden attack.

Three months after the mill closed, the population of the settlement, which had risen to two hundred,[62] was reduced to three. This small remnant stayed on as caretakers of the company farm. The land granted by Douglas for the settlement remained in the possession of the Andersons in England. The first mill had blazed an important trail in what was to become a long and successful history of forestry in the Alberni Valley.

Stamp and Rogers went on to build another sawmill in 1865, on Burrard Inlet, in Vancouver. Rogers went into business as a logging contractor at English Bay. When he died in 1879, his mourners called him "the greatest logger on the coast."[63] Sproat left the lumber business, took various government jobs, and eventually became British Columbia's first agent general in London.

The first white girl to be born in the Alberni settlement was Alice Patterson, daughter of Emily Susan Patterson and John Patterson, a sawmill mechanic from Portland, Oregon, who worked at the Anderson Mill. Alice was born on February 26, 1864, in a house near the old sawmill, near where the Somass Hotel now stands. When Alice was nine the family moved to Burrard Inlet where John became a master mechanic at the Hastings Mill. Alice married Robert C. Crakanthorp, who predeceased her in 1892. She reminisced about her childhood in Alberni:

> When I was born, the only white people who lived where Port Alberni now stands were mill employees and their families, about forty all told. A handful of white settlers also farmed on the banks of the Somass River, where Alberni now stands.
>
> I remember those Alberni days, especially the Indians, many of whom were bad. When they got very dangerous the cookhouse bell was rung as a warning for all the white employees to come up from the mill, and the wives and children to gather at the cookhouse. Fearing to return to our homes, we sometimes slept there, but I recall no serious trouble other than threatening demands for food and payment for the trees. It was the frightening appearance of the Indians which scared us most, especially the women and children newly arrived from England.[64]

Alice Crakanthorp died October 9, 1961, at the age of ninety-seven.

Daniel Clarke and a Scot named Charles Taylor stayed on; Taylor to caretake the Anderson Farm. Also Walter Underwood, nicknamed Watty, remained behind when he married Polly, a Tseshaht woman.

During its tenure in Alberni, the Anderson Company tried different ventures. "It tried to establish copper mines at Tzartus (Copper) Island and Santa Maria Island in Barkley Sound."[65] And while unsuccessful, these tentative beginnings encouraged other prospectors to investigate the possibilities in the area. The Company also established a fishing station at Effingham Island, "the first such commercial enterprise in Barkley Sound."[66] It was reported to be in operation in August 23, 1861.

The H.M.S. *Scout* visited the Alberni Valley in August 1866. A diary of the cruise described conditions:

> It was distressing to see the lately prosperous little settlement of Alberni fast becoming a heap of ruins, only one white man by the name of Drane is there, who takes care of the machinery connected with the sawmill. The pretty little gardens of the settlers are overgrown with weeds and the houses falling to decay. We afterwards, visited the farm up the river; there

is some excellent land farmed by a man named Taylor, a Scotsman, who pays a nominal rent of $1 a year. He has some very fine looking stock.

The empty mill and other buildings stood derelict for a number of years. Then news reached Victoria on September 4, 1879, via the H.M.S. *Rocket* that the mill had been destroyed by fire. When the ship reached Alberni little remained of the small mill, which had burned a few days earlier. The fire was believed to have been caused by an out-of-control campfire of the Cape Flattery Indians. An unsuccessful attempt was made to save the mill buildings by the only two white men there, Charles Taylor and Daniel Clarke. Only the chimney remained standing as a testimony to the once small and thriving community.[67] Clarke eventually left the area but returned later to become one of the pioneer settlers.

Vancouver Island Exploring Expedition

Much of Vancouver Island was still unknown when the Vancouver Island Exploring Expedition took place under the direction of Robert Brown during 1863 and 1864. Brown began his survey in Alberni. Gilbert Malcolm Sproat arranged the opening stage of the expedition by giving him passage on the company schooner to Alberni. He arrived May 25, 1863, and began exploring the surrounding area. He named Sproat Lake in honour of his new friend. Then he named some of the surrounding mountains for his Scottish sponsors.

The longest arm of Sproat Lake he named after a member of his party, Charles Taylor. The Somass River he described as being alive with salmon and beaver. "This creek would afford good water power for mills of any description. The timber is very fine, and we believe Messrs Anderson & Co of Alberni, intend establishing logging camps both on the river and lake."[68]

Brown also described some curiously carved rocks at Sproat Lake, carved by Indians years before. Later he travelled to Great Central Lake, but heavy rain prevented him from discovering the length of the lake. By October he was back in Alberni determined to find out the length of Great Central Lake. On October 22 he arrived at the lakehead. He discovered the lake was eighteen miles long, not the forty or fifty miles it was said to be.

The following year, on August 1, 1864, the expedition left Nanaimo. Brown's group went by sea to Comox, then travelled down the island to Alberni by canoe. The journey took twenty-four days.

The other group travelled to Cowichan Lake by way of Nanaimo Lakes, meeting Brown in Alberni.

When the expedition was about to end in the fall of 1864, Brown and a companion, the Reverend C. Knipe, a missionary in Alberni, attended a potlatch given by a member of the Opetchesaht tribe named "Kayquash" for a group of Tseshahts. The expedition party was at this point based in Alberni, waiting for further directions from Victoria. They were invited to the great feast by Tseshaht "second chief" named "Quatjenam" who had travelled with Brown in 1863 when he explored Sproat Lake. Brown wrote of "really pleasant memories" of the Opetchesaht potlatch.

Confederation

When Canada was born July 1, 1867, it was little more than a collection of farms, villages, and frontier settlements. Only 12 percent of the population lived in cities, with only seven cities having a population exceeding twenty thousand, according to the 1871 census. In the east, people lived in a rural world stitched together by a network of dirt roads. These were the horse and buggy days which are now often looked back on with some nostalgia. But life then was harsh.

British Columbia was still a frontier land – the gold rush colony. The great Fraser River gold rush of 1858 had moved northward to the Cariboo country, to Barkerville, which today remains a monument to gold fever. In March of 1867 Alaska had been purchased from Russia by the United States for $7.2 million.

The British government decided it did not need two west coast colonies, Vancouver Island and British Columbia, each with its own stamps, officials, and capital. The two were joined together forcibly in November 1866, under the name of the mainland colony, with the capital located in Victoria. This union did not end British Columbia's tribulations. The American acquisition of Alaska made British Columbians distinctly uneasy.

With Confederation came renewed faith. The province, however, was still very much as Governor Frederick Seymour had described it "a wagon road, with a gold mine at one end and a seaport at the other."[69] The total white population was 5,625 on the mainland and 5,959 on Vancouver Island, along with 25,661 Indians.

The lieutenant-governor selected as premier John Foster Mc-Creight, a prominent lawyer, but not a politician. The legislature consisted of twenty-five members, thirteen from the mainland, twelve from Vancouver Island. This balancing of power without regard to population continued until 1894.

British Columbians felt then, as they often feel now, like they were at the end of the boondocks, cut off from everything. To send a letter from Victoria to Ottawa, it had to have an American stamp on it as well as the B.C. one, otherwise the American post office at San Francisco would not accept it. Why not be Americans, some thought. What did the new Dominion of Canada have to offer?

For one thing, British Columbians wanted a guarantee of at least a wagon road from Winnipeg to Burrard Inlet. As it happened, when the British Columbia delegation went east to plead their case, Sir John A. Macdonald was ill and George-Étienne Cartier was in charge. "What on earth do you want with a wagon road? It's no good at all in winter, and monumentally slow even in summer. Why don't you ask for a railway?" he suggested. The delegation couldn't believe it, and the Canadian terms were enthusiastically accepted: the railway itself would be completed within ten years. Cartier had committed the Canadian government to building and completing a railway to the west coast by July 20, 1881.[70] One of the many routes proposed would reach the coast at Bute Inlet, bridge Seymour Narrows, and run down Vancouver Island to Victoria.

Indian Reserves

In 1871 British Columbia joined Canada, and attention was given to the assignment of native peoples in the province to reserves. However, in 1864, Douglas had appointed Joseph Trutch as Chief Commissioner of Lands and Works. It was Trutch who would have the say in the direction of Indian land policy in British Columbia.

Douglas had always defended Indian rights. He had made it clear reserves were to be laid out in accordance with the wishes of the Indians. The Indians were satisfied with the treatment they had received under Douglas. But Trutch was a different breed of man. In 1872 he told the Prime Minister of Canada that most of the British Columbian Indians were "utter Savages living along the coast, frequently committing murder and robbery amongst themselves, one tribe upon another, and on white people who go amongst them for the purpose of trade."[71]

Douglas had made the provision that if the area demanded by the Indians did not equal ten acres per family then the reserve was to be enlarged to that extent. But Trutch resolved that the reserves be reallocated on the basis of ten acres per family. "Instead of using ten acres as a minimum as Douglas had intended, Trutch used it as a maximum figure."[72]

When British Columbia entered into a union with Canada, the Indians hoped they would receive a better deal from Canada. But they were to be disappointed. Trutch became B.C.'s first lieutenant-governor and was determined to defend the province's policy regarding Indian land.

The Dominion suggested that the size of reserves be calculated on the basis of eighty acres per family; the province considered that excessive. British Columbia countered with an offer of ten. Ottawa wanted control of Indian affairs, whereas Trutch wanted control to remain in the province. However determined Ottawa was, it was not yet prepared to go so far as to reverse a provincial policy. The negotiations over acreage collapsed and it was accepted that no specific acreage would be allotted, but that individual situations would be examined by a commission and a decision reached on the basis of local knowledge of the Indian agents.[73]

In 1875-76, a joint federal-provincial Indian Reserve Commission was set up to allocate reserves on no fixed basis for acreage. The west coast reserves were mostly defined in the early 1880s by Commissioner Peter O'Reilly, who sought to limit them as much as possible under instruction from Trutch.[74]

The Tseshaht were assigned a total of nine reserves by O'Reilly; the largest of these, on which the entire on-reserve band population now reside, was located on the lower Somass River. Of the remaining eight reserves, two were on Alberni Inlet (one was sold early in the 20th century) and six were scattered through the Broken Group of islands and in Barkley Sound. The Opetchesaht received one reserve on Sproat River, one on the lower Somass, and two along upper Alberni Inlet.[75] The restoration of such reserve lands has since become a major issue in British Columbia. More important is the fact that aside from certain limited tracts, the land in B.C. has never actually been surrendered by the native peoples in treaties.

> The traditional native life was suppressed on all fronts. The potlatch, so fundamental in the workings of West Coast society, was attacked by the missionaries, Indian agents, and other whites, as wasteful, wicked, and an obstacle to the introduction of Christianity and civilization among the natives. In 1884 it was officially outlawed, but the law was not enforceable and the West Coast Indians kept on potlatching.

Perhaps more diligently applied were the fishing and hunting regulations with patrolling officers. Again such restrictions were widely evaded, but sadly the natives were deemed poachers in using their own ancestral resources. Even the gathering of cedar bark became subject to prosecution as timber companies logged off the land. Particularly devastating was the white prohibition on use of the salmon weirs that had been so important through the ages in keeping the West Coast people free from want.[76]

The Indians were beginning to realize what white ownership of the land meant, and learning to understand the value of their land.

Christian Missionaries

The coming of Christianity and the missionaries changed the way of life of the Indian people forever. In Alberni, the first brush with the missionaries was when the first church was established by the Anderson Company. Construction of the small Anglican church began in 1863 under the supervision of the Reverend C. Knipe, a missionary for the Society for the Propagation of Christian Knowledge. The church was erected on the site where the first Port Alberni City Hall once stood on Kingsway. From 1863 to 1864, the Rev. Knipe conducted services in the church, which was said to accommodate forty people.[77] The church continued to be used as a mission by the Reverend Jules Willemar and Harry Guillod, the lay reader, even after the mill ceased operation in 1864. The mission was eventually abandoned in 1871. Both Willemar and Guillod had complained they saw too little of the natives to accomplish their goals. They were transferred from the west coast mission to Comox.

When the Anderson Mill was burned to the ground in 1879, the little Alberni church was lost too. In subsequent years, vicars from French Creek and other east coast communities made occasional visits to the Valley, calling on the Indians. When the courthouse in Alberni was built years later, services were held there.

One of the pioneer missionaries who most influenced native life on the west coast was Father A. I. Brabant, who in 1875, established a mission at Hesquiat. Modern Nootkans consider that he put a stop to the intertribal wars that afflicated the coast. He was, of course, actively supported by Canadian law.[78] His journals show his successful proselytizing was a long hard struggle, but he eventually became a dominant figure, and influenced many phases of native life up and down the coast.

In his journals Father Brabant left a series of reminiscences which told of his life among the Indians. With reference to the potlatch,

41

Brabant said, "As for me, I cannot see any harm in it, although I would rather have it abolished. I had no reason therefore of my own, but giving due importance to the conduct of men longer in the ministry than myself, I used all my influence to keep my people from going to the present gift-feast in Barclay Sound."

He said the hospitality of the Indians to visitors or strangers was quite noteworthy. "As soon as a canoe of strangers arrive at a village they are at once invited by some of the residents to carry their belongings up to their house, a meal is prepared for them and lodgings are offered." When Indians travelled they took little or no provisions along, for they always reckoned on receiving hospitality wherever they happened to go on shore near an Indian settlement.

In 1874 Brabant, accompanied by the Right Rev. Bishop Seghers, D.D. visited Alberni. He wrote in his journal:

> We had a pleasant trip up the Alberni Canal. Having left Ekool in the morning, we arrived in the afternoon at China River and called at the house of the miners, but found them absent. As a sign of our passing the Bishop wrote on their door the fact of our calling and wished them success. That night we were received by Mr. Clark, (Daniel Clarke) who was then manager of the farm. He showed us some fine horses of which he had twenty-two: also some of his cattle, saying that he had a hundred and sixty head running all over the settlement. A Mr. Taylor (Charles Taylor) was the only other settler.
>
> Next day we went to visit the Opetchesahts where we were all well received. They were then living above the forks of the river. The Sheshahts were also on the river, but as their Chief had refused to receive us the day before, we passed them by.

Father Brabant served the west coast mission from 1874-1899. He wrote:

> Twenty-five years have now elapsed since I first set foot on the western shore of Vancouver Island. When I first met the inhabitants of that desolate coast, they were savage, immoral and treacherous. Their dwellings were hovels of filth and misery; their attire a blanket of cedar bark, dog's hair or other inferior article; they were addicted to witchcraft and innumerable superstitious practices.
>
> All alone in the wilderness, deprived of the company of friends or white men, with no mails except once or twice a year, I have spent many mournful seasons without seeing any encouraging results of my arduous labours. With Christianity, they have adopted civilization. The people under my charge are now, as a whole, docile and law abiding. They have used their earnings to improve their material conditions. They have built neat and clean dwelling houses; they dress well, both men and women, after the fashion of civilized people; they are regular at church and at the Sacraments.

The journal is signed A. J. Brabant, Hesquiat, October 1899.[79]

Father Brabant also recorded details of the first Roman Catholic mission which served Alberni. On August 23, 1876, he left Victoria on the schooner *Favourite* with Hugh McKay as captain, and arrived the next day on Copper Island, opposite the Sarita Valley and River. Their provisions and tools were carried in canoes to a spot selected for a building close to the Namukamus Village. After erecting a small cabin, they began work on squaring the logs for a new building.

> My work was to look after the Indian labourers and do the cooking. We had a bunk on each side of the cabin, a stove in the middle, and a small table and a bench at the end of the room. Under the bunks we stowed our provisions – bacon, potatoes, rice and beans. The flour we kept in a small barrel as a protection from the mice which infested our odd dwelling. I made bread as often as required. The Indians we fed on biscuit and molasses. One morning, having neglected to cover the bucket in which we kept our molasses over night, I found 24 mice drowned in the sweet stuff. I carefully picked them out, unseen by the Indians. Afterward they continued to enjoy their molasses and biscuit as if nothing had happened. The Indians, unaccustomed to white man's food, enjoyed their fare immensely. The carpenter also was satisfied with my culinary efforts. Altogether we had a rather pleasant time.[80]

The first mass was said on Christmas Day. Brabant left on the second day of the year for Hesquiat in the canoe which had brought his assistant, Rev. J. Nicolaye, to his new mission. "From the beginning of the year all the Indians of Barclay Sound and down to Port Juan inclusive, will be attended to from St. Leo's Mission, of which Rev. J. Nicolaye is the first resident pastor."[81]

It was from St. Leo's Mission that Father Nicolaye served Alberni in 1878. He described in his own words his first impression of Alberni. "On my first visit, which I made in a small canoe, I was amazed at the huge mountains on either side, at the profound silence all the way up, at the insignificant population."[82] Two years later, Father Eussen replaced Father Nicolaye at St. Leo's. In another four years a sad note was recorded regarding the fate of Father Eussen. Suffering from severe hemorrhaging, Father Eussen waded through February snows to reach medical aid in Nanaimo.

> I left Alberni, February 12, a very cold day. I took my knapsack, weighing thirty pounds, and hired an Indian as my guide, who carried my blankets and gun. The trail was covered with snow which made hard walking, but all we had to do was to follow the tracks of wolves and panthers. After a two hour walk we had to climb View Mountain, 1600 feet. Our breathing was much too precious to speak much during the steep ascent. I asked the guide, if we were on the top. He said, "Oh, no, this mountain has a brother

which is much higher." You can imagine that I wished Mount View was an only son.[83]

Father Eussen had walked in the snow to Nanaimo via Qualicum, a distance of approximately sixty-three miles. He returned to Belgium to recover his health, but died there of tuberculosis.

Father Lemmens followed him to Alberni and within a few years was raised to the dignity of the episcopacy. On River Road, just below the site of the Catholic cemetery, Father Lemmens built the first Roman Catholic church. Father Verbeke, from Belgium, became the first permanent pastor.[84] The picturesque little church was close to the road, about eighty yards from the bridge. On the opposite side of the road was a bell, hung on a sixteen foot high timber-framed stand, on the bank of the river.

Verbeke was an energetic young man. He had a small herd of goats, a large vegetable garden, and an orchard. He lived in the rear of the church. A small cemetery was laid out on the hill above.[85]

Pioneer Settlers

Settlers began arriving in the Alberni Valley as early as 1883. They came by canoe up the Alberni Inlet and on foot over the Horne Lake trail. Many came from Great Britain, others from eastern Canada, some even from Australia.

Of the original settlement, only two men remained continuously in the Alberni Valley. One was Watty Watts, the other Charles Taylor. Watty (Walter) was the son of Walter Underwood, an Englishman who worked at the Anderson Mill in 1861. Although his surname was Underwood he eventually took the name of Watts. He married Polly of the Tseshaht Band. In 1886 he was awarded the contract to carry the mail twice a month from Qualicum, travelling on foot over the Horne Lake trail. Later this mail route was extended to Nanaimo, but by then Watty had a horse.

About 1883 he decided to live in the settlement and left the Indian reservation. For several years he voted. However, the lure of his people was strong. He returned to the reservation to live. Watty married twice, having two children by the first marriage, one of whom was Chief Dan Watts. There were nine children in the second family. In his later years he did some farming and gardening, picking Oregon grapes and ferns for Eastern markets. He was a familiar figure around the yard of his home at the junction of the Sproat and McCoy Lake roads.[86] Watty's Road is named in his honour.[87]

Charles Taylor left Livingstone, Scotland, when the California gold discovery attracted him to the Pacific Coast. He came to the Alberni Valley to work for the Anderson Company sawmill and stayed behind to rent the company farm. He grew potatoes and swede turnips. The Indians had acquired a taste for the vegetables, and often tribes located in Barkley Sound traded with him.

He had left behind in Scotland a son, also named Charles. In 1884 the son decided to join his father. Charles Jr., his wife and six-year-old son, also named Charles, left Scotland aboard an Allen Line passenger boat for Boston. They crossed the United States to Tacoma, Washington, and from there took a steamboat to Victoria. A freighter, the *Sardonix* brought them to Uchucklesit (Kildonan), where Taylor hired a man to bring them to Alberni by canoe. Another canoe ride with an Indian named Cultus Jim took them up the Somass River to the Anderson Farm.

Charles Jr. continued in his trade working as a steam engineer on Captain Huff's boat, occasionally working at the various canneries.[88]

George Daniel (Dan) Clarke, a native of St. Augustine, Florida, also had worked for the Anderson Company sawmill. With his new wife and Dan, her thirteen-year-old son by a previous marriage, he returned to the valley in 1871 to caretake the Anderson Company farm. Charles Taylor was now an old man and was resigning his charge.

Young Dan had two brothers from his mother's first marriage. They were Michael and John Sareault. The two brothers preferred to remain in Cowlitz Prairie, Washington State, where the first family lived. Later, Michael would join his mother and brother in Alberni. He, too, became one of the early settlers, building a small water-powered sawmill on Kitsuksis Creek as well as the Alberni Hotel. John visited Alberni but never became a resident.

Dan and his mother built a small house on the eastern side of the Somass River, leaving Clarke senior across the river at the Anderson Farm. The Clarke farm consisted of 320 acres. Their house was built on Mary Street. All the streets in the area were later named after young Dan's daughters. The western portion of the Clarke family land, 160 acres, between Golden Street and Falls Road, became the property of the Roman Catholic Church in 1886.

Eventually Dan senior followed his step-son across the river, and then the farm began to expand. With the help of a team of oxen, acre by acre was made ready for cultivation. It became a well-worked, highly productive farm. Mrs. Clarke senior was responsible for the very early planting of fruit and ornamental trees on the family property, which became the chief local source of fruit for the early settlers of the 1880s.

On several succeeding spring seasons, young Dan was able to join the sealing schooners bound for the Bering Sea and the Aleutian Islands. These schooners with sailing crews and captains from the Atlantic provinces picked up Indian and white sealers on the west coast. In good seasons considerable money was earned.

In December 1881, young Dan married an Alberni girl, Laura Fern. They were married by the missionary priest Father Eussen. Of their twelve children, two died in infancy, and one son, William, was killed during the Great War. Another home was built to accommodate the growing family at the corner of River Road and Mary Street. The house was shaded by two towering maple trees and surrounded by fruit trees.

This must have been a good life for the Clarke children living close to the Somass River which offered not only good fishing, but also swimming and boating in the summer. They also had access to the family orchard of cherries, apples, plums, and pears.

Laura was a religious woman devoted to the Roman Catholic Church. Her home was always open to any visiting priest known on the west coast of Vancouver Island, including Father Brabant, Father Verbeke, Bishop Orth, and later Bishop Alexander Macdonald.

In 1905-1907 provincial legislation was passed allowing timber licenses in separate areas of 649 acres. For an entry fee of $140 per license and with an annual rental of the same amount, experienced timber cruisers took advantage of the opportunity to form small syndicates. Dan, with the backing of an old friend, Dr. Arthur Proctor (the first schoolteacher in the area), staked twenty-five license areas in the Nahmint Valley and a lesser area at the headwaters of Great Central Lake. Later they sold the timber licenses, and both became wealthy men.[89] Dan's son, George Clarke, also sold timber, and with the money he invested in an automobile. In 1907 Clarke's "Red Humber" automobile was reported to be running between Alberni and Nanaimo carrying passengers.[90]

During the 1910-1912 Alberni real estate boom that resulted from news that the railway was coming, Dan decided to sell the farm. Part of the property was subdivided into five-acre parcels, the river frontage into acre lots. The family kept fifteen acres surrounding the homestead and built a new house just east of the old family home. Dan and Laura looked forward to taking life easy but just before they moved in, Laura became ill and passed away, a tragic loss for her family. Dan eventually obtained a smaller home in the Beaver Creek area, where he lived with his daughter Marguerite. He died in December 1941.

The McKenzie family arrived in 1883. Kenneth McKenzie married Alexandrina MacKenzie in Lanark, Scotland. They emigrated to Kincardine, Ontario, where Kenneth had a general store. The first six of their seven children were born there: Hector in 1869, Annie in 1872, Margaret in 1875, Douglas in 1877, Simon in 1880, and Donald in 1882. Acreage in the Alberni Valley was being advertised and it was not expensive, so the family decided to come west.

The family of eight travelled by the Northern Pacific Railway to Seattle, then sailed on the schooner *George E. Star* to Victoria. Kenneth had applied for 160 acres along the Stamp River, where the Ivor Rage farm is now located. He received his pre-emption certificate on November 5, 1884, and the property was conveyed to him by the E & N Railway Co. on June 10, 1891.

Leaving his wife and younger children in Victoria, Kenneth, with his eldest son Hector, now fifteen, came by boat up the Alberni Inlet to a landing known as Fish House Point, on the west bank of Kitsuksis Creek where it joins the Somass River. They used Indian dugout canoes to carry their tools and provisions to their new property, paddling past the Opetchesaht Reserve on the Somass River, then branching off onto the Stamp River to reach their heavily timbered acreage on the east bank of the Stamp River.

There were no neighbours to help with the clearing and building, so father and son felled trees and hewed the logs to build the cabin. Alexandrina arrived in September with the two girls and three young boys. The family travelled by chartered steamer and arrived in the valley with many supplies and some cattle, to be met by Kenneth and Hector in canoes purchased from the local Indians. They paddled up the river to their new home by the Somass and Stamp Rivers. It took six weeks to transport all the supplies by canoe to the ranch.

A month later, on October 17, 1884, Alexandrina gave birth to John Alexander, the first boy born to white parents in the Alberni Valley. Her twelve-year-old daughter, Annie, and an Indian woman, Jenny Little, helped at the birth. Jenny stayed on to help in the years to follow, teaching young Jack to fish, hunt, and trap. Jack told of shooting his first deer at age eight, then returning to the farmhouse to get Jenny to carry it home.[91] He grew up with a great knowledge of the animals in the forest and of the local Indians. He was able to speak to the Indians in their language.

Kenneth and Hector cleared the land, burning the stumps and brush after falling the trees, getting the ground ready to plant potatoes and vegetables. They named the farm "Burnside Ranch." The Indians were often visitors at their home. Alexandrina fed them and sewed clothing for the children with the material she had brought from Ontario. The Indians in turn gave her ducks and fish and mats they wove for her. One visitor was Chief Konawash of the Opetchesaht Band, who was offered raisin bread. When he left, the raisins were found behind a log he had been sitting on. Konawash went barefoot winter and summer and wore only a feather in his long black hair and a Hudson's Bay blanket. When he grew to trust the white people he appeared at the farm once a week. In Chinook he would say "no muck a muck ten as sun," meaning, "I have had no food since the sun was small."

Four years after their arrival, the McKenzies built a two-storey log house. The land was gradually being cleared. High grade trees, mainly fir, were felled and bucked into two foot lengths, which were split to be used in burning out the tree stumps. It was necessary to keep the tree stump fires going twenty-four hours a day, so during the night the family took turns stoking the fires. The air was constantly thick with smoke in the Valley as the settlers cleared their property.

Alexandrina McKenzie was called upon to act as a midwife. She assisted in the birth of Harold Bishop in 1887 at the Bishops' Beaver Creek farmhouse. In 1891 Alexandrina died, at the age of forty-three. She was buried just off the Beaver Creek trail, near Gill school, but was later moved to Greenwood Cemetery.

In 1898, at fifty-nine years of age, Kenneth McKenzie was married for the second time, to Miss Helen MacFarline of Victoria, formerly of Toronto. Six years later he died and was buried beside his first wife in Greenwood cemetery.

The little settlement of Alberni was slowly growing; wagon roads were being built, and farmers were able to ship their potato and turnip crops to market. The crops sold as fast as the farmers could grow them. The clearing of the farmland was never ending.

There have been over 150 descendents of Kenneth and Alexandrina McKenzie – six generations, five of them born in the Alberni Valley and many still living here. A cairn is now erected on the site where the McKenzie farmhouse once stood.[92]

When Henry Hills (Harry) came to Alberni from Ontario in 1885, he was twenty-nine years old. Born in Seasalter, Kent, England, Harry emigrated to Allenford, Ontario, with his brother James, in 1871. He married Janet Loree in Ontario, and they had three children, Jim, Fanny, and Tom. But Harry didn't like the cold winters in eastern Canada. Letters from another Alberni settler, John C. Mollett, told of the bright prospects and mild weather in Alberni. Harry moved west in 1885, and the following year, Janet brought their three children to Alberni. Seven more children were born on the farm. They were Clayton, George, Percy, Jack, Ruth, Kate, and Dorothy. Harry Hills became the fourth mayor of Alberni in 1917.

James Hills joined his brother in Alberni in 1885. He married Elizabeth Nicholas in 1899; they had two sons, Henry James, born in 1902, and Albert George, born in 1904. James became an alderman on the first city council of Alberni in 1913, and he was an alderman at the time of his death in 1927. James died at age seventy, on July 27, 1927, from injuries received when he was kicked by a cow.[93]

Peter Nicholas left Australia in 1885 to come and join his uncle, Peter Merrifield, who was in poor health. Merrifield, who had left the mines in Nanaimo, had pre-empted 160 acres in the Beaver Creek area. Peter Nicholas, deciding to stay, sent word to Australia that his wife Sarah and their four children should come to Alberni. Then he built a house for his family. The following year, after a long voyage from Australia, Sarah, with her four children, Bertha, Henrietta, William, and Alfred and her brother-in-law, William Nicholas, walked over the Horne Lake Trail to join her husband.

The Nicholas homestead was located beside the Horne Lake trail. The log building, which stood for many years, was recently demolished before efforts could be made to have it declared a heritage site. In the spring of 1887 Sarah gave birth to her third daughter, Johanna, the first born in their new home. Unfortunately, Alfred died that same year. Another daughter, Catherine (Kate), was born in 1889, Ada Gertrude in 1890, followed by three more girls – Clara in 1892, Hilda in 1894, and Lillian in 1897. There were now nine children, eight girls and one boy.[94]

Captain George Albert Huff was born in Brighton, Ontario. He spent nineteen years as a sailor on the Great Lakes, then four years as a merchant in the Bay Island division of the Spanish Honduras, Central America. In 1885 Huff was master of the steamer *Daisy*, running between Victoria and Comox. In August of that year, he came to Alberni, filed on a pre-emption claim of 176 acres, and opened a store a short time later.[95] He was thirty-seven years of age when he came to the Valley with his wife Eliza and their daughter Minnie.

In 1890 Huff sold his land to the Presbyterian Mission for $5,000. This became the site of the Alberni Residential Mission school. Capt. Huff became one of the area's first entrepreneurs. He built the first wharf in Alberni, operated the first store in the small settlement, and was the first resident to own and operate boats that catered to the public. He later purchased a corner lot in Alberni for $900.

On October 5, 1895, Capt. Huff won a by-election in the riding of Cowichan-Alberni and became the area's member of the provincial legislature. Huff was a Liberal; he served three years until he was replaced by Independent candidate Alan Webster Neill, in 1898.

In 1914 Capt. Huff became Mayor of Alberni. Opposing Charles Frederic Bishop, he won the election by only three votes. As mayor, Huff worked with the Port Alberni City Council to bring electric light to Alberni.[96]

His daughter Minnie Huff was born in 1877 at Penetanguishine, Ontario. She married Thomas George Paterson and became known around the world as the "Grace Darling" of the west coast for her part in the dramatic sea rescue of the crew from the barque *Coloma*, which foundered off Cape Beale on December 6, 1906 while she and her husband were keepers at the Cape Beale lighthouse.

Thomas George Paterson emigrated from Glasgow, Scotland, having left home at age thirteen. He owned a large portion of land in Alberni, known later as the Paterson Townsite. For a time before his appointment as lightkeeper at Cape Beale, in March 1895, Paterson operated a stable where locals could hire a horse, buggy, or sulky. He was also the second contractor to carry mail across the island.

Thomas married Minnie Huff on January 19, 1893. They had eight children; the first born was George Andrew, in 1893; Violet Jane, born in 1894, died two years later. Another child, also named Violet Jane, was born in 1898. The others were May Ann, 1899; Agnes Leslie, 1901; Tommy Robert, 1906; Vincent, 1907; and Minnie Belle, born in 1909.

The Paterson family returned to Alberni in 1907. Tommy subdivided his land into residential lots and built a large home just above the railway tracks, in an area then known as Glencoe Heights. He formed a small private company and brought the first telephone to the area. Minnie died in 1911, having contracted tuberculosis in her weakened condition after the sea rescue.

Charles Frederic Bishop was born in Lutton Town, England, in 1845. His wife, Marie Mathews, was born in Adelaide, Australia where her family had gone to make their fortune in a gold rush. The Mathews family never found gold but did well in the baking business. When they returned to England, Marie met and married Charles; they had three children – Anna Maria, Emily Maud, and Edward – before deciding to come to Canada. Frederic had been in ill health and it was thought the climate in Canada would be good for him. They settled in Bradford, Ontario, where they established a baking business before deciding to come west.

The Bishops travelled across Canada on the first scheduled transcontinental passenger train from Montreal to Port Moody on July 4th, then by boat to Vancouver. The Great Fire of Vancouver was still burning when they arrived, and there was no place to stay, so they kept on travelling to Victoria. The Canadian Pacific Railway was advertising land for sale at one dollar an acre in the Alberni Valley. The Bishops set off by small ship up the east coast of Vancouver Island, then came to Alberni via the Horne Lake trail in October 1886. Attracted to the Beaver Creek area, they settled on a quarter section, which was 160 acres. A log house and barn was built by holding a "raising bee," neighbour helping neighbour. They named their new home "Mayfield." Three more children were born here: Frederic Harold, Gertrude Edith, and Ethel May.

Like many of the other early settlers, the Bishops began to think about educating their children. They donated an acre of land for the first schoolhouse to be built. During the spring and early summer of 1887, Capt. George A. Huff and Edmund Gill prepared the logs and split the shakes for the roof of the Beaver Creek and Alberni (Gill) schoolhouses. School officially opened in the fall of 1887 with Arthur P. Proctor as the first teacher, working part-time in both schools.

The Beaver Creek Post Office was located in the Bishop family home. There was also a small store which carried staple items such as flour and oatmeal. In 1895 Frederic was given a contract to carry the mail from Alberni to Beaver Creek, twice a week, a distance of five miles each way. He often walked the distance carrying the mail on his back. For this he was paid sixty-eight dollars a year in quarterly payments of seventeen dollars.

In later years Frederic Bishop told the story of fishing in the Alberni Inlet from a dugout canoe using thick twine. He said he caught a salmon so big he couldn't get it in the canoe and had to tow it around until it expired. The fish weighed ninety pounds.

By the late nineties, mining was driving the economy of the region. Mining companies were looking for someone to open a dining room and bake shop, and Frederic seized the opportunity, moving into town to open the first C. F. Bishop and Son grocery store and bakehouse on Johnston Road approximately where Jowsey's is at the present time. In 1898 a new store was constructed by Thomas Paterson, son-in-law of Capt. Huff, at the corner of Gertrude and Johnston. The new C. F. Bishop and Son dining room and bake shop opened in 1898.

In February 1908, the Bishop family made a contract with Alex B. Wood (Barclay Sound Cedar Co.) to construct a new store. The building, to be used for a grocery and confectionery store and bakery, was erected on a vacant lot at the corner at Southgate and Victoria Quay, the present site of the Somass Drug Store. The family also purchased the Dr. Pybus residence on the adjoining lot to build their new home.

Bishop became a Justice of the Peace and first mayor of Alberni. During his term in office he helped establish the first high school for the district, as well as providing a site for a new firehall for Alberni.

Frederic's son Harold became a full partner in the business, "C. F. Bishop and Son," and opened another store in Port Alberni and a third store at Sproat Lake, where the family had taken up residence. A wharf constructed at the lake became known as Bishop's Landing.[97]

Joseph G. Halpenny also pre-empted a quarter section in the Beaver Creek area. In 1892, with son Heman, he started the Halpenny Sawmill, purchasing logs from anyone who would haul them into their mill. In 1894 the mill was moved to Rogers Creek. Joseph's daughter, Mary Lucinda, married Thomas R. Plaunt. Heman Halpenny married Frances Phoebe Hills, daughter of Harry Hills, then moved to Chemainus.

Thomas R. Plaunt and Ernie Woodward arrived in the area during the winter of 1887-88. The two bachelors lived together on a property on what is now Cameron Road, off Bainbridge Road, in the Beaver Creek district. The Plaunt-Woodward partnership went into farming and engaged as well in several other small enterprises, including unloading machinery for the paper mill, or hauling freight to mines in the area. For the mill job they received two dollars per day. Later they received a contract to haul lumber.[98]

In 1908, Joseph Halpenny deeded one hundred acres of his farm to his son-in-law, Thomas, who undertook to support his father-in-law for the rest of his life. Thomas and Mary had seven children: Elizabeth, John, Margaret, Lois, Thomas, Winifred, and Mary. Ernie

Woodward married Bertha (nee Nicholas) on July 20, 1896. They had one son, Ernest Woodward.

Issac Drinkwater and his son Jack came to Alberni from Ontario in 1887. His wife Maria and their other children arrived in 1891. They had twelve children, eight sons and four daughters: Hilton in 1862, Joseph Albert 1864, Jack 1865, George 1867, Ida 1869, Susan 1871, James 1874, Sarah 1876, Mary 1878, Ben 1880, Frederick 1882, and Alfred 1885. Daughter Susan recalled the family's move to the west from Ontario:

My father, Isaac Drinkwater, was born in Brampton, Ontario on March 12, 1831. His father was an Englishman and his mother was Irish. Grand-father Drinkwater was a small man, though the Drinkwater men were generally tall. Isaac married Maria Shooke in 1860 in Brampton, Ontario. My mother was born in Brampton in 1841. Her father was of Dutch ancestry and her mother was Scottish.

Isaac was a farmer and carpenter. He sold his farm on the Tenth Line near Arran Lake, and bought at Allenford on the Thirteenth Concession. Here the family lived until they moved to Alberni in 1891.

My father along with Duncan McDougall and John Mollet, made a trip into the west. They left on the 25th day of February. I was working at Owen Sound at the time. They were in Manitoba and Montana. My father brought a hammer home with him that we always called the "Bismark." They were in the Yellowstone and Fraser River country, and at one time travelled one of these rivers by raft. They built the raft for use in transportation because of the lack of money to enable them to travel otherwise.

I was sixteen years of age in 1887 when my father made the second trip into the west, going to British Columbia. From Victoria to Nanaimo he travelled by train, then walked to Alberni by the footpath. His trunk was to go by boat. The boat sank and also the trunk. He lost all his gun-making tools, his carpenter tools and all his clothes, including a new suit.

The family moved to Alberni in the fall of 1891. I was at Owen Sound at the time, Joe was in Duluth and Ida at Wiarton, Ontario, when the decision was made to move their home to Alberni on Vancouver Island. The Drinkwater Farm near Allenford was sold to the Newmans. Joe and Ida went to the Coast later. I was married in the spring of 1892 and came to Manitoba. Susan married Andrew Morran and lived in Manitoba from 1892 to 1961. Brother Hilton and his wife and sister Sarah had previously gone to the Coast and walked to Alberni by the footpath.

Mother, Johnny, Mary, George, Jim, Ben, Fred and Alfred, went in to Alberni by stagecoach. The family was a musical one. The boys all played the violin, but Hilton. My mother taught each of them to play. George especially was a very good violinist. By nature, the Drinkwaters were hunters, woodsmen, explorers and prospectors.[99]

Issac was an expert axeman, and besides clearing his own farm in the Beaver Creek area, he was in demand for hewing timbers for other farms. The Drinkwaters were appreciated for their musical talents.

Fred and his fiddle were very much a part of the early entertainment of the settlers. Alf, the youngest, was the carpenter of the family, having learned the trade as a boy from George Forrest, another settler. George Drinkwater was the Valley's first barber. His shop was located in the area now known as Victoria Quay. All of the Drinkwaters were interested in the outdoors.

In 1899 Joe Drinkwater discovered Della Falls, which is 1,443 feet high, and he also staked out some mineral claims which became the Big Interior mine. His discovery of the falls resulted from a bet with a geologist who thought it was not possible to cross Vancouver Island from Bedwell Sound. Joe took up the challenge, and hiking alone he followed Bedwell River through the rough country to You Creek. The first white woman to see Della Falls and Della Lake was Joe's wife Della, for whom they were named.[100]

Joe Drinkwater built a floating lodge called "The Ark" at Great Central Lake, and it became one of the most famous floating hotels on the west coast.

Brothers George and Andrew Smith, and Walter and Frank Stirling, took up land on the north side of Sproat Lake in 1885. The Smith brothers were from Glen Cova in Forfarshire, Scotland, sons of the Rev. George Arbuthnott Smith, a Presbyterian minister, and his wife Jessie. George, the eldest, was born in 1858. His brother Andrew was born on the same date, July 12, in 1860. Another brother William and sister Jessie followed.

George, a surveyor, arrived first, with his wife Evangeline in 1885. He was the government agent in Alberni from 1891 to 1894. The couple had three children, Jessie, Lingen, and Jean. Andrew succeeded his brother as government agent until 1910.

Walter Stirling came from St. Andrews, Scotland, and began farming here in 1884. His brother, Frank, came in 1890 at the age of eighteen and built a log cabin at Sproat Lake. Later Frank Stirling married Jessie, the sister of the Smith brothers, but she died when their first child was born in 1893. Frank, devastated by his wife's death, returned to Scotland with his new daughter to study medicine; he later remarried there. With his second wife and three children he came back to Victoria in the 1900s, where he practised as an ear, eye, and throat specialist. He continued to use the lake property as a summer home.[101]

George Smith had long absences from his home while surveying, and during these periods Walter Stirling looked after his farm. He and Mrs. Evangeline Smith became close friends. Inevitably their friendship turned to love. George and Evangeline were divorced. She and Walter left the Alberni Valley, eventually marrying and settling in the Vernon area. George later married Mary Halliday, and they moved to Los Angeles, California, where George died in 1934.

Rev. and Mrs. Smith joined their children in Alberni. They celebrated their golden wedding in 1907.

Robert W. Thompson was attracted to British Columbia by glowing reports appearing in Ontario newspapers recommending settlers go west. Thompson had come to Canada from Yorkshire, England, settling in the Whitby, Ontario area where he met his wife Ellen.

With his wife and two infant children, Arthur, two years old, and Eva, still a year-old baby, he left Ontario. The young family travelled to B.C. via the Southern Pacific, stopping in New Mexico for a short time where Mrs. Thompson admired the adobe huts, baked clay floors, and thatched roofs.

When they first arrived in Alberni the family lived in a floorless shack on the Daniel Clarke farm on River Road while Robert built a log cabin in the Bainbridge and Thompson road area of Beaver Creek. Three other children, Luther, Oliver, and Nellie, were born on this homestead. The children all attended Beaver Creek log schoolhouse, walking over a trail through the woods.

Arthur kept a dairy which told of the family's early life in the Alberni Valley. He wrote that his mother always wanted to return to Ontario. Despite this desire, she toughed it out, staying to raise her children on the farm. Robert took his young son to a potlach, and the memorable occasion provided a colourful addition to Arthur's diary.

> My father took me to a potlach once. The only one I was ever at. It was held in the largest building they (Indians) had. It was on the right side of River Road, (Opetchesaht reserve). The building must have been 70 or 80 feet long and about 50 or 60 feet wide. The late Frank Heath was there that night. I noticed he was trying to measure it, stepping it off. There were big round timbers on high posts. How they put them up there no one knows. It had a cedar roof of sorts with a hole in the centre for smoke to escape.
>
> The ground was quite hard (earth). A fireplace was burning in the centre right under the hole in the roof. Around the walls were sleeping berths. They had a dance; we did not see it all. I don't know which one gave the potlach but I believe a lot of stuff was given away.
>
> One incident I noticed while there, a small boy was sound asleep. His father took him in his arms and got a piece of charcoal from the fire. He put queer marks on his face which gave him a weird look.
>
> We got an Indian to make us a torch out of cedar splinters bound together fairly tight as it was dark. We had to walk to the old Alberni Hotel where we stayed the night. Surprisingly that torch gave us ample light all

the way. Some of the Indians objected to us Whites being there. Others didn't seem to mind. Father had some sweet biscuits which he gave away to the squaws.[102]

Arthur was intrigued by the Indians and their customs. He described how the Indians used to put their dead in wooden boxes, then hang them in trees.

I saw three boxes much later than that, not very far from the Beaver Creek Road. They did not look big enough to contain a full grown adult, possibly children, although I was told they broke the legs and doubled them over the body. They would have had to go to a lot of work to make a box. To make a 3 × 5 inch plank they hewed a cedar log on both sides until they got the desired thickness in the centre.[103]

He said the Indians were very shy people. They would hide behind trees and peek around anxious to know what a white woman looked like. He was told one was bold enough to try to get into the house. His mother had to push her out. "They had blankets around them from the Hudson's Bay Co. The Indians were treated most scandalously. They (the HBC) demanded a great deal more in furs, beaver, seal and otter, than a blanket was worth."[104]

Arthur's later journal describes the day-to-day life on the farm at Beaver Creek.

George Alexander Spencer, aged twenty-one, came to Canada in 1892, from Bedford, England, where he had apprenticed in carpentry and stonemasonry. He took three days to walk from Victoria to Alberni. Alex, as he was known, had his first Christmas dinner in Canada with Mr. and Mrs. George Smith, the surveyor at Sproat Lake. He first built a log cabin on a quarter section in the Beaver Creek area, approximately twelve miles from Alberni. In 1894 he returned to England and married Jennie Roff. When Alex and Jennie returned to Alberni they built a log cabin at McCoy Lake, where their first son, Norrie, was born.

Every creek or stream around Great Central Lake and down the Alberni Inlet was prospected by the Spencer family and their friend Ephraim Colman, the local blacksmith. Then, in 1900, Spencer purchased another 160 acres of land in Alberni; this quarter section bordered on Compton Road, Margaret Street, Leslie Avenue, and Arrowsmith Street. The Spencers built a family home on Glenside, near Kitsuksis Creek. The Gertrude Street bridge cuts through what was once the Spencer farm. Jennie loved gardening and their home became a showplace complete with tennis courts, resembling an old English estate. They had a dam built on Kitsuksis Creek with water rights for a water supply. Three other sons were born to the couple: Geoffrey Boden in 1900, Brian Roff in 1907, and Alwyn Roff in 1912. Alex Spencer became an alderman on Alberni's first council.[105]

Other pioneer settlers included Edmund Gill, John Love, and John Fisher, who came over the Horne Lake trail in 1886. Mr. and Mrs. Thomas Kirkpatrick arrived in the spring of 1887. In August, Thomas walked to Nanaimo to guide his daughters to Alberni. The three had two horses between them. While one horse carried the luggage, Sadie and Edith took turns riding the other. Edith married Ed Gill. Sadie became the wife of Gus Cox.

Harry Guillod was the Indian agent for the west coast. His reports date from 1882. Before that he was lay reader with the British Columbia Mission which served Alberni in the 1860s. He was the son of Lord and Lady Guillod, of England, and was educated as a chemist. For a time he lived in Comox, where his skill as a chemist came in handy for the early settlers because he could advise on drugs and often acted as a doctor. Harry Guillod married Miss Monroe, sister of Mrs. Willemar, and they had three daughters, Beatrice Josephine, Kate and Edna. The family lived in Ucluelet for a time, then moved to Alberni in 1892 so that their daughters could attend the school.

John C. Mollet was born on the Channel Islands off the coast of France and south of the English coast. He wrote to Victoria's *Daily British Colonist* on June 28, 1884, announcing he had taken up land here and intended to move to the district shortly. His letter was addressed to people in search of land suitable for agriculture. He told of travelling to Nanaimo by steamboat and by trail to Qualicum.

"From Qualicum to Alberni, 20 miles useless, except for timber," was his comment. "The scenery around Horne Lake is beautiful, on one hand clear deep waters of the lake, on the other, abrupt mountains."[106]

He told of reaching the farm of Peter Merrifield (uncle of the Nicholas family) after "a tiresome journey through the mountains; and of spending the night at a farm. There are six or seven other settlers with very good farms and are satisfied with their present and future prospects. Mr. Taylor, the oldest resident, a kind and hearty old man, who has a place of his own, is taking charge of the Alberni farm, a fine piece of land owned by an English company. Mr. Clark has a nice place on the river and his wife has a good garden. Messrs. Little, Clement and Evans are settled some way back. Salmon, trout, deer, geese, duck and grouse abound."

Mollett reported good land sufficient to accommodate one hundred families. Announcing his intention to "remove there shortly," he declared, "It only requires a few enterprising families to join us and we will have a good and thriving settlement."[107]

When Mollet arrived in Alberni with his father and mother, he acquired 176 acres of land. He shipped lumber in and built himself a comfortable home on the banks of the Somass River at the present location of Riverbend Bridge. When his mother died, she was buried at the bend of the river on the high ground overlooking the water. For many years the fenced grave could be seen from the Sproat Lake road.

John C. Mollet became the first government agent in Alberni in 1889 and served in that position until 1893. The system of appointing government agents was adopted from the British system already prevalent in the colonies. It followed the pattern of collectors and district officers who represented the British government in India and Africa. In Africa alone, there were estimated to be 754 district officers. Difficulties in governing British Columbia, largely due to the geography, led Sir James Douglas to make the first appointments of government agents in September 1859. These agents were appointed to act as land commissioners, water recorders, gold commissioners, country court judges, Indian agents, customs officers, sheriffs and mining recorders.[108] Mollet was kept busy dealing with the settler's land acquisitions and mining claims, as well as fielding questions on road building and government grants, and acting as magistrate.

The *British Columbia Directory* of 1887 showed Alberni with a small population of mostly farmers. They included the Coleman brothers, Jim, Ephraim, and Bill. Jim was a baker and pastry cook; Ephraim was a blacksmith, wheelwright, and shoeing smith. Bill, who arrived several years later, was a butcher. They came from Market Harborough, in Leicestershire, England. Jim acquired property twenty miles down the Alberni Canal, while Ephraim farmed on the banks of the Stamp River on the Sproat Lake side. Bill stayed at Jim's homestead.

At the turn of the century Ephraim built a blacksmith shop and house on Margaret Street close to Rogers Creek. He could build a farm wagon, repair worn buggy wheels, or make a very good hoe or garden rake. Behind his shop he had a vegetable garden and fruit trees. Grapes grew on two sides of his home and he made wine from these. Jim, the baker and pastry cook, was much in demand as a cook for survey and other camps. It was said he spent most of his evenings studying cookery books. Bill, the butcher, prepared farmers' cattle for the meat market. All three brothers remained firm friends, living to a ripe old age. They died within a short time of each other.[109]

Other farmers listed in the 1887 directory include Ed. Falwell, who lived in the Cherry Creek area near Horne Lake Road, and Edward Grandy, who married Annie McKenzie, daughter of Kenneth McKenzie, and operated a livery stable on First Avenue across from the King Edward Hotel. Others included John Stull Jolly, Thos. Mulhern, Ed. Moore, James McNeill, Frank McQuillan, John Orr, Robert Pinkerton, William Stoddard, and William Swanson.

Land was being sold in 1887 for eight dollars an acre with four annual payments with interest at 6 percent. The S.S. *Maude* made monthly trips from Victoria.

Building A Community

The first church service for the Presbyterian Church was held November 13, 1886, in a little log cabin across the Somass River on the Anderson Farm, the farm being the focal point for many of the activities of the early settlers. The population of the community was then approximately sixty. The first post office was located in one of the Anderson Company houses, a building that served many purposes for a number of years while it was used as a public hall. It was here Tom Fletcher taught the first school in 1887. John Mollett, magistrate for the district, used it for a courthouse. Fred Saunders had it at night for a bedroom, his store being next door. Reverend Alex Dunn conducted church services here for about six months until Gill schoolhouse was opened and services were moved there.

The Reverend Alex Dunn served the Presbyterian ministry during the years 1886 to 1889. During his tenure in Alberni, Rev. Dunn described the community as almost bankrupt. The farmers had found no market for their produce because the government had yet to provide an access road or regular steamship service to the community. Only two new settlers had come into the area to take up land while several of the 115 settlers had moved away. Despite this, those remaining thought religious services were essential and paid the missionary thirty dollars more than had been previously decided, which was $230 within twelve months. Dunn thought highly of the farmers. He wrote:

> The great majority were intelligent, enterprising, energetic men, who were not afraid to work, and who from previous knowledge and experience of clearing land, could work to good advantage. Besides, most of

them, when they came, possessed sufficient capital to make a good start. Visitors who came into the valley from time to time, who could appreciate its excellence, and who could judge also the adaptation of the settlers to their environment, unhesitatingly predicted a bright and prosperous future for Alberni. The raw material, so to speak, was there.[110]

The first Presbyterian church was constructed in 1892 at the corner of Johnson and Elizabeth Streets. Alfred Carmichael recorded the opening. "Our new Presbyterian church was opened today. It is large and airy, much better than the school house (old log schoolhouse on Beaver Creek Road) which has been used for a church."[111]

The Rev. Stables Smith took over from Rev. Dunn when the new church was built. The first service was held May 1, 1892. During the service Myrtle Gill was christened. The church had cost $1,000 to build and, when it was opened, there was only $150 owing on it. The first collection taken amounted to $47.50. The organist was schoolteacher John Howitt.[112]

Three years later, the Presbyterian Church was having difficulty securing a minister. Carmichael wrote on May 5, 1895:

A new preacher came in yesterday, but Mr. Stit, who was then the preacher, is not away yet, as his money has not come and he is deep in debt. Mr. Thomson has been preaching as Stit did not care to as the church treasury was empty, and he would only get the collection, which only amounted to $1.50. The people think of him more as a horse dealer or auctioneer than as a minister of the gospel.[113]

The next minister, the Rev. George Smith, was rapidly succeeded by Rev. E. G. Taylor, who arrived in August 1896 and stayed until 1904. When Taylor arrived he asked that the next two boys born in the district be named after him. Ed. Cox was the first and the second was Ted (King) Redford, both boys were given the name Edward Taylor. In those days all faiths attended the Presbyterian Church and were active workers. As a result, the old church records contain the names of most of the first settlers – the Guillods, Taylors, Gills, Coxes, Thompsons, Swarthouts, Howitts, Forrests, Huffs, Woods, Redfords, Hills, and many others.

The Rev. James Carruthers came to Alberni in 1910 to take over from Rev. Thomas Stuart Glassford, who had only served three years. Carruthers remained for seven years, and it was largely through his efforts that funds were raised to build a new church in 1916. George Bird wrote:

Everyone who was in the habit of attending church services joined with the Presbyterians in their worship on Sundays at 3 p.m. They kindly offered their church in the mornings. Arrangements were made for the Anglicans to have the free use of their church and organ.[114]

This arrangement continued for some years until the Presbyterians decided they needed their church all day Sunday. Then the Anglicans had to hire Capt. G. A. Huff's hall for Sunday services.

Harry Guillod began the movement to establish the Anglican church in Alberni. At first, because the community did not have a resident minister, the Rev. Bozengate and Rev. C. E. Cooper took turns coming in from Nanaimo. Both were fairly wealthy men. At that time the Alberni congregation could only afford to pay their ministers the sum of sixty dollars monthly. Cooper stayed at French Creek, where he built, on Church Road, a small cedar log church called St. Anne's in memory of his mother.

A committee of the Anglican church congregation meeting in Dr. Alfred M. Watson's home made the decision to build a new Anglican church on land donated by the Anderson Company. A contract was let to George Forrest for less than $1,700. George Bird supplied the lumber. A cousin of Bird's named Robert Ballard built the seats and pews. When the steeple was built it had to be covered with galvanized iron on the platform under the bell, but no one could be found who could do a soldering job. Bird volunteered. Up on the platform he built a bark fire, which he used to heat the soldering iron. Bird recalled it was a very windy day, but despite the difficulties encountered he managed to finish the job. The bell for the church was purchased by money raised by storekeeper Charlie Sells. Dr. Watson was the bell ringer.[115]

The first service in the new Anglican church, held September 3, 1898, was conducted by Rev. Swithin Asquith.[116] John Howitt became the organist, a position he held for fifty years.

A hall and driving shed were constructed later. The shed was needed as shelter for the horses used to transport members of the congregation who came a long distance.[117] The community now had three churches, St. Andrews, All Saints, and the Roman Catholic church on River Road.

The first policeman, C. A. (Gus) Cox, arrived in Alberni in 1883. Cox was born in Ireland and had come with his parents to the United States in 1872, later travelling by train to Marysville, California, where his father tried placer-mining with little success. The family then went to San Francisco where they boarded a paddlewheel steamer to Victoria. Gus was only seven years of age when they arrived in March 1874. His father, Emanuel John Cox, three years later became the first keeper of the Cape Beale lighthouse. Gus grew up at the lighthouse learning to speak the Indian language. In his reminiscences of those early days, Gus said, "I have often spoken to blind Indians and they thought I was one of their own people and asked me what tribe I belonged to."[118]

Cox came to the Alberni Valley accompanied by old Charlie Joy and an Indian named Peter. Joy was a resident of Alberni and had taken beef to Cape Beale. "When I came here there was only the old Qualicum trail, which I crossed in May, 1884, to record a piece of land. The government office being in Nanaimo in those days. It used to take three days to make the journey."[119] The first day he reached Qualicum, the second the old Hirst ranch, and the third Nanaimo, averaging twenty-five miles a day.

Cox did special police work at various times before he was permanently appointed constable in September of 1892 and in 1904 chief constable in charge of the west coast district. He resigned in September 1912.

Crime in the small settlement of Alberni was limited to minor offences which preoccupied the early court records of the Valley. Many liquor charges against both whites and natives passed through the early Magistrate's Court. From 1891 to 1898, regular offenders appeared in front of the presiding Justice of the Peace. Their offences were either possession of liquor or being intoxicated. Fines were twenty-five dollars for possession, or five dollars plus court costs for being drunk. It was against the law to sell liquor to Indians. This did not stop some, who found a ready and willing market. Occasionally there were disturbances among the Chinese.

The excessive drinking habits probably resulted from a population made up mainly of single men, many of whom drifted into town on their way to and from the mines in the surrounding hills. Some were here only long enough for one court appearance; others were repeat offenders. The most frequent charge was "drunk and disorderly."[120] The Court did not sit on a regular basis, going into session only when a crime had been committed.

A licensing board made up of local residents decided who was allowed to sell liquor in town. In June of 1892, the Alberni Hotel, built in 1891 by Michael M. Sareault, petitioned to sell liquor in Alberni. The hotel was the largest building in the settlement. The petition contained 122 names, but there were seventy-nine people in the district who did not sign. Therefore, the board decided it did not have the necessary two-thirds majority for the court to recommend a license be awarded. The hotel eventually did get a license, becoming the first and only place on the west coast where liquor could be purchased. In June 1897 the license was transferred to Augustus (Gus) & George Sareault. When the Arlington Hotel was built in 1893 by Matt Ward, the action in the small community centred around the two hotels, and the saloons of the two pioneer hostels did a roaring business.

The old magistrate court records give testimony of this earlier time in Alberni's history. Those administering justice were locally appointed citizens, such as Capt. George A. Huff, C. Frederic Bishop, C. Talbot Haslam, R. Pinkerton, or George Forrest. The little courthouse was located on the northeast corner of Johnston Road and Elizabeth Streets. The jailhouse was a little log building adjacent to the courthouse and facing on Johnston Road. It was said of the jail that the gaps between the logs were so wide that a bottle could be passed through a chink. If he had friends outside, a man incarcerated for being drunk could be found in the same condition the following morning. Fines were relatively steep and must have cut into the pocket of many a prospector.

Walter Stirling wrote letters home to his mother, Anne Stirling, in Linlithgow, Scotland. These letters, written between July 29, 1884 and October 31, 1886, give some idea of what life was like for the early pioneers. Stirling arrived in Victoria on July 29, 1884, aboard the *Queen of the Pacific* from San Francisco, a trip which took three days. He spent the next two weeks learning Chinook. "It is quite necessary to know if one is going to live amongst the Indians as they are very loath to talk English, even when they know any."[121] He also hired a carpenter named Sinclair, for seventy-five dollars a month, to help build his house.

One of his earliest letters explained how settlers obtained their land. Any British subject could pre-empt 160 acres at one dollar an acre provided he live on the land and give improvements valued at two dollars and fifty cents an acre. The money was payable in four instalments, the first due two years after the claim was recorded and the rest at forty dollars a year until all was paid at the end of five years.

His location was "about three miles from salt water by road." Stirling's chief expense was erecting a cabin. For this, he bought lumber valued at eighty dollars. He described the contents of his new home. In his comments he appears to have taken in a companion: "We have two wooden bedsteads, also a very nice table, and for mattresses, use dried fern or hemlock branches. We sit on boxes. The house is on the top of a bank 30 feet high which slopes to the river. There are enormous Douglas fir trees everywhere."

His nearest neighbour was John C. Mollet, who was Justice of the Peace for the district and who was married with three children. Another neighbour, Kenneth McKenzie, lived with his family two miles up the river from Stirling. Two other men, Hector McKenzie and Neil Quigley, who arrived in October 1884, lived on the other side of the river.

> The worst of Alberni is that there is no post office there and no store. Up to quite lately the settlers have had to be content with getting their letters twice or thrice a year. Nanaimo, 64 miles away is the nearest post office, but Victoria is the most convenient. I think there will be a regular monthly mail very soon as a petition has been sent in for me.
>
> The principal things raised here, at present, are pigs and potatoes. Pigs cost very little to raise as they run out in the woods all the time and find their own food there, and potatoes do very well and grow to a great size. There is a market for the latter, as they are all bought by the Indians who come long distances to buy them.

By November, 1884, Stirling wrote there had been sixty lots of 160 acres each, taken up since he arrived. A school and store were expected to be built the following year. The population was expected to increase to thirty male residents allowing Alberni to have a representative in parliament at Victoria.

Stirling began circulating a petition to have a government official appointed to Alberni to act as a tax collector and officiate land transactions. Until this time, this procedure had to be done in Nanaimo. He managed to get twenty signatures on the petition. On March 22, 1885, he wrote:

> There are fifty-four whites of which forty-seven are males and seven females. Of the former thirty-nine are men and eight are boys, and of the latter four are women and three are girls. Besides this, there are about eight half-breeds. Less than a year ago there were only seven white men. The government guide visited and said he had seven more men coming this week to look for land. One of these men has a wife and ten children ranging from twenty-five years old down.
>
> Potatoes here sell at $1 per cwt. which is a good price. The spring run of salmon has begun. The Indians want 25 cents for one, later on about half that, and in the fall almost for nothing. But in the fall they are not good. The Indians are getting rather a nuisance so many of them coming wanting to sell salmon or clams. The chief invited himself to dinner today. His name is Kon-e-wish. He is an old man dressed in a sort of kilt made out of an old blanket and with long black hair hanging over his shoulders, rather uncanny looking altogether. As he cannot talk either Chinook or English, our conversation was rather limited.

By May, Stirling became friendly with George Smith, the surveyor from Scotland, with whom he was staying. The two had a mutual interest in golf, and Smith had visited and played golf at the course in St. Andrews. Smith intended to purchase land in Alberni if he could sell his property near Seattle, Washington. When Stirling arrived back home from his visit with Smith, he found his cabin had been burned and everything inside destroyed. "There has been so much fire in the woods lately with the dry weather and so many settlers coming in."

Stirling decided to move to the lake next to the Smith brothers. "The land on the lakeshore is getting settled up very fast. Three months ago there was no one at all here, now there is a population on the lake of eight men, four women and four children."

On August 23, 1885, the long dry summer was causing bush fires. For three weeks, Stirling said, there was a terrific bush fire everywhere as the weather had been so dry. "We have seen hardly any sun at all, and what sun there is has been blood red, and the air has been so thick with smoke that one's eyes would smart. One day some of us were out in the lake in a canoe and we all got lost, the smoke was so thick we could not see the shore a hundred yards off."

Stirling didn't think much of the new five mile road being built from the lake head to the settlement as it was only six feet wide, "but it will be better than nothing." The only communication the settlement had with the outside world was by scheduled boats from Victoria every five or six weeks.

He was feeling rather optimistic in October 1885 when he wrote of more people moving into Alberni and two stores opening. "There is going to be a wagon road made from Alberni to Nanaimo so when that is done and I have a horse, I can ride into town in one day, then in a few months there will be a railway between Nanaimo and Victoria, so that it will be soon easier to get in and out of the place."

The winter had already begun in November, leaving Alberni pretty well isolated, as there would be no more boats until spring. The mountains were already covered with snow. For at least two months mail would only arrive once every two weeks.

In January 1886 Stirling wrote about a gathering he had attended on Christmas day at Sproat Lake. The day began with a shooting match followed by a dance in the evening. It was not a large gathering, only five men and three women, "but it was good fun all the same." The dance was held at Mrs. Wilton's house two miles up the lake as her house was the largest. Mrs. Wilton once operated a dancing school so was able to give everyone dancing lessons.

The road to the settlement was finished but it was of little use as no one could take a horse and team over it, "hardly even a horse alone." The road was very rough and wet, and in one place it travelled through a swamp which had a foot or two of water in it. The settlers decided to meet and discuss the road condition and try to get the provincial government to make some improvements. Neither of the two roads that have been constructed in the valley were of any use, Stirling claimed, yet everyone was taxed the same as those in places where there are good roads and schools. "I am going to the meeting as I think the government needs stirring up occasionally. We are going to try and get a member of parliament."

Stirling and Smith decided to go into partnership in farming, concentrating mainly on pigs, which paid better than anything else. Smith had lived on a farm for two years and was considered somewhat of an authority on the subject.

In April 1886, the government allocated $7,500 towards a wagon road through to Nanaimo. Smith was appointed to do the surveying for the road. There were more complaints about the roads in Stirling's letter to his mother written May 24, 1886. "Everyone here is grumbling about roads. There is not a decent road in the place yet."

In June, there was a good deal of excitement in the settlement, for the Canadian Pacific Navigation Co. had started a bi-weekly service to Alberni and there was to be a school opened. The residents had elected school trustees to administer it. On July 7 there would be a provincial election, but Alberni did not have a representative and would have to wait four years for the next election. "For the present, we are attached to Nanaimo. I have got a vote." (The first election was held four years later, on June 13, 1890, when Thomas Fletcher ran against John C. Mollet. Fletcher won by 29 votes to 12.)

> There are a great lot of salmon in the river now. One day we caught between thirty and forty with a net on the end of a pole like a large butterfly net. We sometimes spear them too, but we never catch them with a rod and line as they don't seem to take fly.

Stirling was looking forward to the settlement's first celebration of Dominion Day on July 1st when sports canoe races would be held.

His letter in August described the oddball collection of animals he had assembled and named. "I have got such a lot of animals here. I wish you could see them all. There are two oxen called Bully and Bright, a cow called Daisy, a calf called Strawberry, and a dog called

Betty. Then there is a cat called Tom, a pig called Bluebeard, there are twenty-two pigs altogether. Besides that there are four hens and a cock and fourteen chickens. Daisy is very tame. One day at breakfast time when no one was in the room, she walked in and ate some porridge that was on the table and walked out. Strawberry is red and white. She eats porridge and milk out of a bucket."

In September Walter Stirling had moved to his other place three miles away on Sproat Lake, six miles by water. He built a log house there, two-storey with four rooms. Everything was moved down in canoes, except the pigs. He noted his intention to make a golf club as it had "a fine open place, although the grass is rather long."

His letter in October 31, 1886, replied to some astonishing news. His mother, Anne, had written to say she knew of a woman who had lived in Alberni twenty years before.

> You mentioned in one of your letters about Mrs. Dundas having been here twenty years ago. That seems queer does it not? At that time there was a big sawmill in Alberni and some 300 men employed. You can see traces of them all over, stumps of trees cut down, old log shanties and so forth. The company that owned the land have surveyed some into town lots.

The sixty mile road to Nanaimo was now completed and was good enough for a buggy to travel over. A rail line linked Nanaimo and Victoria. Stirling considered there would soon be a railway to Alberni from the east coast to bring coal across to be shipped from Alberni. "It can be shipped from here at less expense as big ships cannot sail up the East Coast, they always employ tugs, whereas the biggest ships can come right in here."

British Columbia joined Canada in 1871 on the promise of Prime Minister Sir John A. Macdonald that a railroad would be built to the Pacific, and that the western terminus would be Esquimalt, near Victoria. Little thought had been given to the fact that the railway would have to cross water to reach Vancouver Island. However, when this was brought out in a Canadian Pacific Railway survey, it was still hoped the line would run north to Nanaimo.

When there was little progress made on the railway by 1875, islanders became impatient. Alexander Mackenzie, then Prime Minister, introduced a bill in Parliament to build the line. This bill was passed in the House of Commons but defeated by the Senate. British Columbia was offered $750,000 cash to drop its demand for an island railway, but that proposal was rejected. Even though he lost his seat in his Kingston, Ontario riding, Sir John A. Macdonald was returned to power in 1878, after winning a by-election in Victoria. Now, as the member of Parliament from Victoria, he had more reason than ever to push for the construction of the island railway.

When Macdonald announced Burrard Inlet would be the new western terminus of the railway, islanders were notably upset. However, in 1881, Vancouver Island colliery operators Robert and James Dunsmuir reached an agreement which would see them, with their associates, build a railway between Esquimalt and Nanaimo in return for nearly two million acres of land. The land grant was a twenty mile strip on the east coast of the island, running north from Goldstream to Campbell River.[122]

When Robert Dunsmuir opened the Comox coal mines in 1884 he wanted to build thirty miles of railroad and arrange to ship his output from Alberni, because he realized it would be two hundred miles nearer his market. He offered the Anderson & Anderson Company $95,000 for their 1400 acres of Alberni waterfront. But the Anderson Company refused the offer stating it wanted $150,000. Dunsmuir decided instead to establish his shipping base at Union Bay, and never ceased to regret his failure to get a foothold in Alberni, because the value of his shore property destroyed by the teredo worm would more than offset the cost of building the railroad to Alberni. Piles driven at the site of the old Anderson mill were found to be sound and strong half a century later.[123] The natural deep-sea harbour in Alberni has a large volume of fresh water flowing from the Somass River, making it difficult for a teredo to survive. The teredo worm prefers salt water and likes to burrow into the timbers of ships, piers, and wharfs, thus destroying their stability.

In 1886, the capital of British Columbia was transferred from New Westminster to Victoria, which then had a population of 14,000. Construction had begun on the E & N Railway in April 1884; by 1886 the line was almost finished. The two construction crews, who had started north from Esquimalt and south from Nanaimo, met at Shawnigan Lake. The last spike was driven by Sir John A. Macdonald, on August 13, and regular passenger service began in September. Two months before, on July 4, 1886, the first scheduled transcontinental passenger train had reached Port Moody, 2907 miles from Montreal. The new western frontier was about to open, and settlers began arriving in Vancouver by train. It was several years before the railway on Vancouver Island reached the Alberni Valley.

About this time the Anderson Company considered disposing of some of its land for development. In 1886 James G. S. Anderson and Capt. Slader, acting for the trustees of Thos. Bilbe & Co., paid a visit to

Alberni. They travelled by small steamer to the Qualicum River from Victoria. They took a tent and packhorse and were said to have had a one week supply of whiskey for the twenty-two mile walk. When they arrived at Alberni, after camping overnight en route, they planned a small town site. This became known as Alberni.[124]

First Schools

To accommodate the new settlers, the first schools in the Alberni Valley opened for business in 1887 at Beaver Creek and Alberni. Prior to this, the children had been educated in one of the buildings at the Anderson Farm, under the guidance of teacher Tom Fletcher. Fletcher taught until June 30, 1887, and received a salary of $50 per month. This was the salary most rural teachers received. Fletcher also served as government agent from 1897 to 1901. He had previously served as the Alberni member of the provincial legislature after winning the 1890 election.

During the spring and early summer Capt. George A. Huff and Edmund Gill had hewn the logs, split shakes for the roofs, and built the Beaver Creek log schoolhouse. It measured sixteen by twenty-four feet and stood on an acre of land donated by pioneer farmer and businessman, C. Frederic Bishop. At the same time, Gill and Huff also built the Alberni School. This was later named Gill School, in honour of Ed Gill, who had donated the land. Both buildings were ready for occupancy in August of 1887. The original assessment of the Gill school was $600.

When the Beaver Creek school opened, the pupils were Douglas, Margaret, and Simon McKenzie; Heman and Mary Halpenny; Marie Bishop; Fred, Harry, Robert, and Septimus Waring; and Bertha Nicholas. The school term, however, got under way with only one teacher, Arthur Proctor. He taught in both schools, holding classes three days a week in each location.

The *Sixteenth Annual Report on Public Schools for British Columbia* for the year 1886-87 showed there were twenty-one boys and thirty girls enrolled during the year, with an average monthly attendance of eighteen. The total expenditure for the year was $573.87. The cost of each pupil on enrollment was $13.99, while the cost of each pupil on average attendance was $47.74. School board trustees visited the school nine times. The report notes the school opened with the Lord's Prayer.

Proctor was only twenty years old when he became the Alberni Valley's first permanent schoolteacher. He rode on horseback or walked to school each day from his cabin in the Cherry Creek area. Occasionally C. Frederic Bishop, who had come from England the previous year, would take charge of the Beaver Creek classes. The total value of the two properties was only $800. There were forty-one pupils in the two schools, and the teacher salary for the year totalled $600. When Miss Anna Green became the first full-time teacher for Beaver Creek school Proctor was able to teach full-time at the larger Gill school at Alberni.

It was Proctor's intention to attend medical school to become a doctor. A story is told that while he was here an Indian got his leg caught and practically severed in a bear trap. There was no doctor in the area at the time, so Proctor and one of the settlers finished the amputation with a butcher knife and a meat saw.

Proctor's replacement as teacher was John Howitt, who came in 1890 expecting to stay only six months and eventually retired in Alberni after forty-four years as teacher and principal. Howitt taught in the Gill log schoolhouse and in the one-room frame building which replaced it. When the two-room Alberni School was built on a site on the hill on Johnston Road, Howitt became teaching principal. Parents took turns running the school, three trustees at a time. The first board, administering both the pioneer schools, was made up of Capt. Huff, Harry Guillod, and Kenneth McKenzie.

Arthur Proctor had taught for three years when he left the Valley in 1890 to enroll at McGill University. The final stretch of the Canadian Pacific Railway had been in operation for four years, so he was able to travel by train across the country. However, the climate in Montreal did not agree with Proctor. He developed lung trouble and was advised to go to a drier area. Following graduation from Manitoba University as a medical doctor, he returned to British Columbia to make his career. For a year after receiving his medical degree, Dr. Proctor held the appointment of surgeon for the CPR at the Donald, B.C. divisional point. In 1898 he moved to Kamloops, where he practised until 1906. The remainder of his life was spent in Vancouver, except for a period of service during World War I.

He married Christine Mitchell in Inverness, Scotland. The couple had four children, three daughters and a son, who became Dr. A. P. Proctor Jr. The former teacher became well known in his profession. In 1909 he was appointed chief medical health officer for the CPR in B.C. He became active in the campaign against tuberculosis, playing a leading part in establishing the Tranquille Sanitarium at Kamloops. From 1912 to 1934 he was the registrar for the College of Physicians and Surgeons of B.C. He died on August 20, 1934, as a result of a wound received eighteen days previously when he was shot by a CPR engineer whom he had signed off as unfit for work.[125]

For a time, the Beaver Creek school had a problem meeting the requirements for government grants. One little boy, Bobby Dickson, went to school at age four, just to maintain the enrollment. His name was placed on the register in October 1890. Later, around the turn of the century, teacher Alexander Shaw had an answer when the enrollment became dangerously low. He sent to Nanaimo for three of his grandchildren.

Shaw was one of the early pioneer teachers on Gabriola Island. He was born in Ayrshire, Scotland in 1833. He arrived on Gabriola in the late 1850s and soon afterwards began teaching local children to read and write. But Shaw felt handicapped because he had no formal teaching instruction. He decided on a course of self-education and later rowed to Victoria to sit for his teacher's examination, which he passed.

Alexander Shaw moved to Nanaimo in 1888, where he became that city's first E & N station agent. However, teaching was still his profession and he returned to Victoria to renew his teacher's certificate. Again, he passed. When he began teaching at Beaver Creek school in August 1900, Shaw was sixty-seven years of age, with failing hearing and a large grey beard. Shaw's gentle nature was tested many times, for the educational philosophy of the day was to keep children in order, preferably with the use of a stick. He carefully recorded all corporal punishment in the school records – one boy was caned for telling a small lie and another for using obscene language.

Alexander Shaw started Sunday School classes in the schoolhouse and was often called to take Sunday services for the Presbyterian Church in Alberni. His teaching career ended in 1907, but he continued as postmaster of Beaver Creek until he retired to Nanaimo in 1912. When the Great War broke out, Shaw joined the Home Guard and was extremely active. He died in 1916 at eighty-three years of age.[126]

In 1896 the Gill log schoolhouse was replaced by a one-room building of lumber. In 1900 when the one-room school on Johnston Road was opened, the Gill School continued to serve the families in the largely rural area, while the Johnston Road building was attended by students of Alberni and New Alberni.

Roads

Since Mayne and Brown's historic trailblazing efforts in the early 1860s, and the possibility of development of the new community in Alberni, attempts had been made to interest the government in putting through a road to give new settlers access to a market at both ends, Nanaimo and Alberni. In December 1881, a petition was circulated in the areas concerned asking that by 1885 the provincial government construct such a road in order to accommodate the great influx of settlers expected between these two towns. The petition suggested it would be a good investment of public funds as each new settler would add much to the prosperity of the province.

In April 1885, Mr. S. Price, the road superintendent, and Mr. Albion Inkerman Tranfield left Nanaimo to locate a trail to Alberni via Cameron Lake. They were looking for a route with easy grades and one which would cut many miles off the current route, the Horne Lake Trail.

The following month Joseph G. Halpenny, from Alberni, a provincial government guide, along with young Hector McKenzie, made the trip from Alberni to Nanaimo. Halpenny believed there would be no great difficulty in making a road by the route he took. This same month a delegation headed by Mayor Mark Bate of Nanaimo met with the Hon. J. Robson, the Provincial Secretary. Claiming many local surveyors and guides had already explored the best line for the road, the group pressed strongly for a road to Alberni. They were very anxious to see a large number of settlers on the lands while they still had the right to purchase at the low price of one dollar an acre. Robson felt the government would favour their project.

When Robson returned to Victoria, he sent a telegram to Mr. Rabould MPP stating the government had decided to construct the required road on a route that would open up the largest area of land suitable for settlement. Mr. Bray, Associated Commissioner of Lands, received instructions to explore the best of the already surveyed routes. The original trail was cut through by Mr. Kinkade, Mr. Priest, Mr. Tranfield, Qualicum Tom, Mr. Love, and surveyors from Alberni.

Tenders were called for the road construction, which would be divided into four parts. Contractor John McPherson won the bid for sections 1, 3, and 4 for the sum of $4,085.00, while John Fraser won the contract for section 2 for $3,000. John Love was superintendent for both contracts, with work to begin in 1886. Section 1 extended from the Alberni Inlet to the west side of Cameron Lake. Section 2 ran for four miles along the lake. Section 3 was from the east end of Cameron Lake and French Creek, a distance of 8½ miles, and section 4 was to meet the Comox road south of Craig's farm.

The forest was cleared throughout for fourteen feet, close chopped for ten feet, and side hills were graded to form a roadway ten feet wide. All small streams were bridged and swamps corduroyed. Trussed bridges were required over Qualicum River, French Creek, and Englishman River.

Fraser's crew found the work very heavy on their section due to rock slides and falling boulders and also because of the steepness of the hillside along the route. By November 1886 this road was completed, but for some time it was in very poor condition. A wheeled conveyance could not use it during a good part of winter. In 1887 Love applied to the government for $4,000 to make the road usable. His report claimed the road needed stumps and roots grubbed out or covered up and a number of culverts put in and ditches dug to carry the water. "All these things need to be done before it will be a safe road to travel on with a conveyance of almost any kind," said Love.[127]

At the same time, the settlers in Alberni also had roads on their minds when they held a public meeting on May 31, 1886, to decide on the best routes for the three roads to serve the Alberni Valley. The meeting also decided that the government road-building funds should be divided equally between the three roads in proportion to their mileage. The final business of the meeting was to urge the government to survey the balance of the land in the valley, or at least to relieve the settlers of the exorbitant cost of the survey by setting a price on the work to be done.[128]

The Alberni Valley was divided for road upkeep purposes into three areas – McCoy and Sproat Lake Roads; Beaver Creek Road and tributaries; and Cherry Creek, Nanaimo and the settlement district. The government annually awarded road grants, and the government agent allotted the money to be spent in the different areas. Every settler had the chance of bringing to notice any improvements thought necessary on the section of road he used.[129] Many of the valley farmers survived the lean early years by working on the roads.

Another important travel route for a few years was a trail from the present Mt. Arrowsmith highway summit to Cowichan Lake. In 1892 there was great excitement in Alberni as new mining properties were found and rumours flourished. There was a comparatively large settlement then in the Cowichan Valley, and it was only natural there would be a clamour for a trail between these two areas. The thirty-eight mile wagon road was built in 1892-93. A traveller reported:

> Started up the Nanaimo road from Alberni, for some six miles to where the Cowichan road turns off. At the turn-off we found written on a tree, we had 32 miles before us. This was staggering news, for we had heard in Alberni that the whole way was about 22 miles. As a fact, there seemed the utmost ignorance of the length of the road in town. For the whole of the way we found what might best be called an unfinished wagon road. There were stretches of miles where a buggy might be driven with ease, then again, places where it would be utterly impossible.[130]

George Smith, with his brother Andrew, came to Alberni in 1885, George as Superintendent of Public Works. The brothers took up land at Sproat Lake. When George was seventeen, he apprenticed with the engineering firm of I. & F. Salmond, in Dundee, Scotland. He relates in his autobiography how he came to Victoria after a stint in New York and in the iron mines at Lake Superior. He went to work for Harris & Hargreaves. A year later he was sent by the provincial government to survey the new settlement of Alberni. Smith surveyed the Nanaimo Road from Alberni to Englishman River, over the Beaufort Range, by Cameron Lake. He described the road as a sledge-road. "When we came to a big tree we had to back down and run a line around it. After the first year you could ride a horse through, if you were careful."[131]

It was a great day in Alberni when the party started out from the old Saunders Store. The government had supplied the men, and inhabitants, with food and Hudson Bay rum. Every man was presented with a bottle. Smith wrote, "We were told in no uncertain terms that unless we got a road through it would be good policy not to come back." At that time the only way to Victoria was either by the Horne Lake Trail, or by the sailing vessels *Hope* or the *Maude* around Cape Beale, once a month.

When Smith first surveyed the roads through the Valley, it was the "shortest way between two points." One rancher complained to Victoria that the road Smith had built into his place was so crooked it gave him a headache to travel on it.

In the fall of 1891 Smith was appointed government agent for the Alberni District. The mining boom was just starting, and many claims, mostly of copper and gold, were being recorded. Survey crews were kept busy with mining claims and timber limits. Again, not everyone was happy with the government agent's performance. Another letter to Victoria complained: "George Smith, the Government

Agent, is all the time surveying and taking up mining claims and land and timber limits, and the rest of the time he is not in the office." A copy of the letter was returned to Smith with a note attached: "We are glad to see that somebody is doing something in Alberni."

One of the toughest jobs Smith had as a surveyor was the Sutton Timber on the west coast where salal was up to ten feet high. "Mosquitos and sand flies were everywhere." Another job was surveying a route from Alberni to the Union Mines, via Comox Lake. Smith said he never knew what the object of the survey was, although he had heard many weird and wonderful tales about a line via Comox to a bridge at Seymour Narrows, "with the China boats waiting at Alberni." No one had considered Vancouver at this time. But Smith and his crew of Jim Redford, Jim Hills, and Frank Stirling were optimists and were interested in any proposition which might benefit isolated Alberni.

Later, George Smith worked on the survey of the townsite of Port Alberni, the right-of-way surveys on the CPR line from Wellington to Port Alberni, and the Canadian Northern right-of-way from Victoria to the Alberni Inlet. Smith said all these were mere child's play to the survey boys after their experience on the west coast. Assisting him were George Roff and Billy Marshall. Occasionally the men suffered what George Roff named "Bootitis" – everybody's boots seemed to need repairing periodically, and "a man just had to go to town."

The District Lot System was the most widely used method of surveying in the province because of its flexibility for use in unsurveyed areas. It allowed a certain amount of opportunity for a surveyor to demonstrate his sense of values. This was clearly illustrated in Smith's description of the survey he did of the Alberni Valley.

In the matter of the survey of the ranches in the Alberni Valley, it would have saved a great deal of worry and considerable hardship if the land had been surveyed before the settlers took it up. Sometimes a man lost just the piece of alder or maple land he wanted. I remember a very bad quarter- of-an-hour I had when surveying a quarter section for a rancher. The day before I had passed the log house and they were showing me the garden his wife and the children had cleared and planted around the house. One very big stump took them three weeks to burn out. Her hands were scarred and rough, but they were small and nicely shaped. Now, unless one has actually done clearing, you can have no idea of the work it was to dig out even one of those big fir stumps.

Well, we had started at the corner post and had run around three sides and were on the last line. In looking through the transit I noticed a long way off a peculiar brown-looking patch. It did not look quite like a stump.

Suddenly a thin wisp of smoke began to rise. I knew then it was the chimney in the centre of the shack.

I closed up the business for the day and went back to camp. Something had to be done to get that narrow strip of extra land. To get this strip they were up against a whole lot: the Laws of the Medes and Persians, i.e. the B.C. Land Act, the Settlement Act, and God knows how much red tape. However, next day we finished the survey. Just why there were one hundred and sixty-four acres instead of the orthodox one hundred and sixty in that quarter section was never explained, but the great Coal Baron (Dunsmuir) who owned the land, and who had a kind heart, if he had known, would not have had it different. It was a regrettable error, the chainman's fault of course, or it might even have been put down by some to "a poor brand of Scotch". Ah! what did it matter, the kiddies got their garden.[132]

The official Alberni Townsite map was eventually dated March 12, 1909, replacing older maps 197 and 197A when errors were found in the Map No. 197, from the 1887 survey.

Smith later moved to Los Angeles, California where he died on July 25, 1934.[133]

British Columbia's First Paper Mill

In 1891, when the population of Alberni was 191 or about sixty-five families, a second industrial venture came to the Alberni Valley. Herbert Carmichael of Victoria, then the Provincial Assayer, set out to build British Columbia's first paper mill on the banks of the Somass River.

Carmichael was a graduate of the Royal Academical Institute in Belfast, Ireland, and Owens College in Manchester, England, where he had achieved high honours in chemistry. The potential of the Alberni Valley for paper manufacturing must have impressed him, because shortly after his arrival in 1889 he formed the British Columbia Paper Manufacturing Co. Ltd. Carmichael showed faith in the company by subscribing to 150 shares. A shareholder in Santa Barbara, California, W. Alexander, took twenty shares. There were five directors in the company, each holding one share. They included William P. Sayward, a pioneer lumberman; J. Stuart Yates, a barrister, for whom Yates Street in Victoria is named; Thomas M. Shotbolt, a druggist; Joshua Davies, an auctioneer; and Herbert Carmichael. Four people in Alberni also held stock. They were James Thomson, a contractor; A. D. Faber and Frank Stirling of Sproat Lake; and George A. Huff, of Alberni. William Hewartson, a retired English paper maker who lived in Victoria, became the technical adviser for the group. He also held a share in the company. Other shareholders were Victoria and area businessmen and farmers.

The year 1891 was a busy one for Carmichael. In April in New York he married Miss Josephine Mince, of Belfast; in August his paper company was incorporated and he was made secretary. Also in 1891, Carmichael was appointed Provincial Analyst for the B.C. Mining Department.

On April 27, 1891, the paper company purchased Lot 7, Alberni District from John Mollett and John C. Mollett. On July 24, 1891, Carmichael signed the contract with Robert H. Wood for construction of a dam on the Somass River, about two miles upstream from Alberni. The site chosen is presently known as Papermill Dam Park. This location on the Somass River provided unlimited fresh, clear water for the production process. There was also an excellent supply of timber readily accessible and untouched. Unfortunately, the contractors and management did not know the river. After a few days of heavy rain, the partially completed dam was washed out and all the work was lost. Every man who had been employed lost most of his wages.

But the dream was not lost. Again, in 1892, Robert H. Wood signed another contract for the construction of another dam, sawmill, and paper mill buildings, as well as a 5 × 10 foot flume to connect the dam with the water wheels that were installed below the two mills.

In the spring of the year, at high tide on the Somass River, a flat-bottomed light draft steamboat called the *Barbara Boscowitz* arrived, laden with the machinery of an old, dismantled paper mill in Scotland. The ship had come all the way around Cape Horn from Scotland with a cargo that included tanks, cog wheels, and circular grinding stones, which William Hewartson had purchased.

During the summer a gang of men worked at the machinery, scraping off the rust and polishing it. As each piece was finished, it was hauled by oxen to the mill site by Andrew Service. Another small boat called the *Lily*, whose engineer was George Bird, was not even seaworthy, but was bought for carrying supplies on the river from the old Anderson Mill wharf to the site by the flat rocks in the area of the present River Bend Bridge. Teams of oxen carried the supplies the rest of the way.[134]

Alfred Carmichael, cousin of Herbert, arrived to help in the construction of the mill. As the mill construction proceeded, several homes were built in the vicinity, which had now adopted the name "Milltown." These homes were built for Ben Tubman, John Cameron, Alfred Carmichael, Mrs. Cox, and George Bird. The Company built one for Wood and one for James Dunbar, the second manager. Stephen Wells walked to work from his home on Beaver Creek Road, and Andrew Service came from his ranch on the opposite side of the river to the Prairie Farm, crossing the water at the mill in a canoe.[135]

Two women also worked at the mill, Mrs. Frances Morrison and an Indian woman, Emma David. Frances was the sister of Gus Cox and like her brother was raised on the west coast lighthouses. She came to Alberni to keep house for Gus. Her vigour and wit became so well known in the Valley that when, in her seventies, she broke her arm as she jumped a ditch, no one was surprised.[136]

Herbert Carmichael, in the meantime, had been busy. His first report as public analyst presented a record showing an analysis of mineral springs at Alberni. This same report also told of "excellent building stone on Haddington Island," on the west coast. The stone was later used in the construction of the Parliament Buildings in Victoria.

Paper was actually produced only during 1894 and 1895. It was limited to wrapping paper. The first finished paper came over the machine on July 24, 1894. Tom Fleming of Everett, Washington, was the machine man, with Alfred Carmichael as his assistant. The first step in the process of paper-making, which consisted of cutting rags, old clothing, and ropes into short lengths with a machine similar to a farmer's chaff cutter, was handled by two Chinese workers. The material was transferred to two globular steam digesters which revolved slowly under steam pressure for several hours, about half-filled with the material and the necessary amount of soda.

The cooked mass was then raised upstairs to the beater, or rag engine room, where five machines with sets of knives attached revolved over a heavy roller. Water circulated around the pan, passing the material between the knives. Slowly the fibres of the material were separated and reduced to the right length and condition. If bleaching was needed, chloride of lime was added, then sizing made of resin and soda was added. It was then ready to be made into the finished paper.

The paper machine was driven by a twenty-five horsepower turbine. The mass flowed over a five foot wide brass wire cloth which vibrated sideways to distribute the fibres in the paper. Endless square rubber bands travelling on the wire formed the edges of the paper. Water was drawn from the paper by two steam vacuum suction boxes. The paper left the wire, travelling over a woollen felt, then a cotton one, before passing through two sets of heavy rollers to the drying cylinders. When the paper left the cylinders it had enough strength to carry itself to the calendar rolls and onto the winder where it was cut into width requirements.[137]

Hours of work at the mill were long. From Monday to Friday, employees worked from 6:00 a.m. to 6:00 p.m. Saturday from 6:00 a.m. to 12:00 noon, and Sunday from 12:00 midnight to 6:00 a.m.

Equipment and labour, including the dam to provide power, had cost $77,000. The equipment was old, and getting an adequate supply of rags in a country where the population had trouble clothing itself was difficult. Coast towns were searched for material, but by the time it reached Alberni, the cost was prohibitive. Everything from ships' sails to construction overalls was used; ferns, manilla rope, and wood were all tried. However, the steam pressure was only sixty pounds, insufficient to cook the fern and hemp, with the result that particles of this material often appeared in the finished product. Attempts were made to use wood as a raw material. The first wood pulp was actually made on October 1, 1894, but it was not of sufficiently high quality to become a saleable product.[138] The only wood pulp machinery installed was a chipper and a crusher. Some wood was chipped and the chips crushed and put into the rotary digesters, with a liquor of caustic soda. The result was disappointing; the wood would not digest.

The directors called for Hewartson's resignation, and James Dunbar, a paper maker, was brought from Scotland to manage the mill. However, on his arrival and inspection of the plant, Dunbar gave little hope of ever producing paper from wood pulp.

Carmichael tried to refinance the paper mill. During this transitional period, the sawmill continued in operation under Alfred Carmichael and George Bird. They made enough money to pay their living expenses for one month. Dunbar returned to Scotland.

In May 1895, Herbert Carmichael considered operating a sawmill. He arranged for H. B. Winsby, the Dog Tax Collector for Victoria, to manage it. Winsby knew nothing about sawmilling and soon returned to Victoria. Alfred and George Bird took over and began producing rustic siding, clear edge grain flooring, and bridge planking.

But the Carmichaels had not given up hope of producing paper at Alberni. Alfred returned to England in November 1896 and met with a family friend, John Boyd, of Bothwell, Scotland. Boyd was then the owner of the Shettleston Iron Works. Boyd was introduced to Dunbar, and he became interested in the Alberni project. Alfred Carmichael said Boyd's interest may have been on account of his ailing son Bertie, whom he thought might benefit from a change in climate. Negotiations began between Herbert Carmichael and John Boyd. Bertie returned with Alfred to Alberni.

A new company, the B.C. Wood Pulp and Paper Mills was formed with a capital of $35,000. Boyd and his friends contributed $16,050, and Herbert the other half. In the meantime, Boyd had written to James Ormiston, a retired Scottish engineer living on Denman Island, asking him to inspect the suitability of the Alberni site for a modern paper mill. Ormiston reported against the project and suggested a better location might be Powell River. This was the final blow for the Alberni project.

Alfred Carmichael, and Albion Inkerman Tranfield from Nanaimo, began exploring areas north of Vancouver. The potential of Powell River impressed them, and as a result, they recommended Powell River as the best site for a modern pulp and paper plant. When their report was received several of the shareholders withdrew from the company. Boyd was willing to attempt to refinance the development of the power and the construction of a mill at Powell River, but he and Herbert Carmichael could not agree on terms. Boyd finally withdrew completely from the project. The B.C. Pulp & Paper Co. Ltd. was wound up and subscriptions returned to shareholders. Bertie Boyd returned to Scotland where he died shortly afterwards.

With the collapse of the B.C. Pulp & Paper Co. Ltd. Herbert Carmichael and J. J. Shallcross of Shallcross McCauley & Co., Insurance Adjusters, formed the B.C. Power Corporation to secure water rights on Powell River. Alfred was paid sixty dollars by the new company to stake the water rights on Powell River. When the job was completed he joined an expedition to the Atlin Gold Fields.[139]

Herbert eventually retired from public service with the Department of Mines at the close of 1912. He joined his cousin Alfred, who by this time had returned from Atlin and formed the real estate firm of Carmichael and Moorhead Ltd., to act as agents for Alberni Land Company, placing lots and acreage in Port Alberni on the market.

CHAPTER TWO

1893–1906

A NEW CENTURY

The Alberni settlers of the 1890s were full of optimism about their new community, an optimism the rest of the province shared. A statement in the *British Columbia Directory* of 1893 read:

Alberni is destined, at no distant date, to become a place of importance and wealth. All it requires to ensure this position is development of its resources and railroad communication with other places. All kinds of grain, fruit and vegetables grow readily. In their season may be seen the peach and grape, the water and musk melon, tomato and Indian corn, growing to perfection.

There were over 22,377 acres of land taken up in the settlement, which was then assessed at $80,276. Land could be purchased at five dollars per acre, payable in four yearly payments with interest at 6 percent. Roads and bridges were being constructed and improved so that settlers could enjoy the luxury of a buggy or carriage drive.

Three new industries were worthy of mention. The first was the discovery by Germansen and Ethridge of a valuable quick-silver mine on Cinnabar Creek, Barkley Sound. The second was the British Columbia Paper Manufacturing Company built on the Somass River. The third was a small water-powered sawmill owned by Michael Marvin Sareault. The mill had been in operation since 1887 and was located near the present E & N Railway tracks, on Kitsuksis Creek. Logging was done with broad axes and oxen. The mill supplied the timber for the first frame houses in the district, and for Sareault's Alberni Hotel.

The population was estimated at two hundred, excluding Indians and Chinese. The community already had two stores operating to serve the settlers – the Alberni Trading Co. and Huff's store. They were located by Kitsuksis Creek bridge and wharf. Supplies were received twice a month from Victoria. As well, there was a boarding house to accommodate newcomers or transients. It was operated by Mrs. Cox, mother of Gus Cox, the policeman.

The nearest railway station, banking point, telegraph and express offices were in Nanaimo. But the Canadian Pacific Navigation Company's steamer *Maude* was paying twice monthly visits to the Alberni wharf on the west coast schedule. The fare from Victoria was seven dollars. Mail was brought overland from Nanaimo once a week by William Armstrong, farmer and stagecoach driver. Alberni's first postmistress was Agnes Erickson.

The eighty registered male settlers included Alfred Dennis Faber, a civil engineer who became a resident in the Sproat Lake area in 1888, taking a large tract of land, 1270 acres between Stirling Arm and Sproat Arm, plus another 130 acres on the south side of Stirling Arm. An orchard was planted near his home. On the south side of Stirling Arm, on the property which he called Fosselli, Norwegian for "waterfall in a valley," he cleared ten acres to grow hay and potatoes. To harvest these, a raft was built by Valentine Ingram, a farmer who lived near McCoy Lake. The raft, complete with horse and wagon, then was towed by rowboat across the Arm. Mrs. Faber, who was English and a singer, was not happy at the lake because she loved the theatre and concerts.

Tragedy struck in the summer of 1894 when two nieces from England visited. The Fabers' daughter Dorothy, aged four, and the two nieces, Emily Faber, twenty-one, and Mary Josephine Faber, eighteen, were swimming when Mrs. Faber called them to lunch. There was no reply. All three girls had drowned just a short distance along the lake from the home. Since there was no cemetery in Alberni at the time, the children were buried on the Faber property. The tragedy didn't end there. Mr. Faber contracted typhoid fever and died during a business trip in 1899. He was buried beside the three girls.[1] Mrs. Faber returned to England with her remaining two daughters and son. The son was later killed in World War I.

There was no permanent resident physician yet, but the district was served by a young physician, Dr. R. R. Robinson. He didn't stay long; there weren't enough patients to keep him busy. George Albert Huff, better known as Capt. Huff, served a triple role as Justice of the Peace, storekeeper, and secretary of the school board. The only meat market in the district was operated by the Redford brothers, James and John. Their slaughterhouse was situated on the bank of the river near the small bridge on the road at Lupsi Kupsi.

Beaver Creek, a rural settlement six miles from Alberni, had it's own small post office which was operated by C. Frederic Bishop. Mail arrived twice a week. The area had great potential for farming, as the *British Columbia Directory* noted: "There is excellent farming and timber lands, which can be obtained from the E & N Railway Co, or on reasonable terms from the pioneer settlers." The small community could boast of having one church, a public school, and a sawmill: as well, "a trunk road runs through the district, which is being carried on to Comox."[2]

The traditional way of life for the Tseshaht and Opetchesaht tribes was being reshaped as the settlers made an impact. Church and government officials worked to save them from what missionaries called their "heathen darkness." However, the natives continued to assemble in February for the annual seal hunt off Barkley Sound. While the men hunted seal, the women gathered a harvest of shellfish, herring, and herring spawn. As soon as the sealing was over, they often travelled to potlatches, or to Victoria, New Westminster, or Washington State for goods. The success or failure of the sealing season depended on the price paid for the skins, which could fetch between nine and twelve dollars each.

In 1882, Indian Agent Guillod reported a few of the young men of the tribes were anxiously waiting for plots of land to be given to them to build good houses. By 1885 several of the Opetchesahts had built small houses on their reserve. Others built their houses outside the rancherie, leaving the Indian village for the older people. The houses were of frame construction and expensive to build because of the high price of lumber. Rough lumber cost twenty dollars and twenty-two dollars per thousand, delivered on the wharf at Alberni; dressed lumber was eight dollars more. A few paid to have their land ploughed like the white farmers did. The two groups eyed each other with curiosity more than suspicion.

The natives had trouble with cattle wandering into their crops, for they had yet to master the art of constructing a good fence. One Indian cleared a piece of land for an orchard. Several hundred fruit trees were planted and eighty of them soon produced fruit. The tribes then owned twenty horses and six spring wagons. Occasionally the men got work from the settlers, and the women washed and picked potatoes when they were in season.

Even though the potlatch was banned, the tribes continued to enjoy their traditional celebration. Alfred Carmichael attended such a celebration in the 1890s and wrote of the event.

> ... when I first knew the Seshahts, they still celebrated the great Lokwana dance, or wolf ritual, on the occasion of an important potlatch. I remember well the din made by the blowing of horns, the shaking of rattles, and the beating of sticks on the roof boards of Big Tom's great potlatch house, when the Indians sighted the suppositional wolves on the river bank opposite the Village.
>
> In those days we were permitted to attend the potlatches and witness the animal and other dances, among which were the Panther, Red Headed Woodpecker, Wild Swan and the Sawbill Duck. Generally we were welcome at the festivals, provided we did not laugh or show sign of any feeling save that of grave interest.[3]

One of Alfred Carmichael's Indian acquaintances was Ka-coop-et, better known in the district as Mr. Bill, "Keeper of the Songs." Of him, Carmichael said, "Mr. Bill is a fine type of Seshaht, quite intelligent and with a fun sense of humor."[4] The elderly native was respected for his knowledge of Indian legend and folklore. Mr. Bill was only twelve years old when Capt. Stamp worked at the Anderson mill.[5] He often talked about the kindness shown him by the early white settlers.

Another Indian well known in the community was Cultus Bob, the younger brother of Mr. Bill. Bob had quite a personality. Carmichael described him as "handsome, swarthy man with good brains which he used to his advantage in his dealings with the whites."[6] Bob was in the habit of borrowing things from people and not returning them. On one occasion he asked if he could buy a pair of pants from John Cameron, a friend of Carmichael. He promised to pay for them after sealing time. When the season was over he never paid Cameron for the pants, and when the two met, Cultus Bob explained it had been a bad sealing season. He again promised to pay after the next sealing season. Another season came and went. Bob again failed to make an appearance. In the meantime, Cameron heard someone else had become his victim. When the two next met, Bob again said he had got few seals and had no money to pay for the pants.

"Bob," said Cameron sternly, "it is no good you telling me that. Everybody says that you are no good. You are called Cultus Bob, which means "no good Bob."

"Mr. Cameron, you read the Bible?"

"Yes, I do," answered Cameron.

"You know what the Bible says, "No good if all men speak well of you."

Cameron was speechless. Cultus Bob never did pay for the pants.[7]

The population of the Tseshaht tribe now was 150. This included forty men, forty-eight women, and sixty-two children and young people. The population of the Opetchesaht tribe was sixty-one. Of this number, eighteen were men, twenty-four were women, and nineteen were children.[8]

Alberni Residential School

A few of the native children attended the Alberni school. Harry Guillod reported in 1889 that they were making good progress. But the education of the large population of native children concerned the Presbyterian Mission, who thought something should be done to accommodate them in their own school.

The following year Capt. George Albert Huff sold his land to the Presbyterian Mission for $5,000. Three years later, in 1892, the Rev. J. A. McDonald opened a school close to the Tseshaht Indian Reserve. Miss McDonald was the first teacher. She had twenty-five pupils, both boys and girls, under her direction. "They seemed glad to come to school and made good progress," reported Guillod.[9]

The school had a few difficulties to contend with in 1893. Money had not materialized to build a suitable school building. Then Miss McDonald had to leave because of ill health. She later died of consumption (tuberculosis). The new matron, Miss Lister, also died, of pneumonia. There was more bad news when the Rev. J. A. McDonald, who had started the mission school, had to resign, too, because of ill health. However, the work started by him was carried on by a new matron, Miss Johnson, and teacher Miss Minnes. The outside work was done by Mr. McKee, who also helped with Sunday school and Christian teaching.

Until the new schoolhouse was built, the day school was held in a comfortable frame house on the reserve, loaned by an Indian known simply as "Santa." The seats and desks were provided by the mission. The school now had ten girls and two boys, aging from six to sixteen, boarding at the home. This was all the home could accommodate. Some of the children attended Sunday school at the Indian village. Many of the adult Indians attended services at the Presbyterian church in Alberni.

By 1895 construction work was in full swing on the new Presbyterian Girls' Home. Guillod reported: "It will be a substantial and commodious building on a fine site overlooking the river on the

Tseshaht Indian Reserve."[10] There were twenty-seven pupils ready to move in as soon as the building was completed.

The annual report of 1896 from the Indian Girls' Home, came from B. I. Johnston, who complained about having to make a report to the Department of Indian Affairs, as the W. F. M. Society of the Presbyterian Church in Canada had been paying the bills.

> If the department wishes to establish an industrial-school at Alberni, we shall be very glad to have the change made as soon as possible. Indeed, on account of the boys I think it is absolutely necessary. These children are taken into the home out of the filth they live in, made clean and comfortably clothed with good, warm clothing, and good boots and shoes. They are put into clean beds, in nice, large, airy dormitories, and they are given good, substantial food, nicely prepared.[11]

The girls were learning all sorts of "women's work in the home," such as bread-making, laundry-work, knitting, and dressmaking. But there was no provision for the boys other than gardening and wood-cutting. One boy had been sent to the village to learn carpentry and was doing well. Another showing talent for instrumental music was sent to an instructor. There were now twenty-seven children in the home; eleven were boys from five to fourteen years, and the girls' ages ranged from eighteen months to eighteen years.

Besides caring for those children in the home, the mission school also cared for the adult sick in their own home. Johnston reported that plain coffins were made so the Indian dead could be decently buried. Three of the boarding pupils had died, one from the effects of chicken-pox and two from tuberculosis.

By 1900, the number of children boarding at the school had risen to thirty-three. The staff then included principal James R. Motion and his wife, who served as matron. Mrs. Cameron was the teacher and Charles Ross was assistant instructor. Seventeen of the children had come from outside the district, from some of the eighteen different tribes and 150 reserves in Barkley Sound. Guillod reported in 1903 that a small brass band was under instruction at the school.

Pupils of the school gathered October 12, 1907 to help celebrate the golden wedding anniversary of the Rev. George Smith and his wife, who lived at "Riverbank." The pupils included Freddie Jones, Alice Dick, C. E. Guillod, Tom Shewish, Ruth Young, J. Steven, Otto Taylor, Jas. R. Motion, Lily Haslam, Ina Roberts, H. G. Motion, and Mary Motion. Also present were A. W. Neill, the Rev. Glassford and teachers Mrs. Stephen and Miss Guillod. The pupils presented Smith with an illustrated copy of Longfellow's poems while Mrs. Smith received a bouquet of flowers. "After enjoying a hearty tea the venerable minister challenged his young friends to a trial of strength at the Highland feat of putting the stone. He was so severely beaten that he declined to carry out his intentions of trying a race with them," stated the newspaper report of the event.[12]

The school had grown considerably by 1909 when James R. Motion filed his annual report.[13] The Presbyterian Church then owned the 156 acres connected to the school. Several buildings circled the complex. The main building was three storeys high with a wing two storeys high. The old school buildings were used for laundry, bakeshop, and carpentry. Other buildings included a classroom, woodshed, driving shed, root house, stable, and hen house. There was accommodation for sixty children and a staff of seven. The main building was heated by hot air furnace and the new addition by stoves. Coal oil lamps were used for lighting. Fire protection consisted of four Keystone fire-extinguishers, six Haverhill Eclipse and twelve fire buckets distributed throughout the building.

During 1909, forty-seven pupils were on the attendance roll, twenty-three boys and twenty-four girls. During the year, four boys were admitted; two pupils were discharged, while four girls died, two from tubercular meningitis, the other two from pulmonary trouble. Motion said the death of the girls "was the saddest in our experience." Two of the girls were sisters, who died within a short time of each other. Another girl had cold ulcers on her legs. She was allowed to go home on sick leave. While there, her lungs became infected and she died four months later. The fourth girl died from consumption.

The Indian male students were now learning farming, gardening, carpentry, painting, shoe-repair, and baking. The bigger boys were expert fishermen and during the winter they made a new net. The boys also built a stable. The girls were taught housework, cooking, laundry, breadmaking, dressmaking, and the care of milk and butter, also canning fruit, sewing, and music. All the mending of clothing and darning of socks was done by the girls. As a reward, once a week they were taught fancy sewing work.

Motion considered the students were making excellent progress. Some had won prizes at the Alberni fair for their pencil drawings, baking, and needlework. The school was visited monthly by Indian Agent A. W. Neill. It was inspected in June and February by School Inspector Green.

Many of the children must have wondered why they had been sent there – some so far from home and parents – but others looked on it as an adventure. When the school first opened it had been difficult to get children. The parents did not like to part with them and a lot of coaxing and persuading was needed. Among the Indians dislike of the boarding schools was slow to disappear.[14]

Stamps and Stables

Sending and receiving mail was one of the irritants new settlers faced. They relied entirely on the steamers from Victoria, and letters arrived only twice or three times a year. The Nanaimo post office was the closest, but Victoria the more convenient. In 1884 a petition was circulated to attempt to get a regular monthly mail service, and a year later, the first Alberni Post Office was established by E. H. Fletcher. The mail carrier was Wattie Watts. Once a week the mail was brought by steamer to Qualicum, where there was a roadhouse kept by a man nicknamed "Qualicum Tom." Walter Stirling described Qualicum Tom in his letters:

> So many people are coming into Alberni and they generally stay the night at this place on the way, that Qualicum Tom has thought it advisable to start a hotel. He has invested in tables and, I think, chairs, also some brand new mattresses, knives and forks and all kinds of delicacies. Then his sisters do the waiting on the guests. They dress up in a wonderful manner and they all try to talk English and have everything quite correct, just as the "King Gawge" men have it. "King Gawge" is the Indian way of saying English. None of them can sound their "R's" so they call it "Gawge." I think it must be rather funny to see all these grand articles of furniture in a house without flooring, windows, or chimney.[15]

Wattie Watts took charge of the mail from Qualicum and carried it over the mountain via the Horne Lake Trail. An old building over the river served as a post office. Charles Taylor, son of the pioneer settler Charles Taylor, became postmaster, although it was his wife who performed the duties as postmistress. When the Taylors moved to McCoy Lake in 1886, the father maintained the position for a short time until the station was transferred to Frank McQuillan's store. Frank was postmaster until Agnes Erickson replaced him in 1892. When the young Taylors moved to the lake area, a post office was established to provide service to the Sproat Lake residents. Taylor was in charge until the station closed in 1890.[16]

In 1889 a new wagon road was opened, allowing for better mail service. The first contractor to carry the mail was William Armstrong, and he was followed by John Patterson. Afterwards Joe McCarter, the proprietor at the Halfway House at Errington, got the contract. There was keen rivalry every three years when the government called for bids for contracting the mail service.[17]

McCarter was only eighteen years of age when he was awarded the contract to haul mail to Alberni. At first he made only one trip a week, but over the years the frequency of mail delivery increased, and soon Joe was hauling both mail and passengers. The McCarter house quickly became known as the Halfway House. It was there that the stage passengers were fed during the change-of-horses stopover.[18] "Accommodation at the Half-way House was quite comfortable. Deer were plentiful around Englishman River. Game laws in unorganized districts were not enforced and McCarter was quite a hunter, so venison was often on the menu. There was no shortage of good farmhouse fare and home-like hospitality prevailed," recalled George Bird.[19] The Halfway House consisted of nine rooms – two kitchens, a dining room, a lounge, a living room, and four bedrooms on the upper level. It remained in service until the railway put the stage-coaches out of business.

In 1892 Agnes Erickson came with her two children to the Alberni Valley to join her brother, Malcolm Shaw. She had a rough trip up the Alberni Inlet in the old flat-bottom wooden steamboat the *Barbara Boscowitz*, owned by the Boscowitz Steamship Co. Agnes Erickson eventually served as postmistress for twenty-three years.

The post office was in a two-storey building on Victoria Quay, opposite the Kitsuksis Creek bridge. Next door to the right lived George and Alfred Drinkwater. Further right was Arthur Norris, an old bachelor who lived in a small shack. Further yet to the right was the Alberni Hotel, operated by Michael Sareault. On the left was the Alberni Trading Store, the largest general store on the west coast of the Island. It was owned by Henry Saunders and managed by Dave Riddell, who lived upstairs with his wife Margaret and their two daughters, Nancy and Dot.

There was a good sized wharf on the river bank fifty yards from the store entrance. It was here Capt. Huff's hall and store was located. For some years, the vessels *Willapa*, *Queen City*, and *Tees* navigated up the Somass River at high tide to unload freight right at the post office doorstep. Frequently they had to wait for the next high tide to get away. In later years they docked at Port Alberni Wharf, and the wooden stern-wheeler *Willie*, owned by Capt. Huff, transferred the cargoes aboard and unloaded them at the Alberni wharf.

In May 1894, James Thomson opened a small store in Milltown for the convenience of those settlers living near the paper mill. Thomson, with his wife and five sons, had come from Vancouver in 1891 and had purchased the J. C. Mollett property at the river's bend. For many years River Bend bridge was named Thomson's Bridge. Thomson was originally from Bridge-of-weir near Glasgow, Scotland.

The Indian hunters traded with the Thomson store, taking on supplies needed for their trips and potlatch celebrations. As the Indian seal hunters were paid for their catch entirely with silver, Thomson was compelled to make frequent journeys to Victoria to bank his money.

After the paper mill closed, Thomson, with son John, constructed Thomson's General Store at the corner of what is now called Southgate and Margaret Streets. It opened for business in 1900, and John took over as manager in 1902. The store was a landmark in Alberni for forty years.

Once a week, a four horse stage brought the mail from Nanaimo. Mail night was a big night, for practically everyone in town came down to the post office to wait for the wicket to open. There were some angry voices heard when the wicket didn't open on time, or if the weather was poor.

Some of the more prominent citizens had private letter boxes along the wall next to the wicket. They included C. Frederic Bishop (grocer); Dave Riddell (manager of the Alberni Trading Store); Leonard Frank (photographer); Rev. E. G. Taylor (St. Andrews Church); Matt A. Ward (Arlington Hotel); James Thomson & Sons (grocers); Gus Cox (police chief); and Alan W. Neill (Indian agent).[20]

When the mail service was extended to New Alberni in 1902, W. Woodley and S. Vipond held the contract. Their stable and feedbarn was built on Waterhouse's property (site of the present Somass Hotel). The next contractors were Harry Fitzgerald and Jack Burke, whose headquarters were at Alberni Livery Stables, across the road from the Arlington Hotel. In 1909 the contract was lost to a company in Nanaimo, who held it until the railway reached Cameron Lake. Then, for the last period of its operation, it was managed by Sam Roseborough.[21]

One of the first items of business at the first meeting of the Alberni Board of Trade on May 4, 1908, was to get an improved mail service. A committee was established to look into the matter. On May 20, a special meeting was called in the Royal Bank to again discuss the postal service. Chairman Richard (Dick) J. Burde stated, "the service was quite unsatisfactory."[22] A Mr. Fletcher replied that the present service was only designed for the summer months, and that commencing November 1st the mail would leave both Alberni and Nanaimo at 7:00 a.m. three days a week. He suggested if that was not adequate then it could be changed. McCarter offered to bring the regular mail in at 6:00 p.m. with a special delivery Tuesday night, which would bring in the semi-weekly papers from Victoria. McCarter was invited to submit an offer for a daily service.[23]

The livery stable owned by Harry Fitzgerald and Jack Burke was one of the favourite meeting places for settlers. The harness room, furnished with a stove and a coal oil lamp, smelled of horses, polished leather, and hay. There was a certain comfort derived from sitting around the warm stove on a cold winter night, discussing the affairs of the day with neighbours. Settlers dropping in were always assured of the latest news, or gossip, about who had arrived in town. Since there were no newspapers, this was an essential part of the life of the small community.

Here were found all the essential ingredients of a successful livery stable. Outside the building stood the buckboard, democrat, and sulkies ready to be hitched to the horse, or vice versa. From the loft above the stable came a ready supply of hay to feed the animals. A horse trough was nearby for watering. It was here the stagecoach from Nanaimo stopped overnight. Every stagecoach was equipped with a crosscut saw and axe, without which they could never make the trip over the mountain.

These were the days of the horse and buggy, the time of the livery stable and nose bag, when a man was judged by how he handled a team of horses, and when every horse was a personality. There were many well-known horses in the district; in fact, the horses were almost as well known as the people who lived here. If a horse was mentioned in a conversation, which was quite often, no one would think of showing his or her ignorance by asking who was the owner of that particular horse. Jack Burke was the foremost authority on horses in the district. He was always careful and considerate towards his horses, and he fired a number of men for their mistreatment of the animals.

Burke was born in Watertown, New York, in 1869. A papermaker, he came to Alberni in 1895 to work at the first paper mill. When he arrived, the mill was not in operation, so he began working for Mike Sareault driving a horse team. He stayed in Sareault's Alberni Hotel. He also did some hauling jobs between Alberni and Bobby De Beaux' store on the road to the Golden Eagle mine.

91

In 1897, Burke married teacher Margaret Fraser, in Nanaimo. They had eight children: Vina, Nancy, Kitty, Dick, Nell, Anne, Norah, and Bill. George Bird told a story about Burke having raised a large family. His first few children were all girls. Someone congratulating him on the happy event said, "Which is it this time, Jack, another girl?"

"No," said Jack with a happy smile, "it is a teamster this time."[24]

Burke's partner Fitzgerald arrived in 1892, having been invited by Robert H. Wood to work on the construction of the first paper mill. When the mill was completed, Fitzgerald joined with Burke to open the Alberni Livery Stables, taking over the business from Thomas Paterson and Capt. Huff.

The old barn was located on Margaret Street. Meg Trebett recalled it was here the Valley's first plush-covered barber's chair was located. "Guests sat in this 'seat of honour' and looked at walls covered with pictures of race-track horses, which were heroes of the century, and pictures of horses from Burke's stables."[25]

As their business grew, Burke and Fitzgerald built an annex to accommodate additional horses, wagons, and buggies. Before long they had about twenty horses in the barn. They hired teamsters and stable help. One of the teamsters was Bill Derby, the Alberni personality who would receive the first Canadian Old Age Pension cheque.

Later, Fitzgerald sold his interest in the business and moved away to farm in Chilliwack. Burke remained in business until the automobile replaced the horse and buggy. In 1925 he operated the Arlington Hotel. He was a very popular man in Alberni, especially at social events when he frequently acted as master of ceremonies. He often called for square dances. In his later years he loved to tell stores of the early lives of the settlers. In the twenties, Burke sold the last of his horses and started an automated hauling business.[26]

Service by Sea

For many years, Alberni's only means of communication with the outside world were the steamers that used to service the west coast of Vancouver Island. The arrival of the steamer was an important day in the lives of the pioneer settlers, for these vessels brought much-needed supplies for the farmers and miners, and they carried mail and passengers – hunters, fishermen, prospectors, surveyors, judges, and politicians.

The first steamer to make a call at Alberni was the old *Barbara Boscowitz*, which arrived with supplies for Saunders Store. She tied up at the bank of the river at Victoria Quay. She also carried equipment and supplies for the paper mill. The *Hope* was the next to make regular trips when freight and passengers warranted it. Then, in 1893, The Canadian Pacific Navigation Company put the small side-wheeler S.S. *Maude* into service.

For a time, the *Maude*, skippered by Capt. Roberts, connected the settlers in Alberni with the rest of the world. When the *Maude* was out of service, the *Rainbow* replaced her. The trip cost seven dollars from Victoria to Alberni. Built for the Gulf of Georgia and Fraser River service, the *Rainbow* was too top-heavy for safe and comfortable travel on the open ocean. George Bird described a trip in the old wooden boats:

> Their cabins and galley were arranged around the meal table, adjoining the engine room. It took a pretty good sailor to escape from sickness. They were not much, if any, over one hundred feet long, and what with the motion of the boat on the ocean swell, the combined odours coming from the food cooking in the galley and the hot oily engine room, there were plenty of victims.[27]

The *Maude* was purchased by the Canadian Pacific Railway in 1901. She ended her days registered under the B.C. Salvage Company. Then came the *Willapa*, a bigger and faster boat, more of a passenger boat. This was followed by the *Queen City* under Capt. Townsend, which was originally intended for a sealing schooner and had been remodelled. Eventually, a reliable little ship named the S.S. *Tees* began servicing the west coast.

The *Tees* held a special place in the memories of those early settlers. She was built in 1893 at Stockton-on-Tees. "She rides the water like a duck,"[28] remarked Captain Adam Smith, who brought the little vessel from England via the Strait of Magellan into Victoria in 1896. Capt. John Irving, her owner and captain, made the inaugural trip to Alberni. After the first special trip on the *Tees*, August 22, 1896, William Wilson, a passenger, presented Capt. Irving with a document which was signed by the guest of honour and read in part:

> As a lasting expression of our esteem and friendship we ask you to accept when made, a breast pin from the first wash-up of the Duke of York claim, the pioneer successful hydraulic mine of Vancouver Island. Your enterprise in placing such a comfortable, commodious and seaworthy vessel as the *Tees* upon the West Coast route, will, we are sure, be appreciated by everybody interested in the development of mining, agriculture and fishing interests.[29]

The *Tees* brought the first sight of electricity. "The *Tees*, fully lighted up, lying at the wharf on the Alberni waterfront, looked quite a brilliant spectacle to us. We were accustomed only to the light of coal oil lamps and lanterns and to the lights on the steamer *Maude*," recalled George Bird.[30]

Irving sold the *Tees* in 1901 to the Canadian Pacific Navigation Co. The *Tees*, now skippered by Capt. Edward Gillam, a Newfoundlander, was not equipped with a wireless when she first appeared on the Alberni run. When she got a wireless set in 1914, she was the first ship to be so equipped. Her time of arrival in the early days was always a matter of guess work. At the approximate date she was expected, those living in the vicinity of the water would have their ears pealed for the sound of her whistle, and by the time she was tied up, half the population would be down to meet her. Boys used to amuse themselves by imitating her whistle.

The story is told of a time when one of the homesteaders and his daughter came to town and were staying in the boarding house over the Alberni Trading Store, waiting to board for passage to Victoria. Not expecting the boat until morning, they had retired for the night, when there was a whistle from the river bank. They jumped out of bed, dressed, and were down on the dock with their luggage before they discovered it was a false alarm.[31]

Community Social Life

The small settlement at Alberni was not unlike many of the villages and frontier settlements springing up all across Canada. Social life and hard work were intermingled with recurring barn raisings and quilting bees. Neighbour helped neighbour. Women were confined to their homes, either hand-milking cows, churning butter, or weaving. Some women were pressed into service as midwives – the nearest doctor was in Nanaimo. Smallpox, scarlet fever, diphtheria, whooping cough, and tuberculosis were still rampant. Freight was moved by stagecoach and travel limited to horse, buggy, or steamer. Men spent their recreation time fishing or hunting. The Alberni Valley was a sportsman's paradise.

Another great form of recreation was religion. The new immigrants felt the need for revival and redemption. Preachers warned them against the pleasures of the flesh. Sunday was the day of rest. Liquor was the most sinful vice. Although getting drunk was a favoured recreation among the single men, the time was ripe for the beginning of the temperance movement.

In June 1883, Frances E. Willard, of Victoria, organized the first Woman's Christian Temperance Union (WCTU) in British Columbia. This group of Christian women pledged total abstinence, pledged to protect the home, educate the youth, promote good citizenship, and influence public sentiment to obtain laws "which shall bring about release from the evil results of intemperance in our land."[32]

The "Alberni Band of Hope," already in operation in March 1890, held similar ideals. A letter to the Hon. John Robson from William Smith, secretary, stated:

> I herewith enclose resolution which was carried unanimously at the entertainment given on Monday evening March 3rd. Moved by John C. Mollet, seconded by John S. Jolly. "That this meeting of the Alberni Band of Hope workers and members, tenders its sincere thanks to the Hon. John Robson for his support given and fearless statement made on behalf of the Temperance cause on the occasion of Mr. Beaven's Municipal Bill dealing with the licenses to all intoxicating liquors in the cities of this province.[33]

The letter was signed by chairman Arthur Norris.

Social gatherings in the community were held at the government office, and later at Alberni's first school. Special causes for celebration were the 24th of May and Dominion Day on July 1. Residents of the fledgling community selected a suitable clearing, the flats on the Somass River or the Anderson Farm, and out came baskets laden with homemade goodies and the odd bottle of homemade beverage, "while games were organized, small prizes awarded and an evening dance anticipated."[34]

Bill Erickson, son of Alberni's first postmistress Agnes Erickson, wrote of the social life in the valley. He recalled the concerts held in Brands Hall, located at Southgate, in December 1890, with a dance after the concert. James R. Motion was chairman.

> Mrs. Jimmy Hills sang "This is the end of a perfect day," and Captain George Huff sang, "Yip-i-yaddi-i-a." Now Capt. Huff had no singing voice, but he just loved to get up before an audience. This night he was not on the programme and the big crowd in the hall started to clap their hands and shout, "We want Capt. Huff." Up to the platform went the Captain amid loud applause and really gave it everything he had.
> George T. Alexander of Beaver Creek – a man with a wonderful tenor voice – sang "Where is my wandering boy tonight." His parents in Scotland had purchased land far up Beaver Creek road and had sent him out here to try and make good as a farmer. "Willie" Erickson played a violin solo and Miss Groves was at the piano. John R. Packard, a notable character about town, brought in the first gramophone to the Alberni Valley. And he too was up on the platform playing records on an old original "Victor," complete with needle changer and horn. After the concert, the

chairs were all moved back to the walls and dancing went on until the small hours of the morning.[35]

Capt. Huff did much to keep up the spirits of the small settlement. Frank C. Garrard wrote in his memoirs about a mock parliament.

During our time in Alberni, especially in the winter, when there was not much work to be had, we got up a mock parliament to spend some of the evenings. Mr. Huff being the Speaker, and having had experience in the Provincial House, was able to advise as to procedure. Some of our debates were quite amusing and perhaps edifying.[36]

Ed Cox remembered the Bachelors' Ball in the Arlington Hotel and Huff's Hall as having

an all time record for elegance. The six-piece orchestra from Nanaimo was the first one ever to be brought into the district. The players were up on all the latest in dance music – two step, polka, and hesitation waltz. The hall was decorated and programs were printed. As the hotel dining room could seat only ninety people, several sittings were scheduled. For the benefit of the ladies in their long evening gowns, a plank walk was laid from the hall to the Arlington, with a rope handrail on which lanterns hung to light the way to dinner.[37]

The first attempt to form an "arts" association occurred in 1892 when the Alberni Mutual Improvement Association was formed. In a letter dated February 1, 1892, Alfred Carmichael, who was then working with the paper mill, wrote to his mother:

The Alberni Mutual Improvement Association is going to do great good to the valley. It will cause everyone to read and think more. A circulating library has been established. We have proposed to begin a society journal to which members will contribute and the paper will be read at each meeting.[38]

Once again he wrote to his mother on February 22, 1892:

The literary meeting is to come off tomorrow. Our programme is as follows: Essay on readings from Scott, by James Thomson: Dickens, by Mr. Howitt: Shakespeare, by the Rev. Mr. Smith, and if there is time I may give a reading from Longfellow.[39]

The following year, on January 3, 1893, Carmichael attended a concert, at which the bachelors of the district had to provide the refreshments. Capt. Huff was again the star of the evening. Carmichael wrote:

The concert was highlighted by a song given by George Albert Huff. He sang "Polly, Wolly, Doodle all the day". Mr. Huff has no voice at all, but he thinks he has. It happened that he just arrived in time to hear his name called for a song. The people cheered him over and over again. Mr. Huff liked this so well, he bowed to the audience. There was only one book with words and music, and the accompanist took this. So George Huff tried to remember the words. He broke down. He did not mind. The people cheered and cried "encore". He looked at the words again, and battled through to the end. The people roared with laughter, and when he finished, cheer after cheer, rent the air. Huff sang the song again, and would have a third time, if the chairman had permitted him to do so.[40]

Carmichael appreciated the finer things in life. Once he traded 1,000 Foot Board Measure for an old leatherbound book entitled, *The Holy War and the Holy State* by Thomas Fuller, published in London in 1648. This exchange was with an English settler named Wiggs, who lived in Beaver Creek.[41]

Medical Services

It was a great day for the people of Alberni when Dr. R. R. Robinson came over the mountain and set up his office in the shack he shared with one of the first ministers. Dr. Robinson was listed in the 1893 *B.C. Directory* as residing in Alberni, but he did not last long because the practice was not large enough to keep the young and energetic man busy. Dr. Pierce was the community's next physician. He, too, stayed only a few months. Another young doctor who practised during the mining period was Dr. Ross. He used to ride a horse to all the mines in the area.[42] Teacher Arthur Proctor also applied his knowledge of medicine and saved the life of a local Indian.[43]

What medical care the native Indians received was administered by the Indian doctors, missionaries, or Indian Agent Harry Guillod. Guillod's annual reports tell much of the tragedy and suffering among the eighteen tribes and 150 reserves and fishing stations he visited.

In 1883 the death rate was unusually high, Guillod reported.

In a heavy gale of wind during the sealing season thirty-six men were drowned at sea. Whooping cough and measles carried off over twenty adults and fifty children at Kyuquaht, while whooping cough was prevalent in all the tribes and proved fatal to many young children, especially to those whose parents called in the Indian doctor. At Hesquaht where the Rev. Father Brabant has stopped this superstition, no child died.[44]

Guillod spoke out against the Indian doctors and advised the Indians to take proper care of their children. He noted the need for "simple medical attendance."

I have successfully vaccinated some two hundred children and adults this year, (1885) but it is difficult to get the adult Indians to submit to the operation in many cases as it produces unhealthy sores which do not heal for a long time, and one boy at Clayoquot unfortunately died while his arm was very bad. The news spread all along the coast as being caused by vaccination.[45]

There were a number of cases of smallpox in 1893. But Guillod said the Indians were beginning to understand the virulent character of the disease and many were vaccinated.

The Indians had great faith in their Indian doctors and in their Creator. In an interview, present Tseshaht Chief Adam Shewish told about what happened at Effingham Island when a child swallowed a coin and could not get it out. An Indian doctor was called. "She chanted a song. Put her lips on the child's throat. The coin came out. She said she was not doing it, she was just the instrument."[46] Chief Shewish explained how one native doctor received his medical knowledge.

> Doctor Ned was a medicine man well known on the west coast. He had great powers. He wanted to be a doctor so bad, he went into the woods and prayed for the knowledge to be the best. The longer he stayed in the woods, the more knowledge he would obtain. When he came out he was able to help the people with his gift of healing.[47]

Guillod's report of 1896 gives the first indication of a local doctor administering care to an Indian. The doctor was probably Dr. Pybus. "Two men of the Tseshat tribe had tumours removed by the local doctor with a good recovery in each case."[48]

Dr. Alfred John Pybus was was born at Stockton-on-Tees, England, having graduated from London, Edinburgh, and Dublin Universities. He emigrated to Australia October 3, 1884. While there he suffered a serious attack of sunstroke which almost finished his medical career. Looking for a climate where he might find a cure for his illness, he was attracted to Canada. For a short time he practised in Victoria, but prospects in the city were disappointing, so he decided to move to the interior of B.C. where he bought a ranch at Whonnock.

There Dr. Pybus met an old schoolmate, the Rev. Alexander Dunn, who advised him to "Go to Alberni – there is no doctor of any kind there. One is badly needed and the government realizing this need, is going to pay a doctor for this territory."[49] Dunn had served the Presbyterian ministry in Alberni from 1886 to 1889 before moving to Whonnock.

Pybus pulled up stakes once again and moved to Alberni in 1894. His high credentials easily secured him the position as first doctor for the district. He was also appointed medical officer for the Indians. He purchased ten acres of land at one dollar an acre and employed Chinese laborers to clear and cultivate it.[50]

Out of his stipend Dr. Pybus purchased five hundred dollars' worth of drugs and set up a small pharmacy behind his office. He wasn't in the community long before there was a stampede of miners to China Creek following the discovery of gold. With the miners came new settlers and increased business. Pybus struggled on, suffering frequent lapses of bad health. One of the settlers was a druggist who opened up for business, leaving Pybus with much of his stock still intact.

The druggist was Clifford M. Pineo, who arrived in 1907 with his father, the Rev. Albert J. Pineo; two sisters, Evelyn and Emmeline; and two brothers, Holmes De Wolfe and Lew Albert. All three Pineo brothers were druggists. The Pineo drug store sold everything from pills to pianos. At the time of the Pineos' arrival, Dr. Pybus was in bad health, but was still serving as health officer. The family sought his approval to install Alberni's first septic tank.

Alfred Carmichael wrote to his mother of a visit he had from Dr. Pybus over a toothache.

> About this time I was troubled with severe toothache. Two molars in the lower jaw on the left side were badly holed. I plugged the holes with cotton wool soaked in tincture of cloves. There was no dentist in Alberni, but there was Dr. Pybus, an old English doctor. I told him about my aching teeth. One day he called at our cabin. He did not say a word about my teeth. After some conversation I asked him if he would like to see my garden. He would. We walked down the trail through the high bracken ferns. There was a log beside the trail. "This is a good place to have those teeth out," said Pybus. He sat me on the log. Putting his right hand in the pocket of his jacket, he pulled out a pair of extractors.
>
> Put your head back and open your mouth," he said. I did just that and pointed to the offending molars. Dr. Pybus then attempted to extract them. He twisted and pulled to no purpose. Both teeth broke off at the gum. On my first visit to Victoria I had them crowned by Dr. Garesche, a well known and popular dentist.[51]

Pybus was a lovable old character, always whistling half under his breath as he walked the streets of Alberni, taking life easy. One of his interests was stamp collecting. He also claimed the distinction of being the first to own and drive an automobile, a 1901 Oldsmobile. The old car never ran very well and practically every time he took it out it was either towed home by a team of horses or pushed home by a group of young boys. When Alberni became a municipality and taxes were levied, Pybus had to relinquish his property for taxes owed.

After that he lived in a small cottage on the bank of the Somass River at the end of Southgate and Victoria Quay.

Dr. Alfred Marchmont Watson arrived in Alberni in 1895. He was born September 9, 1840, at Lucea, Jamaica. He married Fanny Elizabeth Eaton, at Ancaster, England, on May 24, 1866. The couple had eight children, all born at Penistone, York: Edward Marchmont 1869, James Kenneth 1870, Eleanor Mary 1872, Winifred McKinstry 1873, John Freeman 1875, Freeman George Herbert 1877, Marjorie Leslie 1881, and Phillip Alexander 1884.

When the family came to Canada in 1891, Watson practised in Cowichan for four years before finally settling in Alberni. The decision to build All Saints' Church was made in his home. Three stained glass memorial windows in the church have since been dedicated to the Watson family. Dr. Watson died in 1906.[52]

The next doctor to serve the community was Dr. Arthur David Morgan, who came in 1906. Notice of Morgan's imminent arrival was sent to Dr. Pybus on August 22, 1906: "I am today notified by the Indian Department that a gentleman named Morgan has been appointed permanently Indian Medical Officer, held by the late Dr. Watson. The temporary arrangements with yourself will therefore cease when Dr. Morgan arrives and takes over the duties which I believe will be on Sat. 25th. Yours faithfully, A. W. Neill."[53]

Arthur Morgan was born in Nanaimo in 1876, the son of Thomas Morgan, a Welsh coal miner who came to Canada to work in the coal mines in Nanaimo, eventually becoming government inspector. Dr. Arthur Morgan graduated with honours from McGill University in 1901, and he returned to B.C. to take up his first practice at Quesnel. He married Mamie Bentley of Montreal in 1902, then practised for three years in the Cariboo before coming to Alberni to establish his medical practice.

Later, along with Waterhouse, MacIntyre, Burde, Cox, and Leonard Frank, Morgan helped form the China Creek Water and Power Syndicate to bring electric light to the community. He was also a member of the committee known as the "Citizens' Committee of Eleven" who worked towards making the community a municipality. His name appears in many early records of Alberni.

Dr. Morgan's patients fondly remembered his brown mustache and sometimes abrupt manner. His was a far from conventional bedside manner, but it seemed to have a stimulating effect – his wisecracks were as good as medicine for his patients. Dr. Morgan was never known to turn down a call – day or night, whatever the weather – and his bills were pruned to fit the purses of his patients. He pedalled a bicycle on calls, although occasionally he hired a horse and buggy from Jack Burke's livery stable across from the Arlington Hotel on Margaret Street. Morgan loved a fast horse; he loved politics; and he was very active in the life of the small community.[54]

He practised in Alberni until 1917, when he joined the Canadian Army Medical Corps and served overseas, then in Vancouver at Shaughnessy Military Hospital until the close of the Great War. Later Dr. Morgan returned to Alberni, where he served until his death in 1934.[55]

Agriculture

Agriculture was an important part of early pioneering life in the Alberni Valley. Many settlers and their families established roots in quarter sections in the outlying districts of Beaver Creek, Cherry Creek, and Sproat Lake. A big help for the farmers was the annual government allotment for road maintenance. Nearly all the farmers worked in the summer on the roads and made enough money to pay their year's taxes and bills. "Those who have independent means stay on their places, but the majority work on the roads. If this government aid was stopped, a place like this would cease to exist, as the greater part of the community are altogether dependent on the road money. Their places would be taken over by men of means, or the deer and wolf."[56] In 1892 fruit was cheap. Fifty cents could pay for a 2½ gallon tin of strawberries or any other fruit. Oxen were used instead of horses. Although the animals were slow, they were able to work in places horses could not. Carmichael had a pair he used for logging; they were named Tom and Dick.

With no fences, cattle were allowed to roam free. Alfred Carmichael wrote:

> You would think it strange to see everybody's cattle running wild in the woods: they are very wild too, and some quite ferocious. When a man wants to kill an animal for sale he takes his rifle and goes to the spot he thinks his cattle are and then shoots the one he wishes. Then he brings his "jumper", as sleighs are called here, and takes the carcass to the river. After refreshing it, offers it for sale. This is how the "fleshers" do business in this country.[57]

A visitor to the area, C. M. Cathcart, wrote about the F. M. Walker ninety acre farm, 4½ miles from the city:

> Nearby we inspected a wonderful market garden farm, where F. M. Walker has 90 acres of viable river bottom soil under cultivation. Potatoes, he told

me, should always yield ten to twelve tons per acre. He has twelve acres in potatoes and many acres of corn, beans, peas, turnips, cabbage, berries and practically all other kinds of vegetables and fruits. He told us that his fourteen dairy cows gave him an average return of $10 a day, although he got but 10 cents a quart for the milk. He said this was an earthly heaven for poultry, as well as for hogs, and he could not imagine a man of reasonable thrift and thought, failing to make money here at any kind of intensive farming. Some 75 acres of the land adjoining this splendid 90 acre garden, including 35 acres of river bottom loam is owned by S. M. Read & Co.[58]

Cathcart estimated the cost of the land at $1,000 an acre.

In 1897 the Farmers' Institute was first organized in British Columbia, with the objective of promoting agriculture, distributing products and improving the conditions of rural life, and making new settlers welcome. The province was divided into ten districts, and these district institutes met annually or semi-annually.[59] It wasn't until November 5, 1905, that a meeting was called for the purpose of forming an Industrial and Agricultural Association in the Alberni Valley. At the meeting Fred Cowley was elected president and James Redford vice-president. The directors included William Leason, Robert Thompson, John Best, and Harry Hills. The Rev. T. S. Glassford (Presbyterian minister) was elected secretary and treasurer.

A handwritten minute book shows the Association's main occupation was dealing with business related to the annual agriculture fair. The first Alberni Fall Fair was held in 1904.[60] It was noted the membership was one dollar a year and this included entry to the 4-H hall and fair. Non-members would be charged ten cents. The fair was held on Strick Road, which runs parallel to Beaver Creek Road, now accessed via Pierce Road. A hall was built at the site.

In the minute book there is one sad notation dated August 4, 1906, reporting the position of vice-president was now vacant due to the death of James Redford. Redford had been going about his business on the family farm when he was accidentally shot by James Rollin, who was hunting on horseback. Redford's body was brought into Alberni and tended to by Dr. Pybus, while someone rode horseback to Nanaimo to get additional help. But it was too late for James Redford. His wife gave birth to twins in August.[61] She was left with eight children to raise.

The *Pioneer News* reported September 21, 1907 that the third annual fall fair of the Alberni Agricultural Society was a remarkable success and the display of field and garden produce was equal to the best ever seen in the Province of British Columbia. Two mottos were noticeable: "Watch Alberni grow" and "The farmer is a most useful man." The fair had six hundred entries, double that of the previous year.

The first farm in the district, the Anderson Farm (now Somass Dairy Farm), for many years had the only cattle. As a result, there wasn't sufficient meat to supply the increasing demands of the settlers. Many resorted to canned beef, bacon, and salt pork, purchased from the store. When the farms became established, meat became more plentiful because a farmer could kill a pig or slaughter a cow. There was no refrigeration; therefore milk and butter were difficult to keep during the summers. Again, many were compelled to purchase canned milk.

The Alberni Creamery Association reported in 1908 that 18,522 pounds of butter had been made during the previous year, an increase of 1300 pounds. About one-half of the product was for local consumption and the other half exported. The farmers had received an average of twenty-five cents per pound for their butter. This was a good year for local farmers as the government appropriations for roads were increased by five thousand dollars. Government agent Herbert Charles Rayson was praised for the increase, which allowed for an unprecedented amount of work on roads, trails, and bridges to get under way. The original appropriation was $10,450.[62]

There was an abundance of locally grown fruit and vegetables, which included apples, plums, cherries, and raspberries. Winter vegetables included potatoes, carrots, parsnips, turnips, and cabbage. If the hens were laying, then the settlers had eggs. Prices for produce went according to the law of supply and demand. Farming in the district was actively promoted, especially when there was a hint of a railway coming into town. The Canadian Pacific Railway advertisements read:

> What are the prices of land? Acreage varies from $20 to $100 an acre for bush-land, and from $100 to $400 an acre for cleared land, according to quality and location. How much farming land is there? About 60,000 acres. What kind of farming pays best? Mixed farming, on plots of land from 10 to 20 acres, especially fruit-growing, dairying, hog and poultry raising.[63]

Mining Boom

Vancouver Island is dotted with abandoned mine sites that give testimony to the broken dreams of the early prospectors, who sought to get rich digging gold and minerals. The hills around Alberni had their share of dreamers. Despite a mining boom in the 1890s, better described as a "claim-staking boom," by Ben Hines in his book *Pick Pan and Pack*, a history of mining in the Alberni region, "the Alberni area garnered not one producing mine from the mass of locations put under claim in the 1890s."[64]

Between September, 1895 and March, 1901, the Alberni mining recorder received 2,009 claims. At first it was the rumour of gold that brought the Chinese to the Alberni district, later it was the mineral possibilities that lured the early white prospector. Some of the mines established in the 1890s included the Duke of York, the Golden Eagle, Hayes Mine, the Thistle Mine, King Solomon Mine, and Alberni-Consolidated.

Leonard Frank and his brother Bernard came to Alberni from Oldenburg, Germany in 1898, drawn to the area by glowing reports of mining opportunities. A copper discovery the previous year at Uchucklesit Harbour, eighteen miles down the Alberni Inlet, had brought a rush of mining activity. The Franks staked claims at the Monitor and Happy John mines north of Nahmint Bay, but neither mine brought the wealth anticipated. When the price of copper dropped in 1902, the Monitor was closed. It reopened when the First World War created a new interest in copper mining.

The Raven and Eagle mineral claims were owned by the H. S. Law group. They were situated on the west bank of the Alberni Inlet about 2½ miles from Alberni. The three veins in this property showed values in copper and gold. The Forfarshire Mines Company staked three claims – the Mountain Treasure, the Pacific, and the Pheasant – about a mile from the mouth of Anderson Lake. This property was under the management of J. Cameron. Adjoining the Forfarshire mines was the Marmot Group of six claims, owned by Pemberton and Luxton. On the east side of Anderson Lake was the Lake Shore Group of three claims, owned by McKinnon, Shafer, and Jackson. Next to them was the Florence Group of four claims owned by Young, Johnson, Langley, and Avery.

Interest in developing the mines was hindered by the terrain and by lack of access. Often a mine would be developed only if the miner was willing to carry his tools and equipment over the thickly forested trails. For some, the Alberni Inlet became a lifeline, bringing in supplies and shipping out the ore.

The Duke of York Mine, "well on its way to being one of the most sophisticated and extensive mines of the period",[65] had every appearance of a little town, having a dozen houses in the neighbourhood. About seventy-three men worked steadily through 1896 on the three hydraulic mining claims, the Duke of York, the Cataract, and the Constance.

During the hot summer of that year, two bush fires threatened the town. The Duke of York lost its stables, a blacksmith shop, assay office, and 7500 feet of lumber. The Cataract got a scorching – the dam, sawmill, and 300 feet of flume was burned. Headlines read: "Alberni on fire: Tremendous Destruction of Mining Property by bush fire."[66]

The first manager at the Duke of York was Frank McQuillan, who later left for the Atlin area. He was succeeded by a Californian named Loveridge. Pert's sawmill was operated at the camp. Andy Watson ran the cookhouse and a store. Dan Watty used four pack horses to bring supplies into the mine until the government built a road.

Sid Toy managed the Golden Eagle where a $40,000 stamp mill was installed. The operation belonged to Alberni Consolidated, a Dunsmuir subsidiary. About eighteen miles of road were built for the show, which never produced anything better than low grade ore. It was at the Golden Eagle that Alberni mines recorded the first fatalities. Two miners, William Dixon of Beaver Creek and William Sareault of River Road, were killed by the explosion of two sticks of dynamite which had been drying out in a pan over a store.

The Minnesota was one of the most promising claims. Loveridge paid the prospectors three hundred dollars for the claim and paid two miners four dollars a day throughout the winter to put in a three hundred foot tunnel, only to find that the vein had run out.

Then there was the Thistle, one of the richest mines in the area, discovered by Pat Sullivan and Joe Plasket, grubstaked by Andy Watson. It was situated on the 2,500 foot level on the headwaters of the Franklin River on Mount Douglas. A San Francisco syndicate took over the property and decided to build a nine mile long wagon road to the mine from Underwood Cove on the Alberni Inlet. They employed between one hundred and two hundred men for about two months, but wet weather prevented completion of the road.

Another mine with visions of greatness was Hayes Mine, about fourteen miles down the Alberni Inlet from Alberni. It was under the supervision of Colonel G. H. Hayes, of the Nahmint Mining Company of Portland, Oregon. Organized in 1898, with a capital of $100,000, the mine pushed six hundred feet of tunnel on four full-sized claims and three fractions near the mouth of the Nahmint River. During that year, the company shipped 120 tons of ore containing copper, gold, and silver. Investments at the minesite had been

105

heavy, including the building of a boarding house to accommodate thirty men, two ore-sheds, wharf "suitable for the largest vessels," warehouse, office, manager's residence, storeroom, stable, and smaller buildings. From the wharf a wagon road zigzagged for two miles up the steep mountainside to the mine.

Three months later, Hayes' company faced an unexpected obstacle when the provincial government, then under Premier Joseph Martin, declared an eight-hour working day in the mining industry. When the men refused to accept less than their $3.50 per ten-hour shift for the shorter work day, Hayes ordered the mine shut down.

The legislation had a dramatic impact on the mining ventures. The Victoria *Colonist* reported: "The various properties in and around Alberni are now principally shut down."[67] It was the miners, and those connected with mining, who were the consumers of the farmers' produce. As well, practically all the lumber sawn in the Alberni Valley was for mining camp buildings or mine timbers.

Political Changes – Alan W. Neill

A farmer, Alan Webster Neill, became one of Alberni's longest serving politicians. He would serve both as a Member of the Legislative Assembly of the province and later as Member of Parliament for Alberni-Comox.

Neill came to the Alberni Valley in 1891 and farmed a quarter section of bush land. He reported he had walked from Nanaimo in early winter and said that timber wolves followed him.

Born in Montrose, Scotland, on October 6, 1868, Neill was the son of a farmer. Before coming to Alberni, he lived at "Gourdie" Lochee, Scotland. In 1892 he enlisted in the Royal Canadian Artillery at Work Point Barracks, and a few months later went with them to Quebec. In 1894 Neill returned to Scotland to assist his father, but just three years later he was back in Alberni farming. He sent for his bride-to-be, Jeanie Rutherford Douglas, and they were married in Vancouver on November 19, 1898. The couple had two children, Helen Douglas, born June 1, 1900, and Victoria Webster, who was born January 20, 1902 and died on March 18, 1920. The Neills farmed about three miles out of town in the Cherry Creek area. In 1907, the family moved to a nine acre plot of land fronting the present Margaret Street, then called the Creamery Road.[68]

How Neill entered politics was one of his favourite stories: A fellow workman on the road told him of a political meeting being held that night and suggested they attend. More out of curiosity than anything else, he went. During the nomination period a man on the opposite side of the hall rose and pointed a finger at Neill. "I nominate that man," he said, not even knowing Neill's name.[69]

For the second time the district had been enumerated as a separate riding with one sitting member. Neill hoped to be that member. The Alberni Representation Act of 1886 had been amended in 1871 to include Nanaimo District and "all that tract of land included in a circle which may be described with a radius of 25 miles in length from the site of Stamp's mill, situate at Alberni, as the centre of such a circle."[70] Andrew Haslam, of Alberni, had been elected in a by-election in June 1889 following the death of Robert Dunsmuir.

The riding was changed in 1890 to include only Alberni. On June 13, 1890 Thomas Fletcher ran against John C. Mollet. Fletcher won by twenty-nine votes to twelve. Again the riding changed faces when in 1894 Alberni was joined with Cowichan, with two representatives. These were Theodore Davie and James Mitchell Mutter. Davie resigned a year later to accept the appointment as Chief Justice to the B.C. Supreme Court. A by-election was held April 18, 1895. Capt. George Albert Huff, from Alberni, and Thomas Anthony Wood both received 172 votes. According to the *Victoria Colonist* of July 30, 1895, Returning Officer John C. Mollet allowed two questionable ballots, giving Wood 174. Wood was declared elected. However, Huff claimed that some votes had been missed and that there were other irregularities. He appealed to the Supreme Court.

The official report of the Deputy Returning Officers confirmed by a Supreme Court count, gave Huff 173 and Wood 172. Huff formally claimed the seat. Another by-election was held October 5, 1895, resulting in Huff obtaining 253 to Richard Beauchamp Halhed's 177. Later the Redistribution Act of 1898 created the Alberni electoral district with one member.[71]

On July 9, 1898, Huff ran against Neill, losing by one hundred votes to seventy. Neill was declared elected by a comfortable majority. However, he resigned that same year because he had unwittingly accepted money from the government for road work done after the election. He was re-elected in December 15, 1898, beating out William Arthur Ward. In the next election held June 9, 1900, Neill won over James Redford and James Bain Thomson.[72] He represented the district until 1903. Neill's scrapbook, which is now housed in the Alberni District Historical Society archives, gives some indication of his interests during those years and the legislation he helped implement.

The year before Neill's first election win, a rich gold strike had been found in the Klondike. By 1898, the province had an unprecedented stampede of people from all over the world. For a time everything prospered. But by 1900 the Klondike boom was past its peak and the immigrants began settling in the towns and villages. A large number of Chinese and Japanese immigrants, who had come to the province to work on the railway, in fishing, or in the mines, decided to stay. Racial tensions were high. An editorial from the *Free Press* is one of Neill's first items in his scrapbook. It stated:

> The influx of Mongolians into B.C. is now out of all proportion to the requirements of the country and the character it has assumed is fast becoming a menace to the common weal and so much so that it is a source of consternation, not to say anxiety, to all deep thinking impartial and unprejudiced persons. What the outcome of it will be time alone can determine, but the present evil is so abundantly apparent that we cannot longer blind ourselves to the fact that strong restrictive measures must be instituted to counteract the change, and at once.[73]

Another article, from the *Daily Columbian*, pushed for greater restrictions on the importation of Chinese into the country, and on the Japanese "who have invaded our fisheries to an extent that has crowded hundreds of white fishermen and Indians out of employment, and threatens to entirely capture the industry before long."[74]

A petition was presented in the legislature stating the fifty dollar tax per capita on the Asians had proved "wholly inadequate" and suggested a tax of five hundred dollars would restrict the immigration. The document claimed that

> these Chinese are non-assimilative and have no intention of settled citizenship, are immoral, social and sanitary status usually below the most inferior standard of western life, and, being usually single men imported as coolies by labor contracting organization, accept less than the lowest living wage of white labor, yet expend but little of their scanty earnings in the land of their temporary adoption.[75]

In 1903 the Asiatic head tax was raised to five hundred dollars. Neill commented, "precautions had been taken to protect coal miners from the dangers arising from the employment of ignorant Asiatics, and the same measures should be taken to guard all classes of miners."[76] Neill had to take care of his constituents, many of them miners.

Neill said the remedy was rigid exclusion and a system of registration.

We do not want to imitate them in their low standard of living or in the way they work, their lack of recreation, lack of comforts and lack of culture. From the Atlantic to the Pacific Ocean I see that great Canada peopled with one great white race, the worthy descendants of the two races that now occupy Canada; I see one race, speaking perhaps the two languages still, but one race in their unity as a nation, one race in their allegiance to the flag they follow, one race in their adherence to the God they worship.[77]

Meanwhile, at the turn of the century, the Placer Mining Bill was approved. Neill served on the mining committee. The bill was intended to "protect the magnificent natural resources of the country from the untaxed, non-contributing alien and to let our own miners, capitalists and workers have first chance."[78]

Another bill, which also passed, was the Labor Regulation Act of 1898, which excluded Japanese and Chinese from working in the coal mines.

Neill was accused in one article of being a follower of Joseph Martin, then premier, because road appropriations in Alberni had been cut down to five thousand dollars. Constituents also complained because the Gold Commissioner's office had been taken away from Alberni and the government agent's salary cut. Neill always sat as an independent member, supporting either party as he saw fit. One newspaper article read:

These are little rewards that the Alberni people set for their change of allegiance, and now they are making very angry faces as they swallow the medicine administered by Martin. However, no doubt the good people of Alberni will smile happily again if the government offers to put a few toll gates around the district.[79]

Martin had been the Attorney General in the Turner government when Neill got elected in 1898.

It was now over thirty years since Confederation. The non-party system had not worked. During the past five years there had been five governments – Turner, Semlin, Martin, Dunsmuir, and Prior.[80] These were turbulent years in the House, and Neill was right in the thick of it all, having served under all five. When the Conservative party under Richard McBride won the election in 1903, Neill's term as MLA was over.

The Alberni election of October 3, 1903 was the first provincial election in B.C. fought along organized federal party lines. William Wallace Burns McInnes, a Liberal, took the election against Robert Humes F. Hickey, a Conservative.[81] McInnes resigned on May 20, 1905 when he was appointed Commissioner of the Yukon. A by-election was held July 22, returning William Manson, a Conservative. Manson lasted only two years being defeated in the 1907 election by Liberal Harlan Carey Brewster.[82]

Alan Neill continued to serve his community and the province. He was appointed Indian Agent and served in that capacity until 1913. In 1903 he was appointed Stipendiary Magistrate for the Counties of Victoria and Nanaimo. In 1907 he was appointed Notary Public in B.C. From 1911 to 1927 he built up and operated the Pioneer Feed, Coal and Oil Co, in Port Alberni. Neill's first run at politics had only whet his appetite. He would emerge once again in the 1920s as a representative from Alberni in Ottawa.

Simple Pleasures – Stephen Wells Diary

In the first decade of the twentieth century the air was fresh with renewed confidence. The success of the Canadian Pacific Railway opened lines of communication and travel unheard of previously. Coal-oil lamps still lit Alberni homes. The smell of homemade bread came from settlers' kitchens as cast-iron stoves were fired up by a plentiful supply of wood. Large pots of soup bubbled constantly. Cupboards were full of canned salmon and condensed milk. Jams, jellies, and pickles were made from home-grown fruits and vegetables. Roads were still nightmares. The livery stable, blacksmith shop, and hitching posts were familiar sights.

Pleasures were simple for the early settlers – a visit with neighbours, a church service, fishing on the river, or reading a good book. Planting a garden became a necessity of life. Stephen Wells, a young man who came to Alberni to work at the paper mill, left a diary which chronicles details of his life over several years at the turn of the century. He lived in the Beaver Creek area with his many cats, and walked to work at the paper mill.[83]

A typical breakfast for Wells consisted of graham flour cake and canned mutton, tea with condensed milk, and boiled peaches. For variety, he would have biscuits, canned salmon and potatoes, tea and condensed milk. The graham flour cake was his specialty, and he even included a recipe for it in his diary: "That night I made a cake 'of exceptional quality' it had three eggs, about a quarter pound of butter, two handfuls of unwashed currents, not having time for such trifles,(as washing) baking soda, sugar and salt." (He forgot to mention the flour.)

In March of 1899, while at the store, Stephen Wells spoke with the police chief Gus Cox and the Presbyterian minister Rev. E. G. Taylor about

> the Indians versus the whiskey question. The Indians were not allowed whiskey and any white man found giving them whiskey was fined $50, or three months in jail, or the chain gang. I thought it didn't look right to see men on the streets who had been sentenced for a criminal offence, nor did it look right to see men in chains working on the streets in a civilized country. The minister thought it was alright. I asked him if he would like to be put in the chain gang, and to this he did not know what to answer. The company present thought it would be a good plan to let the Indians have all the whiskey they like for a month to see what (tricks) they would play.[84]

Each Sunday, Wells faithfully read from the scriptures. He took a bath before retiring. Depending on the time of year, his days were spent either chopping wood, working on the road construction, working in his garden, which was extensive, helping a neighbour, or working at the George Bird sawmill. Falling large trees was quite a problem for the settlers. Often it meant boring holes in the trees with an auger and burning them down from the inside out. There was one "big tree" which Wells worked hard at falling. He wrote in his diary: "After breakfast, I piled in a lot of bark and stuff to start up a fresh fire. I did this twice during the day, which continued wet. Just about dark, the big tree fell with a great crash amid a thicket of small timber."

Another time he went to the settlement, to the lower wharf (Waterhouse's) to buy fifty pounds of stumping powder and some dynamite and fuse. William Nicholas came to help him with the dynamite for blasting, which first had to be thawed out. They used over two pounds of the powder, blowing out stumps over two feet in diameter, "leaving a clean hole which would take two wagon loads of soil to fill in." By the next day, they had blasted out or cracked nearly one hundred stumps.

Wells, in turn, went to help William Nicholas dig a drain. "These people have a good farm and live well." After supper he went to look at Mrs. Peter Nicholas' garden. "She owns a splendid fruit garden which she tends and tills herself and has likewise a large family of eight girls and one fat son – in different stages of development."

On a visit with his neighbours, the Thomas Kirkpatricks, who had just recovered from "the effects of la gripe," they discussed the matrimonial prospects in Alberni, as a large number of bachelors were now getting married. (Kirkpatrick was the first established blacksmith in the district.)

A near neighbour, living less than a mile from here, named James Hills, having just come into some money, has just been accepted by a friend in the prime of life, who would not consider his case six or seven years ago. Whether money has worked these wonders, it's not right for human nature to judge, for a little love and a little money together, may accomplish what a little love alone could not do. There have already taken place three or four weddings this year in Alberni and I wish them all a long and happy married life.

Two weeks later, the subject of matrimony was still on his mind as he visited with Johnny Drinkwater, who owned a log house in the forest two miles from another person. "We discussed road-making and bachelors marrying, and the advantages of being a husband of a good wife, especially in a country like this." A little poem followed this insert.

> When many a heart has grown cold and hard,
> Without a mate to match,
> The Rooster is lord of all the yard,
> With never a hen to scratch.

Wells didn't think kindly about what he termed "starvation farmers." During a day in March 1899 when he had spoken with one of the Hills brothers, he noted;

he being one of the joes that believes in feeding stock during March and April. Most of the starvation farmers don't grow enough hay to feed through the winter, so the cattle have to go short after the first of March, which is a very bad policy that a man with any conscience wouldn't endure without making an effort to procure food for his cattle.

His garden produced large amounts of strawberries, which he distributed generously to anyone in the neighbourhood who cared to call. He also took some into town for George Drinkwater the barber, and for Capt. Huff. There were visits from local Indians who wanted plants. On one occasion two women arrived wanting strawberry plants. Wells allowed them to dig up two hundred plants, and he gave them a few seedling apple trees "as they continued to point to the trees exclaiming – nice apples."

He had a certain sympathy for the native people. On one occasion when he was working at the George Bird sawmill Fred Brand came in with a number of Indians. Brand was trying to make a bargain by using them to bring down some logs from a slough. The Indians wanted seventeen dollars for the job. Brand argued them down to six. The job was said to be worth at least fifteen dollars. "Thus do the so called Christian white men impose on the poor savage." At various

Adam Grant Horne and his wife Elizabeth (nee Bate). They were married February 22, 1859 in Nanaimo. Note Hudson's Bay Co. uniform. Circa 1855.   BCARS A-8365

Captain Edward Stamp, pioneer businessman of Victoria, and the founder of the Hasting's Mill in Vancouver. He was so impressed by the great forests in the Alberni region, he convinced two shipping companies in London, England, to finance the construction of the Anderson sawmill. He became manager. Circa 1860.   BCARS A-1768

Anderson Sawmill, or Stamp Sawmill as it was first known, was constructed in 1860 at the present site of Alberni Harbour Quay in Port Alberni.   AVM PN444

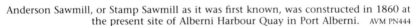

Harry Guillod,
Indian Agent
BCARS A-7529

Gilbert Malcolm Sproat was sent to Alberni
as the shipping company's representative.
In 1872 he became the first Agent-General for
British Columbia in London, England.   AVM PN538

The *Willie* was an old sternwheeler which had seen service on the Fraser River when it
was brought to Alberni by Capt. Huff. The small wood-burning steamer was kept busy
carrying freight and passengers to and from mine sites along the Alberni Inlet. Photo of the
Willie at Thistle mine wharf.   AVM PN3752

Captain George Albert Huff.
Photo courtesy of granddaughter
Mrs. Belle Sherwood.   AVM PN11871

C. Frederic Bishop.
Photo courtesy of grandson
Fred Bishop.   AVM PN11182

Marie (nee Mathews) Bishop,
wife of C. Frederic Bishop.
Photo courtesy of grandson
Fred Bishop.   AVM PN11181

F. Harold Bishop, born in Alberni
in 1887. Photo courtesy of son Fred Bishop.
Circa 1922.   AVM PN 11880

Logging by oxen team.   AVM PN449

The B.C. Paper Manufacturing Co. Ltd. on the Somass River. Circa 1892.   BCARS D-579

Kenneth McKenzie.
Photo courtesy
Lila McKenzie. PN139

Alexandrina (nee MacKenzie),
wife of Kenneth McKenzie.
Photo courtesy
Lila McKenzie. PN11888

Hector McKenzie,
son of Kenneth and Alexandrina.
Photo courtesy
Lila McKenzie. PN11889

Steam schooner, the *Barbara Boscovitz*, which
transported machinery up the Somass River in
1892, to the B.C. Paper Manufacturing Co. mill.
Leonard Frank photo 42015. AVM PN743

Klick-sim (Cultus Bob) Tseshaht
in blanket and feather headdress.
Joseph Clegg photo.
AVM PN1891

First Alberni Residential School.
Circa 1891. AVM PN1974

Alberni Residential School class of 1910. AVM PN3653

Opetchesaht Indian Reserve along the Somass River.
Note several plank houses and canoes on the beach. Circa 1897.
National Museums of Canada photo no. 29146.   AVM PN1998

Arrival of the last stagecoach in December 1911.
Location is at the corner of Elizabeth Street and Johnston Road, Alberni.
Leonard Frank photo.   AVM PN333

Scene outside the Alberni Livery and Feed Store operated by Jack Burke, circa 1902. The barn was located on Margaret Street, Alberni. Left to right: Bill Carky, Herman Halpenny, unidentified man, J. R. Plaunt with driving wagon and Jack Burke with driving buggy.   AVM PN396

Waterhouse's Wharf and ticket office. Waterhouse home is to the extreme right of picture. People identified as left to right. Mr. Brown, Mr. Carmichael, Waterhouse, fourth person unknown. Sign at rear: New Alberni Townsite, Lots for Sale, A. D. Cooper & W. Moore & C.P.N. Co. Ltd. Ticket Office. Circa 1902-03.   AVM PN147

Arthur E. Waterhouse.
Photo courtesy of grand-daughter
Mrs. Belle Sherwood.   AVM PN7122

Dr. Alfred Marchmont Watson.
AVM PN95

The SS *Tees* approaching Waterhouse Wharf in New Alberni.   AVM PN392

Dr. Arthur David Morgan.
AVM PN91

Dr. Caleb T. Hilton.
Joseph Clegg photo.   AVM PN92

Early class at Alberni (Gill) School, Circa 1890. Schoolteacher Arthur Proctor.
Students identified as Henrietta Nicholas, Eva Thomas, Bertha Nicholas, George Sareault,
Henry Thomas, Dan Watts, Charles Mollet, Willie Clarke, John Mollet, Gus La Belle,
A. P. Proctor, Wm. Nicholas, Richard Clarke, Maggie Lauder, Josephine Clarke, Jean Thomas,
Minnie Tinkley, Harvey Tinkley, Willie Tinkley.   AVM PN297

The George Bird family. Back row: George H. Bird, wife Florence; Centre: Eldest son George and youngest son Thomas on knee. Standing left to right: daughters Charlotte, Doris, and Florence. Another daughter Esther was born in 1907. AVM PN106

George Bird's sawmill at Paper Mill site. Circa 1900. PABC AVM PN134

Minnie Huff with husband
Thomas George Paterson, lightkeeper at
Cape Beale lighthouse. Photo courtesy of
daughter Mrs. Belle Sherwood. AVM PN11870

Richard J. Burde,
first newspaper publisher.
AVM PN2335

Courthouse, jail and Government Office in Alberni. Circa 1900. AVM PN16

Barclay Sound Cedar Company, the present site of
Alberni Pacific Division of MacMillan Bloedel Ltd.   AVM PN3907

Arlington
Hotel,
Alberni 1907.
AVM PN688

Victoria Quay in Alberni showing Alberni Trading Co. store, post office and the Alberni Hotel. Circa 1908. Wright Porritt photo.   AVM PN1143

Corner of Victoria Quay and Southgate Street:
Bishop's store on left, Brand's Hall and home; Thomson's store in background.
Circa 1900. Leonard Frank photo.   AVM PN14

Engine No. 494, the first passenger train into Port Alberni
December 20, 1911 stops to take on water.   PABC PN558

The first train passengers are shown at the Cameron Lake Chalet stop.   AVM PN661

Cameron Lake Chalet. AVM PN455

The E&N railway station at Alberni. AVM PN962

points in his diary he noted: "Spotted a few Indians today on the other side of the river."

The diary is full of names of the early settlers, even the arrival of the new doctor, who Wells declared,

> was quite a young man and I believe is subsidized by the government, while the two old doctors who have been here many years, will no doubt feel 'snubsidized' – whose main faults seem to have been making their eternal bills, above the quality of pills, so the people made their will, as they never cured their ills.

Springtime was the happiest of times for Wells. All winter long he had poured over seed catalogues and ordered seeds from all over the world, often necessitating getting them through Customs. Now he could delight in his garden and the constant flow of visitors to his homestead in Beaver Creek, at Malabar. He left another poem:

> The winter has now left us and away,
> All nature is smiling and gay,
> The birds are all singing and the birds are telling,
> of a brighter and happier day.

During the Great War, Wells left Alberni for Australia. When he returned he had lost his homestead, so he built a small cabin and lived there with his many cats, perceived by the residents to be a hermit.

Anderson Land Company

When the transcontinental railway reached Port Moody in 1886, and settlers began arriving in British Columbia by the thousands, the Anderson Company of London, England decided it was time to make an effort to develop the land it owned in the Alberni Valley. James George Anderson, representing Anderson, Anderson & Co., and Capt. George Slader, who represented Bilbe & Co. trustees, came to Alberni to see what could be done. They travelled by a small steamer to the Qualicum River from Victoria, then hiked across the Horne Lake Trail to Alberni. Their gear included "a tent and packhorse and one week's supply of whisky."[85]

After looking over the settlement situation, they decided to lay out a small townsite in 1886. This became Alberni (the Old Townsite). Lots were sold at various times, others were donated for churches, schools and other public buildings. Later, when New Alberni began to develop, another townsite was developed to the south. There were

113

now two potential townsites, although it was never the intention of the company to develop two towns. The Anderson Farm was already rented to Charles Taylor.

In 1902, on the way home from a visit to Australia, Alan G. Anderson visited Alberni and found "utter stagnation in the matter of settlement and demand for land in the Alberni district." He recommended that in order to simplify matters in connection with the sale or lease of lots, or making agreements, the various trustees who owned the property should form into a limited company. The company was registered on May 12, 1905 in the name of the Alberni Land Company. Herbert Carmichael became the agent for the new company.[86]

The Anderson Company was a forerunner of the Peninsular and Oriental Steam Navigation Co., or P & O Orient Lines. James Anderson was just a boy when he was first employed by Thomson & Co., the firm that financed the Anderson Mill. He became a partner in 1842. Three of his nephews joined the company in 1863–1870. The firm became successively Anderson, Thomson & Co., then Anderson, Anderson & Co. In 1959 the Anderson name still appeared but with the addition – Anderson, Green & Co., managers of the Orient Line. Sir Austin Anderson was a cousin of Sir Donald Anderson, managing director of the P & O line. Both of these men were well known in Canadian shipping circles.

Early Forest Industry

It was the forest that first attracted industry to the Alberni Valley in the 1860s with the establishment of the Anderson Mill. But it would be many more years before the forest industry would become a permanent part of life in Alberni. Over the years, a number of small sawmill operators earned a living by supplying the lumber to build the first houses, stores, mines, and farms in the Valley. Trees were still considered a necessary evil in the clearing of land, cutting trails, and making roads. These mill operators included the Perts, Halpenny, Sareaults, Frasers, Motion, and George Bird.

Oxen were used extensively in the early days with the accompanying corduroy roads, or skid roads. These roads were built by laying logs across the roads, much in the same manner as ties are laid for railroads. The logs were kept well greased. The oxen or the horses skidded the saw logs over these roads.[87]

When Mike Sareault first started his mill on Kitsuksis Creek in 1895, he faced the almost impenetrable forests with his water-run sawmill and logging equipment that consisted of little more than a team of oxen and a falling axe. Sareault's mill cut the lumber for the first frame houses of the early settlers and for his own Alberni Hotel. Later the Sareault operation used a method of logging that was unique in the district. The logs were parbuckled on top of a type of two-wheeled truck with very high wheels and a very long tongue; the oxen were hooked on and the logs hauled out. Parbuckling was a way of rolling or loading logs on ships or trucks using two lines. Very heavy or extra long logs could be put aboard safely.[88] As a considerable amount of the log would stick out over the wheels, the long tongue kept the log off the oxen.

There were no government lumber inspectors. The saw was set to fit the individual requirements. What came out of the mill was a size to satisfy the customer.

Pert's mill was at the Duke of York mine in China Creek. It was a portable unit; the steam engine was mounted on a truck drawn by horses. The day after it was drawn up the mountain road to the mine, Pert had all the machinery set up. In less than twenty-four hours they were cutting lumber for the flumes. After the mine closed, the mill was moved back to Alberni.

Joseph G. Halpenny was not a mill man by profession. When he first came to Alberni he did some survey work, and later in life he worked as a carpenter. But when the small settlement needed a mill, Halpenny jumped at the chance. He and his son Heman began operating their mill in 1892. They bought logs from whoever could haul them into the mill and cut lumber for some of the men who supplied their own logs. The mill first operated at Mineral Hill. When the King Solomon mine closed, the mill was moved then set up on a cement foundation beside Rogers Creek.

The mill, called a "Mulay" mill, was operated by a two-man crew and easily moved from place to place. It could be compared to an oversize sewing machine. The saw was four feet in length and took quite short strokes. It could handle a log up to four feet in diameter. The lumber was very even and of good quality. Some young boys earned candy money by pulling logs into the mill with a rope. The mill had a vertical saw, which the boys referred to as "up today and down tomorrow."[89] John Shirley Richardson operated the mill on a lease for a short time.

George Bird first began a small sawmill near the site of the first paper mill. In 1899 he moved the operation to the foot of Argyle Street. Bird had come to the Alberni Valley in 1892. He first worked in the construction and operation of the British Columbia Paper Manufacturing Co. Ltd. before operating his own sawmill business. By November, 1911, the Bird mill was cutting about 25,000 feet daily.[90]

Fred Brand, who worked for some of the sawmills, remembered hauling logs with his oxen down the skid road that is now Redford Road, across the property at the foot of Redford Road where Shaw Cable is now located, and on to the Alberni Inlet. Once he and another man brought a boom of logs up the Inlet to Bird's sawmill from a hand-logging show. After booming the logs, they erected a sail on the front. When the usual afternoon breeze came up, they set sail on their boom and steered with the sail. They had made more than half of their journey when the wind died down. Making it fast to shore, they took down part of the sail to make a tent for themselves and spent the night on the boom. The next day they caught the afternoon breeze to finish their journey.[91] Brand set up his own sawmill in the Cherry Creek district. It ran for many years.

When Premier Richard McBride took office in 1903, he threw open Crown lands to syndicates or individuals – Canadian or foreign – who were allowed to buy as many timber licenses as they pleased. The licensees only had to pay the annual interest on the value of timber when it was cut. After two years, the licenses became transferable, and the timberland could be resold. From April to August of 1907, when the provincial government land and timber office was opened in Alberni, over twelve hundred timber licenses had been filed.[92] There was massive speculation until late in 1907 when the granting of licenses and leases was discontinued.

Many of the investors were American. One of the first investors to buy up large tracts of land in the Alberni area was John D. Rockefeller Jr. of New York, who purchased eighteen thousand acres in 1902 in the Ash River Valley for ten dollars per acre. This would later be sold to the H. R. MacMillan Export Company, precursor of MacMillan Bloedel Ltd. [93]

Another investor was the Red Cliff Land and Lumber Company Ltd. of Duluth, Minnesota, who purchased 22,287 acres in the Alberni Valley. Edward T. Buxton was treasurer of the company at the time. He kept a journal in which he related a series of events that led to the purchase. He explained why the CPR was interested in Alberni.

"The frequent delay of the Canadian Pacific Liners voyaging from the Orient to Vancouver, B.C., caused by storm and fog off the entrance to the straits made it often necessary to rush the mail trains at very high speed across the continent in order to comply with the terms of the mail contract. Steamers being able, at all times, to run into Barclay Sound and from there to the head of the fjord at Alberni, the Canadian Pacific Railway decided to build a railroad across the island to provide for the mail service."[94]

When the company heard that the CPR had decided to build a railroad across the island, Red Cliff's general manager, Arthur Gilbert, came to Alberni to look over the timber and conditions for a lumber operation. His report was favourable, and the company secured the option to purchase land from the CPR.

Frederick Gilbert was president of the Red Cliff. As he did not want to get involved in the new enterprise, Buxton agreed to organize and finance the new company and purchase the properties. They went to Calgary, where the headquarters of the CPR land department was located. There Buxton discovered the CPR knew little of the land west of the island mountains, and he wondered how they could come to an agreement. He decided that if he could draw on the back of a map a circle encompassing all the territory his company wanted, a deal could be made. This was done. The officials of the land department referred it to the office of the CPR in Montreal. President Sir Thomas Shaughnessy wired back giving the Red Cliff Company the contract.

The contract was drawn on the back of an E & N railway map showing the circle of land allocated. There would be a 10 percent reduction if the company paid cash. This made quite a difference on the deal worth several hundred thousand dollars. When it came time to close the deal, the Red Cliff Company was met by "some badly fussed (railway) officials." After an exchange of wires with officials in Montreal, the Calgary officials were instructed to carry out the terms as previously agreed. The claim and certificate were immediately registered.

Along with Partelow Miles, "an old and trusted employee," and a crew of thirty cruisers, Buxton arrived in Alberni for the first time. The crew camped out while the other two men were cared for "in a little home of an English woman who provided for the very few hunters or fishermen who came to the hamlet." He was surprised to see a pelt of a large mountain lion tacked up on the door of the house. It had been shot by the ten-year-old son of the hostess. Buxton now knew he was in a wilderness.

The company purchased a house and lot with a large barn. The barn was fitted out to house the surveyors and draughtsmen and to serve as general headquarters for the company in Alberni. Miles was left in charge of the properties until such time as the company decided to build a plant and start up a forestry operation.[95]

The forest industry has been continuous in Port Alberni since 1904, when the Barclay Sound Cedar Company was established on the present site of the Alberni Pacific Division of MacMillan Bloedel Ltd. The success of this venture was due to the four Wood brothers, Robert, Alexander, Norman, and James, and a fifth partner, Sam Roseborough, a logging foreman and brother-in-law.

Land for the mill was purchased from the Anderson Company. Lumber to construct their living quarters, a cottage on the mill site, was bought from George Bird's sawmill. That cottage later became the company's office building. Machinery was purchased from Joe Halpenny's mill at Rogers Creek. To get the equipment to their own mill, Alex and nephew Roland Wood took a scow up the Somass River and poled, pushed, and pulled it up Rogers Creek to the Halpenny mill. After loading and taking advantage of the tides, they managed to get it delivered to the mill site without incident. New machinery was also purchased from the Robert Hamilton Agency. Robert Wood was a good friend of Hamilton and had installed some of his equipment throughout British Columbia.

Daily production of lumber and shingles began in 1905 with a crew consisting of Robert as manager; Alex, millwright; Norman, sawyer; George Bird, engineer; Fred Brand, engineer; Roland Wood, son of Robert Wood, general helper. Sam, a Chinese man, became fireman. Harry Truman, a relative of Jack and Clayton Hill, also was part of the first crew. These ten men turned out 25,000 board feet of lumber per day, enough for two average-sized homes.

Before the mill was constructed Robert and son Roland had cruised timber and staked limits on Barkley Sound near the entrance to the Alberni Inlet. They also possessed limits around Silver Lake. However, the major logging area was in and around the townsite of Alberni. A skid road was built east of the mill in the Bruce Street area. Douglas fir logs were hauled from there by company-owned horses. Fred Brand also logged the area of the present hospital. Logs from there were dumped into the Inlet at the bottom of Redford Street.

Logging foreman and fifth partner Sam Roseborough also managed the logging of cedar shingle bolts at Useless Inlet. The camp buildings were on Vancouver Island proper, but logging was conducted across the Inlet on Sedall Island. The shingle bolts were cut mostly by local Indians. Three of the shingle makers were Billy Youkum, Tommy Bill, and Frank Williams.

Log towing from dump to mill was handled by a chartered boat owned by an Irishman known as Black Mike. His boat was named the *Shamrock*. Later the company purchased their own tugboat, the *Troubador*. Some time later the *Troubador* was working near Hell's Gate in the Alberni Inlet when it sank with Norman Wood aboard. Fortunately, Wood managed to swim ashore. The tug was raised and later sold.

Shipping products to customers was no easy matter. There were no freighters running the Alberni Inlet because insurance companies would not give coverage to ships that had to round hazardous Cape Beale. The company therefore had to charter ships to take their lumber to customers outside the Alberni Valley. The first shipment by water was cedar factory stock, dressed four sides. It was shipped on the *Otter Number Two* to Vancouver. Other sales went to west coast communities and to Victoria and Vancouver.

In 1907, recognizing the shipping need, the Alberni Land Company concluded arrangements with the Esquimalt & Nanaimo Railway Co. to extend their line to Alberni in consideration for receiving an allotment of 2,500 acres for their railway development.

In 1908, after three fairly prosperous years of operation, the Barclay Sound Cedar Company sold part interest to Carlin, Meredith and Gibson. Carlin invested $125,000 in the concern. Carlin employed Joseph Hanna as manager, a position he held until the company was sold in 1912. At this time, Walter Harris was clearing the townsite and leaving the logs where they fell. Hanna's son Roy was contracted to provide piles for the foundations of the first dry kiln. He hired a team of horses from Roseborough for ten dollars a day. Two days later, the company quit buying pilings. Roy was making too much money. He had made $142.00 for two days work.

The following year, the Wood brothers sold their remaining interest in the mill to the firm of Meredith and Gibson.[96] The Wood brothers, with their mother and father and sisters Mabel and Mary, had made the long trek across Canada from Ontario and settled in New Westminster. Before Robert came to Port Alberni, he had been trucking material at the Bralorne Mines in the interior of British Columbia. Alex was a builder in New Westminster, and Mabel a teacher. Norman was a bridge builder. James had been the CPR divisional agent for sixteen years in the Kamloops area.

119

Mr. and Mrs. Wood and Mabel remained in New Westminster when the three brothers came to join their brother Robert, who was already established in Port Alberni, to start up the Barclay Sound Cedar Company. When the mill was sold the brothers continued to serve the community.

Robert was born December 25, 1858, at Ashburnham, Ontario. He married Mary Louise Stephenson at Walmer, Ontario on March 15, 1886. They had seven children, three boys and four girls. He came to Alberni in 1892 to help build the paper mill and dam, then spent three years in Vancouver before returning to Alberni to start the Barclay Sound Cedar Company mill. He became mayor of Port Alberni in 1916. Later he operated a small sawmill on the Alberni Inlet near China Creek.

James became the first Federal Fisheries Officer in 1912, serving in that capacity until 1937. Between the job at the mill and the fisheries appointment, he had worked as a telegraph lineman. He was also a forestry fire fighter.

Norman became the government's bridge builder. Bridges built under his supervision included Riverbend, Rogers Creek, Sproat Falls, Beaver Creek, Big Qualicum, and Little Qualicum. Alex became the City of Port Alberni's building inspector. A family story about Alex tells of the time when he was inspector and a storm knocked out the steeple of Knox Presbyterian Church. Alex had it declared unsafe, and the congregation of Knox had to move over to a building on Argyle Street. Some questioned this move as the church was later rented out for basketball practice for many more years. Alex Wood also served as alderman.

Mary Wood, one of five daughters of James, began working in the office of the Alberni Pacific Lumber Co. in 1924. In 1946, the Soroptimist Club declared her the "longest serving lumber office girl in B.C." She retired in 1965 and continues to reside in Port Alberni.[97]

Sam Roseborough and his wife Mary (nee Wood), came to the Valley in 1892, bringing with them a team of horses. Sam first hauled sawlogs into the paper mill. When the paper mill closed he returned to the Fraser and farmed there until he came back a second time with Wood to build the Barclay Sound Cedar Company mill. He eventually left the company to establish a livery business, locating his barn near the northwest corner of Argyle Street and Second Avenue. Sam was so successful, he had an average of twenty-six horses, with teamsters, employed. Eventually he had almost the entire travel and transfer business in the town. In partnership with D. Emory in 1923, he opened the first motor bus line to Nanaimo, eventually selling out to Union Stage Lines. Thus, Sam Roseborough had a part in the change-over from horse travel to modern day transportation.[98]

West Coast Tragedy

The wreck of the *Valencia* in 1906 was the worst tragedy to strike the west coast of Vancouver Island. When news of the disaster came over the telegraph lines from Bamfield to Alberni, on January 22, 1906, everyone in the community was shocked. Those who heard were as helpless as those who watched the wreck from the beach, said George Bird later.[99]

The American steamer *Valencia* left San Francisco on January 20 en route to Victoria with 164 passengers and crew. The following day, due to poor visibility, Captain O. N. Johnson had difficulty establishing his position. He didn't know he had missed the entrance to Juan de Fuca Strait and was on his way up the west coast of Vancouver Island. The ship slowly inched her way along at reduced speed, feeling her way more by instinct than by scientific means.

Suddenly, just after midnight on January 22, there was a grinding crash. The ship came to a halt. Johnson reversed engines, causing the ship to slip deeper into the water. There was a huge hole in her bow where she had run aground on rocks. Water began pouring in so fast there was no hope of making the nearest beach. Lifeboats were lowered, but the panic-stricken passengers caused two boats to capsize, drowning many women and children. Of the six lifeboats launched, four made for shore but didn't reach it. One which did make it to shore contained fifteen people; eight perished. Another had seven on board, but only two survived.

As dawn broke the next day Captain Johnson and the remaining passengers viewed the desolate and forbidding shoreline. The ship had gone aground on Pachena Point, fifteen miles from the nearest village of Clo-oose and an equal distance to Cape Beale lighthouse. The only sign of life was a thread of telegraph wire strung from tree to tree along the shoreline.

Several attempts were made to fire a lifeline ashore, but this proved futile. The *Valencia* settled deeper in the water. Two hand-picked crews set out in lifeboats for shore. One boat with a crew of five landed at the base of a cliff, while the other disappeared with nine crewmen on board. The five who had made it ashore climbed the cliffs and followed the telegraph trail to a lineman's cabin which was equipped with a telephone. In Clo-oose, David Logan, the lineman, answered the telephone. He telephoned news of the wreck to the Cape Beale lighthouse, and Minnie Paterson, wife of Thomas Paterson, the lightkeeper, and daughter of Capt. Huff of Alberni, relayed the news on to Victoria via Bamfield and Alberni.

Two Canadian tugs, the *Salvor* and the *Czar*, plus the U.S. steamship *Queen City*, were ordered to proceed to the scene of the wreck. The *Queen City* arrived too late at night to see anything, so had to wait until morning light. Captain Cousins of the *Queen City* caught glimpses of the wreck, which had about forty people clinging to the rigging. He could do little to help as there was a stiff wind blowing and he was unable to get any closer.

When the Patersons' watchdog began to bark, Minnie, then eight months pregnant, ran out with her children to greet the bruised and bleeding survivors. She mistook them for the shipwrecked crew who had telegraphed earlier. When she learned this was a different group, she went back to her headset and telegraphed the men in the shack down the coast. She learned there were seven passengers and two firemen at the other end with only a few biscuits between them. They didn't think they could last much longer.

Minnie wired W. P. Daykin, lightkeeper at Carmanah Point, giving him the position of the shipwrecked crew. Daykin promised to dispatch a party with clothing, food, and ropes. Minnie warmed and fed the survivors, huddling her own family into close quarters so the survivors could sleep and rest. Her home became transformed into a signal station, news agency, and hospital. All through the night she and Thomas monitored the telegraph line.

When the *City of Topeka* arrived in the morning, the *Queen City* was ordered to return to Victoria, leaving the *City of Topeka* and the two Canadian ships, the *Salvor* and *Czar*, to pick up any survivors. Thirty people were rescued off Cape Beale by the *City of Topeka*. The rescue ships left that afternoon when it seemed no further effort could be made to reach the ship by sea.

Meanwhile, lineman David Logan and Joe Martin, another lineman at Carmanah Point, hiked to the wreck. Logan knew the tough hiking trail well. He was used to hiking over fallen trees, climbing up and down ravines, and crossing swollen rivers. When they arrived at the scene, the two linemen could see scores of people still clinging to the rigging and parts of the hull that weren't submerged. When the passengers saw Logan they cheered, thinking they were to be rescued. But nothing could be done. For two hours Logan and Martin watched helplessly as the seas swept over the wreck. Then, around noon, a huge wave dealt the final blow, turning the *Valencia* over and crushing her to pieces.

With help from Constable Gus Cox from Alberni, the gruesome search for bodies began. Bodies were scattered for miles in each direction, some lodged in crevasses in the rocks, others so beaten by rock and gravel there was nothing left but raw flesh, making identification almost impossible. Of the 164 passengers and crew, only thirty-eight survived. Fifty-nine bodies were recovered. The other sixty-seven were missing and presumed drowned.

There were two Commissions of Inquiry held: one in Seattle, the other in Canada. From the Canadian inquiry came the recommendation to construct a road or trail close to the shore between Otter Point, at the entrance to Port San Juan, and Cape Beale, with shelters at six mile intervals equipped with telephones, etc., for the use of shipwrecked mariners. Work on the West Coast Lifesaving Trail, or Shipwrecked Mariner's Trail, began in the spring of 1907 and was completed in the fall of 1908. A modern lighthouse was built at Pachena Point where the wreck had occurred. A lifeboat was stationed at Bamfield.[100]

Eleven months later, on December 6, 1906, world attention was again drawn to the west coast of Vancouver Island. Eighty-knot winds were battering the tower of Cape Beale lighthouse when keeper Thomas Paterson looked out and spotted a ship in distress. It was the barque *Coloma* that was drifting in the heavy seas. He and Minnie took turns watching through the telescope. The ten men of the crew, convinced the end was near, were clinging helplessly to the rigging as waves pounded their ship. The telegraph lines were down, the winds having snapped the line to Bamfield.

So they could abandon ship, the crew on board the stricken vessel attempted to make a raft from the deckload of lumber they were carrying. Six miles away, the Canadian government lighthouse tender, the *Quadra*, was anchored off Bamfield Creek. The faithful old ship was one of the most respected vessels sailing the B.C. Coast. She brought mail, supplies, and fuel to lighthouse keepers, and also served as the law enforcement vessel. She carried fisheries department officers, even governors-general and royalty.

Minnie decided to go to the *Quadra* for help while Thomas remained behind thinking there might be something he could do down on the rocks. Dressing in a sweater and cap and her husband's slippers, half running, half falling, and with Yarrow, their big Scotch collie, at her heels, Minnie ran down the tramway, the only approach to the lighthouse.

Below, the storm and the tide had converted the rocky peninsula into an island. The water reached to her waist. She plunged in and waded fifty yards to the soggy but firm ground beyond, to the beginning of the Bamfield telegraph trail. She ran through the woods with Yarrow yelping ahead of her, sinking knee deep into the mud and forest muck, splashing constantly through the water, wading through the salt tide marsh called Mud Bay. Often she could find her bearings only by threading the fallen telegraph wire through her fingers. Again and again she fell, until she finally emerged at daylight to cross Topaltos Beach. Then it was back into the forest for the worst stretch yet.

After three miles of climbing over fallen trees and moss-covered rocks, she emerged exhausted and bruised at the head of Bamfield Creek where a rowboat was normally kept, but the boat was gone. The swollen tide had left only a narrow stretch of sand on either side of the inlet. Another 2½ mile treacherous hike lay in the path of help. Minnie started to run, wading through icy water and picking her way through the thick salal until she stumbled up the steps of Annie McKay's house. She alerted Annie to the sea drama unfolding, and together they wasted little time rowing towards the *Quadra*.

Captain Hackett of the *Quadra* was just about to go ashore when he saw the two women coming through the rain. After hearing the news of the *Coloma*, the *Quadra* weighed anchor. It had taken Minnie four hours to get help. The two women returned to the cable station, where a cot and blankets were put out for Minnie. She waved off any concern for her welfare, gulped down a cup of tea, and said she had to return to her baby, Tommy Robert, who was only a few months old and had not yet been weaned. The operators tried to talk her out of it, then finally talked her into taking them along. As they rowed up the inlet, Minnie was so cold her legs and stomach were knotted with cramps. Ignoring her own plight, she urged the men to go faster.

Captain Hackett of the *Quadra* arrived just as the *Coloma* was breaking up.

> The seams were split so wide the lumber from the cargo was floating out stick by stick. The deck was flush with the sea. The longboat of the *Quadra* was lowered over the side and positioned alongside the *Coloma*. A line was put onboard and the men taken off just as the *Coloma* struck a reef.[101]

When news of Minnie's heroic effort spread to the outside world, she captured everyone's imagination. Newspapers in Canada and the

United States headlined the rescue. Minnie was declared Canada's very own Grace Darling. Grace Darling was the daughter of the keeper of England's Longstone Light, in the Farne Island, where she earned fame for rescuing four men and a woman in their rowboat from the steamer *Forfarshire* on September 7, 1838. Forty-three drowned in the incident.[102]

On September 11, 1907, a silver plate was presented to Minnie by the Dominion Government in recognition of her services in assisting the saving of lives of the sailors of the *Coloma*. The *Seattle Times* sent a reporter and photographer to Bamfield to meet Minnie. They brought a gold locket and a purse containing a cheque for $315.15 from the women of Vancouver and Victoria; a silver tea set from the officers and crew of the coastal steamer *Queen City*; and some personal gifts, including a new pair of slippers for Thomas.

The *Coloma* was left derelict. She drifted for weeks, a navigational hazard, until she finally drove ashore on a small island, a total loss. The *Quadra*, after years of government service, was sunk in a collision in 1917. Salvaged, she passed into private hands. Eighteen years later, the *Quadra* again made headlines, when she was captured rum-running and was towed to San Francisco. Thomas Paterson died in 1915 on his way overseas with the army during the First World War. Minnie never recovered her health. She died in Alberni in June 1911.

Business and Commerce

Alberni's earliest retail enterprise was the Anderson Mill Store, which served the small population then working at the Anderson Mill in the 1860s. As early as 1870 there was another store in operation at the mouth of China Creek. Run by a Chinese man, it provided supplies for the Chinese miners and Indians in the area.

When Captain Albert Huff arrived in 1885, he began a small trading store at the Tseshaht Reservation. However, this was not a convenient location, and the store was moved to the corner lot by Kitsuksis Creek. By 1892, the Alberni Trading Co. store, managed by Frederick P. Saunders and financed by Henry Saunders of Victoria, was already established at the corner of Johnston and Victoria Quay. Huff's building contained a number of rooms to accommodate a few travellers. Both stores kept supplies of groceries, which were renewed twice a month from Victoria.

Captain Huff was one of the Alberni Valley's earliest entrepreneurs. An active participant in community affairs, he helped build the first school at Beaver Creek, then later he built the first wharf in Alberni. The wharf was located behind the present Regional District office on Victoria Quay. Here, passengers and freight were unloaded at high tide. Huff also operated various boats on the Somass River and the Alberni Inlet. His first boat was a small steam launch named the *Brant* which had been operating on Kennedy Lake. He and Charlie Taylor brought the boat down Kennedy River, through the rapids, to Tofino Inlet on the west coast. Taylor often talked about the difficulties they had taking the boat down the rapids to salt water. Next Captain Huff purchased the *Hollybank*, a steel steam launch built on the Clydebank in Scotland. In 1897 the *Hollybank* was engaged to take James Dunsmuir and his party to the Franklin River trail.

Later Huff sold the *Hollybank* in favour of a bigger boat, an old sternwheeler called the *Willie*, which had been running on the Fraser River. The *Willie* was a wood-burning steamboat. For a while Huff built and operated a sawmill at Franklin River to cut the lumber and timbers for the overhead tramway, bunkers, and other buildings at Hayes' Mine. The *Willie* was kept busy for some time, running back and forth to the mine site. An advertisement that appeared in the Victoria *Colonist* stated:

> Steamer *Willie* will leave Huff's wharf, Alberni, (Master W. Holmes) every Monday and Thursday at 7 a.m. for Ecoole, calling at Hayes' camp, Uchucklesit (Kildonan), and all other places where freight or passengers may offer; returning to Alberni the same evening. For special trips, freight and passengers, rates apply to the captain on board or to G. P. Huff, Alberni."[103]

The sternwheeler was nicknamed "the Weary *Willie*." Coming up the Inlet at night and hoping to dock in New Alberni, the captain would not know if the ship was near the town or not, for there were no street lights to guide them, and residents often blew out their coal oil lamps early. The boat would be stopped when the captain thought he was opposite the dock. He would blow the ship's whistle, and if they were within reasonable distance and the whistle was heard, a rowboat would be put out to find them and guide them to the dock.[104]

When the *Willie* was sold, Huff replaced her with the *Tasmania*, another steel boat, built by Thorneycroft, of Southampton, England.

Huff's business interests were not limited to boats. He also erected the first hall in the Alberni settlement. Located at the corner of Johnston Road and Victoria Quay, it was known as Huff's Hall. For a time, the Anglican Church services were held there once a month, and the Royal Bank of Canada established a temporary branch in the hall.[105]

Another of Huff's business endeavours was carrying mail between Alberni and Nanaimo. He and Harry Fitzgerald held the contract. After some years, Harry sold out his interest to Huff and moved to Chilliwack to farm. According to George Bird, Harry was a strong Conservative, while Huff supported the Liberals. Therefore it didn't matter which party was in Victoria, any government work which came into the district likely came their way. In 1908 Huff established a whaling station in the Queen Charlotte Islands.[106]

Arthur E. Waterhouse was Huff's equal, if not rival, in the settlement to the south named New Alberni. When Waterhouse arrived he was not very impressed with what he saw. Perhaps he had envisioned a community of greater size than what was before him on that March day in 1896: "The only signs of building were a few stout cedar posts situated on the hill just behind our landing place."[107] These had been the supports for the Anderson mill water tank.

Waterhouse came at the instigation of the Canadian Pacific Navigation Company, to build a wharf. "The reasons why I agreed to come were as follows: the geographical situation of the harbour, the fact that the entire Pacific coast was still feeling the effects of the silver panic of 1893, and consequently there were very few openings showing any promise of success. And also because I had heard something of the attractiveness and of the sport to be had in the Alberni Valley," he later recollected.[108]

Waterhouse chartered the steam schooner *Mischief* to carry lumber and supplies to Alberni, leaving Victoria on March 26, 1896, under Captain Foote.[109] Accompanying him was a male companion Captain T. L. Fox, and Sam Handy, who had been hired to build the wharf.

Fox, born in 1838, was a native of Yorkshire, England. His early career had been in the banking business. He came to Canada in 1882 and for a time worked for the Canadian Pacific Railway Land Department where he helped lay out the present Banff Hotel site. Later Fox served as a volunteer during the Riel Rebellion of 1886. His wife had died many years before he came to Canada; he left two children, a son and a daughter, behind in England.

The group anticipated an uneventful trip, but weather conditions were bad. Hours later they found themselves back again at Sayward's Wharf. The next day they weren't much more successful. They had to tie up at the quarantine station for the night of the 27th. On the 28th, after another struggle, they anchored for the night in Sooke Harbour. The next day they made some progress, but at nightfall they anchored on the American side, at Clallam Bay. "The following day was not exactly a pleasure trip and we were glad to spend our fifth night at Bamfield Creek."[110]

Waterhouse recalled it was a glorious morning when they arrived at Stamp Harbour on March 31st. Sam Handy made a raft of lumber, piled on the supplies, and towed them ashore at the site now occupied by the Imperial Oil Co. The strangers must have aroused some interest from the residents of Alberni further along the shoreline. Waterhouse noted, "Some hours later some curious people came through the bush to ascertain why the steamer, which had made its presence known by whistling, had not come up the Somass River on the tide."[111]

The date of his arrival remained forever in his memory. Many years later, in 1937, he recalled the date in an article he wrote for the local newspaper. "The date, March 31st, remains in my memory for the reason that it was many years before any real development took place, and that had I landed a day later, I should have had some cause to think of April Fool's Day on many anniversaries."[112]

Sam Handy had immigrated to Victoria from Northern Ireland, lured by exciting reports of gold in California. He worked for the Hudson's Bay Company on their early wharf building and repairs in Victoria, and there he met Waterhouse. When he came to Alberni, Handy was prepared to work and brought with him a 1,200 pound piledriving hammer, a double-purchase hand winch, and other tools. His first task was to construct a raft of cedar logs, which became the home for a floating pile driver. Soon he had the wharf and the approach built.

A warehouse was built on the wharf. In this shed in 1896, Waterhouse began his first sale of flour, sugar, tea, coffee, canned milk, and a few lines of hardware, including nails, crosscut saws, axes, and rope. Initially business was slow, until the various mines being established in the area realized it was a shorter distance from their mines to Waterhouse's wharf than to the Alberni wharf and Huff's store. Also, Waterhouse was quick to realize the potential of the mines and a deep water port for shipping ore. He had a road built from his wharf to China Creek, via Bainbridge Lake, a distance of about 9 1/2 miles. This was two miles closer to the mining area than Alberni was.[113]

Waterhouse's enterprise began to prosper. He eventually received his share of district trade. The population of New Alberni began to grow, but the larger, more settled community of Alberni was still drawing much of the settlers' business. For many years, the Victoria boat would call at Waterhouse's wharf only when she carried freight consigned to him. The business interests of Alberni and the Victoria wholesalers were both so determined to prevent any new competition that Alberni had the only regular service.

In 1902, Waterhouse ordered lumber from George Bird's sawmill to construct a new general store. Built by George Forrest, it was located close to the shoreline on piles. At high tide, the water would come in under the building. Two years later, arrangements were made to open a post office and telegraph office. Waterhouse learned how to operate the telegraph. He was appointed the first deputy customs inspector. He also served as Justice of the Peace. Bird supplied more lumber to accommodate the postal business. The postmark was then New Alberni. When mail increased, the area soon had post office boxes.

After a visit to England in 1901, George H. Bird purchased property and built a mill at the foot of Argyle Street in New Alberni. Waterhouse convinced him to move to the new location, where he built a house near his new mill.[114] Bird's former home had been near the former paper mill where he used to work.

No one really knows what happened the night of June 16, 1902, but Waterhouse suspected that a spark from Huff's boat, which had been tied up at the wharf earlier in the day, ignited a fire which destroyed his warehouse. The building contained two tons of dynamite for the mines, but fortunately it did not explode. The wharf received little damage and the warehouse was rebuilt. However, the fire caused two expensive lawsuits, one heard in the Admiralty court in Victoria, and the other, arising out of the first trial, heard in Nanaimo. Waterhouse charged that Huff's wood-burning steamboat, *Willie*, caused the fire. The *Willie* had called at the wharf on the way down to Franklin River, where it was to pick up a boom of logs to tow to Bird's sawmill.[115] No doubt this incident increased the tension between the two businessmen.

After the fire destroyed his warehouse, Waterhouse erected a small building on Argyle Street, which did duty until a new building was constructed adjoining the Somass Hotel.

In 1896, the partnership of Chalmer and Armour built the Armour Hotel, at the corner of Kingsway and Argyle Street. The building was more functional than fancy. It lacked siding or paint, but it was a real acquisition for New Alberni in its growing competition for supremacy over Alberni, now considered the "Old Town." Only a trail connected the twin settlements. It was a pleasant, woody trail which ran along the inlet and river. Argyle Street was little better than a rough trail when Tommy Armour celebrated the opening of the hotel with a house-warming party. Most of the people in the district were invited. A year later, due to financial difficulties, the hotel had to close. In 1898 Waterhouse purchased the Armour Hotel. Later he built the New Alberni Hotel, which he renamed the Somass, adjacent to the Armour Hotel. The Somass Hotel was a much more impressive building than anything seen in the area to that date.[116]

In 1903 Waterhouse organized a drive to build a dance hall in New Alberni. Six people were interested enough to put up ten shares of $100 each. Only two held more than one share, Waterhouse and Bird. Bird's two shares were paid for by the lumber he supplied from his sawmill. George Forrest agreed to put up the building, taking one share in part payment. The lot chosen was on First Avenue, between Argyle and Kingsway. Flooring was cut from tough butt logs from the Franklin River area, which were very hard. Waterhouse was a dance enthusiast. Under his special care, the floor gradually achieved an excellent surface. Large oil lamps lit Waterhouse's hall. Later a badminton club was formed.

In March 1911 fire again destroyed Waterhouse's store and wharf. Early on a Sunday morning the town awoke to a fire alarm. Flames spread to the warehouses and other buildings located on the same wharf, and within two hours the wharf had been swept bare of buildings. The headquarters office of Jannse and McDonnell, railroad contractors, was also destroyed. No cause of the fire was known, although one theory had it that the fire might have been started by rats gnawing at matches.[117]

Waterhouse now found ownership of the hotel and the management of the store to be a bit too much for him. He formed a partnership in 1911 with Charles Green, who had been employed by him for some time. This arrangement continued until 1916, and when the partnership was dissolved, Waterhouse retained the firm name of Waterhouse and Green.

Until this time Waterhouse had been a bachelor, whose constant companion was the elderly Captain Fox. The beautiful gardens of their homes on the New Alberni waterfront were photographed many times over the years and were a source of great pride for the two English gentlemen. A cutting from one of the lilac trees now blooms at City Hall on Argyle Street.[118] On October 4, 1918, Waterhouse married Claire Helen Beale, who had come to the Alberni Valley with her first husband, Oscar Beale. Oscar was killed during the Great War; his wife, who had followed him to England, returned to Port Alberni when the war ended.[119]

Arthur Waterhouse died quietly in Victoria on February 22, 1940. He was the first merchant and hotel owner in New Alberni. He was also the first mayor of the city following incorporation in 1912.

Another of the early pioneer businessmen, the eccentric Bobby De Beaux, was born in Hamburg, Germany, but had lived for a time with his family in Minnesota before coming to Canada. He had come from a part of Germany which was sometimes under German rule, and sometimes under French. Bobby De Beaux was proud of his French heritage and boasted that his grandfather had fought for Napoleon Bonaparte at Waterloo.

When De Beaux came to Alberni, he acquired two quarter sections of land at Bainbridge, near where the R. B. McLean sawmill was later located. With money received from clearing and grading land for a government road, De Beaux took a trip to the 1893 Chicago World's Fair. When he returned he built a stable and a hotel at the junction of Mineral and China creeks. The hotel, described simply as a log cabin, accommodated the workers at the stamp mill at Mineral Hill, and it was also a halfway house for prospectors going to or from the Golden Eagle mine and other mines in the area of China Creek. The hotel consisted of a store and restaurant on the ground floor, with a dormitory of twelve beds upstairs.

De Beaux was known for his stinginess. Among old-timers, stories of his exploits abound.

> Mike Comerford, on his first meal at De Beaux's, twice invaded the butter dish, when once only was the rule; Bobby was watching and said, 'Be careful, that cost me 35 cents per pound' Mike said it was worth it and took some more; then he was ordered out. His whiskey glasses were the size of egg cups with an elevated bottom, yet he sold a lot. He might have done more business and still be a frugal soul."[120]

De Beaux recognized that Port Alberni would have a future. When the mining boom faded, he purchased two lots on the corner of Argyle Street and Third Avenue, and there he built a store with bachelor quarters. He cultivated a garden on the southwest corner and specialized in growing loganberries and strawberries. His was the second store in New Alberni. Items for sale were described on a board De Beaux painted and nailed to a tree at the side of the road near the summit of the mountain. "Robert De Beaux, New Alberni; Dealer in boots and shoes, phonograph records, sporting goods and ladies underwear."[121] This was a source of great amusement to commercial travellers and others using the road.

De Beaux was short in stature, he had a slow incisive drawl that could sting anyone he disagreed with, and he never used a smaller word when a fancier-sounding one would do. When he left for a few days' business in Vancouver, he left a clerk in charge of the store. He posted a sign in the window stating: "Gone to Vancouver. My prostitute is in charge." He had mistakenly used "prostitute" instead of "substitute."[122]

The numerous stories of De Beaux's exploits only added to his image as a colorful character. One day he was writing a postcard to Simon Leiser Company of Victoria asking them to ship a box of miner's candles. However, after checking in his room he discovered he still had some left. He returned to his postcard, adding a postscript to the order. "Don't ship them for I went to my room and there I found some."[123] He mailed the card.

On another occasion De Beaux planted a charge of dynamite too large for the gold ore within his claim "the Missing Link" and blew it all down the mountain into the canyon, [124] providing one more good-humoured story for the legend of Bobby De Beaux.

The building of the King Edward Hotel by James Rollin brought to six those businesses locating in the community of New Alberni. These included the Waterhouse wharf and store, Bird's sawmill, De Beaux's general store, the Barclay Sound Lumber Co., the Somass Hotel, and the King Edward Hotel. A Dunn and Bradstreet report for July 1907 stated the population of Alberni was 502, but this figure did not include New Alberni. On the Alberni list of businesses, along with Huff's store and wharf, were C. Frederic Bishop's store; Ephraim Coleman's blacksmith shop; George Forrest, a carpenter and builder; A. W. Heath, a carpenter and undertaker; Saunder's Alberni Trading Store; Thomson's General Store; Matt Ward's Arlington Hotel; and B. H. Williams, a butcher. Alberni was still the larger of the two settlements.

Fishing Trade

In the early days there was no fishing industry as we know it today. The Hudson's Bay Company (HBC) was the first to export salmon from British Columbia. From the year 1821, the company had the exclusive right to trade with the Indians. At first, the HBC obtained salmon mainly to augment the food supplies for its various fur trading posts. When the fur catches failed to equal the rich harvest reaped in the northern departments of the company, cured salmon became a welcome addition to the articles of trade.

The export trade the HBC developed to the Orient and Europe was too far away to make shipment of cured salmon economical. However, the gold rush brought a large influx of new settlers who created a good local market. Fishing soon began to have an impact.

As early as 1858, W. E. Banfield, in articles written for the *Daily Victoria Gazette*, described the incredible numbers of herring that existed in Barkley Sound. He suggested the possibility of lucrative salmon and halibut fisheries in the area. He was also optimistic about the possibilities of a whaling station.

The Tseshaht and Opetchesaht bands of the Alberni Valley used a variety of fish and other marine life found in the coastal waters, and workers at the Anderson Mill in 1860 had learned a great deal from them about harvesting the sea. It was a common thing in the evening to see young Indians shooting with bow and arrows at the fish as they leaped out of the water.

Captain Edward Stamp was a pioneer not only in the lumber industry of British Columbia but also in the fishing industry. The Anderson Company, under Capt. Stamp, established the first commercial fishing station on the west coast at Effingham Island.[125] After he left Alberni Stamp began one of the earliest canneries in the province at Sapperton on the mainland.

Long before the arrival of Europeans on the coast, the native people had developed an elaborate, complex culture based on the abundance of fish. The most simple and efficient method of catching salmon required construction of a weir, a fence-like structure with narrow openings, across a steam or river. The Indians usually built their weirs at places where the water was shallow and slow-moving; this made it easier to erect the structure and easier to catch the salmon.

A large complex of fish weirs and harbour seal traps were located adjacent to the Tseshaht winter village at Lupsi Cupsi. Weir remnants were once visible at low tide along the Somass River near its mouth and in Kitsuksis Creek.[126] However, fishing was mostly done from a canoe, with one person steadying the craft while the other went after the fish with a harpoon, gaff, or long-handled net. Night fishing was done by feeling the fish rather than seeing them.

In 1860, B.C. Indians began to shift from traditional subsistence fishing to commercial fishing in response to fish canning and increased contact with whites. The increased demand for salmon brought experienced fishermen and this in turn meant competition with the Indians for the fish. Natives no longer controlled the fishing waters that were their traditional source of food. The industrialization of the fisheries meant that Indians were required to pay for white goods rather than bartering for them as in the past. The native response was to get involved in commercial fishing.

Concerns were expressed about the alleged destruction of the salmon-spawn by the natives, but these charges were dismissed by the B.C. Inspector of Fisheries, Alex C. Anderson, in his report of 1878: "I have yet failed to discover where the practice exists. I have already expressed my conviction that their modes of catching salmon in the upper waters, is unobjectionable. Any interference with the native, therefore, under hastily formed judgment or frivolous pretext, would be imprudent as well as unjust".[127]

Anderson referred to the pamphlet published by the provincial government on the Indian land question and the treaties of several tribes. In all of these treaties the following clause appears: "It is understood, that the land itself, with these small exceptions, becomes the entire property of the white people forever, it is also understood that we are at liberty to hunt over the unoccupied lands, and to carry on our fisheries as formerly."[128]

Fourteen tribes, under distinct treaty, had their fishing rights secured. Anderson recommended that the Indians of the province be formally exempted from the application of the general fishery law.

Anderson had been an employee of the Hudson's Bay Company and had seen service in the B.C. fur trade. He was also Victoria's first postmaster. In 1877 he was named Fishery Overseer for the province, a position he held for five years.

Reports of the movement of the Indian tribes were made periodically by the missionaries and by Indian Agent Guillod. J. X. Willemar in his report of the Columbia Mission in 1869 reported the Tseshaht tribe had left early for their fishing stations because a trader had offered a high price for oil. In 1882, Guillod reported: "The Tsehahts had left their winter quarters and were making fish oil in the canal in December last year, but all assembled at the sealing stations in February."[129]

The Alberni Indians were among the first sealers on the coast. The best sealing grounds were off Barkley Sound. The Indians were the most proficient with the spear. Tseshaht Chief Adam Shewish recalled how his father was renowned for spearing. At the site of Paper Mill Dam there was a large rock where he would stand and fish. He was able to pick out a male fish from all the others. Chief Shewish said the Indians always went for the male fish, leaving the females with their eggs. If an Indian caught a female fish, he would be teased by other tribe members. "It is a matter of pride."[130]

In 1896, Guillod reported the sealing schooner *Maud* had taken a crew of Alberni Indians to the Bering Sea. He also reported one canoe with Tom Nahwaik and family had gone to the Fraser River salmon fisheries.

> One Alberni Indian came back from sealing with $65 cash. He spent $60 in lumber and started to build a cottage, endeavouring to borrow money to buy windows and doors, trusting to $5 to buy flour and groceries for himself and wife, until he could ship for another season.[131]

When the white settlers arrived in the Alberni Valley in 1886 fishing guardians were appointed by the provincial government to keep a watch over the rivers. Guardians were employed on the Cowichan, Nanaimo, Comox, and Alberni rivers. They reported whether the natives observed the weekly close time set by the department for the opening and closing of weirs on small streams.[132]

Thomas Mowat, Inspector of Fisheries, made a deep sea fishing expedition around the coast on the schooner *Pathfinder*, visiting several harbours on Vancouver Island, including Alberni. At Ucluelet, Mowat met Guillod, "Fishery Guardian and Indian Agent," and Rev. Father Brabant. Brabant told him, "the Indians do not go much outside for fishing, as sealing is lucrative. They make enough during the summer months to support themselves and families all winter."[133] Mowat also learned that the Indians used to catch the "skil" or black cod, at a distance of about fifteen miles from shore. But these fish were so large and fat they were almost unfit for food and were seldom brought home except for the purpose of extracting the oil, which the natives used for household purposes.

After the expedition, Mowat concluded: "Were a colony of fishermen to emigrate here with the prospect of receiving some subsidy or bounty from the government for a couple of years, on the quantity of fish caught, I have no doubt whatever but that, under such a system, the fisheries would be developed much quicker than by any other mode."[134]

Guardian Guillod, of Alberni, reported in 1887 that the only firm engaged in the fishing business was the Barclay Sound Fishing Company. Owned by W. P. Sayward, the Barclay Sound Fishing Company was located at the mouth of the Somass River and Kitsuksis Creek, a location fondly named by locals "Fish House Point." This was the first fishing operation in the Alberni Valley; it also served as a post office with Frank McQuillan as postmaster.[135]

Salmon was important to the white settlers of the Alberni Valley, whose outlying homes were remote from stores where supplies could be obtained. The standby for a main course dinner was fish, especially salmon. Farm equipment could be oiled with fish grease, which also served as a lubricant for hinges and harness leather. Men even cleaned their guns with fish oil. Logging operations used the oil to lubricate the skidroads to facilitate the hauling of logs.[136]

Technical change in the fishing industry placed the Indians at a disadvantage. They were forced to give up their traditional gear and invest in modern equipment. Also, regulations were imposed on all fishermen in an effort to preserve fish stocks, which were being depleted by increased fishing. Indians were especially affected by this government intervention because the new laws limited what the natives considered a natural right to obtain fish for food.

The General Fishery Regulations of 1889 prohibited Indians from using drift nets and spears when subsistence fishing. Then, in 1891 under the Fisheries Act, new fishing regulations were implemented which allowed Indians or their bands free license to fish during close season for the purpose of providing food for themselves, but not for the purpose of sale, barter, or traffic. More regulations in later years curtailed their fishing rights even further, especially with regard to catching spawning salmon in rivers and streams.

When the Clayoquot Fishing & Trading Co, the first cannery on the west coast, opened in 1895 at the mouth of the Kennedy River, local Indians began selling their salmon catches to the company.[137] The cannery was owned by Earle & Magneson. Later, in 1905, its plant at Clayoquot Sound introduced commercial canning to the west coast of Vancouver Island.[138]

Praise for Alberni

There could not have been a more glowing pronouncement about the future of the Alberni Valley than that made by William Roff in 1907. Roff, with his wife Mary, visited this area during a round-the-world trip which included Australia and Japan. Roff came to visit his daughter Jennie, who had married George Alex Spencer, a large landowner and one of Alberni's first councillors. Descendants of the Spencer family still live in the Valley. The family donated land on the north side of Kitsuksis Creek for Spencer Park.

When Roff returned to Bedford, England, he gave a series of lectures on his world trip. He also gave a talk to local residents before he left for home. In the portion pertaining to the Alberni Valley, Roff could see a great future for this little west coast community. It is interesting to note that much of the information on Vancouver Island came from the Canadian Pacific Railway advertising department. His footnote: "This company not only owns the railway but an enormous quantity of land through which the road passes, and they are anxious to obtain emigrants to settle upon it, and if any of you desire to go they will give you every information."[139] Roff's glowing report may have kindled a yearning for life in the colonies.

> Alberni District presents Islands, mountains and valleys and scenes different to other countries, but with a grandeur and beauty all its own – while left to itself. But with the coming of railway men, lumber cruisers, and loggers, much of its natural beauty will be lost. Gone will be its forest with its majestic trees, lowly dales, its humble valley flowers and creepers which grow along the banks of the creeks and lakes and woodlands. Gone will be its graceful bounding deer to seek a home farther away.
>
> Gone will be the blackened stumps which now stand monuments sacred to the memory of the axe and cross saw. Gone will be the fallen logs which now occupy such a prominent place in the landscape. Gone will be the log houses and shacks which now dot the country and have been happy homes where ranchers have dwelt in peace and reared their families around the log fires.
>
> But in place of these will rise more glorious things, for the earth was made for the habitation of man. You will have buildings of architectural beauty and stately proportions along the esplanade on the banks of your river. Your township will be laid out with broad streets and avenues down which electric trams will run, and business and private houses built on either side.
>
> Your valley and hills will be planted with waving corn, thousands of cattle will be grazing in the meadows and flocks of sheep will bleat with the job for the richness of the pasture. Your canal will be alive with ocean liners and craft from every corner of the globe will be sailing along its peaceful waters. Your old mailstage will have passed into the museums of curiosities and the fast flying engine will bring and take away your business letters and loving communication of friend. And your old time pioneers will look on it in wonder and tell the tales of how things were in times gone by.

When Roff visited, there were seven hundred residents living in the Valley. Hopes were high that a railroad soon would open up the country and provide direct communication with the mainland.

At present, there is only one railroad near them (Alberni residents) and that is 53 miles away. This line has been secured by the CPR and the extension of it has been commenced. The right-of-way through the forest and over the mountain has been cleared, but the construction has been temporarily delayed by the slump in the timber trade and the markets generally. The terrible crash in the New York money market which occurred three years ago is being felt throughout the whole American Continent and throughout the world. Alberni and its splendid Canal connection with the sea, makes it almost certain it will become the ocean port for the Orient, and the terminus of the Canadian Pacific Railway.

Roff was a wise man. Although his visit was brief, he could see the future of the Valley would come from the forest, something the community hoped for but had yet to see happen. The forest is so abundant that if cleared with judgment and discretion, British Columbia contains sufficient to supply the needs of the market for three hundred years. It is, and likely to be, for a long time, the principal source of revenue of the province.

He described the logging camps which operated during the spring, summer, and fall, then broke up for the winter.

The work of the logger is to cut down the trees about four feet from the ground. Trim off the branches and where there are streams, float down the logs to the lumber mills where they are sawn into planks. The loggers earn one pound to three pounds a day with all provisions. While in camp there is no opportunity to spend these large wages. The thrifty men have enough for all their needs during the winter months and save in the bargain. Unfortunately they are not all of this nature. As soon as the camps break up and they get into the cities, they find their way into the drinking saloons with their money in their pockets. They soon find their way out again into the streets full of drink, but with empty pockets.

This is the fruitful cause of poverty in nearly all the cities of B.C. and the colonies generally. The saloons are the most terrible curse of the colony. It is generally reported that as soon as a man is a little way in drink, he is supplied with raw spirit, strong enough and vile enough to kill within five miles. It makes him dead drunk.

His audiences may have been shocked at the hard-drinking, hard-working logger in the colonies, but may have been equally intrigued about Alberni's natives.

There are two tribes at Alberni. The Seshaht live on one side of the river, and the Opechesahts on the other. In older times the Indians were all a warlike people ever making raids upon each other. It is illegal to supply, either by sale or gift, any strong liquor to them. There is a heavy penalty. While I was there several convictions took place of whitemen giving whiskey, and fines were inflicted. In one case with a notification that another conviction would mean imprisonment.

138

The government of Canada has appointed an agent in every district whose duty it is to look after the welfare of the Indians and see that they are protected in every way. I don't know whether they are musical by nature, but the gramophone has captivated them and in many homes you will hear one playing as you pass by. The young men, under the captain of the president of the Mission, play football and hold their own well.

Roff was very impressed by the fishing potential in the area and told his audience:

The enormous catches of salmon which have been going on for some years is endangering the supply and making it necessary for the passing of strict laws for the protection of the fish and also the introduction of hatcheries under government supervision. The fall in the salmon industry was in 1906, two and a half million dollars below that of 1905. There are two runs of salmon, one in the spring and one in the autumn. Halibut are caught in large numbers. The value of the catches of this fish rose from $445,000 in 1905, to $5 million in 1906 for the whole of B.C.

Roff visited a whaling station and didn't like the smell.

There are two or three whaling stations on the Island. The one I visited was at Sechart and I saw a whale which measured 85 feet or 95 feet being cut up on the stocks. Indians are principally employed and they eat the flesh with avidity. The Japanese being the principal purchasers. The whale bone is used for stiffening purposes in dress. I spent about nine hours at the station. I found the stench arising from the guana was terrible.

Roff may have visited for only a short time, but he left behind a more optimistic population. He may even have captured a few adventure seeking souls in England with his lectures.

CHAPTER THREE

1907–1912

ALBERNI – PORT ALBERNI

New Alberni began to grow in 1896. The small community had cause to celebrate when the road to China Creek was completed. The mining interests had lobbied for the road, which in turn led to new developments in the mines. However, this "road to progress" was literally "stuck in the mud," as those travelling it had great difficulty steering around the mud holes and stumps. In June, Hilton Drinkwater received a contract from the government to construct a new road to China Creek. About forty men from the Duke of York mine managed to get the road in reasonable condition.

Once again there was great optimism about the future as the little farming community of Alberni looked to the mining industry to enhance its growth. Alberni and New Alberni still were connected only by a trail. However, a prominent Victoria real estate agent, F. B. Pemberton, son of J. D. Pemberton, recognized the potential for development and let a contract to build a road uniting the twin communities to Joe Drinkwater. It was "to be completed in twenty-one days."[1]

In 1897, news came of a rich gold-strike made the previous year in the Klondike. By 1898 there was an unprecedented stampede of people from all over the world to the Yukon. The Klondike gold-strike ultimately depressed mining in the Alberni district. There were some who left the community to seek their fortune. Alfred Carmichael left for Atlin in 1898 and became a mine operator there. Also, Mah Bing, a long-time prospector and local resident since 1873, lost the $4,000 he had made on China Creek in an unrewarding prospecting trip in the Cassiar district.[2]

140

But there were other forces at work to depress the mining industry. Much of the local mineral-bearing land fell under the jurisdiction of Robert and James Dunsmuir's proposed Esquimalt and Nanaimo railroad. The company acquired the right to the base metals such as copper, lead, zinc, and iron. Precious metals like gold, platinum, or silver remained under the jurisdiction of the Crown and subject to the Mineral Act. Those mining in land under the Dunsmuir's railway grant had to pay a royalty on each ton of ore shipped. Needless to say, the miners were reluctant to pay another man for their hard work.

The Coming of the Railway

The nineteenth century, the Victorian Age, and the depression of the 1890s were all over. As the first decade of the new century began to unfold, change was everywhere. The glitter of the Klondike gold rush had started people looking to the west, to new opportunities. Land prices began to soar.

"Almost anywhere in British Columbia, in 1905 and 1906, one could feel a new spirit of optimism. On Vancouver Island, an air of elation accompanied the announcement in 1905 that the Canadian Pacific Railway (CPR) had purchased the Esquimalt and Nanaimo Railway (E & N)."[3] This was a good deal for the CPR, for not only did it receive all of the E & N's assets, but also the land grant for $2.3 million. Keeping the railway's original name, the CPR promised to extend the rails north to Courtenay by 1915.

A road link with Comox-Courtenay had been planned as early as 1893 when the *British Columbia Directory* of that year stated: "A trunk road runs through the district (Beaver Creek) which is being carried on to Comox." Such a road would have helped farming and forestry interests as land was still available from either the E & N Railway Company or the pioneer settlers. In 1904, the Chief Engineer, Public Works Department, Victoria, ordered an exploratory survey for a road link from Alberni to Comox. The engineer placed in charge was Dennis Reginald Harris, who began the survey of the road to Comox with "three axemen and one Chinaman" on September 18, 1904.[4] When he finished he estimated the cost of the proposed road would be $18,900.

Harris drew a detailed map of the area, which showed the topography before the damming of Elsie Lake, then referred to as Ash Lake. The Harris route followed a "man trail" used to pack in supplies to timber cruisers and generally known as the Somers Trail. The survey was completed in 1906.

One year later, the Alberni Land Company concluded arrangements with the E & N Railway Company when it agreed to extend its line to Alberni in consideration for receiving one-fourth of the land, about 2,500 acres, for the railway development. Under CPR control, a preliminary survey of the E & N line from Wellington to Alberni was started in 1906. Frank Sheppard, Provincial Land Surveyor from Nanaimo, was in charge of the survey party. Many lines were run and the topography of the adjacent country was taken before the final route was selected. The work lasted about a year.

The route would take the railway to Parksville, where it would divide, with one line going north to Campbell River and another west to Port Alberni. In 1908 the location line was completed under Harry Hughes Browne, a B.C. Land Surveyor, who was the location engineer. By August, the right-of-way to Parksville was cleared, and by the following year, Cameron Lake was reached. The railway began running a passenger service to Cameron Lake in 1910.

Construction and grading along the north shore of Cameron Lake, over the Beaufort Range and into Port Alberni, continued on through 1911. These were the days before bulldozers and gas shovels, so most of the work was done with picks and shovels, and hundreds of men were employed. The firm of Jannse, McDonnell and Timothy, of Calgary, was awarded the contract for grading the last twenty-seven miles of the E & N extension to New Alberni. Jannse was an old-time railway builder who earlier had a contract to build the E & N from Victoria to Wellington.[5] The Cullinton Bros. built the bridges. For cutting their bridge timbers, they operated a small sawmill at Loon Lake and another one at Bainbridge.

Before work could begin on the railway at Cameron Lake, the CPR was obliged to build a new road on the opposite side of the lake. The new route for the road was said to lengthen the distance to Nanaimo about a mile and a half, but it avoided any crossing.

"Forces preparing to invade Alberni: Evidences of wonderful development soon to be commenced in and around Alberni – Railway location camp is now within five miles of town," blared the *Alberni Pioneer News* headlines on October 26, 1907.

In January, 1908, Alfred Carmichael, who had left Alberni in the winter of 1898 for the Atlin gold fields and returned in December 1907, won the right-of-way contract for clearing the final portion for the E & N extension to the terminus at New Alberni. Carmichael had

142

several camps along the designated line. He promised he would employ "nothing but white men on the work" and expected to employ about 200.[6] The following month in the provincial legislature, the subject of white men being employed on the building of the railway was raised regarding a grading contract from Wellington to the head of Nanoose Bay. A message from the CPR to the Minister of Finance assured the government its wishes were being addressed; only white men would be employed. However, Japanese workers had been put to work on clearing the right-of-way to enable the company to comply with an agreement to start work within a specified time.[7]

Feelings were running high against the hiring of Asiatics following the inter-racial hostility that had erupted in Vancouver the previous year. Those early Chinese prospectors had returned from the gold fields and settled in the Lower Mainland. Some resented their competition in business and in the labour market. "A 1907 economic downturn caused considerable unemployment, resulting in heightened racial prejudice and clashes between whites and Orientals."[8]

An editorial in the *Alberni Pioneer News* followed the race riots in Vancouver:

> Unless something decisive is immediately done at Ottawa, the worst is yet to come. A crisis is fast approaching, and it is up to the government in Ottawa to act on the dreadful warning that has just been given, and cause the individuality of this Canada of Ours to be felt in the motherland. There has been altogether too much sacrifice of Colonial interests on that Downing Street altar of friendship to foreign nations.[9]

Alfred Carmichael later took in a partner to help with the right-of-way clearing contract. He was C. A. Moorhead, who had been working with the Canadian Bank of Commerce in Vancouver.

The building of the railway brought prosperity to some of the merchants in the two Albernis. It was reported that A. E. Waterhouse had sold six wagonloads of supplies for the railway camps.[10]

There was other news with important implications for the future: William Mackenzie and Donald Mann, the heads of the Canadian Northern Railway, planned to come to Vancouver Island to build a railway from Victoria to Port Alberni via Cowichan Lake.[11]

The coming of the Esquimalt & Nanaimo (E & N) railway opened the doors of communication to the outside world for settlers in the Albernis. The railway company also erected one of the most beautiful stations on Vancouver Island at Cameron Lake. The station became known as the Cameron Lake Chalet. Cameron Lake Chalet was "the" place to be. It became a vacation destination for the rich and famous looking for adventure in the wilds of Vancouver Island. In the early years this was the farthest spot on the railway map – the end of the line.

The Chalet was built in 1910 at the east end of Cameron Lake when the E & N railway right-of-way was being extended from Wellington to Port Alberni. While rails were being laid on the mountain stretch between the lake and the Alberni Valley, and until the Victoria-Port Alberni schedule went into effect in December 1911, the stagecoach picked up passengers at the Chalet.

The building had five guest bedrooms on two floors. The beds were large with high headboards. Each room was equipped with a wash stand and the traditional set of chinaware. Pieces of the heavy dark furniture are now housed at the Alberni Valley Museum. A baggage room faced the railway track, and there was a long dining room across the south end and wide verandahs on two sides. It was a beautiful setting for a beautiful lodge.

Some vacationers would come for a week to spend their time fishing or hiking the Mt. Arrowsmith hiking trails to the top of Mount Cokely. During the summer holidays, when the Chalet was full of visitors, a line of tents between the house and the lake accommodated the overflow from the main buildings. The hotel register reveals how the number of tents increased as the Chalet's popularity grew over the years.

Mr. and Mrs. Adam M. Monks were the first to operate the Chalet, and they set the high standard that was maintained for many years. Mr. Monks helped with the management as well as serving as a hunting and fishing guide.[12]

On May 23, 1916, two years after the Great War broke out, Mr. Monks joined the 88th Battalion as a sergeant and went overseas. He was killed in action on August 21, 1917, and the high hopes the Monks had for the operation of the Chalet died with him. Devastated over her husband's death, Mrs. Monks took a year off. In 1920 Mr. and Mrs. George Woollett of Port Alberni operated the facility. Woollett had been manager of the Somass Hotel for the past eight years.

Mrs. Monks returned to the Chalet and persevered for a time, trying to keep it operating. However, after the Chalet was ransacked and robbed on one of the rare occasions when it was left unattended, she gave up. Her good silver and china, many of the furnishings – even the curtains – were stolen and the premises left in shambles. The Chalet then was operated by the Woolletts once again.

The dining room attracted people from the Alberni Valley, Nanaimo, and the Parksville-Qualicum area. Lunches and Sunday dinners were particularly popular. When guests came for tea they sat down to tables covered with embroidered cloths and set with Willow pattern china. A Chinese cook prepared the meals while Mrs. Woollett baked the bread. In a shack nearby lived Bill Stove, a handyman who helped out on many occasions. He had helped build the E & N railway and had decided to stay on at Cameron Lake.

In its heyday some guests arrived at the Chalet by chauffeur-driven cars and accompanied by maid-servants. Many of the Victoria guests travelled by train and stopped over for a weekend. Then there were the day-trippers from Alberni or Qualicum, some in early vintage cars and others in horse-drawn buggies. Farmers, businessmen, and storekeepers from the Valley would drop in to drink tea in the dining room overlooking the lake, perhaps rubbing elbows with the rich and famous. The Chalet became known to the affluent of Britain, the United States, and Europe. who were beginning to discover world travel and were drawn to Vancouver Island to look at frontier life.

The Chalet's old guest registers date from May 28, 1912. The first guest registered was a James Cunningham, from Vancouver. Guests signed in from London, England; Sydney, Australia; Los Angeles, Hawaii, Mexico, Ireland, Scotland, and Paris, France. Mr. Justice O'Connor and D. M. O'Connor, of Sydney Australia; the Duke of Sutherland, from Scotland; and Lady Rosalind Northute of Exeter, England, were only a few of the titled and notables registered.

Perhaps there was a certain prestige attached to visiting Canada's farthest-west hostelry accompanied by maid and chauffeur. The register notes guests who had servants accompanying them. This building at the edge of the forest, overlooking the beautiful lake and surrounding mountains, must have seemed like the last outpost to the world travellers.

After the Woolletts left the Chalet, the building was leased by the CPR through Marathon Realty to a succession of landlords with various plans for the property. But the years took their toll on the old building. It became the victim of a fire in 1966. Little now remains of what was once a proud and prosperous tourist destination. While local and visiting families today can still enjoy the excellent beach facility, it doesn't offer the prestige the Cameron Lake Chalet once enjoyed as a destination for world travellers.[13]

When A. W. Neill's term as Alberni's representative in the provincial legislature was over in 1903, and the Conservative party under

Richard McBride was returned to office with a slim majority, "the lobbying practices of railway promoters in B.C. had been refined to an art. A member of the Assembly could hardly pass through the corridors leading to the Legislative Chamber without being button-holed by a lobbyist. William Mackenzie and Donald Mann were suspected of having financial backing from the Great Northern Railway, who hoped for a subsidy to construct a line through northern B.C."[14]

The public debt in the province then stood at over $12 million, and financial guarantees to railways amounted to more than $1 million, leaving the credit of the government exhausted. "By stringent economies, new taxation and a new formula for sharing school costs with the municipalities," McBride's Finance Minister Captain Tatlow gradually brought the government finances under control. "To the surprise of everyone, he announced a slight surplus in 1905, the second one since Confederation."[15]

Alberni's representative during this time sat in opposition. He was William Wallace Burns McInnes, a Liberal, elected in 1903. This was the first provincial election fought along organized federal party lines. However, "an examination of party platforms show almost complete agreement between Liberals and Conservatives both in theory and in policies. Both urged railway expansion, exclusion of Asiatics, and increase of bonded indebtedness in order to bring population and business into the province."[16] In Alberni, a small farming community, interests of the farmers were paramount. "In 1903 farmers were already learning the value of united action through the Farmers' Institutes; later through the United Fruit Growers and Stockmen's Association."[17]

McInnes resigned when he was appointed Commissioner of the Yukon in May 1905. A by-election was held in July 1905, and William Manson, a Conservative, was elected to represent Alberni. Meanwhile, out on the west coast at Clayoquot, Harlan Carey Brewster, the next sitting member, was making history as manager and part owner of the Clayoquot Sound Canning Company.

Brewster was born November 19, 1870, in Harvey, New Brunswick and spent much of his childhood in his father's shipyard. He loved the sea and acquired a mate's ticket in deep sea navigation. Travelling south to Boston, Brewster took work as a printer, but failing eyesight forced him to give it up. He married Annie Downie in 1892, and together they came to the west coast where he became purser for the Canadian Pacific Navigation Co.

In 1899, when Harlan Brewster was working as a bookkeeper in the store at Clayoquot, he and several other men helped rescue a number of passengers and crew from the ship *Hero*, which was adrift and on fire. He was awarded a gold medal by the U.S. Congress and a medal by the Royal Humane Society.

For a time Brewster managed a cannery on the Skeena River, before returning to Clayoquot as manager and part owner of the Clayoquot Sound Canning Co.[18] Brewster accomplished what had been believed to be impossible. All of the fishing and canning in his company was done by white or Indian labour; no orientals were employed in any capacity. He was able to do this by changing the method of canning salmon. Hand canning had been the bottleneck in the industry, for it required handmade cans, and the crew, often Chinese, who made the cans, also packed the fish, giving the men a longer season of work. Brewster used machine-made cans; these were more sanitary than the old ones and the soldering was less likely to fail than in the hand process. The machine process made oriental labour more expendable, thereby allowing Brewster to operate his non-oriental cannery.

After only a year of Conservative representation in the riding, in 1906, Brewster allowed his name to go forward as a Liberal candidate. In the election of February 1907, he topped the polls, defeating William Manson and James Cartwright. The Conservatives retained power with twenty-six members elected provincially.

Brewster was re-elected in Alberni in 1909 defeating Dr. Arthur David Morgan. Medicine may have been Dr. Morgan's profession, but politics was his love.[19] As a Conservative, he ran against Brewster in the November provincial election. Of the 549 votes cast, Morgan received 256. Brewster narrowly won the election. The Hon. Richard McBride, a Conservative, made almost a clean sweep of the province at the polls. In this election, only one Liberal was elected in the province – Brewster in Alberni. Four socialists formed the opposition, while Brewster was the third party.[20]

In 1912, Brewster decided to take on McBride directly by running as the Liberal candidate in the Premier's own constituency, the City of Victoria. He was soundly defeated. Meanwhile, in Alberni, another Conservative, John George Corry Wood, won the election. Unsuccessful at the polls, Brewster was still held in high regard by his fellow Liberals and was chosen by unanimous vote to be head of the Liberal party. McBride continued to dominate the political scene.

Two Communities Build

With two railways headed their way, the residents of Alberni and New Alberni had just cause to celebrate. However, the two small settlements had their differences, which in turn created rivalry. Alberni, the larger of the two, saw the homes, businesses, and industries being built in New Alberni as a threat to it's own economic survival. The coming of the railway divided the community even further.

In the spring of 1907, Richard John (Dick) Burde came to Alberni to begin the first newspaper in the district. His press was located in the Marcon Building at the northwest corner of Johnston Road and Gertrude Streets. On August 15, the first issue of the *Alberni Pioneer News* came off the press. The community now had a public voice for the first time.

Burde was born in Ravanne, Michigan. He completed his apprenticeship as a printer in Bellingham, Washington in 1890, and he became a member of the International Typographical Union. After a stint at the Bellingham *Herald*, he travelled across the United States. He worked for a time in Winnipeg before following the gold seekers to the Yukon in 1898. There he founded the Whitehorse *Tribune* on a shoestring. Rumour had it that Burde left the Yukon abruptly after a request for financing turned into a dispute with the bank manager. He became editor of the *Columbian* in New Westminster, gathering experience and knowledge of shop operations that would enable him to run his own newspaper. In 1905 he married Mary McClelland. They had one daughter, Margaret. Two years later they were in Alberni to begin the *Pioneer News*.

Burde hired Roy Cox, teenage son of police chief Gus Cox, as a reporter. Leonard Frank, who operated a general store and who later became a photographer with a province-wide following, was a volunteer reporter for a time.

Burde soon became aquainted with the farmers, miners, and businessmen. It was said he had his foot on the barroom rails at the Arlington, the Alberni, and the Somass Hotels. He made contact with government agencies and syndicates to assure his paper of revenue from land and mining advertisements.

The *Alberni Pioneer News* publisher predicted a wonderful future for Alberni. In the first issue Burde predicted, "Just as surely as water will find its level, commerce will find its natural channels, and at the head of Alberni Canal there is soon to be a city, large and important – the metropolis of Vancouver Island – a port to which many big ships will come to carry away the outputs of numerous mines and manu-facturing industries. And this is not a boomer's dream."

In an editorial dated August 31, 1907 Burde hinted of the division that now existed between the two communities of Alberni and New Alberni. "If either of the Albernis was destined to become nothing more than a divisional point on a railway line there might be some room for jealousy between the two towns, but, as it is, any ill feeling is absurd."

The two communities were essential to each other, he said.

Let New and Old Alberni lean towards each other and pull together and there will be nothing lost to either. It is not a case of "United we stand; divided we fall," but it is clearly and indisputably a case of "United we stand stronger." With no jealousies of our own, there will be no cause for jealousy of any other city in B.C. or for that matter, any city on the Pacific Coast.

It was Burde who first made the suggestion to form a municipality: "It is not too early for this community to consider the formation of a municipality . . . and the two Albernis should have a board of trade. We trust that steps for the organization of such a useful institution will be taken without delay."

Not everyone thought this such a timely idea. While William Roff, father-in-law of George Spencer, was visiting from England, he wrote a letter to the editor, suggesting there were other things more impor-tant at the present time, such as water supply, sewers, electric light, tramways, and telephones.

I believe the water rights can be reserved without any cost until the time arrives to justify the creation of a municipality. Another essential for a prosperous city is its promenades and open places for air and recreation. The river frontage is so grand that it commands to be reserved to the public and says to all builders and other obstructionists, hands off.[21]

In the meantime, Capt. Huff's son-in-law, Thomas Paterson, for-merly of Cape Beale lighthouse, had made an application to the provincial government for an act to incorporate a company with authority "to supply power, light and heat for mining, lighting, domestic, manufacturing and other purposes to the inhabitants, corporations, mines, mills, manufactories, situated within a radius of twelve miles of the town of Alberni, Vancouver Island."[22]

Joseph G. Halpenny suggested the application to supply power to Alberni was like "locking the stable door before the horse is stolen and would it not be better for the two towns and the valley to get incorporated as a municipality so we could secure the best supply of water for all uses necessary for all time." In this same letter, Halpenny recommended a scheme should be formulated to erect or lease a building for a hospital.[23]

The idea of forming a municipality took root. Burde reported the two towns were working together "most harmoniously for general advancement."[24]

On January 18, 1908, it was decided the Albernis would have a Board of Trade. Burde proudly proclaimed, "Citizens of two towns unanimously decide on an organization that will represent public opinion and promote the general welfare of the community. The first question the board will have to consider will be that of forming a municipality."

A public meeting was held early in February 1908. Those attending from "the two Albernis" strongly favoured the formation of a municipality. However, it was pointed out at the meeting that a municipality could not be created before the following January. A committee was then struck to take the necessary steps. It consisted of Dr. Arthur D. Morgan, a physician; James Thomson, a merchant; Walter R. H. Prescott, the Royal Bank manager; John Redford, a butcher and farmer; A. D. Cooper, in real estate; W. H. Marcon, also in real estate; Robert H. Wood, the manager of Barclay Sound Cedar Co.; George A. Spencer, a farmer; Robert F. Blandy, sales clerk; George H. Bird, a sawmill owner; and Richard (Dick) J. Burde, the newspaper publisher. Another meeting was scheduled for Waterhouse's Hall in New Alberni.[25]

The "Citizens Committee of Eleven," as it was named, was cheerful and confident as it set off on this auspicious occasion to meet in New Alberni to work towards incorporation. On February 15, 1908, in the *Pioneer News*, Burde described the trip and the meeting:

At about 7:30 p.m. the first municipal ownership, rapid transit vehicle, (a hay wagon) which had been improvised for the occasion, left John Redford's butcher shop with a full load of future aldermen billed for the selected scene of history making where they were to be joined by other fathers of municipalization. The conveyance was the best available. The seven, included old town representatives, convinced themselves it was luxurious enough to fit the momentous occasion, and that a photo of it should be the first picture to be officially hung in the city hall that is soon to be built.

There was no multitude assembled to embarrass the departure, nor did even a small boy disturb it with a cheer. To men on less important business bent, the trip might have been uncomfortable, but to the history makers it was a delightful journey, the splashing slush and the drizzling rain adding to the general interest caused by the absence of springs when the carriage hit the bumps, and the softness of the water soaked hay that answered the purposes of seat cushions.

The new town representation was taken unawares, one at a time. It had not figured on rapid transit and was not on hand in time to welcome the visiting contingent. The hall was dark and silent, and remained that way till the man who was to open it arrived and announced he had forgotten to bring the key with him. By the minds of the elected guardians of destiny who were eager to commence the work of moulding a down-to-date model of a city, it took more than a quarter of an hour plus another ten minutes to unlock the door, but during that time standing was made easier by the ground being made softer. The copious rain drops continued to beat a gleeful tattoo on the heads of the people's representatives, and to splatter merrily in the mud.

Chairman of the meeting was James Thomson. The discussion was informal and touched on the attitude of the CPR, the Anderson Townsite Co. (Alberni Land Co.), and other large owners of property, who would be interested in the movement. It also dealt with Thomas Paterson's application to the province for water power. It was pointed out that if it were intended that the new city should include all of the Anderson townsite, the company owning the property possessed the power to block the scheme since the consent of more than 50 percent of the property ownership, on a basis of assessed value, would have to be secured. It was also made clear that if the large holders (Alberni Land Co. and the CPR) objected to incorporation, the limits of the city could be so drawn as to give the more modest owners control of the situation. Two resolutions were carried:

> That the Anderson Townsite Company, and the Canadian Pacific Railway Company, be advised that the citizens of the two Albernis are in process of forming a municipality, and that said companies be asked how much and what part of their holdings they would agree to have included.
>
> That this Citizens Municipality Committee is emphatically, and unanimously opposed to the application (of Thomas Paterson regarding water power) in its entirety, and that H. C. Brewster, MPP for Alberni, and the chairman of the Private Bills committee of the Provincial Legislature be advised by wire to this effect.

The two real estate agents, W. H. Marcon and A. D. Cooper, were asked to prepare a report on the properties that could be considered in the incorporation proposition. The following week, the Alberni Board of Trade was organized with Capt. Huff as president, vice-president Dick Burde, and secretary-treasurer Clifford M. Pineo, who operated the drug store. The membership listed thirty-six names.

Meanwhile the committee seeking information about incorporation submitted a draft showing the feasibility of incorporation in the

151

event the present large land holders would not fall in line with the common view. By April 11, the CPR let the committee know it was not prepared to commit itself at the present time on the question of its part in the formation of a municipality. The CPR representative, H. E. Beasley said he thought the movement was a little premature. However, the company had large interests here and would like a voice in the question. He pointed out the difficulties of a small number of taxpayers carrying out the responsibilities of government and suggested the community should remain "under the parental care of the (provincial) government."[26]

The Chairman of the incorporation committee, James Thomson of Thomson's General Store, not wishing to offend the CPR, agreed it was a little early yet to incorporate, but the community had to take steps to secure a reserve of water rights. A public meeting regarding the water supply stressed that if something were not done soon, the community would be up against a serious problem. The larger demand for water could not be supplied by the wells. The well water could become contaminated.

The following week, April 18, the Water Committee consisting of Capt. Huff, Walter R. H. Prescott, and Dick Burde began negotiations with Matt A. Ward, owner of the Arlington Hotel, for the purchase of his private water system, suggesting it could be enlarged by building a dam and installing a ram about six hundred feet farther up Rogers Creek than the location of Ward's present supply source. Two weeks later, May 2, a public meeting endorsed the formation of a company (Alberni Waterworks Co.) to supply water from Rogers Creek until such time as the community could establish a permanent system.

When the Alberni Board of Trade officially met for the first time, May 4, 1908, in the Court House on Johnston Street, the businessmen had lots of questions in mind. They were concerned about freight and wharfage rates and better postal service, and there still had been no reply from the Anderson Townsite Company regarding incorporation.

Another public meeting of the board the next week called for the electing of three fire wardens for Alberni. "Every male resident, over the age of eighteen, and not an Indian or a Chinaman, shall be entitled to vote."[27]

Alberni was also concerned about where the railway station was going to be located. At the meeting was H. E. Beasley, divisional engineer of the CPR. When Beasley was asked about the location he said he wasn't in a position to make any definite statement, "but it was almost certain from the nature of the ground that the station and the yards would be halfway between New Alberni and Old Alberni."[28] He obviously did not want to offend either interest.

However, the location of the railway had already been determined. On a visit to Alberni in November 1907, Richard Marpole, vice-president of the E & N railway and general executive assistant of the CPR, made an announcement about the future location of the line. "The mills for which sites at New Alberni were picked out are the Red Cliff Lumber Co. of Duluth, the Alberni Mills and Timber Co., and the B.C. Cedar Lumber Co. The sites will all be situated on the waterfront of the new town and behind the mills will run the main line and spurs of the E & N railway extension across the Island."[29] The CPR were very interested in accommodating industry.

By June a New Alberni ratepayers organization was formed with A. E. Waterhouse as chairman, and a committee of A. D. Cooper, Sam G. Roseborough, Dr. Caleb Thomas Hilton, W. A. Moore, and Wright Porritt. The stated object of the group was to promote the interests of the new town. Cooper, one of the initiators, said every resident of New Alberni should see the necessity of having some sort of organization to represent the public view and promote development of the town. He thought the group should confine its energies to the new town. The old town could have a similar organization, if it wished. Cooper believed in a little healthy rivalry between the two places.[30]

Herbert Carmichael, who had been the provincial assayer after the failure of his paper mill enterprise, accepted an appointment as executive agent for the Anderson Townsite Company (Alberni Land Co.). The move was timely as the two towns were starting to grow and lots were being put on the open market.

But while residential lots in New Alberni were on the market, those of Alberni were being withheld, and residents of the old town began to wonder why. They called another public meeting to discuss the action of the Alberni Land Co. At the meeting Huff reviewed the history of real estate in the Valley and told how the early settlers had bought lots in good faith from the company. Now that there was a chance of development, the town's prosperity was being retarded to the advantage of the new town. A number of people were anxious to buy lots in Alberni but had been turned away. The Alberni residents decided to make representation on townsite plans to the company's headquarters in London, England.

The board also noted there was the likelihood of an early visit from Sir Thomas Shaughnessy, president of the CPR, and a committee was appointed to interview him on behalf of the Alberni residents. This committee consisted of Capt. Huff, James Thomson, and Dick Burde.

By December there were calls for tenders to clear the New Alberni townsite, as Alberni Land Co. had plans to have 100 acres cleared by the beginning of May 1909, when the lots would be placed on the market.

In February 1909 New Alberni formed its own Board of Trade, much to the dismay of the Alberni organization. President was Alexander Duncan MacIntyre, a hardware store owner; first vice-president Charles A. McNaughton; second vice-president, Alfred Carmichael; and secretary-treasurer Robert F. Blandy.

When Blandy came to Canada from England, in 1905, he was twenty-three years of age. For a time he worked in Hamilton, Ontario, then Kamloops, before coming to Alberni. He began working for Arthur E. Waterhouse, but later went to work at Alberni Hardware. Subsequently, his cousin E. Doug Stone joined him, and the two became partners in a ship building business, Stone and Blandy.

The board's first item of business was to appoint a committee to cooperate with the old town Board of Trade in matters connected with the Vancouver Island Development League, an organization similar to the present day Chamber of Commerce. The League was involved in the settlement and selling of Vancouver Island to investors.[31]

The Alberni board members must have asked why this action was taken, because it was reported back to the board on Feb. 22, 1909, "that the New Alberni Board of Trade was formed but solely because the new town felt the need of a local board to act on matters concerning the new town solely."[32]

So upset was the Alberni board about the formation of the New Alberni board, that at one meeting Leonard Frank, then representative on the Vancouver Island Development League, was asked to tell the Alberni Board why he had dared attend a New Alberni Board of Trade meeting. Frank replied, "They invited me."[33]

When Leonard Frank first came to the community, he invested in two copper mines, then he opened a general store in Alberni. The winning of a camera in a raffle prize at the mining camp began a brilliant career that would eventually make him one of B.C.'s most famous photographers.[34]

In March, Capt. Huff was re-elected president of the Alberni Board of Trade. It was noted in the minute book that "all future meetings will be held in the old town." It was at this meeting the board was formally advised of the formation of the New Alberni Board of Trade.

At a New Alberni Board of Trade meeting held in March, a letter was received from MPP Harlan C. Brewster regarding foreshore privileges. It stated the public was barred from access to the foreshore which had originally been acquired by the Alberni Land Co. under an old act. The board felt it should take no action that might antagonize the CPR. It was pointed out that Argyle Street did run down to the water's edge. Any new roads south and north would have to terminate at the water's edge in accordance with the provisions of the existing Land Registry Act.

Work began in May on clearing the New Alberni townsite; acres of forest were being transformed into property suitable for buildings. Sub-contracts were let by Carmichael and Moorhead for thirty acres surrounding the settled part of the townsite.

In Alberni a survey of the Somass River was being done by George Smith to get estimates on dredging the river to see if the flats and river could be improved to enable the deepest draft vessels on the Pacific to steam up to the old town wharf and dock in fresh water.

The railway commission had yet to approve the revised route at the Alberni end of the E & N extension. Property owners on Gertrude Street refused to give free consent to the railway track being laid along their thoroughfare. There was also speculation that somehow the district around Sproat Lake would have a direct connection with the new town and that the old town would be practically sidetracked.

The Alberni Board of Trade was unhappy with the location of the railway line through Gertrude Street. At a meeting held May 3, 1909, Dick Burde moved "that the board consider it the best interest of Alberni that a full and free expression of public opinion be obtained in regard to the railway line along Gertrude Street." The secretary was instructed to call a public meeting for Friday May 7.

Other problems were brewing. The Alberni Board of Trade had formed a hospital committee in 1907 and had begun receiving donations for its hospital fund. An application from the board had gone to the Anderson Townsite Company (Alberni Land Company) for a site to locate the hospital. On November 8, 1909, Burde, speaking for the hospital committee, said the Alberni Land Company had offered to give two lots on Redford Road as a hospital site. The two communities would have to act as one if a hospital was to be built. The site chosen was in New Alberni. The Alberni Board of Trade, chaired by Huff, was quite upset at this turn of events. However, after a few months the Alberni board considered it would ask the New Alberni board to appoint a special committee to act with Alberni's hospital committee.

With one problem out of the way, another soon arose. New Alberni wanted to publish a pamphlet acclaiming the virtues of life in the small community, which, it considered, "had so much potential." When the Alberni Board of Trade was invited to participate in the venture, A. W. Neill suggested the board take steps to publish a pamphlet dealing "solely with Alberni." With the two communities anxious to advertise the virtues of living in the Albernis, in May both were astounded to learn that the Vancouver Island Development League brochure had left Alberni completely off the map. When complaints were lodged with the League, it stated, "The deed had been done, and could not be undone."[35]

On September 25, 1909 the newspaper reported: "There has been a split between the two towns, New and Old Alberni, over the advertising question, and the Board of Trade of the New Town is now proceeding with a publicity scheme independent of the Old Town." The split was a short one, for in October both Boards of Trade were again working together on advertising. At a special meeting of the executive of the Alberni board, it decided to try to reason further with the new town organization.

At the September meeting, the New Alberni board discussed sounding out the CPR on the subject of a new name for the community. All members thought the idea was a good one. The decision was made in October by the CPR. when Vice-president R. Marpole suggested the name be changed to "Port Alberni." Marpole's attention was drawn to the fact that the residents of Alberni had the opinion that the terminal passenger station would be located closer to Alberni than to the New Alberni. He stated:

> The terminus of the Alberni branch of the E & N is, of course, at the head of navigation on the Alberni Canal, at what we now call Alberni. But I think the latter place should be re-christened and named Port Alberni, which will indicate positively that the town is the seaport terminus. In our opinion the station will be close to Argyle Street, the new Somass Hotel, and at the head of the freight yard. If the residents of New Alberni are willing to accept the new title, and if the Alberni Land Co. which owns practically the whole of the townsite, (sic) I will do my best to secure the adoption of the name of Port Alberni. We shall, of course, provide the ordinary railway accommodation necessary for the old town of Alberni and the settlement, and the stopping place will probably be at the crossing of the Nanaimo Road."[36]

On February 26, 1910, the headlines in the *Pioneer News* proclaimed: "New Alberni no more: it's Port Alberni now."

Port Alberni announced, on March 19, 1910, the birth of the first baby to be born in its community, a girl, born to Mr. and Mrs. Alfred Carmichael. The baby was born March 17, St. Patrick's Day, and was aptly named Patricia (Pat).

Despite the wrangling between the two Boards of Trade, both communities continued to grow. In New Alberni, James Rollin built the King Edward Hotel, a three-storey building furnished with all the modern conveniences of the day. It had thirty-eight bedrooms in addition to spacious hallways, parlour, dining room, and bar. "The demand for first-class hotel accommodation in the new town is steadily increasing and Mr. Rollin is doing as much as can be expected of any one man to meet it." Rollin even held a dance in Waterhouse's Hall to celebrate the opening. He also spirited away Sing Long from his business in Alberni to be his new cook. Sing Long had a restaurant in a four by eight foot space opposite the Arlington Hotel. When he left, a sign on the door informed the public that "hereafter 'Charlie' will open the place and cook anytime there is any business in sight."

The Somass Hotel formally opened July 20, 1908. It was reported to be "a little advance of the times, and a credit to the enterprise of A. E. Waterhouse." The hotel was lit by gas and had hot air radiators throughout. In every room there was an electric bell to allow guests to communicate with the office. A large drawing room opened to a spacious verandah. The dining room could accommodate sixty guests. Special attention had been given to fire escapes, which were through French windows opening to wide balconies from the halls on each floor. The sanitary arrangements were said to be up to date. Water was supplied from a deep well to tanks in the attic holding one thousand gallons. The hotel had well-lit sample rooms in the basement for travellers. Also located in the basement were a large ice store, larders, a steam laundry, and the heating plant. Clifford Wise, manager of the hotel, had come from managing the Cowichan Bay Hotel.

C. A. McNaughton opened the Alberni Hardware Co. for business in 1909 in New Alberni, opposite Waterhouse Hall. The store offered a full line of all kinds of hardware.[37]

Over in Alberni, the Alberni Hotel was reopening. Built facing Victoria Quay in 1891 by the Sareaults, this was the first hotel to sell liquor. It was a two-storey building with double decker verandah appropriately gingerbreaded and with three dormer windows on either side of the attic. Later Mr. and Mrs. Gus Labelle operated the hotel until the turn of the century. For a time it was used as a private residence until Rogers and Co. purchased it from the Labelles.

The Arlington Hotel, built in 1893 by Matt Ward, was still the social centre of Alberni. Even before the hotel was completed it was the scene of a dance attended by most of the people in the Valley. "The wet lumber steamed as several heaters were fired to warm up the room for the company. Babies were put down to sleep in corners, and a gay time was had by all."[38] Jack Burke was caller for the square dances held here. Mrs. Ward's piano tinkled out the music as the oldtimers circled and whirled in two-steps and waltzes. In 1908 Matt Ward even ordered an Oldsmobile, which he planned to operate between the two towns to accommodate his guests in the summer months. James A. McNiff and his father-in-law George Meagher operated the Arlington Hotel for a few years. Then Jack Burke and his son Dick ran it for a while before John Militich took it over.

In August of 1907 the community waited anxiously to see which bank would be the first to open. Until this time, all wholesale business had been transacted with Victoria. Storekeepers kept their accounts there. Bets were on that it would be the Canadian Bank of Commerce, for it was known to have prepared furniture and supplies ready for the opening.

However, during a fishing trip to Alberni in 1907, F. T. Walker, assistant manager of the Royal Bank of Canada in Vancouver, saw the possibilities for opening a bank in the Alberni district. Propelled by rumours the Commerce bank was considering opening, Walker wired his head office in Montreal for authority to open a branch here.

While the Commerce was still considering it, the Royal Bank of Canada opened for business on August 26, 1907 with Walker as manager. He arrived on a Thursday night and was open for business the next morning in Capt. Huff's old store where the firm of Marcon and Co. had it's real estate office. The first deposit in the bank was made precisely at 10:00 a.m. by the *Pioneer News* editor and publisher, Dick Burde.

The first permanent manager of the Alberni bank was H. K. Wright, who stayed only six weeks. He was replaced by Walter R. H. Prescott, who remained at the bank until 1912. William Mitchell was assistant manager, and George Bird Jr. was the junior clerk. Two years later Bird transferred to the Vancouver office. In 1908, the Royal Bank of Canada hired George Forrest to begin work on a new building in Alberni, on the northeast corner of Johnston and Margaret Streets on the opposite side of the street to the Arlington Hotel. Prescott was followed as manager by Arthur G. Freeze, who remained until after the Great War in 1918 when the bank closed in Alberni.

Although still a very small village, Alberni was the recognized centre of the west coast of Vancouver Island, and a surprising amount of business came its way. Bank deposits were received from all parts of the coast. New Alberni began to feel it too should have banking facilities. After some discussion the Royal Bank agreed to open a sub-branch in New Alberni. The New Alberni bank officially opened for business on July 10, 1908.[39] In 1910 it became an independent branch, and it continued to serve the community until 1942.

In the summer of 1910 the Bank of Montreal announced it too would open a branch in New Alberni. A year later, on December 27, 1911, the bank opened on Second Avenue between Strathern and Athol. The first manager was E. S. McLintock, the ledger keeper was F. G. McCallum, and the teller was C. F. Pritchard. In 1912 the Bank of Montreal moved to the Carmoor Block at Argyle and Kingsway and added another staff member, W. H. Crowshaw. The bank stayed at this location until 1936.

A. W. Neill sold his forty acre farm and decided to move into town about the same time as C. Frederic Bishop let the contract for the construction of his new store, a one-storey building. The store would be used for a grocery, confectionery, and bakery business. Bishop also purchased the house on the adjoining lot previously occupied by Dr. Pybus.

Robert Blandy and his cousin E. Doug Stone, from England, pooled resources and built the city's first shipyard in 1911 on land leased from the E & N railway. Stone's father owned and operated a shipyard and fleet in England, and Stone himself was a first class designer and practical shipbuilder. He quickly became known in marine circles. His first big achievement was the building and launching of the *Somass Queen*, which for many years served as the only regular passenger vessel for the Alberni Inlet and the west coast. Stone began installing gasoline engines on Indian fishboats. He also purchased the *Oh Mi Mi*, a launch used for transporting people. Later the ship-yard was contracted to build the *May Queen*, the *Mayflower*, and the *Mayfly* for John Kendall, who had built a cold storage plant. The partners Blandy and Stone instituted a water scow business operating from the west side of the Inlet to the sawmill, which had no other source of water at the time.[40] In 1912 Stone staged the first outboard

159

regatta on the Somass River. He won the event himself with a three horsepower Waterman engine.

The area even had the services of a Victoria dentist, Dr. D. E. Kerr, who arrived by boat carrying all the equipment necessary to do "all kinds of dentistry." Appointments could be made at the drug store.

About this time the two communities got a telephone system. It was aptly named the "Hello" system, and despite its shortcomings it beat riding a buggy or a bicycle or even walking, just to speak to someone. Credit for the installation went to Thomas Paterson, the former lightkeeper at Cape Beale, who formed a small private company to install the system. It gave a twenty-four-hour service, but it necessitated having bells ring in the home of every subscriber. If one bell rang, they all rang. Individual calls were determined by a different ring: one short, one long, a long and a short, or two shorts, for example. Everyone soon learned to distinguish their own call and took little notice of others.[41]

An amusing story about the new system appeared in the *Alberni Pioneer News*. Burde, who knew everyone in town, reported on how a group of subscribers got together to decide on the combination of rings required to reach the bartender at the Alberni Hotel.

> All through the day and night of Thursday and Friday a few ingenious subscribers, assisted by a large number of sympathizers, whose names are not on the company's books, tried to find a combination of notes that would bring the mixer of the Alberni Hotel up to the talking place, but music being more to his liking than speech, he declined to interfere with the delightful experiments. The man who presides behind the elbow rest in Rollin's Hotel (King Edward Hotel) became confused over so much bell ringing, and is reported to have, several times, thrown pieces of silver at the phone while he shouted "Hello" at the cash register.[42]

With the large influx of men to the Albernis, Chief Constable Cox requested a constable be hired to help him in his duties. Until this time, he had been a one-man force covering the entire Alberni area. Cox no longer had jurisdiction over the west coast, as a new constable, Ewan McLeod, had been appointed provincial constable for Clayoquot the previous year. McLeod, twenty-six, was born in Dunvegan on the Isle of Skye, Scotland. He had served on the police force in Glasgow for two years before coming to Canada.[43]

A new lighting system was introduced to Alberni in January 1908 at the Athletic Hall. Known as the "Sunbeam," it was a device in which gasoline was forced from a tank by air pressure, through copper tubing. By contact with fire at its outlet the liquid fuel was converted into a gas. The flame was steady and the light powerful.

One light was sufficient to satisfactorily illuminate the hall for a basketball practice. Matt Ward had one installed in front of the Arlington Hotel and five more inside. William Rice was the representative for the company selling the lighting device. The light must have improved things considerably, because a week later it was reported a "lively" interest had been awakened in basketball. A match between the club and the CPR location party had the CPR ahead by a score of eleven points to eight.

A passenger stagecoach service was inaugurated in December 1909 between Alberni and New Alberni by Harris & Roseborough, a new livery firm in New Alberni. It planned to make two or three trips per day between the towns.[44] When the E & N railway reached Cameron Lake, the company took over the mail contract, meeting the train there.

The population of Alberni and Port Alberni had risen to 4082. The new lines of steel would soon connect the Valley with other points on Vancouver Island, making communications with the outside world easier and faster than ever before. The age of buoyant faith in hard work and rugged individualism had given way to a new era, a time when nothing seemed impossible. Those early farming pioneers must have shaken their heads in disbelief at some of the new-fangled contraptions that could bring light or carry a voice over wires. Even women's skirts began to rise, moving from the ankle bone to the boot top. The bicycle was now a common sight; the occasional automobile brought children running to the roadside to witness the spectacle.

Still, the common mode of travel was horse and buggy. This could be a bit tricky if you were dressed in your finest ball gown. Two young women found out the hard way when their horse and buggy ran into a mud bank in front of the Arlington Hotel and dragged them in after it. The women were thrown to the ground; one landed on her face, the other on her hands and feet. Needless to say, they were quickly rescued by bystanders and patrons and given sympathy. Dressed in beautiful ballroom gowns, they were on their way to a big dance at Waterhouse's Hall.

Socially the community was well served. The Alberni District Brass Band was organized in October 1910 with president W. E. Ryder, vice-president Sid Toy, and secretary-treasurer, C. A. Copp. The bandsmen began regular practices under the direction of Captain Fox, who had come to Port Alberni with A. E. Waterhouse.

On June 21, 1911 the band made it's first public appearance at the coronation entertainment in the Port Alberni Public School with a rendition of "God Save the King," followed by "two or three other inspiring selections."[45] There were other musical opportunities in the small community. Private music lessons were being offered by Madame Dupont, from Belgium, who opened musical classes in New Alberni in 1908. She offered private lessons in singing, piano, or cello.[46]

The Alberni Amateur Dramatic Association brought live theatre to the community. It's production of "The New Tutor" got rave reviews, especially the "excellent acting" of Leslie A. Withers in the title role.

Waterhouse was elected president of the Alberni District Orchestral and Dramatic Society following a meeting in the parlour of the Somass Hotel in October 1911. Vice-president was C. M. Wise, secretary treasurer was Dick Burde, and musical director and stage manager was H. A. Grey. The group planned to mount a few musical comedies and comedy dramas during the winter months. A stage was added to the Waterhouse Hall to allow for the productions. The formal opening of "The Port Alberni Theater" on First Avenue was held November 27th with the District Brass Brand providing the entertainment.

The first moving picture show was held December 19, 1910, at the Mertz Hall on Third Avenue. The advertisement in the *Alberni Pioneer News* read: "Big show for three nights only, Dec. 19, 20 and 23 at Mertz Hall. 23 moving pictures." Admission was ten cents for children; adults paid twenty-five cents.

Not all the social events were open to the public. Dr. and Mrs. Morgan held a musical evening in honour of Miss Hettie Morgan, of Nanaimo, who was visiting her brother. She was considered to be one of the most accomplished pianists of the Coal City.

There were also entertainers who visited from outside the community, such as the first minstrel over the summit – billed as the "musical event of the week in Alberni." The minstrel, a coloured man, was travelling the Pacific Coast. He made an unexpected appearance at the rotunda of the Arlington Hotel.

> The rotunda was filled with men who were endeavouring to entertain themselves with a variety of prophesies about the future of the town. The minstrel had come over the summit on foot, carrying his show goods with him. All he wanted in payment was food. After he was fed, he gave a fine performance, both vocal and instrumental. The men passed around the hat and he made a few dollars. A similar performance was given in Port Alberni.[47]

Local Indians continued to hold their traditional potlatch. One such event held by the Tseshaht Indians lasted three days, with the chief entertainer Johnny Youkum. Some of the white settlers were invited. The potlatch was described by Burde as "a mild affair with nothing more exciting then a rasping chorus of voices with a tom tom accompaniment, some bloodless dances, and a pole climbing competition."[48]

Another potlatch was held by Jimmy Santo, also on the Tseshaht reserve. This celebration, held in November, 1907, was in honour of the Ucluelet Indians. About 160 members of the Ucluelet tribe came up the Inlet in canoes and small boats. Jimmy Santo hoped the size of this potlatch would establish a record for the year.

While on a fishing expedition, Santo's son met a beauty of the Ucluelet tribe and wooed and won her. A week prior to the potlatch they were married. It was in celebration of this event that the proud father-in-law of the bride did his best, with the assistance of friends, to give the Ucluelets the time of their lives. The local newspaper reported on the event:

> "The excitement last night when the log fires blazed, and weird noises penetrated the atmosphere for some distance, was only a preliminary affair. While Santo played more the spectator's part in the game, the moving spirits were his friends Cpt. Bill and Tommy Tatoosh. The former provided the muck-a-muck and the latter a hat full of silver, all of which was distributed among the visitors from the West Coast."

The next night was the turn of the Ucluelets to show their best dances for their hosts. Santo had not set a time limit on the celebrations but planned to wait until all his friends had a fair chance to secure social honours. It turned out to be one of the biggest potlatches held that year.[49]

In one of the earliest editions of the *Alberni Pioneer News* a young Indian named Hamilton George explained the legend of the petroglyphs on the rock walls at Sproat Lake and Great Central Lake. Some predicted Sproat Lake would become a fashionable resort. George's description of the monsters of the deep may have put a little fear into those set on building summer homes at the lake.

> Many years ago, no one knows how many, there lived in the vicinity a sort of super-human Indian named Quot-e-yat, and it is believed by some, that he still lives, but that his form is invisible. He had a record for vanquishing fierce and evil monsters that would back St. George of England into heroic insignificance.
>
> Quot-e-yat was a protector of his people whose principal enemies were the monsters of the deep. At every opportunity he gave battle to these evil

things, but was much to his sorrow, unable to extinguish them all. He conceived the idea of travelling about from place to place, and carving likenesses upon the rocks by the waters where they would be seen by Indians afloat in canoes. The pictures served as a warning that such creatures were hiding in water near by, waiting for a chance to attack and devour.

There are Indians now living who most carefully obey these warnings, and make no noise with their paddles for fear that the evil inhabitants of the water will hear them and rise to destroy them. If, by accident, some noise should be made, the occupants of the canoe will immediately rush for the shore. White men say there are no whales or other such monsters in these fresh water lakes, but the Indian has lived here longer, and seen more, and knows different.[50]

There were some prominent people buying homes at Sproat Lake early in 1910. One of those was the premier, Hon. Richard McBride, who bought Arbutus Island. Another was Richard Marpole, vice-president of the E & N Railway Co. It was also reported that work on a fashionable summer hotel at Sproat Lake was now in progress and expected to be opened June 1st, 1911.[51] Arthur E. Waterhouse purchased the George Smith farm at the lake and later leased it to Cuthbert Blandy, who advertised canoes, rowboats, and launches for hire.[52]

Nils Weiner, a Swedish settler who prior to his arrival in Alberni had worked as a miner in the Kootenays, spent the winter of 1912 in Frank Stirling's cabin at Sproat Lake. Stirling had since moved from the Valley. Weiner later purchased land at Brennan's Bay, now known as Weiner's Bay, where he built his homestead. Weiner was a master craftsman. He built boats and houses, made fly-rods and fine violins; he was an expert mechanic and a skilled cougar hunter. His hand-crafted violins became prized possessions.[53]

With a large community of Scottish settlers, St. Andrew's night was not forgotten. "A' Scotchmen wha' are interested in St. Andrew's nicht, 30th. November, will meet i' the Coort Hoose at 8 o'clock Nov. 26," read a notice in the local newspaper. According to George Bird, "two people out of every three were either Scots or of Scottish descent. New Year's Day was the great day with people from the land of the heather." He recalled James Thomson, who was in charge of some of the operations during construction of the old paper mill, being very annoyed when Andrew Service and Bird laid off work on Christmas day and decided to go to work on January 1st.[54]

The English settlers were not to be outdone; they organized cricket matches under the guidance of Waterhouse, John Frank Bledsoe, and P. R. C. Bayne. The Indians got into the sporting mood and formed the Somass Football Club. Also, the white settlers often watched with amazement the Indian talent for spearing fish. On one such occasion, an Indian known simply as Ned speared twelve fish in thirty minutes, much to the delight of an audience on the river.

Little is known of the lives of the early Chinese settlers, who were considered inferior and viewed with great suspicion by the white residents. Gambling was allowed just as long as it was only the Chinese who lost money. Many of the Chinese were single men who had been forbidden to bring their families from China to Canada. However, they were tolerated and did continue to celebrate Chinese New Year with fireworks, which spurred an editorial in the *Pioneer News*:

> One of the objects of a Chinese firecracker demonstration is to frighten away devils that lurk around in space with the intention of making their mark on some Celestial soul, and one of the reasons for which the chief of police of Alberni put a stop to the most recent display in this neighbourhood, was that it was disturbing the sanctity of our Sunday. According to a Chinese version of the interference, the official who acted on behalf of the Christian sentiment put himself in league with the devil."[55]

The small Chinese colony was hit by a tragic accident in the summer of 1910. The heat had been intense during July. A number of Chinese gathered on the Barclay Sound Cedar Co. property wharf trying to catch a cool breeze off the Inlet. On this day, the breeze didn't come, and one of the group stripped and took a plunge into the water, which was about thirty feet deep. He was not an expert swimmer and went to the bottom, finally emerging with seaweed in his mouth. The second time he came up, he grabbed the piling beside him and held on. Even then the Chinese on the wharf failed to realize their friend was in distress and looked upon his unique stunts as something designed especially for their amusement. They were laughing and enjoying themselves, when their companion was finally helped ashore.

The next day the same group was on the wharf again. This time it was Mah Joe, the social leader of the party, who decided to duplicate the episode of the previous day. Only he didn't surface. His friends remained unconcerned for a few minutes. There was to be a meeting of the Chinese Masonic Society that evening and Mah Joe was to be the master of ceremonies. The group called to him to come up, but he didn't respond. Mah Joe had become entangled in a waterlogged tree on the bottom. An Indian named Joe was attracted to the scene on the wharf. He dived to the bottom and tugged at Mah Joe but could not jar him loose from the limbs of the tree. Joe came to the surface and secured a piece of rope and took it down to Mah Joe. Four or five times he tried. When Mah Joe was finally brought to the surface, it was too late to save him. On Monday Mah Joe's body was loaded into a wagon and sent to Nanaimo. Six Chinese accompanied the corpse two miles out of town.[56]

The Imperial Steam Laundry, from Nanaimo, opened a branch in Port Alberni. It advertised "White Labor Only."

The community got the services of another physician in 1908 when Dr. Caleb Thomas Hilton, with his wife Ethel and daughter Betty arrived here from England. The same year Dr. Hilton helped form the New Alberni Ratepayers Association to "represent the public view and promote development of the town."[57] Hilton's home and office were first located at Argyle and First Avenue. His daughter Freda was born there in 1908.

In 1910 Hilton purchased property at the corner of Third and Mar Street where Woodwards is now located. There he built a large two-storey square framed home and office. Two more Hilton children were born at this location: Richard in 1914 and Moireen in 1918. Hilton was an avid gardener, and the grounds surrounding his home became a focal point in the community. One of his prized flowers was an all-white daffodil he developed and named the "Alberni Beauty." He also had some prized lilies and a beautiful rose garden.

In a school essay, Dr. Hilton's great-grandson Craig Geiger described his great-grandfather:

> Nearly every year he would take a trip up Mt. Arrowsmith or to Della Falls, just to collect different kinds of flowers and plants to be transplanted into his garden. People would come from miles around to look at his garden and it turned into a real show place in town. The garden once covered all the area that is now the paved parking lot of Woodwards. There was a water lily and gold fish pond in his garden.[58]

Hilton also served as coroner for the district. At one time he was the only resident doctor. Arnold Hanna, who later became Judge Hanna, was sworn in as coroner because Dr. Hilton said, "I couldn't see any point in sitting on an inquest as coroner and also giving medical evidence to myself."[59] In 1914 Dr. Hilton served with the Medical Corps in the Great War, returning in 1917 to take up his practice again in Port Alberni. Dr. Hilton retired in 1945. At that time he sold his Third Avenue property to Woodwards Store Ltd. He built another home at the corner of Bruce and 11th Avenue, moved all his plants and flowers to his new location, and grew another beautiful garden. Hilton died in 1957.

Memorable Sporting Events

The Alberni Athletic Club can lay claim to being the first to organize sporting events in the community. Even when basketball was still in its infancy in the 1890s, a few of the men got together and learned to play the game. Bill Erickson, son of Alberni's first postmistress Agnes Erickson, wrote of the formation of the first Alberni Athletics, which became the first basketball team.

> Billy Russell was about the only man in town who knew anything about basketball rules. So I rounded up Sid Toy, Alfred and Fred Drinkwater, Willie Piggot, Harold Bishop, and we had a meeting and organized the Alberni Athletics, the first basketball team in the valley. We played in Brands Hall. It was a pretty rough game in those days. Bill Russell refereed. In later years, Ed Whyte, Brother of Bob Whyte of Victoria, came to Alberni, and was a great help to us in keeping the game alive.[60]

On November 9, 1907, a meeting was held in the office of A. French, Margaret Street, to form the Alberni Athletic and Social Club. Honourary president was William Roff; first vice-president J. Redford; second vice-president W. E. Piggot, and secretary-treasurer A. French. The club arranged to lease Brands Hall, (Southgate area) for sporting events. The colours of the club would be blue and white.[61] When Brands Hall had a lighting sytem installed, interest in basketball began to rise. The Athletic Club also sponsored boxing matches and kept rugby alive. On March 3, 1909, the Club leased a large area of cleared land at the junction of Sproat Lake (River Road) and Beaver Creek roads, to be used for sporting events.

Cricket was very popular with the early settlers prior to 1900. Every summer evening, players would be out at Stirling Field for cricket. They included Percy and Stanley Bayne, George Spencer, Willy Piggot, and John Howitt.

In 1898, interest in baseball began. It was quite a job finding enough men whose time wasn't already taken up with cricket. However, Jack Burke and Sid Toy encouraged the young men to learn the baseball rules. After a few weeks of training they thought they were pretty good. As there wasn't another baseball team in the valley to try out against, they challenged the cricket team to a nine inning game. But all the weeks of training were in vain; the cricket team beat them at their own game.

167

The very first Dominion Day celebration, held in 1886, saw the Indians compete in their five or six man canoes. There were three canoes competing and the course was run upstream on the Somass River.

The July 1st sporting events were a big part of the annual celebration. W. Arthur Thompson, a Beaver Creek farmer, wrote in his diary about one such event he attended at the Anderson Farm. An Indian transported him across the Somass River in a large canoe navigated by long poles as the river was low during the summer. On this day the rides were free, paid for by the sports committee. At other times a canoe ride could cost twenty-five cents.

> Some of the young Indians used to compete with the Whites. They always had canoe races, squaws and men, but not mixed. Gus Cox always was M.C. for the races, as he understood the Chinook language. There was always a tug-of-war, Indians vs. Whites. Sometimes the Indians won. The biggest and strongest Indian I ever knew was called Big Frank. He was always anchor man.[62]

Frank C. Garrard recalled one of the first soccer teams. "During the winter months when there wasn't much to do, a group got together and decided to make up a football team and take a trip out of town to Nanaimo and Victoria."[63] To finance the trip, they put together a Christie Minstrel show. Alfred Carmichael was the director. They made enough money to take the team to Victoria. The team included Percy, Stanley, and Talbot Bayne, George Spencer, W. B. Garrard, John Howitt, Robert Ballard, Harry Fitzgerald, Jim and George Drinkwater, Willie Thomson, John Redford, and George Bird. Percy Bayne was the captain. George Bird remembered the game: "The Victorians had no mercy on us and played to beat us right to the finish. When time was called, we found ourselves the losers with no points to our credit, whilst our opponents had scored 65 points."[64] On the return journey they played the Nanaimo Hornets and a team from Wellington. The Hornets had several times been the B.C. champions. They beat the Alberni team by twenty-eight goals.

Native Indians had their own soccer team. In November 1907 the Somass Football Club was formed at the home of Watty Shewish.[65] The team goalie was W. Roberts; full-backs were J. Youkum amd H. George; half-backs were T. Matqua, J. Motion, and W. Haine; forwards were C. Ross, J. Shewish, F. Williams, W. Youkum, and O. Taylor. Club referee was Watty Shewish. In their first game, the Somass team beat the Alberni team by 2-0.

In 1910, the Port Alberni soccer team won the West Coast Association League championship. It had been an exciting season for the five teams in the league, Parksville, E & N, Somass, Alberni, and Port Alberni. Games between Alberni and Port Alberni always drew large crowds. At the first game of the season, held in October 1910, Alberni defeated Port Alberni 3 – 1.

On the Alberni team were goalie A. Drinkwater; backs S. Bennett, E. M. Whyte; half-backs George Ward, R. Erickson, S. Pryde; forwards W. Erickson, G. Blandy, W. Green, C. Cleavely, R. Shaver.

The Port Alberni team consisted of goalie George Bird; backs C. S. Bannell, Roy Hanna; half-backs, R. Wood, J. Mathison, R. F. Blandy; forwards A. Hanna, J. Ogilvie, F. H. Swayne, A. Wood, A. R. DeFeaux. Referee was J. M. Rolston.

By December the standings in the league had Parksville at the top with Port Alberni in second place, followed by Alberni, Somass, and E & N. The final match in January 1911, between Parksville and Port Alberni for the Sloan cup, took place "on the field across the river from Alberni. The weather was perfect, the game fast, clever, clean, and fair. It was free of accidents or serious bungling."[66] Port Alberni won by three goals to two. Waterhouse's Hall was the setting for a big dance which topped off the day. The cup was formally presented to the winners in the parlour of the Somass Hotel.[67]

The same names reappear in many of the sporting event records. This was especially true of the track events. Harold Bishop was known for the one hundred yard dash and Fred Rollin for the mile. The five mile race for a silver cup and the championship of the district became part of the Dominion Day events. In 1910 there were seven entries. These included R. Erickson, John Dick, B. Salmon, Fred Louis, Cecil George, A. Drinkwater, and J. Drinkwater. But the race was really between Erickson and John Dick, last year's winner. Erickson won with a time of 28 minutes and 53 seconds.

On Sept. 26, 1910, a relay race was run between Alberni and New Alberni. Competition was keen between the two communities, rivals in so many other areas. The race was held on a Saturday afternoon. Spectators had a real thrill as it wasn't until the last quarter that either team had any decided advantage. The course was from the Old Alberni Hotel, at Victoria Quay, to the south side of Rogers Creek Bridge and return twice, each runner going only the single distance.

The first pair to start were J. Fox, Port Alberni, and A. Drinkwater, Alberni. Drinkwater had a good lead and started W. Erickson off in good place. A. R. DeFeaux went in chase of Erickson and gained about ten yards but did not overtake him, which gave F. Drinkwater a short start over C. Green. Green made a determined sprint and created a surprise among the spectators by overtaking his opponent and beating him by about twenty yards to the finish line. This gave Fred Rollin, of the new town team, a good start on Harold Bishop, the fastest of the old town combination. He maintained his lead all the way, winning the day for New Alberni.

Fred Rollin and Harold Bishop were the two best runners the district had ever known. Fred, the miler, had many trophies as evidence of his speed in distance races. Bishop took part in his first meet at Stirling Field in 1908, where he won the 100 yard dash, the 220 and 440, competing against John Redford, Otto Taylor, and Alf and Fred Drinkwater. From 1908 to 1914 he participated in every meet held in the Alberni Valley and won every 220 and 100 yard race. Many of the trophies won by Bishop were lost when the Bishop home was burned in 1913. In 1909 and 1910 he brought home the B.C. Championship trophies from Vancouver and New Westminster. In 1910 he came home with the B.C. pole vaulting championship.[68]

The Alberni Tennis Club was actively supported by players and non-players. In May 1910 the club announced the courts would be open to members on June 3rd. "when the mud court will be in a condition to play on. The two grass courts will be ready one month later. The grounds have been levelled and fenced and give promise of being a very attractive and pretty spot for recreation."[69] Subscriptions were $5 for men and $2.50 for women. The tournament held in the fall 1910 was a big success. P. R. C. Bayne reported the Alberni club would be working with the Port Alberni club during the winter to raise funds for both. The Port Alberni club was in the process of acquiring new and enlarged grounds.[70]

When the bicycle was introduced into the valley, cycling joined the list of sports held on Dominion Day. The five mile race became a big event. Jimmy Pryde, a cyclist from Alberni, was out practising for the long distance bicycle race in May 1911. He was going full speed towards the Somass Hotel and had his head down on the handlebars of his wheel when he collided with Capt. Huff's automobile, which was going at good speed in the other direction. The force of the collision caused Jimmy to turn a complete somersault in the air and drop into the back seat of the automobile. Huff's automobile passed over the bicycle and smashed it. Amazingly, Jimmy was only slightly bruised. He was able to resume training two days later. It was a sensational stunt worthy of even the most experienced cyclist. Jimmy went on to win the four mile bicycle race on Dominion Day.[71]

Scams, Schemes, and Speculators

With the advent of the railway, land speculation was at a peak. Everyone wanted to get into the act, and there were some unscrupulous speculators. One wildcat property scam in 1907 involved the real estate firm of McConnel & Taylor, who advertised in Victoria, 33×120 foot lots on West C. Nelson's property near Alberni. Burde editorialized:

> The firm asked the same amount of money for each lot as it had paid for the entire property. It is a daring wild cat scheme. The property is two miles away from the nearest deep water wharf and it is all heavy woods between. Two aged horses died of starvation on it last winter.[72]

The Albernis were outraged. Steps were taken to make the public in Victoria aware of the scheme. No one wanted the reputation of Alberni to be injured by "this rank adventure."[73] A week later, McConnel & Taylor had refunded all the money paid for the lots.

Another wildcat scheme was revealed in 1908 when real estate dealers Bond & Clark offered lots for sale at "$30 or $25, in payments of $10 cash and $5 per month." These lots supposedly placed you on the ground floor in Alberni. Burde called the advertisement "buncoe" and said the subdivision was a swamp, less than a hundred yards from the line of the proposed railway track. The track was about ten miles from its terminus, three miles from the old town and five miles from the steamer landing.[74]

In 1909 when word reached Alberni that the Panama Canal would be completed by 1913, land speculators had a field day. There were now 36,000 men at work on the canal project, which would shorten voyages to Great Britain and Europe considerably. No longer would ships need to round Cape Horn. Ships sailing between Europe and East Asia, or Australia, could save as much as two thousand miles by using the Canal. The United States also saw it as a link in the defense of North America.

> Buy in Port Alberni now before the completion of the Panama Canal – every minute is precious – every date brings rising values and a step nearer to the finishing of the greatest trade factor the Pacific Coast has ever known. Port Alberni is Canada's Pacific Gateway – the terminal of the CPR and CNR. It is fast becoming a second Liverpool. The opening of the Panama Canal will boost real estate values sky high in Port Alberni. Get in on the ground floor now. You can buy now at $250: $25 down and balance

171

in small monthly payments. All lots high, dry and level. Let us tell you more about Port Alberni. Write, call or phone: G. W. Braden, "The Port Alberni Land Man", 213 Eighth Ave. West, Calgary, Alberta.[75]

These kind of adventurers were common everywhere. Needless to say when Calgarians read this account in the Calgary *Daily Herald*, September 23, 1911, they would have been led to believe that Port Alberni would be a good place to invest or to live. Another advertisement that ran for several days in September 1911 read:

> We are the actual owners of Lot 46 and you can buy lots in this property at $150, $175. $200, or $250 now on terms of $10 cash, balance $10 monthly. No interest: No taxes: lots are 33 to 50 feet frontage by 120 feet. Every lot level and free from rock or stone. Suitable for Homes or business sites.
>
> An ocean port for the largest vessels afloat – $100 or $1,000 invested here will bring handsome profits. Better possibilities than early "Vancouver" had. Ask for the "Alberni Gazette" with 18 photos, maps, etc. Call and see the government maps and plans. They are convincing. If the CPR and CNR see millions in revenue here, it should look good to you. The CPR have ocean terminals there now. The CNR are building there. 400 men are at work on the CPR depot construction. A coal seam (Anthracite) is being developed in town.
>
> Port Alberni has sufficient resources at her door to support a 500,000 population. She is growing fast. What an opportunity for investment. A purchase of two or three inside lots now at the prices and terms offered by us will show exceedingly good profit within a year. The development of the town alone will do this. Business is good. Lots are moving off all the time. Get yours now.[76]

Inquiries began coming into the Board of Trade from people in the prairie provinces and as far east as Toronto, where the advertisements had also been seen. People were under the impression they could secure waterfront lots within the limits of "a future metropolis," or close to the boundaries, for little more than the trouble of putting down stakes and squatting on the property.[77]

There were many Calgarians who fell for the advertisements and sold all the family possessions they had in Calgary before moving west to Port Alberni. What they found was not exactly as advertised, much to their dismay. Those level lots free from rock or stone were still forested and far from ready to build on. There was little the families could do but make the best of it. So many Calgarians bought land at that time that one of the districts in Port Alberni was named Calgary district.

Joe Humphries slashed a right-of-way through forest and bush to 14th Avenue and Bute Street. There he built the home he would live in until his death in 1942. At one time he was in charge of the Somass Dairy Farm. He was also associated with the Alberni Land Company. Humphries served as foreman of the city works department. He was also alderman for four years.

Some of the other families included Warnock, Cochrane, Archer, Drummond, Powell, Brierley, and Cain. Warnock and Cochrane became contractors and built houses. Warnock became mayor of Port Alberni. Others went to work in the mills.[78]

W. Hirst, a rancher from Battleford, came looking for a chance to get settled on a nice piece of land where he could raise fruit, vegetables, and chickens. He brought with him his wife and child and his wife's sister. The group did not stay long; after one look around they headed back for Battleford. Hirst's farewell remarks intimated he had seen all he wanted to see of this future metropolis. He said the advertising that was circulated around Battleford was a gross misrepresentation of the conditions in the district.[79]

Everyone believed Port Alberni was destined for a great future. Another flurry of speculation followed the story "Port Alberni on the all red route." The project, first discussed at a Colonial Conference, focused on supplying the quickest possible transportation link between Great Britain, Canada, Australia, and New Zealand. The scheme appeared to gain prominence in 1911 when a powerful British company, the Imperial Steamship Co., announced it would translate the scheme into reality. It proposed a line of 25-knot steamers which would run between Blacksod Bay, on the west of Ireland, and Halifax, and 20-knot steamers which would ply between B.C. and Australia. Port Alberni, the nearest Canadian port to Australia, fully expected to become the Canadian terminus of the Pacific section of the route.[80]

The committee on municipal incorporation fully endorsed the "All Red Route." This decision was supported by Capt. J. D. Milliken, of the steamer *Tees*, who had made many trips through Barkley Sound and the Alberni Inlet. He approved entirely the proposed route. The only concern seemed to be whether the companies could handle the transcontinental part of the "All Red Route." Milliken predicted, "If one of the railways running into Port Alberni was to be used as part of the system there should be no trouble in having this port made a connecting point on the route."[81]

173

A pamphlet promoting the area was finally published by both boards of trade. The pamphlet contained a full-sized map of Vancouver Island, showing the advantageous position of Port Alberni to the various ocean routes, plus a quarter-page illustration showing the harbour and adjacent scenes. However, when the Victoria *Colonist* reported on the pamphlet's content, there was confusion over the names of the two towns. "Although this place is known as New Alberni and Alberni, it has been suggested that it be called Port Alberni."[82]

Of course, the *Colonist* had overlooked the information that the pamphlet was issued jointly by the New Alberni and Alberni Boards of Trade. An editorial in the *Pioneer News* took the *Colonist* to task, explaining the new name of Port Alberni was used for the purpose of distinguishing it as being located on the deep water harbour. "There has been no suggestion to add to or alter the name Alberni. There are now, and are likely to be for some time to come, two separate towns, Port Alberni and Alberni, the former being located on the deep water of the canal, the terminus of the E & N railway extension, and the latter on the Somass River which flows into the canal."[83]

In December 1909 Carmichael & Moorhead began work on clearing 140 acres of the Port Alberni townsite.

Alberni continued to watch Port Alberni grow. To say there was jealousy between the two would be putting it mildly. So anxious was Alberni to try and be one step ahead of Port Alberni, it almost by accident took steps towards incorporation. The incident happened when the Alberni Board of Trade met for its January 1910 meeting. After all the business had been dealt with, a motion to adjourn was made. Suddenly A. W. Neill interrupted the motion with a request for some information from the committee on incorporation. W. H. Marcon gave a brief outline of a proposed city which would encompass the settled and unsettled territory from the Redford Road north beyond Charles Taylor's place on River Road, and a few blocks back from the waterfront. He also produced a map with some figures on assessment.

There were only two out of the seven members present who did not know what either Neill or Marcon were talking about. One was Dick Burde, of the *Pioneer News*. He asked if the committee Marcon was speaking for was a Board of Trade creation. He was told it was not, but was a committee of a number of citizens who had held a hurried meeting in Neill's office two weeks before. The chairman of the old municipal committee had been advised of the meeting.

All attention was riveted on Marcon's map when Burde asked what status the matter had before the Board of Trade. "It has none", replied the chairman. A motion to adjourn was insisted upon and carried.

Somehow Capt. Huff and others believed they had caught wind of a movement to incorporate on the part of Port Alberni people. It was understood that the old town was not to be included in the scheme. The Captain and others were not going to be outdone. A few citizens, selected in a hurry, prepared to get a step ahead of the new town. When the Captain was satisfied the new town did not intend to ram through any snap incorporation plan, the old town proposition was shelved for the time being.

More and more the two towns were developing separately. When the letters from Alberni and Port Alberni reached London, Herbert Carmichael was empowered to speak for the Alberni Land Co. to both boards of trade. He assured them that once the clearing and surveying had been done, more lots would be available. The company was prepared to spend thousands of dollars on advertising as soon as the new lumber concerns which were coming to town began to build their mills.

Regarding Port Alberni's question about foreshore rights, Carmichael said the Alberni Land Co. had transferred the entire foreshore to the E & N Railway Co. He was instructed to oppose, on behalf of the former company, all applications for foreshore rights.

As for incorporation, the company recognized it would be necessary soon to incorporate if only to obtain a water system. Carmichael favoured beautifying the streets and laying out boulevards. He thought it a good plan to sustain a good municipal spirit, and to lay out a beautiful town where people would like to come and live. "This would at the same time mean dollars to the community," said Carmichael.[84] But there were some difficulties, financial and otherwise, in the way. He wanted the company's interests safeguarded.

In Alberni, Carmichael told the meeting the company was waiting for the best time to put lots on the market. But now that the E & N line was to be extended to Sproat Lake, the outlook for an early settlement of the "fruit lands" of the valley was promising. He felt it was time to get down to business. The fruit lands were large tracts of land designated at various points along the E & N railway line on Vancouver Island. This was a scheme by the railway company to sell land to settlers. In Alberni, the fruit lands were located in the Beaver Creek area.

Carmichael said it had been the company's original intention to have only one town, but it now appeared the best plan would be to allow two. "A little healthy rivalry would likely do more good than harm," he said. However, the company did not intend keeping uncleared land as a permanent barrier between the two towns, but would dispose of it as the demand justified.

Perhaps Carmichael was waving a carrot before the two boards of trade, when he said the company was anxious to stimulate outdoor sports. He proposed that five or ten acres of land be donated for recreation purposes. Five acres would be cleared and stumped at the company's expense. He suggested the athletic associations of the two towns should get together and agree on a halfway site that would be good for both places.

The next week, Alfred Carmichael, the local agent for the company, tried to interest the Alberni Agricultural Association in a scheme to have the athletic and fair grounds all in one. The Agricultural Association decided against it. It was now up to the Port Alberni Athletic Association and the Alberni Athletic Association to decide on a park site. They decided should Lot 1 be formed into one municipality, that when the municipality was formed, the land would be transferred to the municipality solely for a recreation park. The site chosen adjoined the Redford Road, a short distance from the waterfront. It was estimated to be about ten acres in size. Another thirteen acres would be held in reserve with an option to purchase.[85]

The Athletic Associations again decided to ask the Agricultural Association to cooperate with them, believing that not only would this provide a stronger force, but also the Alberni Land Co. would be inclined to be more generous. The Agricultural Association again declined.

Carmichael's speech to the Alberni Board of Trade did little to appease the businessmen who were becoming disenchanted. At a public meeting in March, James Thomson, secretary of the citizens committee appointed to deal with the Alberni Land Co. said the company was discriminating in favour of the new town. The letters of reply gave no satisfaction; they stated the company was being guided by the advice of its agent, Herbert Carmichael. Thomson suggested the two were not in touch with each other. There were some very unflattering comments made about the Land Co. before the committee was dissolved.

Fuel was added to the fire already burning in the old town when it was again left off a promotional map, only this time it was in an advertising folder issued by Carmichael and Moorhead. There was a map showing lots and subdivisions in the new town and district. Port Alberni was marked in large, bold letters. All that indicated Alberni was a P.O., meaning post office. Some of the residents decided to issue their own folder indicating the old town with all roads converging on it.

Was Dick Burde upset when he was excluded from the hurried citizens' committee of Alberni in January? There is no documented indication he was, but in May, he announced the *Alberni Pioneer News* would move to a new home in Port Alberni. Work on burning the stumps had already begun on Lots 11 and 12, fronting on Third Avenue. Burde's editorial in the same edition stressed that unity was necessary if the two towns hoped to become a major centre. "For the making of the new city the places are necessary to each other as are the head, the arms, the legs, to the trunk of a human body."[86]

When the plan of the townsite was first put on the market, some wondered why Third Avenue, the main thoroughfare, was not opened up all the way through to the old town. There had been promises that if it should, all the lots would be immediately sold. The plans now had been enlarged to take in two blocks north of the Redford Road. Burde speculated it would be only a matter of time before all of the old town was included. "When the residents of the respective towns are able to get a good, clear look at each other without having to travel a mile and a half over a winding road through tall and thick timbers, they will see more plainly how they are inseparable parts of a whole."[87]

Despite their differences, the two towns got together on July 1, 1910, to celebrate Canada's national holiday.

At a special meeting of the Port Alberni Board of Trade in July, an application for a water record on China Creek was endorsed. The application, from the China Creek Water and Power Syndicate, was signed by Leonard Frank. The group, which included Waterhouse, A. D. MacIntyre, Dick Burde, Dr. Morgan, Gus Cox, W. W. G. McAllister, and Leonard Frank, planned to work with Colin Murray and his associates, who had applied for a water power right on the creek for gold dredging. Murray's application would be withdrawn in favor of the present application, and a joint stock company of both interests would be formed. The syndicate planned to supply electric light for both the old and new towns.[88]

A visit on July 23, 1910, by Dr. H. K. Anderson, from London, outlined the Alberni Land Company's position for Alberni residents. He said the company's interest had been changed since the building of the railroad. When overtures were made by the CPR to the Alberni Land Company, it made sacrifices freely in order to allow the CPR to build. Part of that grant made was two hundred acres for factories, wharfs, and millsites to build up the town. One thing the company could not control, said Anderson, was population. He did not think it wise to sell lots and have no people. The CPR fixed its site for wharfs. "Alberni is specially blessed in having so much agricultural land adjacent," he told the meeting.[89]

When Neill questioned Anderson about land for industries, predicting industries were sure to start when men began to exploit the forest wealth, Anderson replied, "The Alberni Land Co. had the development of industries in view when it arranged with the CPR, believing this would be a seaport." The Alberni Land Co. had reserved five hundred acres across the river for future development and would give assistance to establish industries. When asked how many industries had applied, he replied, "Only one."[90]

Why should Alberni delay incorporation? asked Marcon. The CPR had chosen the deep water for their terminals; the Alberni Land Company had nothing to do with it, Anderson replied. He said he regretted the distrust of his company by the people. However, the company wanted to make some profit out of the land after holding it for so many years, and didn't want to be taxed out of existence if a municipality were formed. "The CPR are partners with us. We will follow the lead of the CPR, and it may be, this end (Alberni) may have to wait a little longer before being developed than the other." He said the company wanted only one town for the whole townsite. As to the time for incorporation, this was chiefly for the people to decide. However, if and when they did incorporate, the company wanted to have the local improvement plan, similar to that in Oak Bay and North Vancouver.[91]

With the company's position clearly outlined, the Alberni Board of Trade again directed its attention to the location of the railway station. A memorandum to the CPR, dated September 2, 1910, read:

> 1) that Mr. Marpole having stated that a station would be where the railway crosses Johnson Road, this board would suggest that the station be built near Rogers Creek on the Scotch Settlement Road, as it would be only a short distance from the centre of town and a level road. As the bulk of freight arriving at Port Alberni comes to Alberni, and camps north and

east of the town, as it is the nearest point to get to Sproat Lake and Great Central Lake for tourists and residents there, we urge that an up-to-date station building be erected.

2) Some time ago the owners along Gertrude Street were asked to consent to the railway of the proposed Lakes Branch being built along this street. Not sufficient time being given for consideration, their consent was not obtained. We believe that if negotiations were opened again, there would be no difficulty in securing consent of owners, and that this board would facilitate this matter to the best of its ability. On the alternate proposed Lakes Branch, the board strongly disapproves of the placing of a bridge across the Somass River between the wharf at the foot of Johnston Road and the mouth of the river, as it will impede and may obstruct navigation in the river.[92]

Another memorandum from the Alberni Board of Trade to the Alberni Land Co. stated the board wanted all streets in the townsite of Alberni to be opened up, slashed, stumped, and rough graded; the triangular piece of land lying north of Nanaimo Road to be sub-divided into lots; and a recreation park to be set aside along Rogers Creek with athletic grounds across the Somass River, opposite the Indian Reserve. Also requested were ten to twenty acres to be set apart from the company farm, which would become a Model Farm for the cultivation of grains, grasses, vegetables, and horticulture. This was expected to increase the value of the farm property, an excellent advertisement for people coming into Alberni.

By September, plans for the E & N Railway wharf at Port Alberni had been accepted, and building was expected to begin soon. The wharf would be located between Waterhouse's wharf and Argyle Street. The railway company announced a tri-weekly train service between Victoria and Cameron Lake would begin October 3rd. A station was being built at the lake.

The Port Alberni Board of Trade moved to incorporate the town in November, 1910. By then, even the Alberni Land Co. had come to realize the need for municipal incorporation. When it was pointed out to the board that with the assistance of the company an area of townsite embracing assessment values amounting to $800,000 could be brought into the scheme, Alfred Carmichael, representing the Land Co., said his company was willing to do what it could to assist incorporation. A committee composed of Waterhouse, Robert Blandy, A. D. Cooper, Dr. C. T. Hilton, and Alfred Carmichael was appointed to take the matter further.[93]

The committee reported back to the board in December. A tentative estimate placed the minimum revenue of the city at $15,000 in land taxation, while the government revenue from any probable city area if left unincorporated would be $9,000 in the year 1911. This was expected to be increased by over $3,000 the following year. The chief disadvantages of incorporation would be a possible increase in land taxation and the loss of government expenditure on roads. In 1910, the government had spent $7,700 on roads south of Rogers Creek, but less than $3,000 per annum in previous years.

By the end of 1910, much of the work on the Port Alberni extension of the railway from Cameron Lake station to the terminus was almost finished. Soon many of the engineers would be leaving the area. To celebrate the occasion the E & N Railway engineers held a "break-up" dinner in the Somass Hotel.

On March 6, 1911, the Alberni Board of Trade was still concerned about the location of its railway station. A motion by Matt Ward suggesting the station be located where the railway intersects with Johnson Road was carried.

In June, 1911, the *Port Alberni Gazette* was published by the Port Alberni Board of Trade. The advertisement publication promoted the city as having a shining future. "Port Alberni, A Flourishing City – The Place for a Home and Opportunity," read the headlines. There was little mention of Alberni.

A notice to incorporate appeared in the *Alberni Pioneer News* on September 9, 1911:

> Take notice that A. E. Waterhouse, A. D. Cooper, A. D. MacIntyre and others intend to apply for incorporation as a City Municipality, to be named Port Alberni; the land to be included within the limits of the proposed municipality is as follows:
> Lots 45, 46, 91 and 113, Alberni Land District, and that portion of Lot one, between the south bank of Rogers Creek and a line running from the S.W. corner of block 95, Lot one easterly to the east boundary of said Lot one, comprising an area of about 2,000 acres.
> Signed – A. E. Waterhouse, A. D. Cooper, A. D. MacIntyre, petitioners, Port Alberni, B.C. August 22, 1911.

The application of Port Alberni to incorporate was discussed at the September meeting of the Alberni board. It was reported the Alberni Land Co. would not wish to include Alberni in the proposed municipality. The first motion proposed that the property owners of Alberni had no present intention of incorporation. They opposed the inclusion of any of Alberni's natural territory in the proposed municipality of Port Alberni. After considerable discussion, when everyone had expressed their views, the first motion was withdrawn. A new one introduced by Neill, and seconded by Jas. R. Motion, that the board hold a meeting September 5 and invite all citizens to be present, was passed.

There were thirty-five residents present at the meeting when Marcon outlined the revenue that would be derived from an area to be incorporated with Alberni. He moved that Alberni should form a municipality. A committee should be formed to proceed with the necessary preliminaries. The motion was eventually withdrawn after some discussion. On a motion by Huff, the meeting decided to protest to the Lieutenant Governor in Council regarding Port Alberni's application to incorporate. A committee of Huff, John Frank Bledsoe (a former financial editor of the *Vancouver World* who had decided to settle in Alberni), and Thomson was appointed to get data regarding municipal incorporation.

There was also overwhelming objection to the lines drawn by the Port Alberni applicants, who wanted to make Rogers Creek their boundary for some distance back from the waterfront. Alberni residents thought it was unfair to have the boundary line so drawn as to shut them off from street access to the south side of the creek where they wanted to have a railway station and freight sheds in the future.

In November, Bledsoe reported back to the board that his committee had met with a similar committee from Port Alberni, "whose attitude was one of indifference to the request of the Alberni board for inclusion in the proposed municipality, or for alterations of the proposed boundaries." He said the government had been informed of the attitude of Port Alberni.[94] The government decided against the petition from Alberni to have the boundary changed in the application for incorporation from Port Alberni.

Alberni's first labour strike occurred in October 1911 when Henry Frenette stood on a soapbox on Argyle Street and Kingsway to try to persuade thirty-four loggers in the Carmichael and Moorhead camp to go on a one-day strike for better working conditions. Frenette had tried unsuccessfully to have every wage earner in town stop work on the same day. The community went about its work uninterested in the strike.

Henry Frenette was a member of the Industrial Workers of the World (IWW). The IWW union, or the "Wobblies" as the workers were nicknamed, had been formed in Chicago in 1905. Frenette was protesting the trial of American worker John J. McNamara accused of bombing the *Los Angeles Times*. He said "capitalists were attempting to murder him by law. One workingman's interest was the same as another," he said, "all should stand together." He argued the best means of protest was a general strike which would show workingmen were strong.[95] When he was challenged on some of his arguments and asked to produce his credentials, Frenette's sister-in-law stepped up on the soapbox.

"You are a lot of dopes. You are a bunch of working stiffs. The capitalist is robbing you. Every day you work, he makes $8.30 profit on you and you get just enough to buy the bare necessities of life," said Mrs. Frenette. When she finished her speech, Henry got on the box again. By this time the crowd began to disperse, bored with the proceedings. After claiming the crowd didn't show much sense, he picked up his soapbox and left, stating if anyone else wanted to make a speech they could find their own box.

The strikers returned to work the next morning, but the trouble continued in the camp. Special Constable Stephens had to arrest two of the strikers in the evening. By the end of the week, Walter Harris, manager of the camp, fired five of the men who had been causing the most trouble. The whole work crew went out in sympathy, and the camp was closed temporarily.

The following week the *Alberni Pioneer News* printed the aims and objectives of the IWW and an editorial as well. The IWW position:

> The working class and the employing class have nothing in common. There can be no peace so long as hunger and want are found among millions of working people and the few, who make up the employing class, have all the good things in life. Between these two classes, a struggle must go on until the workers of the world organize as a class, take possession of the earth and the machinery of production, and abolish the wage system.

Burde editorialized October 14th:

> Sincere and honest people ought to understand each other better. The *Pioneer News* trusts that its every reader has an interest in the improvement of the condition of the workingman and woman and all the rest of humanity as well. The IWW method has appealed to a large number of people, and it is the duty of all to whom it does not appeal to seriously consider the necessity of counter action.

After the strikers left the community, work resumed at the camp. Alberni had had its first brush with a union organization.

Meanwhile, the Christmas present everyone in the Valley had been waiting for finally arrived when the first passenger train over the Port Alberni extension of the E & N Railway arrived at the terminal at 4:25 p.m. on Wednesday December 20, 1911. The train included E & N vice-president Marpole's private car "Nanoose," three passenger coaches, a baggage and an express car – all pulled by engine

No. 494. The conductor was P. Fletcher, the brakemen were H. Williams and W. Pinson, Harry Austin was the locomotive engineer and L. Davis was fireman.[96]

The train had left Victoria at 9:00 a.m. carrying thirty passengers. It picked up more at Nanaimo and other stops along the line. Four of the passengers left the train on its arrival at the Alberni station where the whole town had gathered to give it welcome. The others continued on to Port Alberni, the terminus, where they were greeted by a similar gathering.[97]

The names of those who travelled in the first passenger train included Dr. and Mrs. Lewis Hall, Victoria; R. W. Lindsay, Alberni, with a friend, Walter Grieve, Salmon Arm; Mr. and Mrs. Wm. Russell, Victoria; Wm. Duncan, Victoria; G. S. Seaton, Vancouver; T. P. McConnell, Victoria; C. J. McCrae, Uchucklesit (Kildonan); T. B. McBey, Cameron Lake; R. Bitten, C. N. Ry, W. R. Chandle, Vancouver; Capt. Geo. Heater, Victoria; J. W. Graham, Victoria; S. McB. Smith, Victoria; D. Stephenson, Nanaimo; Judge Futcher, Victoria; Al Davis, Nanaimo.[98]

No special celebration marked the occasion because it was the middle of winter. However, the following April a special train left Victoria for Port Alberni under the joint auspices of the two cities' Boards of Trade. The locomotive was decked out with flags and streamers. Passengers included CPR officials, politicians, civic and industrial dignitaries, their wives and families. The train pulled into the station to the music of the brass band. The reception committee waiting included MPP J. G. Wood and Mayor Arthur E. Waterhouse. Speeches of welcome were given before a crowd of citizens, and there were handshakes all around.

The ceremony, in front of the Somass Hotel, was temporarily interrupted by a near tragedy. The brass band was playing on the bandstand located nearby. To obtain a better view about fifty children swarmed on to the bandstand roof. The sound of breaking timbers was heard, and the bandstand began to tilt. A mad scramble followed as bandsmen and children jumped clear. Fortunately no one was hurt. The supporting timbers had broken under the heavy weight. Meanwhile the speeches continued and the band continued playing on the street.

The visiting guests were later taken on a trip down the Alberni Inlet to an area near Franklin River where construction crews were at work on the Canadian Northern Pacific Railway. There they were treated to a champagne lunch in one of the big mess halls. Immediately afterwards, from a safe distance out in the Inlet, guests watched as one of the biggest charges of dynamite ever exploded in Canada blew half a hillside into the sea.

Back in Port Alberni the visitors attended a banquet where they heard more speeches before beginning the return journey to Victoria. The railway had been officially welcomed into the Albernis in grand style.[99]

The January 2, 1912 meeting of the Alberni Board was a subdued affair, with little progress reported on efforts to have the Port Alberni boundary changed. In other business, Leonard Frank urged the board to ask the Vancouver Island Development League (VIDL) to take strong action with the provincial government regarding the completion of a road via Sproat Lake and Kennedy Lake to Ucluelet and Long Beach at the earliest possible date. The delegates also urged the completion of the Great Central Lake Road.[100] The annual meeting of the VIDL did endorse the road to the west coast.

Meanwhile, the property owners of Port Alberni met to emphatically declare themselves against any municipal union with Alberni. Burde reported the meeting "was highly charged with a mixture of indignation and determination."[101] George Bird presented a petition signed by sixty property owners objecting to the inclusion of the old town. Robert Wood said the petition was a misrepresentation; the people who signed it did not know what they were signing. He said it was first proposed the old town be taken into the municipality by requisition after the first year. This proposition had been approved by Herbert Carmichael for the Alberni Land Co. Now, he said, there was a disposition to shut the old town out altogether. Waterhouse had no recollection of any original proposition to take the old town in. A. W. Neill, of Alberni, appealed for union.

Then Alexander D. MacIntyre made a motion which would exclude the old Alberni settlement. Wood countered with an amendment to incorporate the whole of Alberni into a city and build a high school. Besides, the Alberni Land Co. had promised to donate a city block for the school, the list price being $7,800. The provincial secretary had promised that if the people of the district would get together the government would provide a high school on the Redford Road. Wood said he had little hope his amendment would be carried, considering the charged meeting, but he wanted to go on record. As he predicted, MacIntyre's resolution was carried. Wood and four others did not vote; only Neill and P. R. C. Bayne, both residents of Alberni, stood up to be counted against. Wood tendered his resignation as a member of the municipal committee, and George Bird was elected in his place.

The Alberni Board of Trade had been attempting to get a newspaper into production, and they finally succeeded. On February 10, 1912, the printing plant arrived by steamer and was immediately installed. The first issue of the *Alberni Advocate* hit the newsstand March 8, 1912, under editor and manager John Frank Bledsoe. It was published by the Alberni Advocate Printing and Publishing Co. A one year subscription to the *Advocate* cost two dollars.

Bledsoe had had a nomadic early life. Shortly after the American Civil War, his father sold out his estate, which had been ruined by the war. He bought a wagon train and headed for California, taking his young son along. Halfway across the continent, on the famous old Oregon Trail, the father died. Bledsoe roamed all over the American southwest as a buffalo hunter, wagon freighter, and prospector. His son Frank said his father told him stories of the old west in the frontier days. He claimed to know Buffalo Bill Cody, the outlaw Billy the Kid, and the famous marshalls Bat Masterson and Wild Bill Hickok.

Finally John Bledsoe drifted to California and worked on the *San Francisco Chronicle*. Moving north, he sometimes worked as a miner, sometimes on newspapers. It was as a newspaperman that he first came to B.C. to work, joining the Victoria *Colonist* in the late 1890s. But the lure of mining drew him to Alberni to inspect the gold mines then operating on China Creek and Mineral Hill. He returned to the USA as a representative in the west for a New York mining syndicate.

Before long Bledsoe was back in B.C. as the financial editor of the *Vancouver World*. From Vancouver he made many trips to Alberni before he decided to build a home and settle. He built the former Tidebrook home, now occupied by the Riverside restaurant. When the opportunity presented itself, he began publishing the *Alberni Advocate.*[102]

Burde now had competition. He changed the name of his newspaper from the *Alberni Pioneer News* to the *Port Alberni News*. Meanwhile, to show support for the new newspaper, the Alberni Board of Trade took out advertising in the *Advocate* for a twelve-month period. The advertisement would show the advantages of Alberni and district. Headlines in the first edition read: "Alberni will be on the main line of the C.N.P. Railway on Vancouver Island."

Alberni would make an ideal terminus for the Trans-Canada Highway, the Alberni board reasoned, and so wrote, putting forth a strong argument in favour of this proposal. The planting of a post signifying the terminus of the new highway would be a historic event. Therefore a committee was appointed to take care of entertaining the guests expected to arrive for the event. A special edition of the *Alberni Advocate* would be published and "any deficit would be met by the Alberni Board of Trade."[103]

Government moved slowly, but Port Alberni residents were out to show they meant business. On March 9, 1912, they chartered a special train to take them to Victoria to press their intent to incorporate. The train was festooned with banners painted by local sign writer Tom Costen, trumpeting slogans such as "We Want Incorporation" and "Watch Port Alberni Grow." Waterhouse was the spokesman for the "monster delegation, 33 in number"[104] which met with cabinet ministers.

Alberni had not given up hopes of being included inside the Port Alberni boundary. The following day Alberni sent its own delegation to Victoria. It included James Motion, A. W. Neill, and H. H. Browne. After hearing both sides, Premier McBride announced in favour of Port Alberni. There would be no change in the boundary.

The Victoria *Colonist* reported:

> The new city of Port Alberni is the fifth city to obtain incorporation on Vancouver Island. Great developments in the way of railway enterprise, lumbering and mining are now taking place in the district. The CPR has completed it's connection with the town, and the Canadian Northern Pacific has surveyed its line through to the southern boundary of the new city. The B.C. Telephone has installed a local service during the past few months.[105]

While the Alberni District Brass Band played "inspiring music," on March 12, 1912 the lieutenant governor of B.C. put his signature on the document creating Port Alberni as an incorporated city. The birthday of the new city was spontaneously celebrated when one enthusiastic citizen ran up the national flag. Other flags followed and before long there were flags everywhere in town. That evening, a public meeting was held in Watson's Hall, in the basement of the Port Alberni Hotel. Speeches were delivered by A. D. Cooper, Robert De Beaux, and Dick Burde. A concert program was provided by the brass band. Along one side of the hall was strung a banner, "Welcome to our City." The sign was contributed by E. M. Scoffin, the painter and decorator.

A week later the registered owners of the land within the limits of Port Alberni met to nominate a mayor and six aldermen. If an agreement could be reached, there need be no formal contest. If seven candidates were nominated, they would be declared elected by acclamation.

Returning officer Robert Blandy, before a small and quiet gathering at noon on March 25, read the proclamation for the first municipal election. The meeting was held in the Permanent Exhibit building located at the southwest corner of Argyle Street and Kingsway. For the past three years it had been used as a meeting place for the Port Alberni Board of Trade. There were nine people nominated, but two of the candidates did not show up. At 2:00 p.m. there was only one candidate for mayor and six for aldermen. "I do announce that the name of Arthur Edward Waterhouse has been put in nomination as candidate for mayor," proclaimed Blandy.[106] Aldermen nominated included George Hubert Bird, Frank Herbert Swayne, Alexander Duncan MacIntyre and his brother Joseph Albert MacIntyre, Robert McGinley Ellis, and Alexander Duff Cooper.

The MacIntyre brothers came to Alberni in 1909 from Saskatchewan. Both had been members of the legislature of the territory of Saskatchewan. In New Alberni, Joseph went into the building and contracting business, while Alexander began a hardware business. Frank Swayne left Ireland in 1907 and joined the Canadian Bank of Commerce staff in Toronto. In 1909 he joined the Port Alberni firm of Carmichael & Moorhead. Alexander Cooper came to Port Alberni in 1907 from Ladysmith; he operated a real estate and insurance business on Third Avenue. Robert Ellis arrived in 1901 from Calgary and worked in the building and contracting business.

On March 27, 1912, all were declared elected by acclamation. A ward system was implemented later in the year; there were six wards, each with its own representative on council. Only Alderman Bird thought two wards would have been sufficient for the town.

New City of Port Alberni

The following week, the first council of the new City of Port Alberni sat for the first time. At the noon meeting His Worship Mayor Waterhouse gave a brief speech congratulating the councillors on their election and promising that "all would work out in amity and unity for the city's good." The first motion was to obtain an official seal for the city. Later the urgent matter of street levels came up for discussion. The first official picture was taken by Leonard Frank. The inscription "Permanent Exhibit," which appears directly over the heads of the group in this photo, refers not to the council, but to the name of the hall in which council held its first meeting.

Two designs from Mrs. Thos. Collinge were considered for the city seal. Finally a combination of the two drawings was chosen. The motto of the new city would be "Perseverance and Prosperity." Collinge was paid fifteen dollars for the design. This was the first account paid by the city. The seal itself was made in Seattle and cost eighteen dollars, plus the cost of a special messenger who brought the seal from Seattle to Victoria.[107]

When the question of a city clerk came up, the press was asked to withdraw. Waterhouse suggested it would be better if council were to talk over this question privately. Dick Burde was there representing the *Port Alberni News*, and S. C. Platt reporting for the *Alberni Advocate*. "Is it your will that we should retire," asked Burde, speaking for both. "Then your worship, I must question your authority and assert my right to be present and remain as long as this is a regular meeting of the council."[108]

Waterhouse smiled an acknowledgement and turned to the *pro tem* city clerk Robert F. Blandy for advice. Blandy proceeded to pore over a copy of the Municipal Act. The mayor read aloud the section in which it was stipulated that all regular meetings of the council should be open and that the power of expulsion was limited to cases of disorderly conduct. Mayor Waterhouse abandoned the idea of privacy for the time being. Council decided to place an advertisement in the paper inviting applications. Blandy got the job at seventy-five dollars a month.

The *Alberni Advocate* watched carefully the happenings with the new council and cheerfully reported any difficulties the council might be having in establishing its credibility. One such report suggested there might be "serious trouble on hand, with more to come."[109] It seemed Alderman Cooper viewed with alarm the idea of the city clerk Blandy "chasing around over the country with all the visible possessions of the city tucked away in his vest pocket," and suggested that a safe be purchased at once. To this came the reply that there were no funds and no credit at any bank for the purchase of the safe.

It was proposed to place an immediate tax on pool rooms, dogs and editors, for the purpose of securing the needed funds. It was not explained whether or not the suggested means of revenue were to be regarded as of value in the order named. The finance committee is facing the problem of

188

whether it is best to buy a safe and have nothing left to put into it, or still take a chance on the vest pocket of Mr. Blandy.

The committee of public safety is also causing some worry. Not even the mayor appears to know what the functions of this committee are but suggests that pending an investigation the committee might be employed in guarding Mr. Blandy from any bold highwayman who might attempt to steal the sketch of the City Seal. Ald. Cooper remarked, "Well, if we have no money, gentlemen, I don't see the use of us staying here any longer. We might as well go home."[110]

By June Port Alberni City Council had received notification of its first grant of $5,000 from the province to discharge all financial obligations. Council already had a request for $100 from the Alberni District Brass band to purchase music. Two weeks earlier it had been announced a bandstand would be erected in the neighbourhood of city hall where a program of open air concerts would be given during the summer months. The Canadian Pacific Lumber Company had agreed to supply the lumber. The remainder of the cost would be raised by public subscriptions.[111]

For weeks the finance committee had struggled along with no money. Then a Temporary Loan bylaw was passed which gave the city a credit of $1,000 in the Royal Bank of Canada. But this lasted like "a handful of snowflakes in a Chinook breeze," reported Dick Burde in the *Port Alberni News*. When the provincial cheque finally arrived it was enclosed with a letter from the Minister of Finance, which "begged to enclose a check of $5,000." A grateful alderman worried about how council was going to pay for the new uniform for the Chief of Police remarked, "He need not have apologized."[112]

In June a volunteer fire brigade was organized. The men proudly turned out at the CPR wharf for the first practice with the new chemical engine, a fifty gallon Ajax, under the direction of Chief Richard Venables. The engine, along with ladder, truck, hose reel, and fire buckets, had been obtained from the City of New Westminster. When there was a fire, the horses were supplied by Sam Roseborough. The engine was kept in a shed alongside Roseborough's barn, the rest of the equipment standing outside. The firemen included Frank Harrison, Charlie Fawcitt, Alf Kneen, Henry Porritt, Harry Neal, Pete Johnson, Dave Owen, Freddie Cole, Percy Drakes, George Bird Jr., and John R. Thomson.[113]

The only pay the men received was the ten dollars that went to the first team to reach the engine and be hitched up. In the majority of alarms Frank Harrison reached the engine first, but at times it was Freddie Cole.[114] A month after the brigade was formed, on July 24, the engine was called to a real fire of burning stumps and logs. The blaze was quickly put out.

A fire bell was obtained and erected on a wooden tower. Bucket stands were provided at strategic points around the city.[115] When there was a fire, an alarm was telephoned to the exchange managed by Harry Mertz. He, or someone on duty, would run across to the corner, ring the alarm, then run down the street to the barn to tell the fireman where the fire was located. The bell tower was later wrecked in a wind storm.

The first fire of any size was on February 8, 1913, at the C. Frederic Bishop residence on Southgate Street. There was a foot of snow on the ground when the call came in at 11:45 p.m. Frank Harrison had to use a four-horse team to get over to Alberni. The trip took fifteen minutes. The bucket brigade and buckets were brought over by stage, but when they arrived there was nothing that could be done. The house was totally engulfed by flames. The fire was caused by a small coal oil stove being placed too close to window curtains.

A request for a fire building to house the engine had gone to city council the week before. Richard Venables served as fire chief from 1912-1914.

The Old Town Incorporates

Two months after the City of Port Alberni became incorporated, hundreds gathered under clear, sunny skies in Alberni for the installation of a post commemorating the terminus of the Trans-Canada Highway, a project of the Canadian Highway Association, at the foot of Johnston Road at Victoria Quay. The post, with the letter "E" on it, would face any traveller coming from Port Alberni, Beaver Creek, or Sproat Lake. The Alberni District Brass Band was on hand to liven things up, and about one hundred automobiles crowded Johnston Road. The Reverend Carruthers in his formal address to the gathering said, "This day you (the Canadian Highway Association) have given birth to a great national idea, which I have no doubt shall continue to live as long as the hills with which we this day are surrounded. Now it is "Eastward Ho!" and I can already see your roadway rising away above the great belt of Alberni timber on through the undazzling gold of grain, on till ocean's roar falls upon the ear."[116]

The honour of planting the post went to W. J. Kerr, the president of the Canadian Highway Association. Kerr said:

The ceremony that has gathered us here is one which will long be remembered in the annals of Canadian road building. The planting of this post, on the shores of the Pacific, is an event too important to be lightly considered. The building of this trans-continental highway is a serious undertaking, one that calls for energy, enterprise, and concentration. The planting of this post on the west coast of Vancouver Island is a fitting tribute to the spirit of the west. This is a mighty undertaking but the men of the west are the men who do big things. The building of a cross-Canada road would have been an impossibility twenty-five years ago. Today, there is no big obstacle in its way.

In the audience were Mayor Beckwith of Victoria; Mayor Shaw and former Mayor Planta, both of Nanaimo; H. S. Clements, Member of Parliament for Alberni, and F. H. Shepherd, a visiting Member of Parliament; John G. C. Wood, Provincial Member for Alberni; and W. W. Foster, Deputy Minister of Works. Present by special invitation were Mayor Waterhouse and the City Council of Port Alberni.

The small farming community of Alberni had scored a major coup, and it was justifiably proud. Everyone praised Alberni for securing the post as well as the beautiful drive now open to residents of Nanaimo. Mayor Beckwith said the development of Vancouver Island was the one thing both places had to work for. Then the Mayor of Nanaimo claimed it was Nanaimo who gave Alberni the first chance to exist. "And if for no other reason, Nanaimo would always take a friendly interest in the welfare and progress of the town being honoured. The flow of tourists to Alberni would all have to go through Nanaimo," the coal-city Mayor reasoned.

Perhaps the only newsworthy announcement to come out of the historic event was the announcement by Foster that Strathcona Park was to be opened up and the road to Long Beach was to get underway without delay. Alberni was destined to become the centre for tourist travel to the middle and western sections of Vancouver Island.

Bledsoe, chairman of the event, was happy it had gone off without a hitch. He incensed Port Alberni residents by warning them against laying envious eyes upon the post. "A large bulldog would be chained to the post to protect the symbol," he said.

His warnings – perhaps his challenge – went without notice, as the post was spirited away during the night and replanted in Port Alberni at the corner of Argyle and Kingsway, where for two hours it remained undisturbed. When Mayor Waterhouse heard about it, he ordered a delivery wagon to return the post to Alberni. The incident was closed as far as the mayor was concerned.[117]

Five days later, just before a council meeting, the chief constable of Alberni arrived, prepared to arrest the mayor and aldermen. He presented them with summons, claiming they had been harbouring stolen property. He reasoned the post had been found suspiciously close to the mayor's store. A stay was allowed when Waterhouse explained the post had been returned to Alberni.[118]

Reports of the post stealing were carried in the Victoria *Times*, the Victoria *Colonist*, the *Vancouver Province*, the *Nanaimo Herald*, the *Vancouver World*, and the *Vancouver Sun*. Waterhouse even received a telegram from the Canadian Highway Association. "Press reports post removed to Port Alberni. Sincerely hope it is incorrect." The next day another telegram arrived: "Please wire answer to my question regarding moving post. Important." It was signed, P. W. Luce. Waterhouse replied the post had been returned the following morning.[119]

In June, Sir Kenneth Anderson of the Alberni Land Co. met with the Alberni Board of Trade and was told of "all the promises made before and not kept, and all the things needed for the benefit of the town."[120] Seven requests were presented to the English gentleman. The board wanted better railway facilities and some designated recreation ground. There were lots not subdivided and streets not graded as promised. There was a need to clear and burn scrub timbers. The board wanted the title to the public park secured. Finally, Anderson was asked to provide a subscription to the water works company.

On the matter of the railway facilities, Sir Kenneth promised to use his influence with Marpole of the CPR, but the subdividing of the remaining land and placing lots on the market would depend on incorporation. He thought it would be difficult to find a suitable site for recreation purposes. It was the question of incorporation that caused the greatest amount of discussion. Sir Kenneth emphatically stressed his unwillingness to have the land across the Somass River, the Anderson Farm, taken into the municipality. "The land is absolutely farming land," Sir Kenneth informed them. A heated discussion took place involving Neill, Motion, Bishop, Huff, Riddell, Bledsoe, and Tebo.[121]

The meeting must have left a bitter taste in the mouth of Sir Kenneth, because a week later on June 10th, he again met with the board. The first item of business was an explanation by the chairman that there were no hostile feelings towards the Alberni Land Company. The board hoped everyone would work for the benefit of the town. Sir Kenneth apologized for misconstruing the feelings of Alberni towards the Land Company. During the meeting he agreed to withdraw any opposition to incorporation if the land reserved for the farm was omitted from the municipal boundary.[122]

Meeting with Sir Kenneth Anderson had been fruitful for the Alberni Board of Trade, which now turned its attention to the CPR and tried to flex some muscle there. The Railway Commission decided not to hold a sitting in Western Canada this year, but the board was adamant it would get its point across. Bledsoe wrote:

> The data which has been collected shows plainly that Alberni has been and is now being, subjected to the most petty of all petty campaigns of slight and annoyance on the part of the railway company that is supposed to be built for the benefit of the public and not to further the individual ends of a few officials.
>
> There may have been a time when it was unwise to voice a resentment against any of the methods of the CPR no matter how arbitrary those methods may have been. That time is past. When a company comes forward claiming, and getting what amounts to practical exemption from taxation over a vast area of their holdings, it is right to require that this company show some inclination to listen to the just demands of the public for service that is something more than a name.[123]

About this time, a petition for incorporation was circulated in Alberni. John George Corry Wood, a Conservative, had just been elected to the provincial legislature for the Alberni Electoral District.

There was reason for optimism in Alberni that spring, as a road program for the summer had been announced. Two road crews were now working on the Nanaimo-Alberni road, widening and improving the roadbed from Cameron Lake. An appropriation of $5000 was being requested for the rebuilding of the government wharf to enable freight to be landed at Alberni. But the irritant over the railway station still bothered the Alberni board and prompted this tongue-in-cheek editorial by Bledsoe.

> What has become of the suggestion that the Alberni "station" of the E & N Railway be placed on wheels so that it can more easily be moved out of the way when the hotel rigs desire to turn around. (These were the horse and carriages sent by the hotels to pick up passengers at the station) The counter suggestion of placing handles on the corners of the "building" so that it can be lifted out of the way, has been made, but there is little to recommend it. In the first place it would require four men for this purpose, one at each corner, while by having the wheels one man could manage the job quite nicely. These suggestions should be put in practice at an early date. As the Company is too poor to carry out any such extensive alterations, it is suggested that the same method be used as that which provided the "station" with a sign, namely a public subscription.[124]

The Alberni Board met with CPR vice president Marpole and his divisional engineer Beasley regarding their grievances. The meeting did not accomplish much. Marpole said the present freight and passenger traffic did not warrant the expense of two agents or telegraph operators, but it was up to the Alberni people to make the volume of freight so good, as to compel the company to increase staffing. This comment made the board more than ever determined to present their grievances to the Railway Commission.

Finally, on July 30th, the meeting with Railway Commissioner Scott took place in Victoria. Board representative James R. Motion presented a list of twelve complaints. Accommodation at the station was inadequate for the amount of travel to and from Alberni. Motion argued there was more mail handled there than at any station north of Nanaimo, despite the fact there was no CPR operator or ticket agent to assist in shipping and receiving goods. No tickets were issued for Alberni. There were no means of getting return tickets from Alberni further than Wellington. More complaints dealt with the length of time the train was at the station and the lack of freight accommodation. Alberni was left out of the classified rates printed by the CPR. Considering the amount of freight shipped to Alberni and the high cost of obtaining freight from the nearest freight shed, this was unacceptable to Alberni businessmen.[125]

Motion claimed deliberate discrimination against the Old Town. After he had made his presentation, Commissioner Scott stated, "It looks like a case of the railway company exercising their power to get even when they do not get what they want."[126]

Marpole, the railway representative at the meeting, interjected that the mistake of not having rates given for Alberni had occurred through a confusion of names on the part of the passengers. But the commissioner refused to believe it saying "Old Alberni was known before Port Alberni." Marpole denied discrimination. Motion said the CPR was ignoring Old Alberni because the residents of the town would not allow the CPR to occupy the Gertrude Street route for their line. "Ever since then there has been trouble with them." Marpole argued that Port Alberni had been known first when the Anderson sawmill was there in 1860. To which Motion replied that Old Alberni had been planned in 1887, while the new town had not been planned until 1896. "The CPR favours them, because it owns three miles of waterfront of Port Alberni." Another argument that arose between the two sides was based on the danger of the Johnston Street crossing.

Commissioner Scott decided to send an engineer to investigate the matter.[127]

In August, engineer T. L. Simmons arrived, but passed right through Alberni. Not even taking the time to meet the committee, which he had wired of his coming, Simmons proceeded through to Port Alberni leaving the committee of Motion, Mike Tebo, and John F. Bledsoe standing at the Alberni station waiting for him. The engineer was accompanied by two representatives of the CPR, H. E. Beasley and R. A. Bainbridge. Beasley, the divisional engineer, was becoming a familiar figure in Alberni from his previous visits with the Board of Trade over the railway station location. It wasn't until the next morning the Alberni committee had the opportunity of meeting Simmons.

The three visitors, with the Alberni contingent, toured the Alberni station and the crossing on Johnston Road. Beasley thought that something could be done to the crossing. "He admitted that it cost money to kill people, and that the policy of the company was to avoid this where practical," wrote a bitter Bledsoe of the meeting. It was promised a man would be placed at the station to sell tickets half an hour before the train came in, but he wouldn't stay. Beasley concluded, "The railway company had wrapped Alberni in cotton wool and treated it very tenderly."[128]

The morning Simmons left it was raining. He had to stand in the rain waiting for the train. He finally agreed something had to be done and changes were required at the station. Alberni, or the weather, had proved its point to the railway company.

Alberni's only option was to incorporate. The town had tried and failed to become included in the boundary with Port Alberni. "If 24 registered property owners in Port Alberni can be allowed to call themselves a "city" surely the two hundred and sixty-four registered owners of Alberni may be allowed to make the same demand."[129]

An application to incorporate went to Victoria and was rejected by a meeting of the provincial executive. The conflict that had raged for some time between Alberni and Port Alberni was a source of concern for the committee. It was decided that any action should be withheld until a complete statement of the situation was obtained. Commissioner Thornton Fell was appointed to go over the issue and report back.

Alberni was not going to be allowed to incorporate without a struggle. At the opening of the negotiations with the government, Premier McBride remarked that he did not think he could allow the name "City of Alberni," as it would conflict with the name "City of Port Alberni." The people in Alberni were flabbergasted at this remark by the premier. What conflict? they asked.[130]

Commissioner Fell presided over a hearing in the Alberni courthouse July 25, 1912. The city clerk from Port Alberni, Robert F. Blandy, presented Fell with a copy of an address the council had sent to the provincial secretary, explaining Port Alberni did not wish to oppose the inclusion of the word "Alberni" in the name of the proposed city. "But it considers that the adoption of that name without any prefix or qualification would work a serious injustice to the City of Port Alberni."[131]

Blandy drew attention to several facts. The first white settlement in the district was close to the present centre of Port Alberni. Port Alberni had double the population of the proposed city and four times the assessment. It was developing faster and had the only large industry in the district. As well, Port Alberni had the railway terminus and deep sea harbour.

During the arguments Blandy was forced to admit the townsite of Alberni was registered at a time when there was no settlement at the Port. It was shown in the counter evidence that long after this the Port, and the surrounding country, had been registered as the "First addition to Alberni." The fact that Port had incorporated first and had used the word "Alberni" in the title seemed quite sufficient to demand the old town should only use the word if it had a prefix or qualifying word of some sort.

Alderman Frank H. Swayne also appeared before the commission, not representing the City of Port Alberni, but representing both the Alberni Land Company and the E & N Railway. Swayne's employers, the firm Carmichael & Moorhead, were local agents for the Land Company. Writing in the *Alberni Advocate*, Bledsoe later reported this dual representation was because "it was shown that the two companies were practically so bound up that the case for one was the case for the other." Both companies protested against the inclusion of the land on the west side of the Somass River. The Alberni Land Co. was about to convey to the E & N Railway Co. 316.42 acres of foreshore lands on that side. These lands were to be used for manufacturing and sawmill sites only, and could not be subdivided into lots for sale.

All the water frontage was the property of the E & N on the east side of the Somass River, and the harbour of Alberni is included in the City of Port Alberni. A great many lumbermen will look askance at establishing industries on property controlled in the matter of taxation by a community whose object would naturally be to realise as much revenue as possible from the industry. For this reason it is the desire of the railway company to keep the manufacturing sites on the west side of the river clear from city domination.

The Alberni Land Company again pressed the point for exclusion of its farmland, announcing it had spent $8,513.13 during the last two years erecting buildings and improving the land. It planned to establish a model farm which would benefit the whole district.

An Alberni citizens' commission presented Commissioner Fell with an array of facts and figures supporting their claim for the granting of a municipal charter. "The name of Alberni must be preserved at any cost," their petition insisted. Alberni had a total population of 568 "exclusive of Indians"; there were 254 adult males, all British subjects. There were 264 registered property owners in the area proposed, and enough of these had signed the petition to fully comply with the legal requirements. The area included 1909 acres, which would be reduced if the farm was excluded. However, it expected to produce about $15,000 in revenue. Expenses for the new town would be kept low and would not run over $2,500. Roads, streets, and bridges would take approximately $8,000; a school would have to be maintained.

When the question of adopting a prefix in connection with the name of Alberni came up, there was an absolute refusal to consider anything along those lines. Commissioner Fell suggested "North" Alberni, but the Alberni delegates assured him there could be no compromise on the name "Alberni." Commissioner Fell reported back to Victoria, and in September it was announced that incorporation would be granted to the "City of Alberni," effective January 1, 1913.[132]

On November 9, 1912, a public meeting of Alberni residents discussed incorporation and decided to ask for a federal building to house a post office, Indian Agent, and Dominion Fisheries offices.

By December 1912, there were municipal elections in full swing in both cities. Dick Burde announced he would be a candidate for Mayor in Port Alberni, while in Alberni the names of Capt. Huff and C. Frederic Bishop were being rumoured as possible candidates for Mayor of the new city of Alberni. Huff later announced he was not running. James Motion added his name as a candidate for Mayor of Alberni.

Burde turned over his newspaper to a joint stock company, the Port Alberni Printing and Publishing Co. Ltd. The company included

Waterhouse, McNaughton, Swayne, Rand, Gibbons, and Burde, with McNaughton as president. In January Dick Burde was elected Mayor of Port Alberni by acclamation.

January 13, 1913 went down in history as the beginning of the City of Alberni. Charles Bishop beat out James Motion by fifty-two votes to thirty. The six aldermen elected were George Forrest, A. W. Neill, John Grieve, Frank Gibson, James Hills and George A. Spencer.[133]

Grieve was a farmer who lived in the Cherry Creek district. In 1896, at fourteen years of age, he had come with his family to Alberni from Scotland. George Forrest had come from Ontario in 1891. He was a carpenter and is credited with building All Saint's Anglican Church as well as many of the other early buildings in the community. He also served as undertaker and Justice of the Peace.

The first meeting of the Alberni City Council was held January 20, 1913, at 12:00 noon. It was mainly a ceremonial affair. Rev. James Carruthers offered a prayer, and Mayor Bishop thanked the returning officer S. Johnson and appointed F. H. Cleland as temporary clerk until the appointment of a permanent clerk could be made.

The following evening at 7:30 p.m. council got down to business. The first official task was to find a suitable building to use as a municipal office. Aldermen Forrest and Spencer were appointed to the search. On the agenda under correspondence, there was a letter from Colin Campbell of Courtenay, asking for information on the legal procedure towards incorporating a new city. Two letters were from E. E. Frost and F. H. Cleland applying for a position as constable in the new town. Frost was selected as constable but resigned the position in April when he moved to another community.

Three other letters were received from E. Whyte, Walter Coleman, and P. H. Soule, applying for the position of City Clerk. But council decided to advertise the position. In Februrary, P. R. C. Bayne, a government employee, was appointed City Clerk. He was instructed to purchase a large Underwood typewriter and stationery.

Council decided on Mike Tebo's building as most suitable for a temporary municipal office. A new seal was designed with the city motto, *Magnas inter opes*, meaning "Amid great resources."

Unlike Port Alberni, Alberni was a well established community. It was not plagued by lack of funds for its new city council. One of council's first acts was to open an account with the Bank of Montreal. It flexed a little muscle with the bank by adding the stipulation, "on the condition that the bank open a branch in the city shortly."[134]

The old volunteer fire brigade was disbanded and all its assets assumed by city council. A new brigade was organized under Captain J. B. Scott, Lieutenant E. M. Whyte, and secretary F. H. Bishop. The volunteers included W. C. Clark, J. W. Heaslip, H. J. Gillis, R. Erickson, C. M. Pineo, George Forrest, G. E. Richmond, A. E. Drinkwater, S. Heaslip, H. H. Godron, M. McIntosh, F. Andrews, N. Spencer, P. Stewart, V. Shaver, E. Frost, J. W. Stevens, K. W. Franlow. As a temporary fire hall, Tebo's stables were rented for twelve dollars a month.

The Attorney-General was asked to appoint A. W. Neill as City Police Magistrate. Neill agreed to take the position without salary.

The Alberni Council was always mindful of what was happening in Port Alberni. Once again the rumour mill was at work. Aldermen Spencer and Forrest were asked to speak to the government agent regarding a report that the government offices might be moved to Port Alberni, where a free site had been offered. MPP John Wood assured council there was no foundation to the rumour.

The Arlington Hotel was given permission to turn on electric lights.

In February 1913, Dan Clarke, of River Road, offered to sell to the municipality for $20,000 fourteen acres of Lot 10 for a public park and graveyard. Council asked him on what terms he would lease the land for a period of five or ten years with an option to purchase, but Clarke refused to lease and council decided it was not prepared to deal on his terms.

Council made sure it had a deal with Sir Kenneth Anderson for the promise of a park on Rogers Creek. Alfred Carmichael, acting for the Alberni Land Co. assured Council the recreation grounds would be free for a term of fifteen years. A town hall site would be donated on the condition that the city build a bridge over the Somass River.

After some negotiations with the Rogers Creek Water Works Co., council agreed to pay $2,415.25 to pay off a draft due to the Canadian Pipe Co. on the understanding the money would be used for that purpose and would form the first payment on the assets of the Water Works Co.[135]

Now, all the City of Alberni needed was light.

CHAPTER FOUR

1912–1915

WARTIME

Servicing the Towns

In 1912, both Albernis thought the future had never looked brighter. The E & N Railway now made regular runs into Port Alberni, and the Canadian Northern Railway was heading towards the Alberni Valley from Cowichan.[1] Work had already begun on constructing a wagon road from the Alberni Inlet into Cowichan Lake in preparation for the railway. Two hundred men were working for the contractors Murdoch & Co. to build the thirty-six mile road. It was reported the company had no difficulty in finding enough "white men" to fulfill the contract.[2]

Both communities wanted the terminus of the Canadian Northern Railway to be in their location. The City of Alberni overcame its previous objections to the railroad crossing Gertrude Street; now it agreed to have the railroad cross any of the city streets selected by the company. George Smith received orders to rush the work of surveying the line from Alberni to Cowichan Lake. The survey line showed the railway would travel along the Inlet from Granite Creek to China Creek and then behind Copper Mountain. The route passed through Port Alberni on the eastern edge of the town, making a loop before it reached Alberni near the centre of the settlement.[3]

A few enterprising citizens in Port Alberni could see an opportunity to link Cowichan to Port Alberni with a "permanent" road, and they asked MPP John G. C. Wood to try to persuade the provincial government to take advantage of this opportunity. Murdoch & Co was also approached and offered a "reasonable proposition for assistance." When construction of the railway was completed, there would be little use for a wagon road. Why not make it permanent? The contractors were willing, if only the government would cooperate. The local visionaries could see the benefits to both communities if such a road were to be built. The road from Port Alberni around Cowichan Lake could connect at the other end to Duncan. A petition, showing unanimous consent of local citizens, was sent to the government.[4]

The railway company confidently announced on December 18, 1912 that the thirty-six miles of the Canadian Northern Railway on the Island were actually completed and ready for the rails. The Company anticipated the entire location of the line would be completed by February, 1913. Also in December, there were signs the prospect of the permanent road to Cowichan was unlikely. The Department of Public Works investigator D. R. Irvine said it was regarded by those who knew the country well, "as highly improbable the Minister would look on the proposal advanced as feasible."[5] He reasoned the road cost of approximately $400,000 would serve little as an avenue for agriculture or industrial colonization.

While the debate on the railway continued, services were being established in both towns. In August 1912, the Alberni Board of Trade endorsed a proposal by the Alberni Hydro Electric Power & Light Company to supply electricity to Alberni.[6] The company consisted of local residents, with Dr. A. D. Morgan president and W. W. G. McAllister secretary-treasurer. Within two months every house in Alberni would be lit, the company promised. A steam engine and boiler had been ordered. After Alberni was lit, the company expected to supply Port Alberni with power.[7]

Somehow, Port Alberni beat Alberni to the light switch. Three months later, Port Alberni City Council received a proposal from Mather, Yuill & Co. to install a diesel oil engine to supply power to the city. The cost of the system was estimated at $30,000 and it could be in operation by February 1913.[8] Council agreed to the proposal. The Port Alberni council was taking giant strides towards improving the quality of life for its residents. It had already let a contract to the Municipal Construction Co. Ltd. of Vancouver to supply water to the community at a cost of $91,122.[9] The water was carried in a wood stave pipe from China Creek.

The electric power plant was constructed by Mather, Yuill & Co., on Fourth Avenue, now the site of the Port Alberni Friendship Centre. It was a garage-like structure with a concrete foundation which sank to a depth of eight or ten feet. The 150 hp Atlas diesel engine sat on a concrete platform eighteen inches high. Quinn & Rowley of Port Alberni won the contract to erect 350 sound cedar poles and to string wires for the electric light system.[10]

The city had gone out on a limb financially to install both systems. In February 1913, Mayor Burde got a shock when the Royal Bank refused to advance money to the city for payments due to contractors for the waterworks and electric light systems. The city, piqued, transferred its account immediately to the Bank of Montreal, where it was assured of better credit.[11]

When the lights were turned on in Port Alberni on July 22, 1913, it must have seemed as if a miracle had happened. Dick Burde described the scene:

> Argyle Street and Kingsway presented a vastly more citified appearance than they have ever done previously. There is a feeling in the air that as time goes on, the New York thoroughfare will not be the only "great white way" on the continent. An ingenious and wonderful piece of machinery is this Deisel Oil engine. Turning a fly wheel of some tons weight, the shaft of which is connected with the generator, 150 horse power is obtained with as little fuss as an ordinary gas engine drives a pump. Not a single hitch occurred in the connections. The switch was put on. The electrician said, "let there be light" and instantly there was light.[12]

The official inauguration of the Port Alberni civic water and light systems happened July 30. Even the bandstand was decorated with colored electric lights for the occasion. At 10:50 a.m. the big main at the foot of Argyle Street was opened, allowing a large volume of water to run direct from the source of supply.[13]

At a meeting of the Fire, Water and Light committee of Port Alberni city council, J. Quinn of Quinn & Rowley proposed to buy wholesale from the city enough electric energy to supply a lighting system for Alberni.[14] Alberni, however, did not seem too interested in receiving power from its neighbour. Instead, it called a special meeting of the two city councils to reveal a plan to build a generating plant at Sproat Falls. The question was asked, would Port consider combining with the Old Town in the project?

Mayor Burde said Port already had a contract with Ritchie-Agnes Power Co. to supply power. A bill had already been introduced in the House, and there was no doubt it would go through. There was no hope that Port Alberni would consider any association with Alberni in building an electrical generating plant.[15] However, would Alberni consider receiving power from Port Alberni? A committee was struck to look into the offer.

Three weeks later, the committee reported back that Alberni could have light at about nine cents per kilowatt hour, which was the same rate being charged the Port customers. In order to secure this rate, Alberni would have to take the light for not less than eighteen months. The deal was too good to pass up. By the end of March, Alberni had agreed to receive light from the Port Alberni plant.[16] Both cities now had electricity.

In June 1911, the first telephone exchange in Alberni was established by the British Columbia Telephone Company with Harry L. Mertz as manager. The telephone exchange, located in Mertz' business at Third Avenue and Argyle Street, had sixty subscribers. By October the first telephone directory was published. The second directory, published in June 1912, showed Port Alberni for the first time.[17] The exchange was moved to Fourth Avenue on February 28, 1913.[18] Alberni had 130 subscribers with another thirty-four orders pending, giving the town the unique distinction of "having as many telephones per individual of population as any place in America."[19]

In 1913 Mertz retired to attend to his own business, and a new manager was appointed. He was A. B. Curtis, of the Greenwood exchange. Curtis was only there two months when he was transferred to Victoria, and W. M. Holt became the Alberni manager.[20] The same year, a telephone connection was made with the hospital. By September, a Private Branch Exchange (PBX) switchboard was installed in the Alberni Hotel, making it the first place on the Island outside of Victoria to have a PBX.[21]

Another important service inaugurated in 1913 was the steamship *Princess Maquinna*, which made its maiden voyage in July. When the ship came within sight of Port Alberni, the whistles blew from the Canadian Pacific Lumber Co. mill and the Wiest Logging Company. Gasoline launches, tugboats, and various other types of water vessels gathered around the big ship to bid it welcome.[22]

The *Princess Maquinna* could accommodate four hundred day passengers with sleeping facilities for one hundred. She was the pride of the Canadian Pacific Railway's British Columbia coastal fleet. The ship sailed three times a month from Victoria to Port Alice; during busy summer months the trips were increased to one every week.

Maquinna's timetable had "special arrangement only" stops, some of which were little more than lonely cabins or floating rafts. Messages were sent out several days ahead to notify the ship where and when to stop. The ship's first captain, Edward Gilliam, and others who followed him, were always willing to tie up beside some rickety old dock, or go alongside a floating logging camp, to give service when needed. The *Maquinna* served the community for many years.

Policing was another necessary service being initiated in Port Alberni. Until the city incorporated, it had been policed by Chief Constable Cox of Alberni. One of the first acts of the new city council in May 1912 was the appointment of a police constable. The first police commission included Mayor Waterhouse, Alderman George Bird, and Robert Wood. They decided one constable could do the job and appointed F. Wolfe Stevens to fill the position at a salary of seventy-five dollars a month, with uniform. Cox of Alberni was asked for the temporary loan of handcuffs and other "necessary equipment" needed.[23]

A year later, the commissioners decided an assistant constable was needed. J. R. Edwards, formerly of Coquitlam, was appointed. Apart from making sure law and order was maintained, the two police constables were occasionally directed to watch various Chinese premises for gambling offences and to ensure everyone observed the Sabbath. They were also ordered to watch a suspected house of prostitution. The Chief of Police noted the house had been visited by "various automobiles and scams." If there was sufficient evidence they were to arrest the occupants.[24]

Building A Hospital

Until this time, all of the doctors had worked without the aid of a hospital. They drove a horse and buggy, and later rode bicycles to get around to their patients. When seniors became ill, they were taken over the road by horse and stage to Nanaimo or by sea to Victoria.[25] Often their patients couldn't pay the doctors' small fees, but the settlers did pay – with fresh vegetables or whatever they could afford. Dr. Watson attended the daughter of Robert Thompson in Beaver Creek in 1901. His fee of $3.50 was paid with a bag of potatoes and several dozen eggs.[26]

Because there was no hospital, patients were often admitted into their doctor's own home to receive care. Both Morgan and Hilton built large homes to accommodate their patients' needs. The situation was convenient but the patients could not get the same care as in a hospital, although Mrs. Ethel Hilton was a trained nurse and assisted her husband greatly in caring for patients. Hilton's first patient was a man with a broken back and leg who stayed with the family for three months. Dr. Hilton recalled the incident:

The first logging accident that I had here was one that happened to a man by the name of Eric Udine. He was working for the Wiests (Logging Co), and while trying to put the brake on a rail logging car that was slipping, tripped on the tie that was across the rails to prevent the cars from going off. His foot was pinned just above the ankle between the brake board and the tie being flattened out like a piece of paper.

He was brought into town, the intention being to take him straight to Nanaimo. I, however, prevailed on the Wiests to examine him first. In doing so, and finding both bones in his leg in slivers, I fixed up the leg and kept him at my home for about three months. In about a year's time he was alright again and walking. He was off work for 15 months.[27]

Doctors faced another handicap in not knowing just what kind of treatment they would have to administer on arrival at the scene. Communications were poor. Often they did not know whether it would be pneumonia or a broken leg, so it was necessary for them to carry around enough drugs to cover any and all conditions they might encounter.

Often when a birth was imminent, the doctors would call upon several women in the community to help. One woman claimed to have assisted in the delivery of at least one hundred babies. For ten days the women would look after not only mother and baby, but often the whole family. Fifteen dollars was all they asked for their services.

A temporary hospital, erected east of the city at Loon Lake when the grade was being constructed for the railway, was primarily used for accident cases during construction. In charge of this railway hospital was Dr. McArthur.[28]

The need for a hospital was brought home to the community dramatically when James Redford was accidentally shot by James Rollin while out hunting. Dr. Pybus was unable to care for the stricken man. Someone had to ride to Nanaimo to bring Dr. Hogl to his aid. The doctor arrived on that June day in 1906 in the second automobile ever to come to Alberni. He made a desperate attempt to save the injured man, but it was too late.[29] While he was in Alberni, Dr. Hogl also answered an emergency call to the Beaver Creek Post Office, where he saved the life of Mrs. Bob Orr and her son. Mrs. Orr operated the post office and the travelling library in her home.

When the first newspaper rolled off the press in August 1907, residents had the opportunity to present their opinion on many subjects through letters to the editor. One such letter in January 1908, from Joseph G. Halpenny, a Beaver Creek farmer, suggested a scheme should be formulated to erect or lease a building for a hospital.[30]

The idea took root. When the first meeting of the Alberni Board of Trade got underway a few months later, in May 1908, one of the first suggestions was to form a hospital committee, and "to formulate a scheme for the account keeping of hospital funds." By June, Dick Burde reported from the committee to the board he had received a cheque for fifty dollars for the hospital fund, making a grand total of $136.50 at present. The committee had also written to the Alberni Land Co. to have a site designated for a hospital. In November 1908, word had been received from Herbert Carmichael that the Alberni Land Co. had set aside two lots on Redford Road. The site would be designated for hospital purposes when the land survey was completed.

The following February, New Alberni formed its own Board of Trade, much to the astonishment and dismay of the old town settlement board. By April, the Alberni board decided it would ask the New Alberni board to appoint a special committee to act with Alberni's hospital committee. A hospital site was granted by the Alberni Land Co. in October 1909.

Although attention then focused on forming a municipality, hospital funds continued to accumulate. A reported smallpox scare in Nanaimo and Cowichan in February perhaps hastened the Alberni drive for a hospital. There had been two deaths from the disease, which had affected eighty people in the Nanaimo area.[31] On March 7, 1909, the New Alberni Board of Trade elected a committee to undertake the preliminary work of raising funds for a general hospital. The committee included Dick Burde, Dr. Morgan, and W. H. Marcon. The hospital building would accommodate about twenty patients. It was estimated that $3,000 would be required for the building and furnishing.

A visit from the Alberni Land Co. president, Sir Kenneth Anderson, to the Alberni Valley in July, 1910, brought astonishing news. Anderson said he did not think the designated site for the hospital was a good one. He wanted to consult with the hospital committee to secure a better site.[32] The joint hospital committee met with Anderson and Carmichael of the Alberni Land Co. in the Somass Hotel. Anderson said he did not think the town had developed sufficiently to decide just where the site should be located. He recommended a temporary site. The committee already had the company's promise of a grant of two lots, the location to be picked somewhere on

Redford Road as soon as the land surveys were complete. A more desirable site was considered to be the north side of the Dry Creek park reserve, (10th Avenue at present) about six blocks from the waterfront, a site which had already been cleared. Anderson and Carmichael agreed to leave the decision on the site with the local agents. The committee agreed.[33]

The Alberni residents thought the proposed alternate site was too far away. The site eventually chosen on Eighth Avenue was considered mid-way between Port Alberni and Alberni, and the change in location was expected to do much to remove any friction between the two towns. The company donated six lots and reserved the rest of the block, which was later purchased by the hospital board.

At a joint meeting of Alberni and Port Alberni residents the first board of trustees for the hospital was chosen. Chairman was Charles A. McNaughton; vice-chairman, John G. C. Wood; Dick Burde, secretary and Walter R. H. Prescott, treasurer. Others on the board included John Frank Bledsoe, publisher of the *Alberni Advocate*; Dr. C. T. Hilton (Port Alberni); James Motion (Alberni), a real estate and insurance agent and president of the Alberni Board of Trade; D. Osborn, from Bamfield; and Mr. McClintoch, also from the west coast. Both towns collaborated in raising funds. Some outside points such as Bamfield, Ucluelet, and Tofino, also helped. About $4,000 was collected.[34] The provincial government grant was expected to be at least $5,000.

The firm W. M. Ryder & Co. was commissioned to draw the architectural plans. In March 1912, the plans were sent to MPP John G. C. Wood, who submitted them to Dr. H. Young, the provincial secretary, for approval. The government was asked to appoint two directors to represent it on the board.

The buildings would be two stories high with a concrete basement. The main hospital would have a wing and a central administrative block. The wing would house the men's ward with ten beds. Above would be the women's quarters with four beds and three private rooms. In the central block there would be a matron's room, dining room, kitchen, consulting room, and operating room.

The *Alberni Advocate* reported the site of the hospital was 8400 feet from the Alberni post office, 6600 feet from the Port Alberni depot, and 10,000 feet from the Canadian Pacific Lumber Co. mill.[35] In June came the good news that the provincial government grant could be $10,000, if $7,000 was raised locally.

Work on the hospital temporarily stalled in August when the tenders for construction were opened. It was found that the lowest bid had come from the firm of Warnock and Cochrane. The construction company let it be known it did not want to work under the supervision of the architectural firm of W. M. Ryder and Co. It seemed Ryder and Co. consisted of Ryder and Story, the latter with an interest in the firm of Wood & Story, which had also tendered for the contract to build the hospital. The hospital board considered the objections of the contractors were well founded. The services of W. M. Ryder & Co. should be dispensed with, as far as supervision was concerned. However, Ryder refused to allow the plans to be used unless the firm's services were retained for the supervision. The board decided to appoint a committee to engage another architect to prepare new plans and call for a new set of tenders.[36]

Warnock & Cochrane were again the successful bidders for the contracting job, beating out their nearest rivals by so much that for a while the question was in the minds of the board whether there had been a mistake. The new building was similar to the previously planned one, but some changes had been made to the interior.[37] A contractor, W. Mesher, who was building the Argyle Street addition to the Somass Hotel, had drawn up the new plans. He also supervised the construction work as his contribution to the hospital.

Work on the hospital construction continued to proceed satisfactorily. One payment of $1,500 had been made to the contractor in October, 1912. Then a letter arrived to say the B.C. Telephone Company could not see its way clear at the present time to install a telephone. The company had decided not to do any further construction work in the district for some time to come. To extend the service as far out as the hospital would cost in the neighbourhood of $275, and this, B.C. Telephone considered, would not be profitable. The hospital board was dumbfounded; the telephone company came in for some harsh criticism. The board decided to refer the matter to Port Alberni City Council to use its influence with the company.[38]

Chairman of the hospital board Charles McNaughton took time out from his duties on the hospital board to marry Mrs. Helen Rollin on November 14, 1912. Helen was the widow of James S. Rollin, who built the King Edward Hotel. Rollin had died in May 1910.[39]

On December 27 the hospital advertised for staff.

> Wanted for West Coast General Hospital: a hospital matron, who must also be a graduate nurse, starting salary fifty dollars per month; a graduate nurse, starting salary forty dollars; a certificated male nurse, who will be

Richard John Burde, left, and Leonard Frank with Margaret Burde, (Nightingale) on knee. Circa 1911. AVM PN933

Notable men about town with B.C. Premier Richard McBride. Circa 1913. Left to right George Forrest, unknown, Joe Hanna, Richard Burde, unknown, Leonard Frank, Frank Bledsoe, Matt Ward, unknown, George Drinkwater, unknown, Premier McBride, unknown, unknown. Leonard Frank photo. AVM PN1142

Clearing the townsite of giant trees. AVM PN1136

Argyle Street looking west toward Alberni Inlet, December 19, 1912.
Carmoor Block on left, C. M. Pineo Drug Store on right. Leonard Frank photo.   AVM PN619

Argyle Street looking east showing bandstand and Somass Hotel.
Circa 1913.   AVM PN3899

Beaufort Hotel, on Third Avenue,
New Alberni, decorated for Dominion Day
celebrations. Circa 1910.   AVM PH690

Post Office and
Federal Building,
Third and
Angus Streets,
Port Alberni.
Circa 1914.
AVM PN1138

Alberni football team,
A.F.C. champions
1908-1909.
Back row, left to right:
Sid Toy, Jack Clarke,
Ferguson, Ed White,
Dr. Morgan:
Middle row, left to right:
Harold Bishop, Ferguson,
M. Ward:
Front row, left to right:
Alf. Drinkwater,
Walter Green, Percy Bayne,
Ward, Fred Drinkwater.
AVM PN1068

Port Alberni's first city council 1912. Back row, left to right:
F. H. Swayne, Robert Ellis, Robert Blandy, J. A. MacIntyre, A. D. Cooper.
Front row, left to right: A. D. MacIntyre, Mayor Arthur E. Waterhouse,
George H. Bird.   AVM PN741

First council of Alberni 1913. Left to right: John Grieve, Frank Gibson, A. W. Neill,
Mayor C. Frederic Bishop, George Forrest, James Hills, George A. Spencer.   AVM PN102

Installation of the
post which ended the
Trans-Canada highway at
the foot of Johnston Road,
Victoria Quay.
Bridge over Kitsuksis Creek
in foreground. 1912.
Leonard Frank photo.
AVM PN2438

Alberni Fire Brigade 1910. Back row, left to right: Drinkwater, Fred Drinkwater, George Forrest, D. Ed White, Ferguson. Front row, left to right: Jack Forsyth, Wes Heaslip, George Drinkwater. Joseph Clegg photo.   AVM PN1056

James B. Wood, first Fisheries Officer on the west coast, also one of the Wood Brothers who operated the Barclay Sound Cedar Company. Photo courtesy daughter Mary Wood.
AVM PN11872

Kildonan Fish Cannery. Circa 1918.   AVM PN2638

First West Coast General Hospital
as it looked at its opening
May 7, 1913. AVM PN108

Hospital nursing staff:
Left to right: Miss Kate Hills,
hospital's first matron,
Miss L. Swanson and
Miss Georgina Smith.
AVM PN849

First school in Port Alberni at the corner of First Avenue and Argyle Street.
Teacher is Ellsworth Foy. 1906. AVM PN293

Alberni District Brass Band with their new uniforms,
1912. Leonard Frank photo. AVM PN310

Waiting for the train to take them to war. People identified as Kelly Gill, James Loudon, Wes Heaslip and Clayton Hills. Joseph Clegg photo.   AVM PN854

The Redford brothers
ready for war.
Back row: Douglas,
killed in action, William.
Front row: Ken Boyce and
Edward Redford.   AVM PN852

Port Alberni Swimming Club 1912. Leonard Frank photo.   AVM PN307

Canadian Pacific Lumber Co.   AVM PN535

Harold Dent boating.
Family photo.

Princess Maquinna. Postcard photo.

Bainbridge Sawmill owner
Clarence Hoard, left, with Sam Hoard
taken in Seattle, Washington.
Photo courtesy of
Mrs. James E. Sidey, Tigard, Oregon,
USA, daughter of Sam Hoard.

Bainbridge Sawmill.   AVM PN4682

Bainbridge School May Queen celebration. Back row, left to right:
Tina Marks, May Queen Joyce Hopkins, page Jimmy Flaherty, Nellie Marks.
Front row, left to right: Miss MacKenzie, Miss Flaherty, Meredith Fjarlie,
Mona Fjarlie and Miss Hopkins. Circa 1921.   AVM PN1408

Peace Day
celebration
parade on
Johnston Road
1919.
Joseph Clegg
photo.
AVM PN17

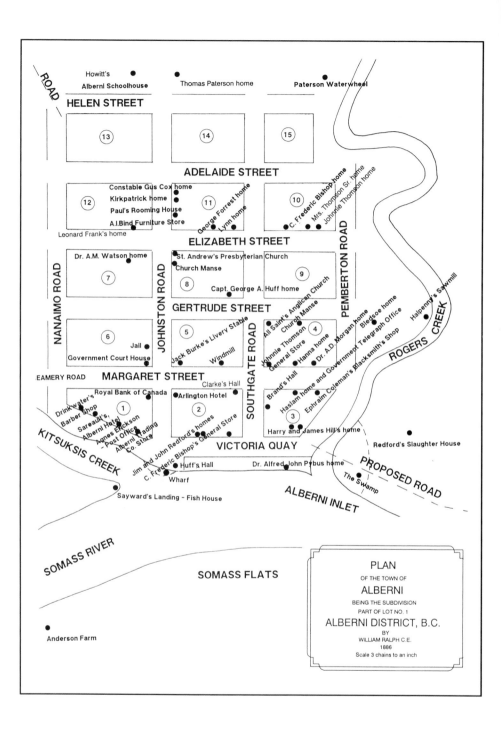

ROAD

Howitt's ●
Alberni Schoolhouse   ● Thomas Paterson home   ● Paterson Waterwheel

HELEN STREET

⑬   ⑭   ⑮

ADELAIDE STREET

Constable Gus Cox home ●
Kirkpatrick home ●
⑫   Paul's Rooming House ●   ⑪   ⑩   C. Frederic Bishop home
          A.I.Bind Furniture Store ●   George Forrest home   Mrs. Thomson Sr. home
Leonard Frank's home   Lynn home   Johnnie Thomson home

ELIZABETH STREET

Dr. A.M. Watson home ●   St. Andrew's Presbyterian Church
                         Church Manse
⑦   ⑧   ⑨
NANAIMO ROAD   JOHNSTON ROAD   Capt. George A. Huff home

GERTRUDE STREET

                    All Saint's Anglican Church
⑥   ⑤   Church Manse
          Jack Burke's Livery Stable   Johnnie Thomson   ④   Bledsoe home
Jail ●   Windmill ●   General Store   Dr. A.D. Morgan home
Government Court House   SOUTHGATE ROAD   Hanna home   Dr. A.D. Morgan
                         PEMBERTON ROAD   Government Telegraph Office
CREAMERY ROAD   Brand's Hall   Ephraim Coleman's Blacksmith's Shop   Halpenny's Sawmill

MARGARET STREET

          Clarke's Hall   Haslam home and
Royal Bank of Canada ●   ROGERS CREEK
Drinkwater's ●   ● Arlington Hotel
Barber Shop   ①   ②   ③
Sareault's ●
Alberni Hotel ●   Agnes Erickson   Harry and James Hill's home
● Post Office
Alberni Trading   Jim and John Redford's homes   ● Redford's Slaughter House
Co. Store   C. Frederic Bishop's General Store

VICTORIA QUAY

KITSUKSIS CREEK   ● Huff's Hall   Dr. Alfred John Pybus home   PROPOSED ROAD
                    ● Wharf   The Swamp
          ● Sayward's Landing - Fish House   ALBERNI INLET

SOMASS RIVER

          SOMASS FLATS

                         PLAN
                         OF THE TOWN OF
                         ALBERNI
                         BEING THE SUBDIVISION
                         PART OF LOT NO. 1
                         ALBERNI DISTRICT, B.C.
                         BY
                         WILLIAM RALPH C.E.
                         1886
                         Scale 3 chains to an inch

● Anderson Farm

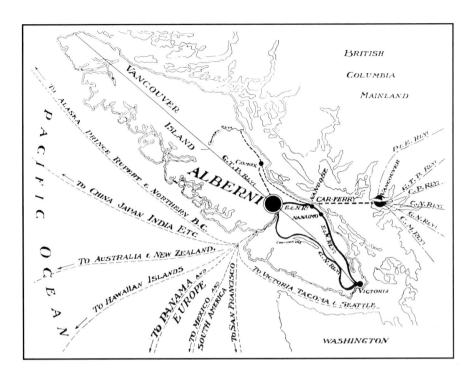

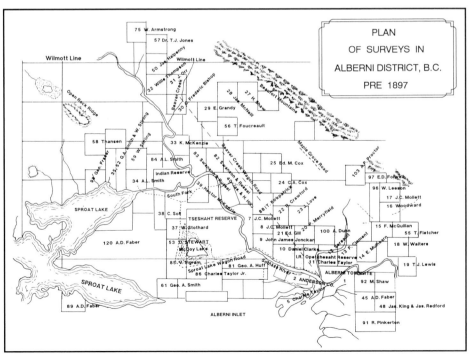

PLAN
OF SURVEYS IN
ALBERNI DISTRICT, B.C.
PRE 1897

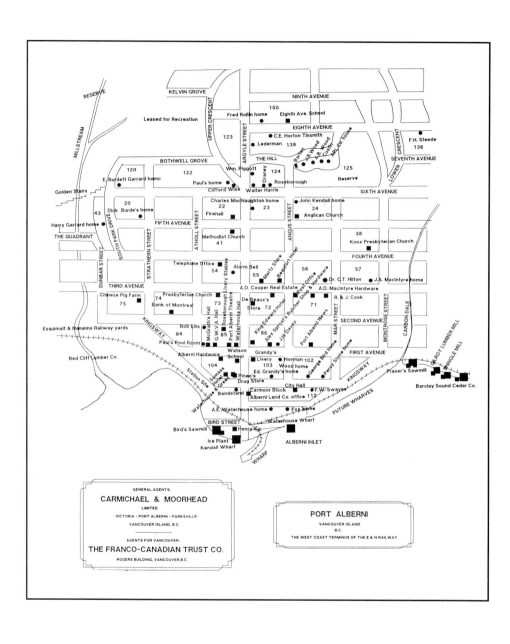

RESERVE

MILLSTREAM

KELVIN GROVE

NINTH AVENUE

UPPER CRESCENT

Leased for Recreation

150
Fred Rollin home   Eighth Ave. School

123   EIGHTH AVENUE

C.E. Horton Tinsmith
Lederman   138

THE HILL

F.H. Steede
136

SEVENTH AVENUE

LOWER CRESCENT

ARGYLE STREET

Bothwell Grove

120   122
E. Burdett Garrard home   Paul's home

Wm. Piggott   124
Draney   Roseborough

125
Reserve

Golden Stairs

Clifford Wise   Walter Harris

SIXTH AVENUE

20
Dick Burde's home
43

Charles MacNaughton
22   23
Firehall

John Kendall home
24
Anglican Church

Harry Garrard home

THE QUADRANT

FIFTH AVENUE

38
Knox Presbyterian Church

THE QUADRANT

ATHOLL STREET

ANGUS STREET

Methodist Church
41

FOURTH AVENUE

DUNBAR STREET

SOUTH PARK DRIVE

STRATHERN STREET

Telephone Office
54

Alarm Bell
55

Mertz Store

Beaufort Hotel

56   57
Dr. C.T. Hilton   J.A. MacIntyre home

THIRD AVENUE

Chinese Pig Farm
75

Presbyterian Church
74
Bank of Montreal

A.D. Cooper Real Estate

Post Office
Sprat's Butcher Shop & Hardware
A.D. MacIntyre Hardware

Livery Stables

73

De Beaux's
Store 72

71

R. & J. Cook

CARBON DALE

OX-BOY LUMBER MILL

Esquimalt & Nanaimo Railway yards

KINGSWAY

Port Alberni Theatre

Bob Ellis
84

McGrath's Hall
G.W.V.A. Hall
Roseborough
Waterhouse Hall

King Edward Hotel

86   Alex Sprat's Butcher Shop
J.N. Davey

Port Alberni News

MAR STREET

MONTROSE STREET

SECOND AVENUE

SHINGLE MILL

Red Cliff Lumber Co.

Station Site

Paul's Pool Room

Alberni Hardware
104

Watson
School

Somass
Hotel

Pineo's
Drug Store

Bandstand

Grandy's
Livery
103
Wood home
Ed. Grandy's home

Norman 102
George Bird home
Percy Stone home

FIRST AVENUE

KINGSWAY

Fraser's Sawmill

Barclay Sound Cedar Co.

City Hall
Carmoor Block
Alberni Land Co. office 112

F.W. Swayne

FUTURE WHARVES

A.E. Waterhouse home

Fox home

BIRD STREET

Henry Co.

Bird's Sawmill

Ice Plant
Kendall Wharf

Waterhouse Wharf

ALBERNI INLET

WHARF

ALBERNI INLET

GENERAL AGENTS:

CARMICHAEL & MOORHEAD

LIMITED

VICTORIA - PORT ALBERNI - PARKSVILLE

VANCOUVER ISLAND, B.C.

AGENTS FOR VANCOUVER:

THE FRANCO-CANADIAN TRUST CO.

ROGERS BUILDING, VANCOUVER, B.C.

PORT ALBERNI

VANCOUVER ISLAND

B.C.

THE WEST COAST TERMINUS OF THE E & N RAILWAY

expected to make himself generally useful, starting salary forty-five dollars. A white woman cook, starting salary thirty dollars. Board in each case. Applications for the above positions, accompanied by testimonials, will be received on or before January 8, 1913, by J. R. Thompson, Secretary, Hospital Board.

The makeup of the board was outlined at a meeting in December. There would be three directors each from Port Alberni and Alberni, two provincial government appointees, plus one director from the west coast district. The board also proposed "that directors in each town be asked to organize a Ladies' Auxiliary in each of their respective towns."[40]

Building began in the fall of 1912. The hospital was opened officially on May 7, 1913, by Dr. H. Young. Two patients had already been admitted on April 19. Young promised:

> If $1,000 is raised by the Ladies' Auxiliaries the Government will send these same ladies $2,000. The sum of $5,000 will be given to provide a Maternity Ward and to furnish quarters for the staff, if the people will raise $2,500. Let the ladies furnish a private ward, and send the bill to me.[41]

The staff hired included a matron, one nurse, and a cook. The first matron was Miss Isabel Hill. The first nurse was Miss Kate Guillod, daughter of Indian Agent Harry Guillod. Both women lived in rooms in the hospital; Hill in the matron's room while Guillod slept in one of the private rooms. The "general all-round man" was Patrick Harrigan.[42] The physicians and surgeons who handled the majority of cases were Dr. Morgan, Dr. Hilton, and Dr. Gerald Harpur.[43]

Rates for the new hospital were set. The private wards cost $20 a week, while public beds had a price tag of $1.50 a day. There were also set rates for the crews of industrial companies and special contract rates for services to the native population through the Department of Indian Affairs.

By October 15, the hospital was plagued by financial troubles. The running expenses were estimated at $600 per month, while revenue averaged about $150 per month. The board had to come to terms with an accumulated debt of $3,000. There was an appeal to the provincial government for more financial assistance. The government came through with $3,000. Both Alberni and Port Alberni contributed another $500 each, resolving the immediate problem. The public was called upon to take more interest in the welfare of the hospital.[44]

There was more financial trouble reported on August 14, 1914, just after the outbreak of the First World War, when the Canadian Pacific

Lumber Company, the Wiest Logging Company, and Carmichael & Moorehead camps all closed down. Each of them had been operating under the contract system with the hospital and making monthly payments to the institution.

In 1916 the first expansion added twenty-seven beds, increasing the capacity to forty-seven. This involved building an east wing and nurses' residence. The nurses' home was built to accommodate four nurses with sitting rooms and bathrooms. It was located at 3831 Ninth Avenue, across from the hospital.

Financial problems would continue to plague the hospital for many years to come.

Until this time the women of the Albernis had gone about their business caring for their families, largely being unrecognized for their worth. They had no vote, nor could they run for public office. Their first names were never mentioned in any official documents or news reports, although few churches would have survived without the fund-raising assistance of the women of the various congregations. Therefore, the official public call to form a ladies auxiliary to aid the new hospital was a challenge few women could resist. The wives of the leaders in the communities typically became the leaders of the auxiliaries.

First to form was the Port Alberni branch of the Women's Auxiliary to West Coast General Hospital. At the first meeting, held January 30, 1913 at 3:00 p.m. in the Church Hall school room, there were forty-three women present. The meeting was opened by Mrs. Dick Burde, the wife of the *Port Alberni News* publisher. She gave a brief report on the hospital. The women must have been impressed with her leadership because they nominated her for president. Mrs. C. T. Hilton was nominated vice-president, and Mrs. C. Wise became secretary by acclamation. Other charter members included Mrs. R. H. Wood, Kelly, C. A. Manning, Maurice, C. A. McNaughton, Lowe, J. B. Wood, Milton, Rolph, Davey, A. B. Wood, E. S. V. McClintock, J. A. MacIntyre, Mitchell, Lee, Dixon, Barnes, Hayne, Miss Lowe.

The Alberni women responded equally to the call to organize an auxiliary. Mrs. C. Frederic Bishop was nominated honourary president, with Mrs. James R. Motion as president. The vice-president was Mrs. W. R. H. Prescott, secretary Mrs. H. M. T. Hodgson, and treasurer Miss Bishop.

On February 10, the two auxiliaries met to discuss the constitution. They agreed to adopt the constitution of the auxiliary to Vancouver General Hospital. They also agreed they would function separately, but "still work in harmony until something definite turns up and we require the two committees to meet."[45]

The early auxiliaries of both communities spent hours making nightshirts and tea cloths and mending linen, while organizing fundraising teas, sales, and concerts. The Alberni Auxiliary paid for the construction of a driving shed and morgue and hitching post. In 1914, the auxiliaries contributed $500 towards the building of the nurse's home and maternity wing. It would be difficult to imagine West Coast General Hospital without its able auxiliary workers, who continue to provide funds for furnishings and equipment. During the early years, these efforts were particularly important.

Early Education

The growth of schools in the district had kept pace with the twin communities. Few of the early teachers had a service record like that of John Howitt. He came to Alberni in 1890 to teach in the Alberni (Gill) one-room log school, which served the entire north end of the Valley. His pupils came on foot from as far as McCoy Lake, a distance of several miles.

Howitt was born in Southampton, England in 1864. Entering the teaching profession at the age of fourteen, he taught in Hampshire, England, for ten years before coming to Victoria in 1890. For a few months he was employed by the Canadian Pacific Railway until he decided to return to teaching.

> I decided to stay in Alberni for six months, as I liked the place, and that stay lengthened into 56 years. The school, a log building, was called the Gill school, but was actually the Alberni school as it served all of that area. Pupils from Cherry Creek, McCoy Lake, and about four miles up the Beaver Creek Road, attended this school, as well as the residents of Alberni proper.
>
> In order to keep the attendance up to requirements, several Indians also attended. They could speak but very little English and with my limited knowledge of Chinook, together with their little command of English, we managed to get along quite well. Strangely enough, considering the distance travelled by a large number of pupils, lateness was quite uncommon. I remember one boy, Charlie Taylor, from McCoy Lake, being late one morning, and he told me that there were wolves on the road and he returned home to get his father's rifle for protection.
>
> For six or seven years I didn't have a visit from a school inspector. The school curriculum in those days was very sketchy, consisting of the Three R's, health, geography, history and drawing.[46]

211

The log schoolhouse was replaced by a one-room frame building. When the one-room Alberni school was built on a site on the Johnston Road hill, Howitt became principal. While the new school was being built, Howitt took a leave of absence to visit England and the continent. In 1905, on one of four such visits, he married Florence. They had one son John William (Jack), and two daughters, Ida (Mrs. Roy Hill) and Stella (Mrs. Carl Lassau).

Alberni school became known as "Mr. Howitt's school." The school became an Old Town landmark standing near the E & N railway track. As the community began to grow, so too did the number of pupils, and another room was added in 1910. Eventually the two-room school became overcrowded, and extra classes were set up in other buildings, including the old Alberni Fire Hall. At one time Howitt had as many as forty pupils, all grades and ages. Then Miss Gammon was hired and took charge of the lower grades. Some of the early primary and intermediate teachers included Miss Pringle, Miss Bury, Miss Beatrice Penn, Mr. E. Berryman, and Miss Agnes Irvine. Howitt remained principal and head teacher until the present Alberni Elementary school was built on Helen Street in 1934. He was probably the best known member of the community as he was active in sports and community affairs. As an ardent sportsman, John Howitt held several local records. For instance, he shot the largest elk brought down in the Alberni district; it weighed seven hundred pounds and had a spread of over four feet between the antlers. Howitt had the head mounted and hung it on the wall of his home on River Road. He shot a huge cougar, mounted the claws on a gold brooch, and sent the skin to England. Every day throughout the year he swam in the Somass River.

When Howitt came to Alberni there was no Anglican church, so he became organist for the Presbyterian church. He was organist there for eight years. Later, when All Saint's Anglican Church was built in 1896, he was appointed organist, a position he retained for fifty years.

Howitt remained for three generations in one school, teaching the children's children's children. One of his pupils, John McGregor Thomson, later became a school trustee. Howitt's long record of service in the teaching profession is almost unequalled anywhere in British Columbia. His scholastic standards were high, and he was a strict disciplinarian. The John Howitt Elementary School was named in his honour. Howitt retired in 1934, the year Alberni Elementary School was built.[47] He was a life member of the Central Vancouver Island Teachers Institute.

On June 28, 1934, teachers and school board trustees of Alberni district attended a private dinner to honour John Howitt. Max Wright, president of the local teachers association, W. G. Bigmore, of the Alberni School Board, and Miss Anne Prescott, senior teacher in the Alberni School staff, all paid tribute to Howitt's record and achievements. Later a banquet was given in his honour at the Arlington Hotel in Alberni.[48]

Four years later, Florence Howitt suffered a heart attack and died while placing flowers on her mother's grave. John Howitt died November 26, 1951.

In the twin city of New Alberni, the first school opened in 1903 in the basement of the Watson building at the corner of Argyle and First Avenue. Elsworth Foy taught a class of twenty-eight, all grades. After the first year, a one-room school was built on Third Avenue. This served the community until incorporation in 1912 when a two-room building was erected on 8th Avenue, at the present site of 8th Avenue Elementary School. Additions and annexes were built as pupil enrolment increased. The first principal was John R. Thompson.

Thompson was a native of Ireland. After graduating from Dublin University he began a teaching career with the National School Board in Belfast. He came to British Columbia in 1906, spending some time in the interior of the province before coming to Port Alberni at the age of thirty-five to take the position of principal. He was killed in action during the Great War. Other early principals and teachers included McTavish, Barker, St. James, Hildrich, Harries, and Murray.[49]

At the official opening of the hospital, Dr. Young made an announcement. "If the two towns will give $5,000, the government will give $15,000 towards a new high school for the district. If the two towns would get together and settle their little local differences, we could create one district for both and place the school in the centre."[50] Young had already received a request for funding for a high school earlier in the year. The subject of a high school arose when the school board met with Port Alberni City Council in February, setting out its requisitions for the year. The secretary of the School Board, E. Burdette Garrard, advised there were ninety-six children on the school register, and the capacity of the school was only one hundred pupils. The school would have to have an addition or a new building erected.[51]

In May, a joint meeting of the two school boards of Alberni and Port Alberni was called to find a way to work together towards the establishment of a district high school. Mayor Burde and Alderman

Bird represented Port Alberni; Mayor Bishop and Alderman Forrest represented Alberni. The committee consisted of Sid. H. Toy and Edward Burdett Garrard. First the Alberni Land Company would have to be approached for a site for the school. The Land Company agreed to give twenty-six lots in the City of Port Alberni valued from $8,000 to $10,000, if a school building was erected at a cost of $30,000. The Department of Education thought this would meet the present needs of the district. The site was in the Calgary district, the present location of Calgary Elementary School.[52]

The new high school was opened in August 1914 by Provincial Member of the Legislature J. G. C. Wood, under principal Miss Mary Mahaffey. The school had two large school rooms, spacious hallways, and a basement. One room housed the high school students while the other accommodated elementary grades.

Business interests flourished in 1912-13. But the new construction that was taking place was mostly in Port Alberni. The building of the Carmoor Block at the corner of Argyle and Kingsway was officially announced in August 1912 by Alfred Carmichael of Carmichael & Moorhead. The first floor had seven stores, with an office entrance on Argyle Street, and the second floor had nineteen offices. Fire protection was provided by two hydrants complete with a fire hose. The whole block was steam heated and lit with electricity. There were toilets and baths. The Carmoor Block cost $25,000 to build.[53]

By October 1913 most of building was occupied. On the first floor were the Alberni Land Co. and Carmichael & Moorhead. On the Kingsway side was a fish and poultry business operated by H. R. Kiln, and adjoining it was the Bank of Montreal. Next door was a distributing store for the Alberni Land Co. farm, which sold fresh milk, cream, butter, and other products from the farm. The second floor housed the headquarters of the Canadian Northern Railway engineering staff and the offices of barrister and solicitor A. T. Sanders and Dr. Gerald T. Harpur.[54]

Perhaps the city's most important new building was the Dominion Government building located at the corner of Third Avenue and Angus Street, the site of the old schoolhouse at a cost of $25,000. To the residents of Port Alberni the construction of this building at a cost of $25,000 clearly indicated that the centre of government work on the west coast of Vancouver Island was to be Port Alberni. The Dominion Government Building housed the post office, telegraph, and Fisheries and Customs offices.[55]

Sir Richard McBride performed the opening ceremonies in June 1914 by laying the cornerstone of the new building. It was a splendid day in Port Alberni; even the weather cooperated. Beautiful decorations were everywhere, on buildings and telephone poles. A public half holiday was declared in honour of the occasion, allowing workers from the Canadian Pacific Lumber Co. mill and Wiest Logging Co. to attend. Just prior to the laying of the stone, Capt. Napier with a detachment of eighteen of the B.C. Horse cavalry arrived on the scene in full dress uniform, adding colour to the ceremony.[56] Local dignitaries were on hand to welcome the Premier of the province and other invited guests.

The Dominion Government building must have been a source of great dismay for neighbouring Alberni. When the report of Port Alberni being awarded the public building was announced at an Alberni Board of Trade meeting, one member suggested it should be "Alberni's turn next."[57]

Construction also began in May of 1913 on Port Alberni's latest hotel, the Beaufort. Located at Third and Angus Streets, the four storey structure was built along colonial lines with spacious verandahs giving a beautiful view of the harbour. The local newspaper reported that the building would be "constructed with a roof garden for the pleasure of guests during the summer months."[58] The proprietors were Thomas Costen and Joseph Albert MacIntyre, both well known Port Alberni residents. E. G. Burleight was the architect. The fifty room hotel with dining room and lobby also had private baths, heating, lighting, and toilet facilities.

Joe Drinkwater's Ark Resort at Great Central Lake was built in 1912 by Joe and Clyde "Snowball" Paxton, and it opened the following year. It was originally a float house, accommodating fishing and hunting sportsmen from all over the world. The float house had sixteen bedrooms, each equipped with a bunkbed, a small table, and a small heater. There was a combined dining-living room with an adjoining kitchen. Joe acted as guide and Paxton ran the boats.[59]

The Presbyterian congregation erected a church at Fourth Avenue and Montrose with a seating capacity of two hundred. It stood on three lots donated by the Alberni Land Co.[60]

Gateway to the Panama Canal

For the growing community of Port Alberni anything was possible, even the building of grain elevators to handle wheat from the prairies. Port Alberni put its claim as a site for the grain elevators to the government Grain Commission chairman Dr. R. Magill at a Port Alberni Board of Trade meeting in March 1913. Magill, from Fort William, had been invited to town by John G. C. Wood MPP, the area representative in the provincial legislature, and Alfred Carmichael on behalf of the Board of Trade.

Dr. Magill was wined and dined at the Somass Hotel by both the Port Alberni City Council and the Board of Trade. Carmichael & Moorhead offered the use of their automobile for the journey over from Nanaimo. Wood even took three days off his busy schedule to accompany the commissioner on a tour of the area. After a cruise of the harbour Magill commented, "It is a wonderful body of water."[61] Then he carefully examined the pilings of the old Anderson sawmill site for evidence of the toredo worm. He was impressed with the condition of the piles after nearly sixty years submersion.

At the Board of Trade meeting, arguments were put forward showing the special attributes of the deep sea port as the site for grain elevators. Port Alberni would be the western terminal of the Island branch of the Canadian Pacific Railway, and the Canadian Northern Railway was heading this way.

Publicity Commissioner for the City, H. F. Burmester, outlined Port Alberni's position. D. McN. Lowe, secretary for the Board of Trade, submitted a review of the water power situation. City clerk Robert Blandy offered a statement on the fuel conditions. Port Alberni's new electric light and water supply were also important considerations. Burmester pointed out that Port Alberni was nearer to the Pacific entrance to the Panama Canal than either Victoria or Vancouver. There were no "narrows" in the Alberni Inlet to threaten vessels with destruction or great damage. There was no need to dredge, "and the natural depth of the channel was such that the mariner is not at the mercy of tide 'races' and currents."

> It would not be necessary for the government to expend $5 million to improve this harbour so that the Lloyds and other marine insurance firms would not look upon vessels entering this port as undesirable risks. Port Alberni is fitted by nature as a site for elevators. There would be no necessity of expending millions in fitting the harbour for the erection of the grain storehouses. Wooden wharves are all that would be needed. . . . the harbour is open 12 months of the year . . . and there is no congestion of traffic.
>
> Where elevators are there are sure to be oatmeal and flour mills, and with such mills, fuel and water are important factors. The grain cars would not go back to Alberta and Saskatchewan empty, they would be laden with

lumber from the heavy forests of the area. Port Alberni is located in the heart of the largest body of heavy timber in North America and is destined to become a great milling city.

Magill must have been impressed by the presentation because two weeks later he stated that Port Alberni was the logical point for the shipment of grain across the Pacific and through the Panama Canal provided that the facilities for handling it from the prairies were provided.[62]

According to Wood, the people of Port Alberni had been doing everything in their power to press the claims of the port before the commission. "There will be nothing to prevent Port Alberni from becoming the great wheat shipping centre on the Pacific Coast. There is not a little reason to believe that the bridge will be completed," said Wood. "The construction of a bridge across the Seymour Narrows would make the distance from the grain belt to the open ocean through Port Alberni 150 miles shorter than by any other route."[63] A railway line was planned from Comox to Alberni.

The Port Alberni promoters had given great thought to the question of how the grain from the prairies would get from the mainland to Vancouver Island, then to Port Alberni. The obvious answer was a ferry service from the mainland. On April 2, 1913, Board of Trade secretary Lowe wrote a long article for the *Port Alberni News* explaining how the grain might be handled and suggesting that the Canadian Pacific Railway had "shown in the establishment of its magnificent passenger ferry service between Vancouver and the Island, a close sympathy with the needs and future requirements of that branch of its interest on this coast and is not likely to fall behind in ferrying of freight should traffic warrant it." In the article Lowe also referred to the ferry system then in operation across Lake Michigan by the Pere Marquette Railway, which operated a car ferry capable of carrying thirty loaded cars per trip, a distance of seventy-five miles, at from twelve to fifteen knots per hour. Running a large ferry in the enclosed water of Georgia Straits seemed much simpler than running one the Great Lakes.

> It has long been understood that a car ferry connection from Nanoose Bay to the mainland would be established by the Canadian Pacific Railway. Consider at 15 knots per hour, the time taken on the trip from Vancouver to Nanoose Bay would be about three hours. Each ferry would be able to make two trips a day during the busy season. Two or three ferries each making two trips a day, each ferry would carry thirty cars of wheat or 30,000 bushels a trip, making 60,000 bushels per day for each ferry, or a total of 120,000 bushels per day.

If the CNR had a ferry running, another 60,000 bushels could be brought to the Island. The total wheat export of Canada for the year 1911-1912 was only 64,500,000 bushels, so that if the movement from the prairies were evenly distributed, it would be possible to handle the grain crop through this port.

Port Alberni's efforts to get the grain elevators located here were admirable, but the attempt failed. In 1914 the federal government built Lapointe Pier and a 1.3 million bushel grain elevator at the foot of Salsbury Drive in Vancouver. But Port Alberni didn't give up the promotion of it's port facilities. In 1914 a big publicity campaign proclaimed: "Port Alberni – The magnetic city: The nearest Canadian Port to the Panama Canal. An unavoidable transfer point on the "All-red Route." With the opening of the Panama Canal, Port Alberni will assume her rightful place in the shipping world."[64]

Even the CPR was pleased with the progress of the city. Sir Thomas Shaughnessy, CPR president, was in town in September of 1912 to size up the opportunities of the farthest western terminus of the CPR system. Looking down the Alberni Inlet, Shaughnessy said, "That is a splendid outlet to the ocean." He predicted that before long the whole stretch of waterfront would be lined with manufacturing industries.[65]

Two big events in 1913 gave the city fathers a chance to show what the community had to offer. The first, in June, was the visit of the Vancouver Island Development League (VIDL) members from Victoria, Duncan, Ladysmith, and Nanaimo. While the band played "The Maple Leaf Forever" the big excursion train of seven cars carrying the representatives of the VIDL rolled into the station. After a welcome by local dignitaries the group toured the Canadian Pacific Lumber Co. mill and Wiest Logging Co. The next day they took a motor trip to Sproat Lake and Great Central Lake, as well as a trip down the Inlet to the headquarters of the Canadian Northern Railway construction work.[66]

The second event, a provincial swim meet held in August, attracted swimmers from all over the province. The host group was the Port Alberni Swimming and Water Polo Club under president David Owen. About eight hundred people lined the shore and wharves when the Swimming Club's first annual gala and British Columbia Championship meet got under way August 6. The event was held under the auspices of the B.C. branch of the Canadian Amateur Swimming Association. The location of the meet was in the small bay to the north of Stone's shipbuilding yard. The swimmers started from a large float and finished at a scow near the new mill under construction by the Port Alberni Lumber Co. A diving platform twenty feet high had been erected.

The first event was the fifty yard championship of B.C. Of the twelve men entered, only four qualified for the final, which was won by B. Bladwin of the Vancouver YMCA. "Never has such speed swimming been seen on this part of the Island" reported the *Port Alberni News*.[67]

The local polo team did well, trouncing the Victoria team soundly by a score of nine to zero. The winning team included Oldridge, Stephens, and Street. This was the first time polo had been played in the district. The relay race included the local team of Oldridge, Street, Stephenson, and Owen. Despite a bad start they were not far behind the winning team from Victoria. The diving event was won by J. Cameron of the Victoria YMCA. When the meet was over, the swimmers were entertained by the local club at a banquet in the Somass Hotel.

The musical aspirations of local residents also got a boost in 1913, when the British Columbia Conservatory of Music announced in May it would open a Port Alberni Branch. Principal of the school was Harry A. Harvey, who five years before had formed the Nanaimo Symphony Orchestra. The school would prepare pupils for any of the standard exams. "It would open departments for vocal cultivation and tuition in piano-forte, violin, mandolin guitar, as well as instruction of all brass instruments." The district manager was H. A. Gilbert. The school was located on First Avenue near Argyle Street.[68] Harvey's assistant was Mrs. Pym, a musician trained in London and Paris who came with very high credentials.

J. H. "Jack" Warren, a printer with the *Port Alberni News*, began the first moving picture show in Waterhouse Hall. He had learned this skill in Nanaimo at the old Crown Theatre before he moved to Port Alberni. He and his wife Louise arrived aboard one of the first trains to come into the Valley. They had three children born here; Alice, Harold, and Evelyn. Later, Warren joined Wingate and Backman, who were using their own electric power to produce moving pictures as large and as clear as anywhere on the Pacific Coast.[69] These were the days of the silent movies, which needed some musical accompaniment, and Mrs. Janet Venables on piano and Mr. Brown on violin were hired to "play the picture." Brown earned $1.50 a night for his effort.[70]

219

The "picture show" then moved to the Jones & Carter building on First Avenue. This new theatre under the management of J. W. Bagman could seat about three hundred people. The opening program was a two reel feature entitled, *The Scapegoat.*

The plans of the Anderson Company were being brought to fruition[71] as the Experimental Farm (the Anderson Farm) across the Somass River was demonstrating what could be done with the soil and climate of the Alberni Valley. Another large area had been cleared and put under cultivation.

A petition to have a road constructed to the west coast was being enthusiastically signed by the residents.

In Alberni, the community was divided into three wards: South, North, and West. Two aldermen would serve each ward.[72]

The first Alberni city council let the contract to build a fire hall to J. H. Gordon, chief of the Alberni Volunteer Fire Brigade. Gordon was asked to put up a bond of five hundred dollars to ensure the building, designed by George Gibson,[73] would be completed and ready for occupancy by February 15, 1914. George Forrest was appointed the new fire chief; his assistant was A. E. Drinkwater.

When the municipal elections of January 1914 rolled around, for the position of mayor it was a close race between incumbent C. Frederic Bishop and Capt. Huff. The election should have favoured Bishop, but Huff won by a narrow margin of eight-five votes to eight-two. Both men ran on the "municipal ownership" ticket, but it was Capt. Huff's position in favour of a plebiscite on the lighting question that won the day for him. The firm of Ritchie-Agnes Power Company now wanted a thirty-year agreement to supply power to Alberni, but Huff thought a thirty-year agreement was out of the question. The community might as well put in their own system.[74]

At an Alberni Board of Trade meeting in February, W. H. Marcon offered his property at the corner of Johnston Road and Gertrude Street for a post office site at a cost of $2,600.[75] Marcon also made arrangements to relocate the Chinese wash house in the vicinity to make the neighbourhood "more desirable."[76] The new post office would be larger than the old one. There would also be 225 new post boxes of the small size and twenty-five drawers. The lobby would have desks and writing materials. There would be two wickets; one for general delivery and stamp sale; the other for money order and registration business. Bernard Frank was appointed the postmaster for Alberni in March, and his appointment was endorsed by the

Alberni Board of Trade. Roy Cox was the assistant postmaster. The new office opened the first of April.[77]

On May 4, 1914, Leonard Frank tendered his resignation to the Board of Trade. The board refused to accept it. The members considered Frank "had at all times proved himself a very valuable citizen and a hearty worker for the good of the city."[78] There was no explanation why Frank wished to resign; however, it was around this time that he became a photographer for the provincial government.

In May, 1914, the Albernis had a visit from two unusual people who caused quite a stir among residents. Two distinguished looking East Indians arrived on the train and proceeded immediately to Stevens' boat house at the foot of Argyle Street. There they chartered the *Serita Queen* for a trip down the Alberni Inlet. They stated their objective was to intercept the Japanese liner *Komagata Maru* on its way to Vancouver. They intended to speak to the commander and some of the passengers on board.

It had been announced in the daily newspapers that the *Komagata Maru* was due to arrive at Victoria on Friday. It had on board 376 Sikh immigrants. Wealthy countryman Gurdit Singh was bringing over the group with the objective of testing the exclusion law recently made by order-in-council at Ottawa. Immigration authorities were instructed not to allow the Sikhs to land in Canada. Some suspected the two visiting Sikh gentlemen intended to acquaint the charterer of the liner with the details of movements to prevent their landing either at Victoria or Vancouver and try to induce him to have the immigrants landed at some point in Barkley Sound or Alberni Inlet.

Shortly after the two men started on their journey down the Inlet, immigration inspector H. Good arrived by automobile from Nanaimo. He held a hurried conference with Customs Collector Garrard before following the men down the Inlet.

The two Sikhs landed on the shore of Pachena Bay and walked over the trail to the Pachena wireless station where they attempted to communicate with the incoming ship. What messages, if any, were exchanged is unknown. But Inspector Good was prepared to prevent any other means of communication with the *Komagata Maru*. It was believed that when the two men learned of the activities of the immigration official, they abandoned their mission and returned to Port Alberni.

Mayor Burde, in his capacity as newspaper editor, interviewed the two men on their return. One was introduced as H. Rahim, editor of the *Hindustan*, published in Vancouver. "He proved to be an enter-

221

taining sort of person, with a fluent command of the English language and a sense of humour which apparently caused him to enjoy the excitement he and his travelling companion had created."[79] Rahim admitted if they had been able to communicate with the *Komagata Maru* they would have advised a change of course and a call at Port Alberni. But, he contended, there would have been no attempt made to land passengers without first advising the immigration authorities at Victoria or Vancouver. The little jaunt he and his companion had taken, he said, ought to be appreciated by the people of Port Alberni, as it meant that the people from the Far East were able to realize that the route via Port Alberni was feasible and a short cut to either Victoria or Vancouver. "You see," he remarked, "our people have a better knowledge of the easiest and shortest way to reach the important points of B.C. than some of your own people in B.C. seem to have."[80]

Burde said there was only one thing that the captain of the *Komagata Maru* lacked information on: that Port Alberni was a port of entry. If he had known, he would have sailed directly here to meet the resistance of the immigration authorities.

The *Komagata Maru* arrived off the Williams Head quarantine station, where it was detained for a few hours for inspection. It then proceeded to Victoria, where passengers were prevented from landing by the immigration authorities. Later the ship proceeded to Vancouver; there, once again, the passengers were not allowed to land. Gurdit Singh, on arrival at Victoria, said he was determined to fight the matter out in the courts because he believed that the people of British India should have the right of entry in all portions of His Majesty's Dominions.

> There are thousands of natives of my country who are anxious to come here. The reason I chartered the *Komagata Maru* was to find out if it was the intention of your government not to permit East Indians to come to Canada. If we are turned back the matter will not rest there. I intend to use every legitimate course I can pursue to make sure if it is true that East Indians will not be permitted to land in your country.[81]

Of the East Indians aboard, he said that 160 had been taken on at Hong Kong, the balance at Shanghai and Japanese ports. He had chartered for the vessel for six months at a cost of $66,000. She carried a crew of forty Japanese and a cargo of coal, which he hoped to dispose of in Vancouver.

All summer long, the people of Vancouver watched the comings and goings of immigration officers to the *Komagata Maru*, which was moored in the harbour. Case after case came into the courts; and as the time lengthened, the rations of the Sikhs became scarce and their plight more desperate. On July 18, after a court declared in favour of the deportation order, a mini war broke out between police, immigration officers, and the passengers on the *Komagata Maru*. Finally, arrangements were made for the departure of the ship. On the morning of July 23, the citizens of Vancouver watched as the *Komagata Maru* was escorted out to sea by H.M.C.S. *Rainbow*.[82]

Canadian Pacific Lumber Company

In September 1910 the Barclay Sound Cedar Company of Port Alberni merged with three other concerns, the Canadian Pacific Lumber Co. of Port Moody, the Anglo-American Lumber Co. of Vancouver, and the Gibbons Lumber Mills which operated on the Arrow Lakes. The consolidated corporation was named the Canadian Pacific Lumber Company and had its head office in Vancouver. Capitalized at $5 million, the company was one of the largest in British Columbia.[83] Robert Abernethy and Percy Roe had started the company in April 1900 with financial backing from Victoria businessman Thomas P. Paterson. In 1910 Abernethy and Roe sold out M. M. Carlin, Robert W. Gibson, and J. D. McArthur. Carlin became president.[84]

The new company announced it would build a large export mill at Port Alberni when the extension of the E & N Railway from Nanaimo was completed. The new mill would handle a large amount of the oriental and Pacific trade besides shipping direct to the northwest and eastern Canada. The old mill would be turned into a shingle mill. The new company would take over all the standing timber owned by the four concerns, estimated to be 135 square miles, with the cruise amounting to 2½ billion board feet.[85]

If Port Alberni expected there would be an immediate boom in the forest industry, hopes were soon dashed in June 1911 when Arthur E. Gilbert, president of the Red Cliff Lumber and Land Co, visited the city and predicted:

> You cannot push the lumber manufacturing industry ahead of its time except to your sorrow, but when its time does come there is no force that can hold it back. I believe it will be two or three years yet before lumber manufacturing on a large scale is commenced in this district. It should not be later than the opening of the Panama Canal billed for the year 1915. You will have to wait a little while for your lumber manufacturing boom. It will be a bigger thing than any of you now imagine.[86]

223

Gilbert's statement cast a gloomy business outlook for the next few years in the district.

The first shipment from the new Canadian Pacific Lumber Co. sawmill was made June 22, 1912. This was a red letter day for Port Alberni, as it marked the dawn of the forest industry. The new mill's payroll was expected to run to $20,000. A number of orders had been received from the west coast. Most orders previously had been going to Victoria and other outside points. The manager of the new mill was J. F. Halle, with Rand Gibbons assistant general manager. Gibbons moved to Port Alberni in order to give the sawmill his personal supervision. In August 1912, the company purchased seventeen city lots to build residences for the married employees in the mill.[87]

Within a year an unexpected opportunity for B.C.'s lumber industry came from the prairies. Immigrants were arriving in Canada in the thousands, and many were heading for Canada's wheat belt. The City of Winnipeg received 5,458 homesteaders in the first half of 1913; of these 2,638 were British, and the rest were from other countries.[88] The demand for lumber for building became tremendous.

In September 1912, the mill filled an order for the CPR for twenty carloads of heavy timbers to be used in bridge building in the mountains and on the prairies.[89] The unequalled demand for lumber caused stocks at various points in the province to be greatly depleted. Shipments from the coast and mountains were moved ahead.[90]

In anticipation of increased export business, the Canadian Pacific Lumber Company's managing director, Thomas Meredith, announced that a new wharf would be built in Port Alberni to handle large ocean vessels. Meredith had been connected with the Anglo-American Lumber Co, one of the partners in the new enterprise. Later in the year, Rand Gibbons, now manager of the mill, said he had an order for twenty-five carloads of lumber to be shipped to points in Saskatchewan.[91]

For a time it looked as though the forest industry was about to bloom. However, things were far from being rosy. The industry was stymied by a shortage of railway cars to carry lumber east.[92] In January 1914 the company was rushing out orders. The mill was running eight hours a day and averaging 90,000 feet a day. Every day a train of ten cars left the mill for points on the prairies and eastern provinces.

Keeping the plant supplied with logs was the business of the Wiest Logging Company. Jack Wiest, superintendent of the logging operations, said his company was preparing for bigger operations in 1914. He expected to be in a position to keep well ahead of the sawmill even with the larger demand for logs. There were now seventy-four people on the Wiest payroll. Of these, sixty were loggers. The company also added to its operation a donkey engine which increased the number of logs delivered each day to the mill.

The Shay engine, now restored and known fondly as the Two Spot, was built by the Lima Locomotive Company, Lima, Ohio. The forty-two ton engine was built to run on very rough track. It was the first steam locomotive in the area, and soon became very popular with loggers.[93] "Starting with the ground lead method and two skidders – an Empire for speed, and a Humboldt for power – Wiest went into high lead yarding at Cox Lake with a five mile logging railway."[94]

By April, the mill had increased its hours of operation to a twelve hour day. It was turning out some very large timbers for shipment across Canada, including one which was six feet in diameter. But the one shipped out April 15, consigned to Halifax, had everyone talking. It measured twenty-two by twenty-two and was sixty-five feet long. There was scarcely a knot discernible in the piece which measured over 2621 board feet.[95]

The Panama Canal was due to open in August 1914. Already orders were being placed for B.C. lumber to be shipped via the Canal to Toronto for the large harbour project underway in that city.[96] On August 4, 1914, war was declared. Four days later the Canadian Pacific Lumber Co. mills in Port Alberni and Port Moody were shut down. The collapse of the prairie market in 1913 combined with the outbreak of the war disrupted shipping and closed export markets. The move was at first considered temporary. Wiest Logging Company announced it would continue logging at least until the end of the month in order to have a supply of logs on hand for the reopening of the mill. On September 2 the mill in Port Moody was destroyed by fire. By October 28 president Thomas Meredith announced the company was now in the hands of receivers.[97]

British Columbia had neglected the export lumber market, so when it was forced to turn to the world market, shipping was at a premium because of the war. Half of the logging camps in the province were forced to shut down.

A Royal Commission on Indian Affairs

Although they had never surrendered their land rights, the Tseshaht and Opetchesaht tribes of Alberni were now limited to life on their designated reserves. They continued to fish or hunt for food, and occasionally they found work in the canneries. There were no jobs in the mills in Port Alberni as employers opted to hire oriental labor. Native lives were in limbo – they were caught between the white man's world and the world of their ancestors.

The issue of native land claims would not go away for the provincial and federal governments. For decades there had been confusion over how much land was enough. Finally the two governments appointed a royal commission to draw reserve boundaries once and for all. The McKenna-McBride Royal Commission on Indian Affairs was born in 1912. It travelled British Columbia listening to testimony from Indian leaders. What was heard in Alberni showed the frustration of native Indians living on a reserve in 1914.

On May 9, 1914 members of the Royal Commission arrived in Port Alberni on the chartered steamer S.S. *Tees*. They included Nathaniel W. White, K.C., chairman, Dr. J. A. J. McKenna, and Mr. Saumarez Carmichael, K.C., representing the Dominion government; J. P. Shaw, M.P.P. and Day H. Macdowall, the nominees of British Columbia; C. H. Gibbons, secretary and James S. McArthur, clerk and stenographer. Inspector W. E. Ditchburn and Indian Agent C. A. Cox accompanied the commissioners in their investigations.[98]

The Alberni Board of Trade was invited to attend one of the sessions to give information on the market value of land in the local reserves. A committee of three met with the commission. They were Walter R. H. Prescott, former manager of the Royal Bank of Canada; John F. Bledsoe, editor of the *Alberni Advocate*; and Ed. M. Whyte, secretary, Alberni Board of Trade. Their comments must have been favourably received by the commissioners because the committee reported back to the Board of Trade meeting in June, "the commission members stated it was the most helpful and well considered (brief) they had received anywhere in B.C."[99]

On May 11th the Royal Commission met with the two tribes. The first testimony heard was from the Opetchesaht tribe. Chief Dan Watts was sworn in as interpreter. He began by expressing concern over reserve boundaries, wanting them resurveyed to find out if they still had the same acreage as before. The big concern, however, was about fishing in the Somass River.

Many years ago the big men told all the Indians they could fish in this river all they wanted for their food, but now those whitepeople try to stop us. I don't know what we are going to do. We live on our fish – we are not like whitepeople – it is hard for us to get a job here. Since the canneries opened there were fewer fish. The purse seiners were gobbling up all the fish.[100]

Chief Dan Watts also complained that the dam built at the site of the old paper mill was restricting fish swimming upstream. There was also concern about hunting deer and ducks the Indians shot for food. The game warden had told them they couldn't do this. The chairman explained they could shoot the siwash duck at any time, but other ducks could not be shot during close season. Indian Agent Cox argued the Indians were not getting a square deal. The Chief wondered why they were not allowed to cut timber on their reserve; they feared fire would destroy everything they had. He considered they should be allowed to cut timber and make a few dollars selling it.

Three years earlier the government had built a road through the Opetchesaht reserve, taking a large portion of land. Water pipes had also been run through the reserve, but Indians were refused water. No permission had been asked nor information given that this work would be done. Chief Watts felt the band should be compensated. The band also feared its land would be taken away as there were now town lots developing all around the reserve.

Following this testimony the chairman began to question Chief Watts about the different reserve lands and his people. The Chief said there were fifty-seven men, women, and children living on the reserve. The chairman offered some advice. "I think that if the Indians turned their attention to the raising and planting of crops and cattle; especially if the fish are getting scarce . . . I think if you turned your attention to farming it would be a great deal better."

The same concerns over fishing were heard from the Tseshaht band later the same day. Hamilton George was sworn in as interpreter. Chief Shewish addressed the commission.

Now the Indians claimed the river, but the whitepeople say we have no rights to fish, and we cannot make a living in any other way. What fish we caught were distributed amongst the tribe. The whitepeople came in here – they thought they would run the place better and thought they would have more fish by having the Indians not use traps. The purse seine came and began fishing at the mouth of the river, and sometimes they caught 10,000 and 15,000 salmon and they caught the salmon before they got up to the spawning grounds. If they keep on fishing with the purse seine they won't have any salmon to take out of the river.

We are entitled to this land. Our great-great-grandfathers lived and were born here. I don't know why an Indian should have a license to fish on this river because we claim the salmon running up here.

A Tseshaht Indian named Mr. Bill testified that unless they were allowed to fish they would not be able to buy the sugar, tea, and flour offered by the white people.

The Government or the Fishery Inspectors did not bring the fish into the rivers after they came into the country – the salmon were here even before we were. We claim the salmon ourselves and it should not have anything to do with the whites. We were here before they were and we claim all the fish.

Mr. Bill said after two years there were only a few herring left in the Alberni Inlet because of the purse seiners.

The laws against Indians were getting more difficult for Indians to cope with, said another Indian named Tom. He said there was talk about a railway company putting a track through the Tseshaht reserve. Tom wondered where the children would play. There were now three roads through the reserve lands and no one had been compensated. The chairman advised it was near 5:00 p.m. and asked them to hurry "unless there is something of importance you want to bring before us."

The Tseshaht people wanted a doctor to look after them when they were ill. The doctor in town was too busy and often had no time to visit the reserve. He was paid fifty dollars a month by the government to attend the Indians but insisted on charging more from individuals, stating his government pay was not enough.

The reason we ask you to give us a doctor was because we have no money. At the present time when there is a child, or a woman or a man gets sick, no one looks after them. Sometimes we go to town for the doctor but he does not come up to see us, and they have to lay there and suffer. We want a sober doctor – one who does not drink.

Chief Shewish was questioned about the number of people living on the reserve. He said there were 136 people. When asked if they worked in the mills, he said that since the orientals and East Indians came the Indians had no chance of getting work. The chief expressed hope that through education the future of Indian children would be better. He wanted permission to cut timber on the reserve to sell. One Indian had been caught by A. W. Neill doing just that and was put in prison, he said.

The chairman thanked Chief Shewish and others for their testimony and stated he had noted what they had said regarding fishing and cutting of timber. He agreed something should be done regarding the timber and promised to make a report about the subject. "We are very glad that you have a fine school here, and a great deal will depend on the education you give your children," concluded chairman White. Two days later the commissioners boarded the S.S. *Tees* headed for Kildonan and another hearing.

A year later, at the old paper mill dam site a mile above River Bend bridge, the dam was destroyed, allowing large schools of salmon to migrate further up the Somass River to their natural spawning grounds. Norman Wood destroyed the dam on instructions from the Dominion Fisheries.

In 1916 the McKenna-McBride Royal Commission on Indian Affairs announced the reductions and changes to the boundaries of reserves. Everywhere the hearings were held, commissioners heard statements and pleas that reserve lands be increased rather than reduced. The commission found the West Coast Agency had 150 reserves totalling 12,385.1 acres. One acre for 1683 persons, providing 7.35 acres per capita. It added fourteen reserves but cut off 600 acres from one and 240 acres from another, leaving a total of 12,200.25 acres. The reductions were made because the reserves were regarded as being "in excess of the reasonable requirement of the Indians."[101] The Tseshaht tribe had 240 acres of the northern portion of its reserve land reduced.[102] The Opetchesaht land remained untouched.

Other concerns expressed by the two tribes regarding timber rights, hunting, fishing, and medical care, were largely ignored as the country entered the First World War.

War Is Declared

For a few days in late July and early August residents of Alberni and Port Alberni felt there was a chance for Great Britain to avoid war in Europe. This hope was soon dispelled. On August 7, 1914, as the crowds gathered at the *Alberni Advocate* office around the bulletin board, it gradually dawned on even the most optimistic that it was only a question of hours before Great Britain would be forced to take action.[103] The *Advocate* bulletin board posted important notices and news events between the newspaper's publishing dates.

Fear of war was not unfounded; Canada was ill prepared, with only a regular army of "3110 men and 684 horses, plus a navy of 300 men." The air force did not exist except for "two canvas planes still packed in crates."[104] When war was declared August 4, 1914, the call went out across Canada for volunteers. Recruiting offices were set up. These were flooded by young men, content to earn only a dollar a day serving their country. Canada had offered Britain a contingent of 25,000 men and was delighted to get far more recruits than were needed.

"The war spirit is alive in Port Alberni," read the headlines of the *Port Alberni News* on August 5. A call for volunteers for active service was received by Capt. W. G. Cunningham, attached to the 88th Fusiliers of Victoria. Cunningham spoke to Mayor Burde, who called a public meeting in the theatre on First Avenue. It attracted nearly three hundred men from both communities. Burde asked all citizens to endeavour to remain calm, cheerful, and tolerant, and he observed that there were two or three people in the city who did not seem to have much sympathy with the British cause. He was referring to those settlers who had been born in Germany.

There were two classes of men enlisted. One group was men willing to leave on the shortest notice for Nanaimo or Victoria to prepare for active service. The second group was left at home unless there was an emergency. The maximum term of war service was eighteen months. Dr. C. T. Hilton asked for volunteers for the Legion of Frontiersmen, who would proceed to Vancouver to be transported to the front. He explained the legion did not belong to the regular troops but would engage in a sort of guerilla warfare against the enemy. Over thirty men volunteered for service with the Fusiliers, while four put down their names as frontiersmen.[105]

The war in Europe was dramatically brought home by the occupation of the Cable Station at Bamfield by the 5th regiment from Victoria. H.M.C.S. *Rainbow* began patrolling the line of the Pacific cable. The ship had just recently escorted the *Komagata Maru* out of the Vancouver harbour and had been fitted out for a patrol of the sealing grounds in the Bering Sea. With the war in Europe, the *Rainbow* became an escort and patrol vessel. There were reports that the German cruiser *Leipzig*, which had been stationed off the west coast of Mexico, was headed towards British Columbia.[106]

Mayor Huff in Alberni received a telegram from Esquimalt dated August 4: "Please give the widest publicity to the following: All Royal Naval Reserve Officers and men are called out by the Admiralty and should proceed to England forthwith."[107]

During the first few days of recruitment in both towns nearly one hundred people had signed up for service. On August 14 a large crowd gathered at the Alberni railway station to see the men off to war. There were few dry eyes as the train pulled in from Port Alberni and the Alberni contingent got on board. The cheers of the crowd on the platform were answered by those on board. Then there was a last look as the train slowly pulled out of the station. Many wondered when the next call for recruits would come.[108]

The departure of the men to the front signalled the beginning of a depression for the twin communities. Business activity slackened and land values declined. There was no work for those left behind. The mill was closed and logging shut down. Construction work on the Canadian Northern Railway would only be carried on according to economic conditions caused by the war in Europe, announced Sir Donald Mann, vice-president of the railway. To get rid of timber stocks and secure revenue for the country, the government lifted the restriction on the export of logs. The immediate future looked bleak.

Mayor Burde made a hurried trip to Victoria to try to induce some continuation of the Canadian Northern Railway construction work. Premier Sir Richard McBride promised he would take the matter up with Sir Donald Mann. In December, Mayor Burde and MPP John Wood reported the Canadian Northern Railway work would begin again in the near future. They had returned from another conference with the premier.

In the meantime, sixty additional soldiers arrived at Bamfield to guard the cable station. Two machine guns were landed for protection of the immediate area. Another ten soldiers were on duty at Pachena.

With the local economy on a downswing, Burde made the decision to publish the *Port Alberni News* only once a week. He announced there would be no Saturday issue until further notice. Like other businesses in the city the paper felt it necessary to retrench.[109]

Rumours circulating that the hospital would be closed were discounted by the board of directors, who had decided to reduce staff. The hospital would remain open, But maternity cases would be treated only on the condition that patients provided their own nurse for night duty.

At the end of September another call for volunteers for the war effort went out from the 88th Fusiliers. Another sixteen men volunteered at a recruiting meeting held in the court house in Alberni. Transportation costs were not provided the volunteers by the military, so arrangements were made by the city councils of both cities to provide tickets to Victoria.

231

This was a difficult time for those Alberni residents of German descent. They were eyed with suspicion; their comments and actions were weighed for any hint of betrayal; their friendships were threatened. Bobby De Beaux, Bernard and Leonard Frank, and Nils Weiner all suffered the scrutiny of an anxious community. Although Weiner was born in northern Sweden, some believed him to be of Prussian descent.

Two letters to the editor appeared in the *Victoria Times* on Monday, November 2, 1914, from James Clark of Alberni. The letters were reprinted November 11th in the *Port Alberni News*.

> This is a matter of national importance and not trifling, and the appointment of a nationalized foreigner should be prevented in the future. Why Leonard Frank should be appointed photographer for the provincial government is past our understanding. I am simply one of a numerous party not objecting to Frank's appointment through lack of ability, but from the fact that he is a foreigner born and there are thousands of Britishers for such a position.

The other letter was addressed to the postmaster-general.

> I wish to draw your attention to a ludicrous position in the post office at Alberni. The old postmistress was dispensed with and a German, named Bernard Frank, a German trained soldier, a pro-Boer of the worst type, fills the post. Are there no native born sons to fill the post? His brother Leonard, ever a worse pro-Boer, has photographed every important position on the coast, including Banfield Cable Station, lighthouses, etc. for government, railway companies advertisements. I understand both of the Franks are under the strongest surveillance.

Postmaster-general Louis P. Pelletier replied to Clark, stating that Bernard Frank had been appointed on the recommendation of the local member of parliament Herbert S. Clements. Burde, outraged at the claim made by Clark, wrote an editorial: "The charge that he is a German trained soldier is absurd in view of the fact that he left Germany when he was 17 years of age. The Franks are both pioneers of this district and have done more than the average person towards its development."

Following the reprinting of the letters and the subsequent editorial, Clark penned another letter to the editor, this time to the *Port Alberni News*.

> Apparently you have no argument to offer and security carries no weight to maintain the ridiculous position of placing a man born in Germany as a postmaster in the British Empire. The Frank brothers have both an uncle and a brother fighting for their country against our Empire and quite naturally their sympathy is with them. The original letter sent to *Victoria*

Times does not agree with the insertion in your paper. In clause three you have no reference to Leonard Frank sending negatives to Germany to be developed and that may have an important bearing on German naturalization.

I notice the local stores retail postcards, views, etc. marked "printed in Germany" but there is a sound British way to deal with retailers of German goods. We should boast this city as the Western end of the "All Red Route" and cry out for manufacturers when even the school pump is German made and from the day it was erected has neither been ornamental or useful, except to the plumber. Does Canada or the British Empire not manufacture pumps good enough for the City fathers?[110]

Burde replied; "If it can be presumed that when one brother has an uncle and a brother, the other brother has the same relations, one point in Mr. Clark's communication can be accepted without question."[111]

In the civic elections of 1915, Mayor Huff was re-elected by acclamation in Alberni. Mayor Burde, in Port Alberni, however, had some competition from A. D. MacIntyre. The vote was close, with Burde taking a small lead. In a spirit of goodwill both mayors publicly praised each other.

With a new mandate to continue Mayor Burde took steps to reduce the salaries of city employees by $5.00 per month. The salaries per month before reductions were – city clerk $100, medical health officer $15, city electrician $100, senior engineer $85, waterworks foreman $80, chief of police $90 with an additional $10 a month for services as sanitary inspector. The salary of the city scavenger was $100 a month, plus $30 a month for the upkeep of the horse. The city scavenger's salary was discontinued. Those benefiting from his work would have to pay him directly.[112]

This was the first election in Canadian history where some residents whose names were on the voters list were not allowed to cast their votes. Deputy returning officers in municipal elections throughout Canada were instructed to prevent from voting those former residents of German, Austrian, and Turkish nationality who were not naturalized Canadians. While their names appeared on the voters list as occupants of property, they were prevented from voting. All voters of foreign nationality, whether naturalized or not, had to be sworn in.[113]

As well, all aliens in Canada were forbidden to have in their possession arms or explosives. Those whose countries were at war with England had to surrender their weapons to the authorities immediately. Bobby De Beaux did not surrender either the rifles or the ammunition he had in his store on Argyle Street, but, like others from Germany, he was under surveillance.

A referendum to abolish the ward system in Port Alberni, which had been in operation since November 1912, was passed.[114]

The large number of unemployed was of great concern to both towns. Mayor Burde, working with MPP John Wood, convinced the provincial government to loosen its purse strings and provide some financial assistance in the amount of $5,000 to inaugurate permanent street improvement work that would be completed over three months. Unable to induce the resumption of construction work on the Canadian Northern Railway, the government considered another plan for relief work. Mayor Burde spoke about the unemployed in Port Alberni, noting how the unexpected termination of payrolls had brought about the serious conditions. Anyone who wished to work on the civic works program had to register at city hall. Only urgent cases for relief would be considered.

In January 1915 the Alberni District Home Guard was organized in Alberni. Mayor Huff presided at the meeting. Hubert Mervyn T. Hodgson, a well known civil engineer, was elected captain; A. W. Neill and Albert Wood Lee were elected lieutenants. All three had military training. The purpose of the corps was to acquire military instruction in infantry drill and musketry. All male British subjects capable of bearing arms were eligible, and the applicants had to agree to serve for six months. Forty men signed up; of these twenty had some service experience. The corps used the rifles of the Alberni District Civilian Rifle Association.

The hospital was again in financial trouble. Two debts were outstanding: the Canadian Pacific Lumber Co. (CPLC) and Wiest Logging Company had failed to pay employee deductions. The CPLC debt amounted to $215, and the hospital board needed the money. Letters were written unsuccessfully to Thomas Meredith, managing director of the CPLC, and to the receivers, requesting the debt be paid. Meredith replied that since the account was not paid before the company went into receivership, it was out of his hands. The hospital board decided to take legal action. Wiest Logging Company explained its overdue account would be paid before March.[115]

The hospital appealed to both communities for financial help and asked each to provide a municipal grant. For some time it appeared the hospital would be cut from the provincial grant. In contrast to the quarter of a million dollars the province had provided for hospital purposes in B.C. during the previous year, in 1915 there was only a few thousand. However, the hospital board was delighted with the good news that came in a letter from Provincial Secretary H. E. Young informing them the hospital would get another $1,000.[116]

Dr. Morgan's lectures on St. John's Ambulance work were proving popular. His class had fifty-seven members.

Letters from the front began arriving back home. One of the first came to J. Thompson in April from Pete Johnstone, one of Port Alberni's fire department volunteers.

> I am still alive and kicking. We have been twice in the trenches and they are a good deal better than I expected. The ones we are holding now are more a series of small forts than trenches, made of sand bags and of a three quarter circle formation. The trouble is in relieving and being relieved as you have to cross an open space of 150 yards right in front of the enemy's line before you get under cover. You are continually sniped and are often under the fire of their maxin guns. They keep sending up star shells, which made things as bright as day, putting C. M. Pineo's efforts in the shade, then you have to either stand steady, or flop in the mud. Their snipers are remarkable shots, often sending bullet after bullet through our loopholes.[117]

Two months later Corporal Pete Johnstone became the Albernis' first casualty of the war. He was killed in action at the battle of Ypres on April 22, 1915. Johnstone had joined the Seaforth Highlanders in Vancouver at the outbreak of the war and left Canada with the first contingent. After distinguishing himself in a bayonet charge he was raised from private to lance-corporal. "He was the stuff that real war heroes are made of."[118]

Bamfield Cable station came under attack in May. While it would not be considered a major attack, nevertheless, two men had attempted to blow the station up. The sentry noticed suspicious movement and went to investigate. Suddenly a rifle shot cracked and a bullet whistled overhead. The sentry fired at two men fleeing into the darkness in a boat. Later, the military guard made a search of the area to confirm a boat had been seen exchanging signals with someone ashore. Extra sentries were placed at the station.[119]

Rumours circulated that the Canadian Pacific Lumber Co. mill was about to be reopened. When asked, Meredith said the question of resuming operations depended mainly on the CPR. The lumber company had entered negotiations with the railway company for more favourable freight rates from Port Alberni to points east. The proposition was now up to the railway officials in Winnipeg. The Canadian Pacific Lumber Co. had been operating the Anglo-American mill in Vancouver, but owing to the expropriation by the dominion government of part of its site and the consequent handicap on operations, both the lumber company and its receivers were unhappy with the situation. If the negotiations with the CPR were successful, the Vancouver mill would be closed and the Port Alberni mill reopened.

When the Canadian Northern Railway heard there was a possibility of the mill reopening, it decided to leave its construction crew where it was for three or four weeks. It had previously planned to withdraw the crew completely but decided to wait to see if the mill did start up.

Work on a new government road summer project began in April. Estimated to cost $5,000, the road was to connect Kinross Street (later renamed Burde Street) in Port Alberni with the Island trunk road at a point near the summit. The road would allow Carmichael & Moorhead to open up their land development, which was said to be enough for twenty small farms.[120]

By July 1915, the first section of the new road was completed. Mayor Burde and Alderman McNaughton could not resist taking Burde's automobile for a spin on the road link. The highway was wide enough for two cars to pass. A mile and three-quarters of the road had been built through the virgin forest to the east of the city. Another two miles needed to reach the intersection with the trunk road at the summit was expected to be completed the following year.[121]

Alberni residents were upset about this new road, which they saw as another example of Alberni being left out in the cold. Travellers coming into the city would go directly into Port Alberni, bypassing Alberni completely. A campaign was mounted in Alberni to stop the construction of the road.

Baron von Alvensleben

With spring came renewed hope for the forest industry. Every day there was a new and more substantial promise it would come back and on a larger scale than before. The British Admiralty had placed an order in Vancouver for ten million board feet of lumber. There were important orders from the railway. The Canadian Pacific Lumber Company was operating its Vancouver mill at full capacity and bidding for more business. Just one more important order could mean the reopening of the Port Alberni mill.

But there were other powers at work which could give greater importance to Port Alberni. An American syndicate of lumber manufacturers, the Red Cliff Land & Lumber Co. of Duluth, Minnesota, owned many thousands of acres of the best timber on Vancouver Island. The company had been preparing plans for logging operations and construction of a mill equal to the largest on the coast. Negotiations had begun with the CPR for manufacturing and booming sites and railway facilities. Eight years before, the company had obtained thousands of acres of timber from the railway on the understanding that the E & N line would extend to Port Alberni and that a large manufacturing industry would be established here as soon as the road was completed.

The prospect of an enormous profit on a turnover tempted the Red Cliff Company to make a deal to sell its holdings for $2.2 million to a German syndicate, represented by Baron Alvo von Alvensleben of Vancouver. Alvensleben, described as a Prussian aristocrat, had arrived in Vancouver in 1904 with only four dollars in his pocket. Before long he had established a real estate and investment company with branch offices in Victoria, Berlin, Paris, and London. He advertised extensively overseas, describing the investment opportunities in British Columbia. Vancouver was then in the midst of an economic boom.[122]

The baron also purchased timber holdings, leases, licenses, and logging outfits. In 1906 he organized the Vancouver Timber & Trading Co. turning over to it all of his forestry holdings. He then returned to Berlin, where he sold shares to his friends and family connections. By 1911, Vancouver Timber & Trading was a $10 million investment. In 1914 the company had an estimated $7 million of German money invested in the B.C. forest industry.

The German syndicate paid $800,000 to Red Cliff Company on its agreement for purchase. The payment on both principal and interest stopped. Tax payments also stopped. Von Alvensleben's Company went into liquidation with little or no hope of being able to complete its payments. The journal of Edward T. Buxton, treasurer of the Red Cliff Company, sheds some light on the deal. Partelow Miles, agent for the Red Cliff Co., informed his company someone wanted to purchase its west coast timber. Miles introduced Alvo von Alvensleben and his brother. The Red Cliff Company agreed to sell at one hundred dollars an acre, or $2.2 million, with a sixty day option to allow von Alvensleben to consult with his principals in Berlin.

The von Alvensleben Prussian estate had been in the family for over seven hundred years. One uncle was ambassador to Russia and another, General Casper von Alvensleben, commanded the 5th Army Corps in the Franco-Prussian war. The father, Count Werner von Alvensleben, was a widower with five sons and two daughters. The sons were in the army. Each year since childhood his Imperial Majesty, Kaiser Wilhelm II, had visited the von Alvensleben estate to hunt in their four thousand acre game preserve. Alvo von Alvensleben had been an officer in a regiment of the Guards, stationed at Pottsdam, and was a protégé of the Kaiser.[123] He had resigned from the army and come to British Columbia, where he tried to interest the Kaiser in several profitable deals in real estate. At the time of the negotiations, Buxton said his company did not know of the von Alvenslebens' connection with the Kaiser. This information was given later. All the company knew then was that the baron was a "man of substantial means and entitled to confidence."[124]

From Berlin, von Alvensleben said he was organizing a company of men of "high standing and financial strength." He asked for an additional sixty days to carry out his plan. The Red Cliff Company agreed. Arthur Gilbert, general manager, and Edward Buxton now thought the deal would go through. Attorneys were advised of the contract and terms of sale. Buxton was invited to Vancouver to continue the negotiations.

> With our attorney, Frank H. de Groat of Duluth, we went to Vancouver. Alvensleben meeting us at the railway station and taking me directly to his home, De Groat meantime going over the matter with our Canadian attorneys, Bodwell and Lawson. Reaching the Alvensleben place, which was quite imposing and substantial, (at Point Grey, in Vancouver) we found the architecture and arrangement of the grounds and buildings to be quite foreign. Those who know said it looked like a part of Germany.
>
> I found there, with von Alvensleben, Baron von Stackhousen, Baron von Roon and Prince Campe and two attorneys. The prince and the two barons were typical German officers – most punctilious and with marked mannerisms; all three were in the Engineer Corps. Von Roon was a nephew of the von Roon who, with Bismarck and von Moltke, formed the trio which fought the Franco-Prussian War. All were most courteous to me, yet I could not help noting that they were rude and arrogant in their treatment of others. The home life of the von Alvenslebens was ideal.
>
> Breakfast was a moveable feast. When ready, one wandered downstairs to the breakfast room. An attendant there informed you what was ready, or would be ready soon, and you gave him your order. Dinner was quite formal. Ladies in full dress, as were the gentlemen and the officers in full regalia. After dinner we had our cigars or cigarettes with a demitasse in the drawing room and then some music. Mrs. von Alvensleben was a fine pianist and her husband had an excellent baritone voice and sang well. The rest of the company joining in the chorus. There was a large billiard room in which we would spend the later part of the evening.

After several days Buxton reported the group had arrived at an agreement. Contracts were drawn up, signed, sealed, and delivered. Papers were placed in escrow with the Canadian Bank of Commerce at Vancouver. The terms of the contract were as follows: The company agreed to sell the property for $2.2 million. After one million dollars was paid, the deed would be given and a mortgage taken for the balance of principal due. There would be a cash payment on signing the contract of $400,000; $200,000 would be paid within ninety days plus an addditional $200,000 the following year. When the final payment of $200,000 was made, the deed would be finalized. All unpaid sums would carry a 7 percent interest charge.

Buxton wrote, "As they had organized a company under the laws of British Columbia, the contract was made with this corporate body. A draft for $400,000 was the first payment on account given to me as treasurer of the Red Cliff Land and Lumber Company Ltd." According to Buxton, he left Frank Duluth in possession of the draft contract and copies of all the papers. But he wondered how it was possible that intelligent and able businessmen, as he was certain these men were, could buy property without first examining it. As far as he knew, no one other than von Albensleben had ever seen the property, and even he had given it only a slight and casual look. The answer to Buxton's riddle came later.

The draft was taken to Henry von der Meyer, vice-president of the German American Bank in St. Paul, Minnesota. Buxton instructed him to collect it and pass the credit to the Red Cliff Company. Von der Meyer was very interested in the draft, as it was on the bank in which the German Emperor and his family and personal friends, were interested. He told Buxton: "You have sold your property to the Kaiser, or to his close associates."

When the Great War erupted in Europe, the Germans had paid on account $800,000. Another payment would be due September 1st, 1914. About the middle of August, Red Cliff Company received via Copenhagen a cable from von Alvensleben asking its representatives to meet him in New York. Gilbert and Buxton complied and met von Alvensleben, Campe, and Dernberg, the latter acting as attorney. The Germans asked for an extension of sixty days on the payment due in September. The Red Cliff Company refused, believing the war would last for some time.

"Prince Campe threw up his hands with a quick gesture and said, "I was in the foreign office in Berlin the day before we sailed and was assured by the officials there that we would be in Paris in a week and the war would be over inside thirty days," Buxton wrote in his journal.

After a lengthy conference, Red Cliff agreed to allow the German businessmen a few days to consult with the German ambassador in Washington, for they had stated that the Kaiser's interest in the property was so large that Ambassador Bernstorf would probably feel the use of government funds to protect the Emperor's interest was warranted. When they returned, they said:

> We will either win or lose this war: although it is hardly to be expected we can lose. If we win the German government will make good – any losses caused by the war – from indemnities collected from the conquered countries. If we lose the war, we would not be allowed to hold property in Canada. In fact, our holding would be confiscated. We will let the matter rest and await events.

Von Alvensleben moved to Seattle, Washington. The United States was not then at war.

While Red Cliff attorneys tried to decide on the next course of action, they were suddenly confronted by a decision of the English highest court that changed the whole status of the case. Lord Chief Justice Alverstone stated in his decision that a corporation organized and operating or holding property under British law, in case a majority of the stockholders were foreigners, was in effect a foreign corporation. Red Cliff was advised by its attorneys that this decision would affect all British possessions and would make the Canadian corporation, which had purchased its property, a foreign corporation. The company would be unable to bring them into court until the end of the war.

Various plans were proposed. Taxes and carrying charges on the property were large, and there was no way of obtaining an income from it until the company could get possession. Taxes alone were about $60,000 a year.

Red Cliff consulted with B.C. Premier Sir Richard McBride as to whether the property should be confiscated because of the German interest. It learned that both the provincial government and the government of Great Britain were in fact fully convinced that Red Cliff's property had been purchased by the German Empire for use as a naval base on the north Pacific. The provincial government decided the property was just as safe in the Red Cliff Company hands. The government was in no condition to take on additional financial burdens. However, it did agree to help in any way to recover the title.

Judge Nesbit, of Toronto, who represented several corporations with difficulties similar to the Red Cliff Company, went to London, England, to find a way out of the problem. Eventually a plan was worked out. After legal action was completed, the property would be returned to Red Cliff. The Province gave an indefeasible title. This meant that should the German government or any party attack the title, the Province of British Columbia would defend the action and guarantee from loss.

When Judge Nesbit returned to New York, Gilbert and Buxton met with him to go over details of the plan to recover full possession of the property. Buxton related the following conversation:

> Do you remember a little Jew named Frank who was employed by your people as a draughtsman while you were locating, surveying and estimating this property? It seems that this young man had appeared at Alberni at a time when I was making one of my frequent visits to overlook the work and consult with our men. He had applied for a position and held good references as a skilled draughtsman and was at once set to work and remained in our employ until the work was completed.

Judge Nesbit stated that he had learned through the British Government Secret Service that Frank had copied all maps, estimates, and plans for heavy concrete foundations for a mill plant and in fact all papers of any value. These had been forwarded to Berlin. He said the German government was fully informed, and when von Alvensleben approached Red Cliff to buy the property his principals already knew all about it. When Edward Buxton heard this, his riddle over the non-investigation of the property before purchase was solved. The man Buxton referred to in his journal was Leonard Frank, the settler from Oldenburg, Germany who had settled in Alberni with his brother Bernard in 1894 and had since become a photographer for the provincial government.

Buxton speculated in his journal as to why the German government would have an interest in the Red Cliff property in the Alberni district. He believed it was because of their need for a north Pacific naval base. The Alberni Inlet would be an ideal safe haven for German ships, and there would also be no trouble in providing ample supply of coal for a large fleet of ships. The plans for heavy concrete foundations for a mill plant could easily be disguised to accommodate heavy cannon. "The very reasons which made it a strategic site for a large lumber operation and for the easy and economic distribution of a bulky product made it also an ideal place for a naval base," wrote Buxton.

Germany already had a naval base near the entrance to the Panama Canal. They had also, said Buxton, obtained from Mexico a naval base on the Gulf of California. In order to complete their plans for world control, a naval base was needed on the north Pacific. This had to be obtained under cover, as neither the United States nor Canada would ever permit such action if its purpose were known. Buxton was not sure what other facts had convinced the governments of both Great Britain and Canada that the Red Cliff property was to be used for a naval base, but he was sure "they were conclusive."

Despite this disclosure, Buxton said he respected von Alvensleben. "I became quite fond of this family. And while in the aftertime disaster overtook them, and war and its cruelty, and its many causes for adverse criticism, caused disparagement and hatred, yet in intimate personal and quite frequent meetings with both von Alvensleben and wife, in his home and mine, I never saw reason to change in my respect and esteem."

The Red Cliff Company applied to the court in Vancouver for a foreclosure and was granted the application, allowing a couple of months time for the defaulters to make good. There seemed little doubt that in the end the Red Cliff Company would again be in full control of practically all the best timber within the E & N Railway belt in the Albernis.[125]

Police files from the war years are full of reports casting suspicion on von Alvensleben as a spy,[126] most of it based on hearsay and unsupported evidence. The United States government eventually interned him in 1917 at Fort Douglas, Utah, on a suspicion of espionage that was never proven. He lived near the Bremerton naval base at Puget Sound, and it is known he opened his home to the captain of an interned German vessel.

A letter from a Marshall Bond to M. White, of the U.S. Secret Service, dated July 13, 1917, stated von Alvensleben frequently associated with a "suspicious German Jew," and read him letters he had received from Germany about the country's shipping, army, and food supplies. Was this friend Leonard Frank? Did Bond label his friend "suspicious" simply because he was Jewish? Buxton also seemed to think Frank was a spy. However, in forming an opinion, it is important to keep in mind the distrust with which Canadians and Americans regarded all Germans during the war years.[127]

Von Alvensleben died in 1965, a year after the death of his wife, leaving a small fortune to his three children.

The Albernis Struggle On

In June 1915, one of Alberni's finest buildings, the Presbyterian Church, was destroyed by fire, and the manse was badly damaged. About 8:30 a.m. the blaze was discovered by Mrs. R. L. Fraser, who was living at the manse with her parents Rev. and Mrs. Carruthers. The Alberni volunteer fire brigade under fire chief George Forrest was the first to arrive at the scene. With water from a nearby hydrant the brigade began attacking the flames, but the hydrant was so close to the heat that some of the hose was badly scorched. The Port Alberni brigade under fire chief W. M. Holt was called in to assist in protecting the surrounding buildings. All the contents of the church, including the parson's valuable library, were destroyed. There was $2,000 insurance on the church building, which had cost in the neighbourhood of $6,000 to build.[128]

The benefit of the Panama Canal to the forest industry in British Columbia was being realized. Orders were being received from parts of the world previously beyond the scope of trade. Once again, the link and shipping advantages of Port Alberni were being acclaimed by the *Port Alberni News*. "Port Alberni is closer than any other B.C. shipping port to the Panama Canal".[129]

Hopes were raised once more when representatives of the Canadian Pacific Lumber Co. and the Dominion Bank inspected the company's property and a portion of its timber limits adjacent to the mill. President R. W. Gibson said his company was endeavouring to make arrangements for an early reopening of the lumber mill in Port Alberni.[130]

The slump in real estate was beginning to show on the records at Port Alberni City Hall. There were 750 lots advertised for sale in July. Of these, twenty-two were sold. Council took steps to exempt from tax sale any of the properties owned by people who had gone to war.

The district of Alberni West began collecting funds to purchase a machine gun to be used by the Canadian troops in Europe. George Spencer and Cluny Luke were in charge of collecting the money. The gun was sent to the 62nd battalion in March 1916.

The Alberni Ladies Patriotic Society was in full swing. The Ladies decided to send fifty dollars to the Red Cross to establish a bed in one of the society's hospitals. Another ten dollars was to be donated to the Overseas Tobacco Fund.

Alberni followed the lead set by the Port Alberni council and cut the salaries of the city clerk and the police magistrate.

The previous November Dick Burde had spoken out in newspaper editorials against the allegations made regarding Leonard and Bernard Frank. Ten months later he found himself in court making a charge of his own. A conversation Burde had with Leonard Frank came out during a trial for assault on a charge made by Frank against resident Cluny C. Luke.

Luke, from Edinburgh, Scotland had made his money sheep ranching in Argentina. He and his French wife travelled all over the world big game hunting. In 1912 they built one of the Alberni district's most beautiful homes, the Hermitage. Residents must have looked on amazed as the 18th century style lodge was constructed on acreage on the high bank of the Somass River on the old Mill Town Road (Falls Road). The ten-room mansion, with attached servants' quarters, had oak panelling from England, bricks from Italy, and plumbing fixtures imported from France.[131] A massive stone chimney rose from the gabled roof. A wide staircase curved up from the hallway in which a huge fireplace was located. Each room had its own fireplace with fireboxes located nearby; the fireboxes were so large a child could walk into them. Chandeliers hung from the ceilings. The great hall measured thirty-five feet square. It was panelled with imported English oak. A full suit of armour stood in the main entrance. Each bedroom had a pedestal sink with French lettering on the hot and cold water taps. The Lukes each had their own apartment, one in blue, the other in pink. Each had its own matching fireplace.

The entrance walls were lined with heads of wild game animals, trophies from hunting expeditions around the world. Among them were deer, elk, caribou, mountain lion, mountain goat, and an eagle. Pelts of animals adorned the floors of the spacious rooms. A stuffed Kodiak bear stood near the entrance, and on the giant staircase leading up to the second floor was a stuffed cougar. Cluny Luke was credited with having bagged the best head of moose in twenty years, and Mrs. Luke held the women's record for caribou.

Luke had been talking with Burde the week before the incident that led to the assault charge, and Burde had told him of a conversation he had had with Leonard Frank. "We have beaten Russia, and we are going to lick England. You are foolish to enlist," Frank told Burde at that time.[132]

A few minutes later Luke was talking with Herbert S. Clements, MP, when he saw Frank approaching. He went forward to the top of the steps of the Somass Hotel, and told Frank to "Get out." Frank refused. He demanded to know why he should leave a public place. A scuttle followed and blows were exchanged between the two men. Frank laid a charge of assault.

Five witnesses were called to the trial to detail the incident. Leonard Frank had been in the company of Robert Wood when he was confronted by Luke. Frank insisted he had the right to come and go as he pleased. Under cross-examination, Frank was asked to explain his relations with a man named Flockerman and his conduct when the news of several disasters to the British and Russian forces reached Port Alberni. Frank denied there had been anything out of the way in any of his actions.

Burde was sworn in. He said it was about the first of August he was approached by Frank. He had been talking of enlisting, and Frank appeared to be trying to get him to refrain from joining up. Burde invited Frank to his house. Frank is reported to have said, "I can talk to you as you are not prejudiced. We have the Russians beaten. But you do not really think that the British are licked. They are licked now. We have them beaten. The war will be over before you can get to the front. You are a fool to enlist."

After hearing the arguments on both sides, Magistrate A. W. Neill found Cluny Luke guilty. He imposed a fine of thirty dollars and refused a request to bind Luke over to keep the peace.

Burde enlisted in the 67th Canadian Scottish regiment as a lieutenant. He was granted a leave of absence from his position as Mayor until the expiry of his term in January 1916. Alderman Edward Exton was elected mayor for the balance of Burde's term.

The First Canadian Pioneers, under Major McDonald, came to Alberni in September of 1915 to recruit more men. Those who signed up included A. Fleming, H. G. Rogers, D. Kershaw, N. A. R. Spencer, G. C. Roff, W. J. Wear, J. Manuel, J. Forsythe, and E. A. D. Jones. Spencer was in California surveying when the call for more men came. He gave up his position and left immediately to join the Alberni group. The number enlisted from Alberni and Port Alberni now rose to 160 men.

Raising money for the war effort often stretched the imaginations of the fund-raisers, but few events were more dramatic than the "war game" of living chess played out in national costumes, which was staged by the Patriotic Fund. The event, held in Lord Best Hall on Johnston Road, was a big success.[133]

War loan bonds, or Victory Bonds as they were known, went on sale for the first time in the history of Canada in November 1915. The call to arms also meant the call for cash to finance the war effort.

Those with savings earning only 3 percent could now invest in bonds worth double that amount. The bonds were issued in denominations of $100, $500, $1,000 and $5,000.[134]

Like many other businesses in the Albernis during this period, the *Alberni Advocate* newspaper had been in financial trouble for a few months. After repeated appeals to subscribers to pay their subscriptions, in October 1915 Bledsoe called it quits and ceased production of Alberni's only newspaper. The last issue was dated October 8. The business of reporting the news fell into the hands of the *Advocate's* rival, the *Port Alberni News*. With Burde off to war, the *News* was now run by Jack Warren, a full-fledged printer who had worked for the *Nanaimo Herald*. Burde still remained the managing director of the publishing company.[135]

Before he left for war, Mayor Dick Burde had been to Victoria twice to try to convince Sir Richard McBride's government to influence the Canadian Northern Railway to continue with the line from Port Alberni to Victoria. Premier McBride was criticized for extending the time limit for construction of the railway. The financial straits of Canadian Northern became desperate in August of 1914, when the company's credit in London was exhausted. McBride telegraphed Donald Mann, one of the principals of Canadian Northern: "Would be very disastrous to me if Island work shut down. Must insist imperative lay some steel and carry on so as at least keep up appearances."[136]

In September 1915, the Canadian Northern Railway was able to float a loan in New York for $11,500,000. This money was earmarked for the development of the company's terminal and other projects in British Columbia. The announcement raised hopes in Port Alberni and Alberni that their economic plight might soon be lightened by the arrival of the railway crews to resume construction of the rail line to Victoria. A week later these hopes were dashed by a comment from the railway company's chief engineer, D. O. Lewis, who said it was the intention of the company to proceed with tracking on a portion of the west coast section of the railway, as well as the Patricia Bay line; "but the work will in all probability be done on the Victoria end and not on the Alberni Canal."[137]

McBride, who had been premier for almost thirteen years, announced on December 15, 1915 that he was resigning to accept the position of Agent General for British Columbia in London, England. William Bowser formed the next government.

Premier Bowser tested the political waters by calling two by-elections, one in Victoria, the other in Vancouver. He was defeated in both. Harlan Carey Brewster, now leader of the Liberal party and former member from Alberni, saw an opportunity to once again make a try for McBride's old constituency of Victoria. With no change to his platform from 1912, Brewster won the Victoria by-election with a healthy majority, beating out A. C. Flumerfelt, McBride's Minister of Finance. Brewster took his seat in March 1916.

The women of British Columbia demanded recognition of political and professional equality. From ministers of the Gospel and prominent business men came a cry for temperance legislation. Brewster indicated the Liberal party would be responsive to these requests.[138]

In the Alberni district, canvassers in favour of Prohibition went door to door. H. J. Knott, of Victoria, the Island organizer for the People's Prohibition Movement of B.C., came to town, held organizational meetings, and succeeded in recruiting a small army of people to assist in his work. The canvassers had cards demanding a vote be taken on the question of prohibition of the liquor traffic. The government was asked to bring in legislation subject to the approval of the People's Prohibition Movement.[139]

A provincial election was called for September 14, 1916, and Harlan C. Brewster became a Liberal candidate in both Victoria and Alberni. There were two other candidates in the Albernis: Capt. John G. C. Wood, the Conservative standard bearer for the district, who was serving in France with the Canadian Expeditionary Force, and Alan W. Neill, who decided to run again as an Independent.

When Premier Bowser visited the district in June 1916, he made no rash promises regarding the resumption of railway work. Instead, Bowser stated he hoped when he came back during the election campaign to be able to offer some definite promise as to when the Canadian Northern would again resume operations.[140]

The Liberal campaign in the Alberni district got into full swing in July when Brewster attended a Liberal meeting in Port Alberni, chaired by Charles McNaughton, president of the local Liberal Association. McNaughton, noticing a large number of women in the audience, said he was pleased so many had come, as women's suffrage was one of the planks in the Liberal platform. Brewster, tongue in cheek, said he missed Dick Burde in the audience. Burde, one of the leaders of the Conservative movement in Port Alberni, was still serving overseas. Brewster attacked the government regarding the railway work in the district, stating there was no excuse for the noncompletion of the Canadian Northern Railway on the Island because the company had received enough money from the sale of government bonds to complete the line.[141]

Independent candidate Neill had strong support from local farmers. He argued for the abolition of patronage and advocated a return to the system in use when he was a member of the provincial House at the turn of the century, when road foremen were elected in each section by the general public. This put the power in the hands of local people, he said. "Such other patronage as could be handled directly by the public, I advocate placing in the hands of a committee elected annually by the people so that every section would have representation in a similar manner to the school boards."[142]

Meanwhile, the Conservative meeting focused on the new road being built from Port Alberni to the Nanaimo Highway summit. The Conservatives promised $3,500 would be spent by the government on the road that year.[143] Letters and a petition from Partelow Miles, Alberni agent for the Red Cliff Lumber Co., claimed the road would interfere with its logging operations. However, after investigation by the Minister of Public Works, the government decided to proceed with the construction work. The opposition to the road was considered unjust.

The Prohibition Act received a lot of play in the local newspaper. The *Port Alberni News* reported:

Bill appears to have been framed as a direct blow to workingmen.

To the man of means, who is accustomed to buy his liquors by the bottle or case from the wholesale store or retail shop, the Prohibition Act means absolutely nothing, as he can still order his supply from a neighbouring province or the States, as easily as in the past, only he will have to pay a higher cost for transportation.

To those accustomed to buy his liquor by the bottle or glass, the Act means the ordinary working man is not given the opportunity to lay by money sufficient to provide for his sending away for a case of liquor hence he is under a handicap which does not interfere with the rich men. Then again, the working man's usual beverage is beer and on shipments of this class the freight rates are so high as to make the price almost prohibitive for him.[144]

Brewster's Petticoat Government

When the September election results were tallied they showed Brewster had been elected in both Alberni and Victoria. The *Port Alberni News* headlines on September 20, 1916 read: "Liberals victorious in province. Capt. Wood defeated in Alberni. 39 Liberals, 7 Conservatives and 1 Socialist elected. Women's suffrage carried by a large majority and the Prohibition Act was carried by about 8,000 majority."

Brewster had topped the polls in the Alberni district with 393 votes to the 355 of his nearest opponent Wood, and Neill's 253. Port Alberni had always been a Conservative stronghold; therefore, it came as a great surprise to the community that a Liberal should win. Alberni Liberals had mounted a strong campaign. In the same election Alberni voted against prohibition by a margin of 117 votes. The electoral franchise for women referendum in Alberni was a more decisive vote. Those in favour won by a margin of 322.[145]

It was weeks before Premier Bowser knew the results of the soldiers' votes from the Canadian military camps, and from the base hospitals in England and the Front. While it was clear the Liberals had won, it was not until November 23 that Bowser relinquished his office, and Brewster became premier. Now a member in two ridings, Brewster resigned his seat in Alberni in favour of Victoria. His home riding waited for a by-election to be called.

Brewster finally gave up his job at Clayoquot cannery, for he felt that to be Premier of B.C. during the war required all his attention. It speaks well for Brewster's judgment that he chose for cabinet posts three men who were to become future premiers. They included John Oliver, John Duncan MacLean, and Thomas Dufferin Pattullo. Almost at once Brewster injected new vitality into the party by giving a sympathetic hearing to popular demands for a programme of reform.

His integrity and fair-mindedness commanded universal respect. But the political favours demanded of him soon brought difficulties. The "hungry" Liberals, starved of patronage for years while the Conservatives held office, now waited for their turn. To their disappointment, the new premier announced he was opposed to patronage. He had decided on an extensive program of retrenchment.[146]

All during 1917 Alberni district waited for the by-election to be called. Bowser made frequent trips to the region, each duly reported in the *Port Alberni News*. Premier Brewster, the Liberal, however, made no such headlines. His activities as premier went without fanfare in his former home riding. Finally a by-election was called for January 24, 1918. Capt. Huff was appointed the returning officer for the area.

With a by-election now scheduled, the Alberni Conservatives resolved once again to nominate Capt. John Wood as an Independent Conservative. But the Conservatives on the east coast of the Island, from Wellington to Qualicum, decided to form a central association to include Alberni. It was agreed at the December 1916 meeting of the Alberni Central Association that unless a local candidate could be induced to run, the seat should not be contested in the by-election. The meeting also decided A. W. Neill should not receive the party's support. "It is essential Neill should not be elected and so be able to claim Conservative support in his use as an Independent,"[147] said the Association. Instead they chose Richard Pateman Wallis, a farmer from Nanoose Bay, as their standard bearer.

John Frank Bledsoe, former editor and manager of the *Alberni Advocate*, was the choice of the Liberal party in Alberni.[148] Bledsoe and Wallis each addressed public meetings in both towns. Bledsoe felt there had been criticism of him for leaving the district when his business venture with the *Alberni Advocate* failed. He said, "If I cannot make a living here it is nothing to anybody. I have left the district on several occasions and after making a stake have returned, and where have I spent my money? Any old timer here can tell you, I have always spent it in the Alberni district."[149] Bledsoe said he had been in contact with shipbuilding interests, visiting yards and sites in the United States, but none could compare with the Port Alberni site. "We will have to quit party strife to reap the benefit of our advantages," he said. He added that he thought the time was at hand when the province should have control of the fisheries.

Over the previous year there had been growing opposition to Port Alberni completing Kinross Road, now renamed the "Burde Road" in honour of the former mayor. Bledsoe said not to count him among the dissidents. "What rot this! It is the only thing you people of the Port ever asked from the Provincial government and you are entitled to it. I would be in favor of paving it with the bricks that have been thrown at me lately," he said.

Wallis said he had been a resident of the district for the past thirty years. He knew the people of Alberni would have liked to have had a member from their town, but he assured them he would take just as much interest in the Alberni constituency as any local man. "My interests are just as much here and on the West Coast, as they are on the East Coast," he added.

Wallis, the Conservative, won the by-election. The vote was a close one with Bledsoe capturing the majority vote in both Port Alberni and Alberni.[150]

Brewster's government was under siege. The Prohibitionists wanted the Prohibition Act implemented immediately, but it was delayed by the investigation into McBride's conduct during the recent voting. When the negative result of the soldiers' vote overseas became known, McBride was accused of being in league with liquor interests. Brewster sent a commission of inquiry overseas to investigate the complaint. It recommended the entire overseas vote taken after September 14, 1916 be disregarded, thus favouring the Prohibitionists. Also, women wanted the vote. Here Brewster complied, but his action didn't endear him to the soldiers, who had registered a negative vote on the franchise referendum as well. Brewster's government was tagged the "petticoat government"[151] by opposition members because of the women's franchise vote.

The Provincial Election Amendment Act was passed in April 1917, extending the provincial franchise to women. This act also repealed the Woman Suffrage Act of 1916. The Prohibition Act came into force October 1, 1917.[152]

Meanwhile, Brewster's Attorney General M. A. MacDonald had to resign after an investigation showed campaign funds had come from the Canadian Northern Railway. MacDonald was replaced by J. W. deB. Farris. Another cabinet position left vacant when Minister of Finance Ralph Smith died was filled by the appointment of John Hart. Adding to Brewster's worries was the collapse of morale as the war news became increasingly depressing. In the summer of 1917, when conscription was being considered, he said Canada might become a second Ireland if conscription were enforced without proper precautions. British Columbia now had a manpower shortage. "Its population had dropped by one hundred thousand since 1914."[153]

In October, 1917, Prime Minister Robert Borden asked Brewster to come to Ottawa, suggesting he would make an offer for the premier to join his cabinet. Brewster went to Ottawa to hear what the prime minister had to offer; however, he was not anxious to give up his Victoria seat. No final decision was made on whether or not he would join Borden's cabinet. In late February, 1918, Brewster began his return journey to British Columbia. On the trip he became ill with pneumonia, and at Medicine Hat a special nurse joined the party to care for him. A decision was made to take Brewster to Holy Cross Hospital in Calgary, where he died on March 1, 1918. His body was returned to Victoria.

During Brewster's absence from Victoria, John Oliver had been appointed acting premier. On the evening of March 5, 1918, after the state funeral of the late premier, a Liberal caucus selected Oliver, a farmer from Delta, as its new leader.

Brewster left three daughters, Edna, Marjorie, and Annie, and a son, Raymond. His wife Annie had died in 1913, so the children were left orphans. Raymond was killed overseas just prior to the signing of the armistice in 1918. The legislature voted to provide $5,000 to help educate the young children.

During his brief term in office, Harlan C. Brewster, the west coast canner, had given women the right to vote and brought in prohibition.

Sir Richard McBride enjoyed his appointment in London, until he became ill with Bright's Disease. The former premier then asked the new Liberal government for financial aid to help him return home. They provided him with funds, but he had just completed the final arrangements for the ocean voyage when he died on August 6, 1917.

Kildonan Cannery

Kildonan Cannery was one of the largest fish processing plants to be established on the Alberni Inlet. Located approximately twenty miles from Port Alberni, at Uchucklesit, it operated for fifty years, turning out millions of cases of canned fish ready for market.

The cannery first began operation in 1903 with owners Capt. D. Macdonald and C. Ternan under the Alberni Packing Company, later known as the Uchucklesit Cannery. The property was acquired in 1910 by the Wallace brothers, Peter and John, who renamed it Wallace Brothers Packing Company. A year later the company reorganized as Wallace Fisheries Limited. The original site name of Uchucklesit Inlet was changed to Kildonan after the brothers' home town in Scotland. In 1911 a cold storage and ice plant, wharves, and buildings, were built at the site. The plant, which employed two hundred men, was plant No. 2 for Wallace Fisheries, who also owned another plant in Prince Rupert.[154]

Because the cannery was built at the foot of a mountainside, the entire development was set on pilings. Power for the plant came from a mountain stream at the back of the settlement. A water pipeline snaked down the mountainside to the power house, turning several water turbines to keep the refrigeration machinery in operation for the cold storage plant. The power plant was kept scrupulously clean. It had a colour scheme of green and black for all the machines, with brass and steel. All the cans required for several canneries operated by the company were supplied by American Can Co.

In addition to the cold storage plant and cannery, there were various other buildings. The herring building was where the small fish were prepared. The company operated a small general store, and there were several bunkhouses and residences for the employees of the plant. The community had its own electric light, water, and sewage system.[155]

Living conditions at the cannery were described by some as less than ideal. Samson Robinson recalled there was neither union nor any set rate of pay when he worked there. The cannery became unionized a few years before it closed. Women employees were paid by the can. Accommodation was supplied.

> Everything was built on stilts. The shacks were made of shiplap, which left gaps when dry. There were bunkhouses, one each for single women and single men. Three or four for Chinese; about 20 family houses, and five or six longhouses for Indians. All were segregated from the White workers. The cannery owned a small store, but the workers paid high rates for their groceries. The *Princess Maquinna* brought in supplies. The store shut down when a store opened in Port Alberni with better rates. Wages of $1.75 to $3.50 was (*sic*) considered a good wage in the cold storage section. There was also a small school. Power was generated by a big waterwheel. Wallace Bros. Chief engineer was Dave Luzlow.[156]

When Wallace Fisheries began canning herring, the local market expanded into the fresh fish trade. It started Scotch-curing herring with the help of young women brought over from Scotland's Orkney Islands. The product was shipped to the orient. Two men who worked at the cannery, Pete Gregory and Stan Littleton, recalled the women were called "herring chokers," as they ate a lot of dry salt herring and potatoes "with their jackets on." They spoke only Gaelic. "The girls later travelled back and forth like loggers to Kildonan, Butterfield & Mackie Co. at Ecoole, Gosse-Millard at Ritherdon Bay. They were making big money packing."[157]

Margaret McRae was one of those women brought over from Nairn, Scotland. Maggie, as she was known, first came to Newfoundland in 1906 to show workers how to "Scotch cure" herring. Then she returned to Scotland, only to come back to Canada in 1912 with her family to Vancouver, where she worked for "Watson Bros" curing herring as "kippered herring." She had fifty other Scottish women with her and was considered the "forelady."

> Most of the herring were graded and salted, put in barrels and sent all over the world. The company even had its own cooper, a person who makes

barrels. The small herring were salted, crated, then sent to China. The women followed the herring run which started in Pender Harbour, the Gulf Islands and finally the Alberni Canal.[158]

While the company began by processing herring, it was salmon that became its mainstay. According to Gregory and Littleton, "There were so many fish in those days, from the Somass run and Henderson Lake. Old Peter Wallace said he could clean them out in twelve years, but he did better than that, he cleaned them out in eight."[159]

Mabel Taylor, a well known Indian basket-weaver, worked at the cannery and remembered the white dress and hat she was required to wear, the hat to prevent hair from falling into the can. "We had two sets of clothes and had to wash them each day. We looked like cooks with the white dress and hats." She said canning dog salmon, herring, and pilchards was the worst job. Sometimes she worked for three days and nights without any sleep. Only half an hour was allowed for eating supper. A time card was handed in at the end of the day's work. She got paid according to how much fish was processed. "If you didn't work everyday, you would be fired. Even if you were sick or something."[160]

News from Kildonan began to appear in the *Port Alberni News* on a regular basis. The small fishing community was included in many Alberni Valley events. During the Great War all the employees of Wallace Fisheries contributed a day's pay each month to the Canadian Patriotic Fund, which had been established to help the dependents of the men at war.

Two other smaller fish processing plants established in Port Alberni were competing with Wallace for fish. John Alexander Kendall opened an ice plant in 1912 to keep meat and fish frozen for use by the residents and the railway crews working on the Canadian Northern Railway. He also constructed a wharf and contracted to Doug Stone, of Stone and Blandy shipyard in Port Alberni, for a gasoline boat, the *Mayflower*, to be used in collecting fish from the fishermen. The Kendall plant employing fifty men began operation in November 1912.[161]

Kendall was an interesting character. The blusterous sea captain was born in Newfoundland in 1862. With his family, he came to the Alberni District in 1901. He earned the title of "captain" from his fishing business. Residents remember Kendall "always walked around wearing a sea captain's cap and smoking White Owl cigars."[162] His on-going battle with local Fisheries Officer James B. Wood brought the two face to face in court several times. Wood was always found innocent of the charges laid by Kendall, who perceived he was being persecuted by Wood. The conflict between the men made good copy for Burde in his weekly newspaper. Always interested in politics, Kendall was not above writing letters to the editor, or to city council, complaining about some aspect of life in the small town.

Butterfield & Mackie Company, wholesale fish merchants and curers, established a plant in Port Alberni in 1913, next to the CPR wharf. The company had branch plants in Vancouver, New Westminster, and Prince Rupert. Salmon and halibut were shipped both fresh and smoked. The manager Mr. Christison had twenty men working for him. In 1916, the company moved the plant to Ecoole where it began operating a fish reduction plant.[163]

As the war dragged on, fishing in Barkley Sound in 1917 was never better. Fishermen were receiving a price for their catch that had never been equalled before. But all was not well in the fishing industry in Barkley Sound. Fishermen believed Wallace Fisheries and other canneries were depleting the Inlet of fish. There were also serious allegations made against Fisheries Officer James B. Wood and his superior Edward Taylor of Nanaimo, who were suspected of collaborating with the cannery operators. It wasn't long before the whole fishing industry was under investigation in an official government inquiry.

CHAPTER FIVE

1916–1922

THE HOMECOMING

Although the war in Europe was far from over, in 1916 thoughts had already turned to helping the returned soldiers. A local branch of the Returned Soldiers Aid Commission was organized in Port Alberni to look after the needs of soldiers when they returned from the front.

A Roll of Honour was published periodically, listing the men from both cities who had enlisted for active service. The roll listed those dead, wounded, or missing in action and was a grim reminder of how much the European war had cost the small communities. In Alberni, of the eighty-eight who had enlisted, twelve were either dead or wounded. In Port Alberni, of the seventy-eight enlisted, ten were either dead or wounded. Another nine people enlisted as munition workers or nurses. The west coast enlistment stood at twenty-five.[1]

The Firing Line

The former mayor of Port Alberni, now Lieutenant Dick Burde, kept up his professional skills by writing from "somewhere in Flanders." One letter to Charles Clarke was published September 27, 1916 in the *Port Alberni News*.

> Night and day there is always a familiar sound around here. You catch it at times between the noises of the high explosives. Sometimes it is like one sawmill and sometimes again, it is like a dozen sawmills all going in different places. It is the noise of the aeroplane. The air is filled with them and they soar about with all the assurance of the most graceful bird that ever flew the air. Anti-aircraft guns are constantly trying to bring them down on both sides, but I have as yet seen only one fatally winged and that was a German.
>
> The noise all over caused by artillery is terrific. Nothing we ever heard can begin to compare with it. The air and the earth and everything planted

on it, quiver, shiver and shake, and in the trench zone proper, the bullets fly just as fast and as thick as hail stone drops in the prairie storm area. I don't think anything you have ever read about this war is an exaggeration of the facts. Our battalion has had some losses, but they have all behaved admirably. A man has no idea of what he can stand till he gets a couple of tests of this life.

In 1917, Capt. Burde sharpened his writing skills further, when he began editing a new "trench" paper entitled *The Shell Hole Advance*. Another letter from Burde arrived in January 1917, just after he had won the Military Cross for "zeal and untiring energy in the performance of his duty while under fire."[2] He was decorated on the field with the medal after Vimy.

How does a man really feel when shells are bursting around him, shrapnel is bursting overhead and machine gun and rifle bullets are perforating the air all around him? He does not analyze his feelings at the time. You are going ahead at something. You don't want to stop till something stops you. You have a desire to get up to the source of your danger and try to stop it. You invariably believe that you can get up, and that you can stop it when you get there. There are also times when fear becomes subordinate to curiosity.

Burde, always thinking of home and perhaps of his own mortality, sent a souvenir to the residents of Port Alberni. This was a German shell case picked up on the battlefields and artistically engraved. It had been made in Karlsruhe, Germany, June 1915, by Patrone-Neubrik, and was similar to the British eight pound shell. The panel was inscribed: "To the Mayor, Council and Citizens of Port Alberni, B.C." On it was engraved a picture of a soldier falling among barbed wire and the words: "Yes – Let Me Like a Soldier Fall Upon Some Foreign Strand." Below was written, "From Lieut. R. J.Burde, Mayor 1913-14-15." The souvenir went on display at City Hall.[3] The shell is now on display in the Alberni Valley Museum. The shell was known to the British as a "whizz-bang." Burde later elaborated on the souvenir:

The contents of one of these struck the edge of a trench where I was doing duty in the Ypres salient on Aug. 15 last year, the second day of my real war experience and caused me to be buried under a few sand bags. Hence my interest in them. The one you have was the first I was able to find. I found it on the Somme, the day after we got beyond the famous old Regina trench, near Courcelette.[4]

Mr. and Mrs. Ed Gill received a letter from their son Keith. He wrote:

We are in the thick of it now, and I don't get much time to write, as we are in the trenches as much as we are out of them. We are getting pretty well used to the firing now. I have fired quite a few shots at the Germans, but I don't know if I have killed any of them or not. I got hold of a German rifle and ammunition the other day and I used it to shoot at them with. This saved my own from getting dirty. I don't know what they would say if they knew we were shooting at them with their own rifles. The trenches are so close that we yell back and forth to one another all the time. The most of them can speak English, so we can tell what they are saying.

I am feeling fine myself, and getting along fine. This country might be all right in peace times, but is sure badly battered up just at present. I guess they will build it up again when the war is over. I wish it was over now because I would like to be back among the timber and the mountains. I am getting tired of this settled country.[5]

Keith returned home a hero in October 1915. The announcement of his pending arrival home read: "Today, Keith Gill, native son of Alberni, and hero of three of the fiercest fights the world has ever known, is expected home. When Keith gets his medal, on it will be bars carrying such names as Neuve Chappelle, Festubert, and Ypres, names never to be forgotten while the hearts of men vibrate to the tales of heroic deeds."[6]

Of the three sons of Mr. and Mrs. James Redford, Alberni, who went overseas to serve with the 88th Victoria Fusiliers, only two returned home. Douglas was killed in action. William was the first to return home in November 1916, disabled from further military service and still suffering the effects of shrapnel and gunshot wounds. The citizens of Alberni and Port Alberni turned out in great force to give him a rousing welcome. The train was met by the mayor and council, and an automobile decorated for the occasion transported the wounded hero and his mother to the city center where a formal welcome was read by Rev. J. Carruthers.[7]

Edward Redford, or Teddy, as he was known locally, returned home in March of 1917. He had gone almost unscathed through nine months of severe fighting; then when he was struck, his wounds resulted in the loss of his left arm and serious injuries to his hip and leg.[8] Edward's unfortunate accident occurred when he and some other young men found an unexploded German shell and decided to clean it out, polish it up, and send it home as a souvenir. While they were doing this the shell exploded, blowing Edward's arm off and killing the two other men who had been helping him.[9]

Early in 1916 the British Colonial Secretary cabled the Governor General of Canada suggesting a battalion of lumbermen be formed as "1500 men fellers, haulers and sawyers were urgently needed."[10]

Skilled lumberman were given an opportunity to join the 230th battalion of Foresters. Trench warfare and bridge building in Europe required the quick production of large quantities of lumber. Owners of forests in England and Scotland had given the timber; now skilled lumbermen were required to cut the timber and transform it into dimensions needed for bridge, road, and railway buildings.[11] Robert Barnes and Hugh Fowlie joined.

Schoolteacher John R. Thompson became another district hero when his death was announced in October, 1916. Thompson left in 1915 to enlist in the 88th Fusiliers. Later, he was transferred to the 62 Battalion and went to England as a corporal. But he gave up his stripes in order to get into action sooner, and he was drafted into the 29th Battalion. His brother Lieut. William C. Thompson was still serving with the 5th Regiment in Victoria.[12]

The Dan Clarke family also had two casualties. William was killed in action, and his brother Jack was seriously wounded. The young men left with separate battalions. Jack, who went with the 20th Battalion, had been previously wounded at Ypres, but after recovery he had returned to the firing line. Eighteen year-old William, who had enlisted with the 48th Battalion, met his death on the battlefield.[13]

In May 1917, Mrs. Florence Bird, wife of sawmill owner George Bird, received the devastating news from Ottawa that her son George, aged twenty-six, had died of wounds received during recent heavy fighting in France. George had left with the 62 Battalion in the spring of 1916 and had taken part in the capture of Vimy Ridge. George Bird Sr. was also overseas, in Great Britain, serving with the 2nd King's Own Rifles, Lancaster Regiment. George Jr. had come with his parents to the district in 1892. He was an ardent sportsman and athlete and was the goalie for the championship soccer team of 1910. Before he went to war he had been working for the Royal Bank of Canada in Vancouver.[14]

Alberni Mayor Alan W. Neill discovered to his horror that two lots belonging to soldier Douglas McKenzie, who was at the front, had been sold in the city tax sale. Neill said the lots should never have been put up for sale and suggested the purchaser be asked to take his money back and cancel the sale. Council voted unanimously to redeem the lots and advise the purchaser T. Paterson of its decision.

When the death of "Shorty" Thompson somewhere in France was reported July 4, 1917, the headline called him a "famous adventurer" for his role as the instigator of the "post planting" episode of 1912, which had caused Alberni so much distress. Finally, what really had happened became known. The post had been placed at the foot of Johnston Road in Alberni by the Canadian Highway Association to symbolize the beginning, or end, of a cross-Canada highway system expected to be completed within three years. It seems Shorty and his friend decided to capture the post and take it to rival Port Alberni. Late at night Shorty succeeded in uprooting the landmark. He jumped into the Somass River with it, and clinging to it, floated down to the mouth of the river where he was met by his friend in a rowboat. They then towed the post to a suitable landing spot and carried it to the main business corner in Port Alberni.[15]

Keeping the Home Fires Burning

As the soldiers began returning home, the Avecourt Girls Club organized special evenings for them. One such event was a chicken supper held April 4, 1917, in the Somass Hotel dining room. The supper was followed by a dance in the club room in the Watson Block. Guests of honor included Henry Davey, Sidney Fry, and Fred Street of Port Alberni; Edward and William Redford, Keith Gill, Wesley Heaslip, and Edward Homewood, from Alberni; also Lt. J. R. Simpson, of the Imperial Army, a former resident of the city. Sidney Fry had just been appointed customs collector at Kildonan.

Parcels of socks, cigarettes, tobacco, and chewing gum were being assembled and sent overseas by the local Patriotic Society. Local school children held concerts in McGrath Hall for the War Prisoners Fund. The Canadian Patriotic Fund was not doing very well in Port Alberni in comparison to other communities. The local secretary drew attention to the small amount of money being contributed. Every person in Canada had been asked to contribute what they could afford. "Do your 'bit' today and you will feel better for it."[16] Port Alberni City Council decided the community could do more to help those families left behind when the breadwinner went to war, and a committee was appointed to approach the management of local industry to secure monthly employee contributions to the Patriotic Fund.

In 1915, the drain of men going to war left some of the local services shorthanded. The Port Alberni Fire Brigade, for instance, had to be reorganized, as the brigade was practically defunct because there were so few men.

Port Alberni Alderman Robert H. Wood resigned his seat as alderman to allow him to construct the new dominion government wharf at the foot of Argyle Street.[17]

The provincial government made an offer to help relieve the unemployment in the Alberni Valley by offering jobs for fifty men in logging camps in various parts of the province. Mayor Edward Exton duly reported the government's offer, but no one took advantage of it, or was willing to leave the city, and the offer came in for considerable criticism. To local residents it looked as though the government had no intention of doing any further work on the new road from Port Alberni to the Summit; nor would the Canadian Northern Railway line see any further action.[18] The Port Alberni Conservative Association wrote in January 1916 to Premier Bowser, once again appealing to him to do something for the district, which "was on the verge of distress." They pleaded:

> The grading of the road stops some five or six miles from Alberni. If this could be continued and the timbering proceeded with to Cowichan Lake and with local and not imported labour, it would relieve all this distress, not only locally, but along the West Coast amongst homesteaders who would then be able to keep their homesteads and continue to improve them as soon as happier times arrive.[19]

The January 1916 municipal elections saw Robert Wood elected as Mayor of Port Alberni, and the number of aldermen reduced from six to four. Elected were Archibald Campbell Macfie, David Wallace Warnock, Edward Exton, and Anthony Watson. Wood had been opposed by John Kendall and R. M. Ellis. Wood was full of optimism for the future when he made his inaugural address. "A district with the potential wealth of the Alberni district should come through the present crisis in good shape. I have no doubt but that it will come out with flying colors."[20]

In Alberni, Alan W. Neill was elected Mayor, along with Aldermen Henry Blakemore, George (Alex) Spencer, John Best, James Hills, and C. T. Harvey. Both councils endorsed a resolution to the provincial government presented by Alderman Exton for the completion of the Nanaimo road as a general district relief project, and called for the resumption of work on the Canadian Northern Railway.[21]

The winter of 1916 was quite severe. A blanket of snow five feet deep covered the twin communities. The Alberni Inlet froze over as far down as Coos Creek, giving skaters a wonderful glassy surface to skate on at points close to shore. The snow also caused some destruction. The roof of the Port Alberni theatre, previously known as

Waterhouse's Hall, collapsed under the weight of the snow. The building, which had become a landmark on First Avenue, was built originally as a dancehall by the social club and was for many years the only building of its kind in Port Alberni. The new addition to the hall, consisting of a stage and living quarters at the rear, was undamaged. Another old building demolished as a result of the heavy snow was the Alberni Land Company barn on the flats near Dry Creek, which had been the headquarters for the work crews during the days when the land for the townsite was being cleared.[22]

The high price of copper caused by the war in Europe resulted in a flurry of activity in the mining industry in the Valley. The price had risen from an average of $.13 lb. in 1914 to $.27 lb. in 1916,[23] and rumours circulated that big transactions were underway. A leading mining and smelting company began negotiations for the purchase of the Monitor mine on the Alberni Inlet fifteen miles from Alberni. Local miners considered that finally the mining business was coming into its own in Alberni.

A year later, a new ore body was discovered at the Monitor mine. The new discovery, at a site first located by Leonard Frank some time ago, looked very promising. J. A. Skene, the mining engineer in charge, named the new ore zone the "Leonard Discovery." In January 1917, the Monitor mine was shipping tons of ore to the smelter in Trail, getting $50 a ton; 9 percent was in copper.

In March 1916, news came that the road to the Thistle mine, which ran inland from the Alberni Inlet at a point near China Creek, was to be completed and development work would be done to the mine during the summer. The Thistle, a rich copper-gold sulphide deposit, was owned by American business interests in San Francisco. It had been sold fifteen years ago by Alderman Watson, who still held the position as local manager for the company.[24]

A gold and silver mine owned by Alderman Watson and C. Dawley at Elk River on Clayoquot Sound was also receiving attention.[25] Two new copper mines fourteen miles from Alberni were the Canadian, near Coleman Creek, and the Happy John on Handy Creek, adjoining the Monitor just north of Nahmint Bay and owned by Leonard and Bernard Frank.[26]

Forest Industry Revitalized

While the mining companies brought an increase of activity in the district during this period, it was the forest and lumber interests who created the new prosperity in the Albernis. When news came on February 25, 1916, that the Canadian Pacific Lumber Co. mill had been leased by a Seattle syndicate, local residents rejoiced. It was as if the heavy mantle of despair and unemployment that had weighed upon the district since the mill was closed in 1914 had finally been lifted. Howard A. Dent, of the Dent Lumber & Shingle Co. and A. W. Mylroie, of the Anchor Supply Co., both of Seattle, announced they had taken over the property of the lumber company and promised to reopen the mill by March 10th. They purchased timberland from the Red Cliff Lumber and Land Company.

Dent and his partner were impressed with the advantageous geographical location of the local mill for supplying the Alaskan and northern B.C. lumber trade. The mill was expected to employ two hundred men and would create a payroll of approximately $10,000 a month. When logging operations began, this was expected to greatly increase.

The logging operations were to be carried out by the Wiest Logging Company, from Oregon. The mill was quickly put in shape by mechanics and millwrights. The entire mechanical staff of the old mill company were retained by the new company.

Although a portion of the mill staff was oriental labour, the mill company promised to employ white labour as soon as possible. Married men would get preference. The new mill management was under the direction of E. E. Houston, of Seattle, and A. W. Mylroie, one of the partners. As promised, the mill, now renamed the Alberni Pacific Lumber Co. (APL), was running at full capacity on March 10, 1916.[27]

Clearly, new prosperity was expected in the community, for the city clerk and electrician each received salary increases of five dollars per month. The clerk's salary increased to ninety-five dollars, the electrician's to eighty-five dollars per month.

By May 1916, trade with Alaska had already begun. The company purchased the steam schooner the *Southcoast* from Capt. C. H. Sooye, in San Francisco. The boat travelled between Port Alberni and Anchorage, Alaska, towing the company barge *Bangor*.

The Wiest Logging Company began logging operations at Cox Lake to supply the mill with logs. Francis Wiest, the manager of the logging outfit, had to go to Vancouver to hire more men. There were now sixty men working in the logging operation. The Two Spot once again was tuned up ready to roll. Brakie Albert (Al) Naslund arrived in April 1916. His brother William (Bill) Naslund was head brakeman.

The Wiest Logging Co. was very much a family operation. Ed Wiest was engineer, Cyrus Wiest was fireman, and Jack Wiest was head foreman. John B., Ed, and Gordon Wiest also worked in various capacities at the camp.[28]

By June, APL was despatching an average of fourteen railway cars daily in addition to three shipments of lumber for Alaska. All went well for the mill and the logging camp until September 1916 when bush fires began breaking out in the area. One fire, fanned by a terrific breeze, swept down on the logging camp at 2:00 p.m. and destroyed seventeen buildings at the Wiest Logging Company camp. Only six buildings in the camp remained. These included the blacksmith shop and the engine house, the water tank and a few of the homes. But the cookhouse, four bunkhouses, several homes, the oil house, saw filing shop, the office, and some other buildings were totally destroyed. The fiery storm came so rapidly it was impossible to save anything from the buildings. Several families lost everything they possessed but still considered themselves lucky to escape with their lives. Fay Massey, daughter of the cook, Jim Massey, was only a little girl at the time but still remembers being thrown out of the window and landing in the ashes.

> The Two Spot saved the day. The fire came up so fast we couldn't open the door. There was no loss of life, but we lost all our possessions. Mother always lamented about the pictures she lost. They could never be replaced.[29]

Employees of the company made heroic efforts to fight the fire. The crew of Two Spot kept on the job until the whole camp was in the grip of the flames. Employees grabbed some of their prized possessions and jumped on the train, which took them to town. "A dash was made through about three hundred yards of a seething furnace of fire on the short trip to town."[30]

The fire played some strange tricks. There were ten pigs in the fire and all but one was killed. This one did not have a bristle scorched on its hide, while the others were actually roasted alive. At one point a framework for a tent remained unscorched, while on each side the vegetation was burned to dust. At the very edge of the fire zone was a small cabin which contained some inflammable material. It remained untouched, while a building no more than fifteen feet away was completely destroyed. The heat was so intense, it melted the windows of the building into odd shaped masses of glass. The refugees from the fire were taken to the new Beaufort Hotel where they were housed until they found other accommodation.

264

The fire was a devastating blow to the logging company. The ashes were still smouldering at the camp when the company began reconstruction. By the following week a new cookhouse had been erected and several smaller buildings were being put up so that logging operations could be carried on. The logging railway, also damaged in the fire, had to be repaired. Several small bridges were rebuilt and fallen trees were cleared from the right of way.

Bush fires continued unrelentingly during the month, tasking firefighters to their limit. One fire on October 11th swept down from Anderson Avenue, through the ferns, new growth, and logs, in the direction of the mill and residences on the south end of the city. Somehow it was contained. But for three terrifying days the local fire brigade under Fire Chief William Holt fought the spreading flames with fire, water, and every other conceivable means. A crew of men from the mill and another from the logging camp helped to fight the blaze.

When the lease on APL expired, so too did the contract entered into at the same time with the Wiest Logging Co. APL now had to make alternate arrangements or the mill would have to be closed for lack of logs. Such a closure would have been devastating for the city, considering it was just recovering economically after the major depression of 1915.[31]

In November, Howard Dent went to Port Alberni City Council to plead his case to have the city sell some of its timber holdings to his mill. Thomas Meredith had previously indicated to council the mill's plight. If it could not secure a sufficient quantity of logs at a reasonable price to keep the mill going for another year, it would close down.

Council's original price was $1,000 for forty acres of standing timber. Dent questioned if the city was not taking advantage of the company and holding it up for "so exorbitant a price."[32] He argued he wanted to be reasonable with the city but felt the estimate of the timber was too high as there were less than three million feet in the entire district lot. As the city only controlled one-third of that, he refused to consider the city's offer of $1,000. After a lengthy discussion in council, Dent finally made an offer of $400. Alderman James Macfie countered with an offer that the timber be disposed of for $500. This was accepted. The mill now had a secure source of timber to keep it operating.

In December 1916, Dent and Mylroie dissolved their partnership. Dent continued to operate the mill, while Mylroie devoted his time to the Alaska trade, which had been absorbing more lumber than was anticipated when the partnership was formed over a year ago. The mill's shipments of finished lumber to Alaskan points totalled approximately six million feet.[33]

Dent noticed that many of the orders he received for lumber also called for shingles. As there was no shingle manufacturing plant in Port Alberni, he was compelled to import all shingle requirements to fill the orders. Dent decided to do something about it. He purchased the Port Alberni Lumber Co. mill and converted it into a shingle mill.

The Port Alberni Lumber Co. mill had opened in the spring of 1913 under the partnership of Victoria businessmen Nixon and DeSalis. Located on the waterfront just north of "Hayes Point," it had a capacity of 40,000 feet a day and was considered a small mill. A wide variety of products were produced there, including doors, windows, mouldings, and rough and dressed lumber.[34]

The announcement of the purchase came in December 1916. Dent expected the mill to have the capacity of about 100,000 shingles per day.[35] Dent's brother Fred went to Vancouver in May and purchased $10,000 worth of new logging equipment to be used in the production end of the shingle mill, which had been operating on a double shift.[36] In 1919, the Dent Shingle Co. mill was sold to Harris and Squires from Vancouver.[37]

In May 1917, the George Bird sawmill, idle since Bird went overseas, was leased for five years to D. Burgess of South Vancouver, who had been operating a shingle mill at Cassidy's Siding, near Nanaimo. Burgess constructed a large dry kiln and overhauled the mill to meet the requirements of a four line shingle plant. He added a new boiler to feed the dry kiln and rebuilt the main building to give upstairs accommodations. The mill became known as the Acme Shingle Co. mill. Also in May, a fire at Cherry Creek wiped out Brand's sawmill. The plant was totally destroyed and the machinery badly damaged.[38]

Along with this industrial activity in Port Alberni, logging operations now assumed considerable importance in the area. When APL opened a new logging camp at Copper Island for supplying their shingle mill with cedar logs, they installed a large amount of first class logging equipment. There were now three camps supplying the needs of APL. Once again the Wiest Logging Co. began operating east of the city on D.L.113, where the main camp was located, and also at No. 2 camp at Murdock's Landing. Another logging camp opened at Grappler Creek, near Bamfield, to supply the new Acme Shingle Co. mill with cedar bolts. The manager was Mr. Jardine, of Vancouver.[39]

By January 1918 the Acme Shingle mill was idle owing to a stoppage in bolt supply. There were enough bolts but they were just not getting to the mill. F. W. Fearman and Alex Plummer had been taking out about one thousand cords of wood a month at the site near Bamfield. A hitch developed in the delivery service, resulting in an accumulation of bolts at the camp and none at the mill. The distance from the camp to the mill was about twenty miles, and the contractors decided to handle the towing themselves.[40] There were now four machines operating at Acme, and a night crew had been added in the spring. The machinery for the mill came from the Old Star mill at Cassidy's Siding.

The City of Port Alberni leased a portion of the Coal Creek ravine to R. L. Fraser of Alberni for another sawmill with a capacity of forty thousand feet per day. This is the present site of the Port Alberni Harbour Commission office. The five year lease cost fifty dollars a year. Fraser had applied to the E & N Railway for a lease near the "Wye," a turnabout on the tracks at Lupsi Cupsi Point. He was refused because the railway had been reserving this site for a large mill. The Industrial Committee of Port Alberni City Council, which was anxious to increase the payrolls in town, tried to interest Fraser in the Bird sawmill, but Fraser considered this too small for his needs and preferred to get his own site and machinery. He had already made arrangements with the CPR to secure a waterfront site at the mouth of Coal Creek. He moved his mill, which had been located on Rogers Creek, four miles northeast of the city.[41] Fraser's new mill, which became known as Coal Creek Lumber Co. Ltd., opened in March 1918, with a crew of twenty-five working in the mill and another forty in the logging camp. Fraser's good fortune did not last long. In January 1919 the mill was assigned to Alexander Cruickshank, in Vancouver, following a meeting of creditors held in December. In November 1920 the mill was sold to W. A. Gilroy and T. G. McKay and became known as the Gilroy McKay Lumber Co.

Almost a year later, on July 12, 1921, the Gilroy McKay Lumber Co. was completely destroyed by fire. The loss, estimated at $75,000, was only partially covered by insurance.[42]

Just a few minutes after the plant had closed for the day, the blaze broke out in the boiler room and got out of control, destroying the mill and nearly two million feet of lumber. A brisk wind did not help the efforts of the volunteer fire brigade from both towns who concentrated on saving adjoining property and nearby residences. Fire twice threatened the roof of George Bird's residence but was quickly extinguished. The engine driver of the E & N Railway rushed his locomotive to the scene and saved some loaded cars that were on the mill siding. Fireman Dick Spencer had an arm broken when a pile of lumber fell on him.

About a mile north of Alberni and a quarter mile east of the Beaver Creek Road, the Beaver Creek Lumber Company was turning out fish boxes for Wallace Fisheries at Kildonan. The Beaver Creek Lumber Company was owned by three former employees of Alberni Pacific Lumber Co., C. J. Clarke, B. I. Hart, and Norman McEachran, who had decided to go into business for themselves.[43]

The three sawmills owned by the Canadian Pacific Lumber Co. in Port Alberni, Vancouver, and Pingston Creek were all under lease, and as the leases neared their expiry dates the company gave thoughts to reorganization. The change was forecast in an application by the receiver to the Supreme Court for permission to send an agent to England to interview the bondholders, to try to get additional capital to continue operations at the three mills.[44]

When the previous lease arrangements were terminated, the APL acquired all the logging equipment from Wiest Logging Co. including the forty-five ton Shay locomotive (the Two Spot), twelve logging trucks, seven donkeys and miscellaneous gear. APL was now a subsidiary of the Red Cliff Land and Lumber Co. who now owned twenty thousand acres of timber in the Alberni district, as well as an undeveloped mill site on the city waterfront.[45]

Howard Dent began to open up the company's extensive timber holdings. To do so required additional miles of main line roadway and miles of branch trackage, and at the same time the location and construction of new camps began. Logging operations were under the direction of George J. Rayner of Vancouver, who had done similar work at Half Moon Bay. Another locomotive was added to the No. 2 camp in August 1919.

The settlement between Dent and the previous owner Thomas W. Meredith, of the Canadian Pacific Lumber Co., was far from final. In October 1919, the dispute between the two was such that Meredith came to Port Alberni, and with two assistants, attempted to put the mill out of business by tearing up the rails of the track that delivered logs to the mill. Dent responded by closing down the logging camp and paying off the employees. The interference with railway services did not stop the working of the mill, however, which had a supply of logs on hand to keep it going for another two months without interruption.[46]

Whatever the outcome of the personal dispute between the two men, the business details were finalized when Dent purchased the mill outright in February 1921. In May, the London and Canadian Investment Co. Ltd., from Vancouver, officially informed Port Alberni City Council that it had sold out its mill holdings to Alberni Pacific Lumber Co. The investment company had in 1920 purchased the mills and timber holdings of the Canadian Pacific Lumber Co., which was then in liquidation.[47]

The waterfront in Port Alberni was a very busy place in the summer of 1918. Stretched out like an industrial ribbon along the Alberni Inlet were the Alberni Pacific Lumber Co. sawmill, Dent's shingle mill, the Acme Shingle Co., plus Fraser's new sawmill, the Coal Creek Lumber Co. On the surrounding hillsides and along the Inlet were numerous logging camps cutting deep into the forest to feed the mills.

Bainbridge Lumber Co., began sawmill operations in March 1918 at Bainbridge station, about six miles from Port Alberni at the Loop on the E & N Railway. The mill was constructed by Mr. MacKenzie of Vancouver, who was the local manager for the Municipal Construction Co. when the Port Alberni waterworks system was installed. The mill was considered "modern in every way." It cut the finest grade of big timber suitable for shipbuilding and was equipped to handle very large logs. Owned by Clarence Hoard of Victoria, the sawmill originally employed eighty men.

Clarence Hoard and his brother Sam and sister Clara were born on a farm near Covington, Kentucky, U.S.A. Clarence was born in October 1878 and Sam in 1881. Clara was a few years younger. When the children were small the family moved to a farm near Ord, Nebraska, where they lived in a sod house until their home was built. This house is still standing and is owned by Clara's son, Raymond Pocock. Clarence attended the University of Nebraska, where he studied civil engineering. When he came to British Columbia in 1903, he held several jobs as an engineer. Working for the CPR as a civil engineer, he was in charge of building the final stretch of the E & N Railway into Port Alberni. During those years he lived in the Empress Hotel, in Victoria. In 1914, he married Caroline Kinsley, a young woman from Indianapolis, Indiana, and they spent three months in Hawaii on their honeymoon. On their return to Victoria, they lived in Esquimalt and later moved to Rockland Avenue.

Sam Hoard married Nellie May Ollis in Ord, Nebraska, on March 17, 1911. He held various jobs, including one surveying for a logging company at Jordan River. When he worked for the CPR, Sam built the trail up Mount Arrowsmith while he and Nellie lived in a tent on Cameron Lake. He also did some survey work near Cumberland, where their first child was born in 1912. The young family moved again to Graham Street, Victoria, where another child was born in 1915. Then they rented Woodside Farm, in Sooke, before moving to Alberni in 1918, where their son was born at their home on Heaslip Street.[48]

When the brothers worked for the CPR they saw the big timbers in the Alberni Valley and recognized an opportunity. Clarence financed the sawmill, while Sam and his friend Jim Flaherty formed a logging company, the Hoard and Flaherty Logging Company, which supplied the logs for the sawmill operation. The logs were cut from the property of the Alberni Fruit Lands Limited, owned by the E & N Railway Company. The railway snaked along the foot of the mountain and eventually crossed Beaver Creek Road to take out logs as far as the bank of the Stamp River.

The small mill community built by the Hoards had fifteen houses for married couples. These were situated at the end of Bainbridge Road, and the community became known as Bainbridge. Three of the houses stood by the railway tracks about one hundred yards north of the manmade log pond. A separate group of buildings housed Japanese, Chinese, and East Indian millhands, separate from each other.[49]

The bunkhouses had a basin and stool outside where the men could wash, and it was the job of the bull cook to keep the pail by the basin filled with water. A wood heater was situated in the middle of each bunkhouse. A kerosene lamp provided light. Only the mill and lumberyard had electricity. Originally the men supplied their own bedrolls and did not have many blankets. When the stove was on, the men in the upper bunks found it difficult to sleep because of the heat until the fire burned down and the room cooled. Gradually conditions improved. The bunks were removed and replaced with iron spring bunks with mattresses, and blankets and sheets were supplied.

Eight men slept in a room approximately eighteen by eleven feet. They put up with overcrowded conditions, lack of privacy, and sometimes bedbugs. Loggers who stayed at the bunkhouses remember their "tin pants." Their pants were waterproofed by rubbing paraffin wax onto them, and they were so stiff they could practically stand by themselves. The evenings were made tolerable by listening to the good accordian music played by Italians, who had been hired to grade the logging railway. These men graded by hand with only blasting powder used when necessary.

About fifty yards north of the cookhouse on the east side of the railway, Charlie Ryan lived with his wife in a one-storey house with a filing shed attached. There, by the window in the shed, Ryan filed the crosscut saws of the fallers and the bucking saws with their wider blade. He was a skilled broad-axe man and also had the job of making the skids for the donkeys.

The complex also had a barn and a pigpen. The two-storey barn contained hay in the top storey; on the ground level were stalls for the company's team of horses. Company teamster Ed Blackall, with the team and a wagon, managed to keep wood supplied for the stoves of the cookhouse, offices, bunkhouses, and homes.

The first superintendent of the mill was William McCarter, a tall man who died of a heart attack in July 1922. McCarter had been a pioneer lumberman in Victoria. Arriving from Ontario in 1885, he became a member of the Taylor Milling Company in 1891 and about ten years later was appointed manager. His successor at Bainbridge was Sam Abernathy.

Steam engineers were at the mill twenty-four hours a day. Jim Pakenham worked as watchman-engineer. He worked 363 shifts with only two days off at Christmas. A watchman made his rounds and punched the clocks at different places in the mill, which was on the west side of the railway. He made sure steam was kept up. One of his duties was to blow down the burner, as steam was required for the job.

Head millwright was Angus Theriault, who had worked on the construction of the mill and stayed. John West and all five of his sons worked at the mill. Edgar West was a donkey engineer for a number of years. Walter Glanville graded lumber there. His brother Harold recalled he and Walter used a cart to load lumber into boxcars during the early days of the mill. Bruce Wright operated the circular head saw. Steve Jones filed saws for him. Denis O'Brien was a scaler and remembers one shipment of timbers 36" × 36" × 72". N. A. McEacheren, a millwright, saw twenty-four inch square timbers 120 feet in length loaded on three flatcars to be shipped to the Welland Canal. Wes Heaslip was also a millwright, with Stan Littleton acting as his helper. Firemen were Andy Anderson and George Strand.[50]

When Harry Berryman arrived as bookkeeper, he was told he would also have to act as bullbucker. "What is a bullbucker?" he asked.[51] A bullbucker was the boss of the falling and bucking crews.

271

Berryman learned quickly. He also soon established a fine cost accounting system and was able to give his employer the exact cost of each log produced in the show. Another bookkeeper was Adrian Van Pinebroek.

Dennis O'Brien came from Vancouver to relieve scaler Johnny Garrett. When Garrett phoned to say he wasn't coming back, O'Brien said, "I'm not staying." But superintendent Abernethy undertook to make it worth his while and he remained to scale the magnificent giant timber. O'Brien recalled when the company bought a sizable stand of timber from Mr. Wrotonoski, on the west side of Beaver Creek Road. The owner received $2.75 a thousand for the logs, just twenty-five cents less than the asking price. When the logging was finished, Wrotonoski presented the crew with two barrels of beer.

A crew of thirty men worked six days a week and delivered between 80,000 and 100,000 feet of logs each day to the mill. The logs, mainly unbucked, were dumped from the railway cars into the pond at $8 a thousand. At that time millworkers were making 25 cents an hour; fallers were getting $5 and up per per day, and other loggers were getting rich on 50 cents an hour.[52]

O'Brien also recalled a dramatic episode in the history of Bainbridge – a logging train accident.

The locie was pushing a string of empties when a king pin jumped out and the train ran away. Engineer Johnson chased the train down the track hoping to reconnect it. Before he could reach the cars, they crashed. There were three men aboard one of the flatcars, two jumped and the third rode the train until it crashed. Two were killed outright. The other man never recovered from head injuries received in the wreck.[53]

O'Brien remembered picking a huge skunk cabbage leaf to place over the battered head of one of the victims. Fellow workers contributed when a collection was taken for the widow and two small children.

Gilbert Renwick, who worked for a year in the shipping department of the mill, remembered the care with which the timber was handled.

We couldn't use any tools that would ruin the wood. All the timbers were pushed by hand onto the timber deck to special sleighs. Then cranes overhead lifted up the timber very carefully to the trucks. Every precaution was taken not to put a dent of any kind in them. We cut the largest timber in the world. We even cut masts for the British Admiralty.[54]

Lumber was transported in a cart twelve feet long, made of only the framework and four crosspieces which stuck out from the frame. Two men, one on the end to steer and one on the side, pushed the cart which they had loaded.

When Bainbridge sawmill was operating at full capacity, a school was opened at the camp. Ruth Jones, daughter of the sawyer, was teacher. Another daughter, Margaret, taught in Beaver Creek school two miles away, and when enrollment dropped at Bainbridge, she received Ruth's pupils. One of the children who attended both schools was Jack Wright, who later became head pilot of a national airline.[55]

Social activities were an important part of life in the small community, and crowning May Queen Joyce Hopkins was a significant social event in 1920. Joyce's maids of honor included Lily Dobdin, Monna Fjarlie, Merydie Fjarlie, and Kathleen Hopkins. The crowning took place in the schoolgrounds at Bainbridge with John West officiating. The children of the school danced around the Maypole.

For the adults, the Bainbridge workers organized dances in Port Alberni. The first dance was so memorable that a notice of the second was all that was required to get a large attendance. Duguid's orchestra, from Vancouver, supplied the music. The local newspaper commented: "The arrangements were thorough and the first consideration all the way through was shown for the patrons of the dance all of whom decided that the Bainbridge boys not only know how to give a dance but they also give everything that is worth giving without stint."[56]

The mill became famous for the size and length of the timbers it shipped out of the Valley. It could cut timbers up to 120 feet in length and four feet square. Between 20 and 40 percent of timbers cut in 1920 were shipped to Victoria shipyards. At that time, this highly efficient mill was cutting from 75,000 to 80,000 feet a day. About 20 percent went to Victoria for use in the building of Victoria ship-owners' four barquentines. The shipbuilders were using timbers from eighty to one hundred feet long and twenty-two inches square. Other orders were filled for eastern and American markets. A shipment of three-feet square timbers, sixty feet long, was made in December 1923. These were carried by two Canadian Pacific Railway cars, and they were used in the construction of the Welland Canal.

Clarence Hoard, having designed the octagonal farm silo and cut edge grain fir with which to build it, was a pioneer in the field of prefabrication. His design took prizes in Europe.[57] In 1922 the Bainbridge mill began manufacturing these silos and shipped ten to Ireland for use in agricultural exhibitions to show Irish farmers the advantage of wooden silos. These silos were different from the usual silo, as they were built of notched boards lying parallel to the ground instead of standing vertical. This method of construction stabilized the silo. It was, therefore, not affected by climatic conditions which often resulted in expansion or contraction.[58] Hoard planned to develop a market for his octagonal silos on the prairies and in the United States.

Logging, which had begun close to the mill site, eventually moved further and further away. Logging camps with cookhouses and bunkhouses were established in four different locations. The company was running out of large timbers. It could not afford the timber at the head of the Valley, and it had failed to come to an agreement on the price of timber east of the mill.

Then, on October 17, 1927, a donkey engine working the Empire Spur on the face of Baldy was pulling in a large log from the yarder at the same time a heavy log in the air was in the process of being loaded onto a car. The weight put too much strain on the guy lines, and one broke. The whole spar tree swayed as it was falling. The fireman, forty-five year-old Archibald W. Thompson, had been stoking the fire. He went behind the boiler, but when he saw the spar tree was going to fall in his direction, he ran towards the woodpile. A piece of the spar tree broke off, struck Thompson on the head, and broke his neck, killing him instantly.

When word of the accident was received at the mill at 11:00 a.m., management told everyone to stop work immediately. No more regular work was ever done at the Bainbridge sawmill. By this time Clarence Hoard and his family had moved to Seattle, where he began work with the U.S. Corps of Engineers. He worked in Seattle and Portland until he retired to Victoria. Sam Hoard also returned to the United States, to Orting, Washington, where he purchased a small sawmill.[59]

In June 1919, the Canadian Pacific Railway president, E. W. Beatty, announced the construction of a branch line of the E & N Railway to Great Central Lake. The new line would branch off the Port Alberni extension at Solly Siding, and would touch the shore of Sproat Lake.[60] Construction of the line was awarded in December to the Foundation Company of B.C. Work on clearing and grading the road bed, estimated to be ten miles in length, was reported to be almost complete in May 1920, and was expected to be operational by August 1920.[61]

When D. C. Coleman, vice-president of the CPR, visited Port Alberni in July 1920, he announced:

We are building the lines to the lakes for the purpose of stimulating industrial development there. There is a tremendous wealth of timber contiguous to Sproat and Great Central Lakes and our extension taps it in the best possible manner. We anticipate that considerable development will follow its completion. Cruisers estimated there was enough Douglas fir to produce one million feet of lumber every day for thirteen years. On condition that the purchaser would erect a mill and ship lumber on E & N and CPR rails, the E & N was ready to sell.[62]

With the mills working at full capacity, local businesses began to pick up in 1916. Grocery stores were well stocked and prices were considered reasonable. Waterhouse & Greene were selling New Zealand butter for 45 cents, one dozen juicy oranges for 25 cents, and Peek Frean biscuits for 20 cents a package. Vancouver Island potatoes were selling at $2.50 for a 100-pound bag; Old Dutch cleanser was three for 25 cents; and Green's home-baked bread sold for thirteen for $1.00. A pair of boys' blue denim overalls sold for 45 cents; children's dresses were 20 cents; and gents' made-to-measure suits were $25.00. Men's work shoes cost $2.75 a pair.

C. F. Bishop & Son sold a one pound tin of peanut butter for 25 cents, a large package of Quaker Oats for 25 cents, and fresh tomatoes for 15 cents a pound. Watermelons cost 5 cents a pound. Kellogg's corn flakes and Kellogg's Krumbles sold for 10 cents a package. The Alberni Trading Co. store would deliver Golden Seal Flour for $1.65 or 100 pounds of granulated sugar for $9.75.[63]

A babysitter could earn $10 a month but she "must speak correctly".[64] The janitor at the Port Alberni High School was paid $15 a month.

In Alberni, the warm summer weather inspired some to organize a swim from Alberni to Port Alberni. Of the eight competitors who started off from the Old Town wharf to swim to the public wharf, a distance of approximately two miles, only three succeeded. Those who finished were W. Wilkinson, of Port Alberni, who came in first; L. Wrotnowski of Alberni, second; and Margaret Watty, a young woman from Alberni, who came in third. The choppy waves proved to be the downfall of K. Gill, J. Spencer, J. Redford, and J. Harling of Alberni and T. R. Poole of Port Alberni. It was a case of survival of the fittest.

The Alberni Fall Fair went ahead as usual on September 13, 1916, at the Fair Grounds on Strick Road. The membership fees were reduced and no entry fees were charged for entries this year.

Alberni City Council was having a little trouble with the Port Alberni School Board. An account received for tuition was ordered returned with a request for an itemized statement of $188.70 spent on fuel during 1916. Council also refused to pay for stables, built to house the horses used by the Alberni pupils travelling back and forth to school. It took the position that no authorization had been obtained from the Alberni School Board.

The small rural community had trouble with cattle roaming at large on local streets. To curtail this nuisance, council passed a bylaw which would allow cattle to roam at large only between 7:00 a.m. and 7:00 p.m. The bylaw was strictly enforced at night. Horses, on the other hand, were not allowed to run at large at any time under any circumstances.[65]

Two Chinese, applying to open laundries in the community, were advised to get the majority of property owners within a radius of two hundred yards of the proposed wash houses to sign a petition in favour of the opening. If the property owners agreed, the applications would be considered.

Residents of Alberni now knew when there was a fire. A huge fire alarm bell, weighing over six hundred pounds, had been purchased from the City of Vancouver.

A new city clerk was appointed. E. Dinsdale from Alberni succeeded Percy R. C. Bayne, who resigned to take charge of the Alberni Land Company office. Bayne was later elected to Port Alberni School Board following the resignation of F. H. Swayne, who left for Ireland.[66]

The January 1917 municipal election in Port Alberni saw Alexander Duncan MacIntyre elected mayor, along with aldermen Edward Exton, Archibald C. Macfie, Anthony Watson, I. M. Lederman, G. H. Proctor, and Charles Stuart. School board trustees were Mrs. George Bird and Mrs. G. H. S. Cowell.

It was a shocked community who read of the arrest on January 31, 1917, of Leonard Frank. "Leonard Frank, for many years a highly respected resident of the Alberni district, and well known as a scenic photographic artist, was on Monday afternoon committed for trial by Magistrate Hooson of Alberni, on the serious charge of criminal assault, which, it is alleged, he committed on a child of tender years."

The preliminary hearing was held behind closed doors. Little was known of the case, but the gossip continued in the scandalized community. "The fact that he is of German extraction, although a naturalized citizen, may have something to do with the case, but also, the fact that the evidence was strong enough to result in his being committed, gives the whole thing a very serious aspect."[67]

Frank was taken to Nanaimo by Police Constable McKenzie, of Alberni. He was later released on bail pending his trial on February 15, 1917. The results of Leonard Frank's trial remain a mystery, for court records from Nanaimo and Port Alberni have yet to be catalogued at the Provincial Archives in Victoria, and they are not yet available for public use.

Frank never returned to Alberni to live. He left behind the community he had worked so hard to develop, opened a shop and laboratory at 553 Granville Street in Vancouver, and became official photographer for the Vancouver Board of Trade. As well, he carried out assignments for the provincial and federal governments. He became, through time, one of British Columbia's most accomplished photographers. The record of his achievements in developing Alberni and the high regard in which he was held by the businessmen of the Alberni Board of Trade is perhaps testimony enough of the man behind the camera.[68] When Leonard Frank died on February 24, 1944, still a bachelor at age seventy-three, he had spent fifty years photographing British Columbia.

Residents with vacant lots were urged to get into the potato growing business and turn a profit. Why should hundreds of dollars be sent out of the city in exchange for such produce that could easily be grown in the city? Sam Roseborough was held up as an example of what could be done. On his city lot, measuring only one hundred by thirty-five feet, Roseborough raised a ton and a half of potatoes.[69]

The Somass Hotel had some renovations done to the old section of the building to accommodate four pool tables and a refreshment area. Harry Philpott, a returned soldier, who had been employed as a clerk at the hotel, was placed in charge of the new pool room.[70]

The Women's Franchise Act came into force on April 5th, 1917. Three hundred women from Port Alberni and Alberni registered to vote. The Alberni riding received over seven hundred applications for registration.[71]

In May, there was a redistribution of seats and the federal riding known as Comox Atlin, of which Alberni was a part, was divided into two seats. The southern portion would be known as Comox Alberni Electoral district.[72]

In June of 1917 the Alberni Residential School was destroyed by fire. The entire building was burned to the ground and little was saved. The fire had started in the attic and had smouldered for some time before breaking out. The local fire brigade was called on to be ready to answer a call for help. Unfortunately, it was not until the fire

277

was out of control that it was even considered advisable to call the Port Alberni fire fighters. Fire Chief Captain Holt who visited the scene in his own car as soon as the alarm was sounded, tried to help put out the flames, but the lack of a suitable water supply made it difficult to cope with the fire.

A bit of a mystery surrounded the fire, for by peculiar coincidence three mission schools on the west coast had been destroyed by fire during the past few months, and in each case it was said the fire started in the attic. A few weeks previously, the Indian missions at Ahousat and at Clayoquot had been burned down.

A month later five Indian children were remanded in Nanaimo for sentencing on charges of arson in connection with the fires at Clayoquot and Ahousat. At the trial, Judge Barker pointed out to the children the serious nature of their offence. After hearing the evidence, he ordered two of the children released. But the other children were not so lucky. Placid Lucas and Joseph Ignass were both sentenced to two years confinement in the Provincial Industrial School for Boys, and Florence Charlie of Ahousat got a similar sentence to the Provincial School for Girls.[73] There was no mention of the Alberni school in the trial proceedings. A new Alberni Residential School was build by F. Parfitt, a contractor from Victoria.[74]

The Effects of War

By 1916 the first flush of patriotic enthusiasm for war had passed. Farmers' sons had been slower to enlist than their city cousins. Farm produce was necessary to the war effort. For the first time in Canada there was a lag in enlistments, especially in Quebec. French Canadians had never shared the enthusiasm other Canadians had for war, and they held no special emotional attachment to Great Britain. They had accepted the need to fight, but only voluntarily. The Borden government was faced with a declining recruitment and increasing casualties. Throughout the war Borden had insisted that Canada be a full participant. The military commitment had to be honoured. By the spring of 1917, the war far from over, Borden had to face the reality of a new policy of compulsory military service.[75]

The Military Service Act, 1917, came into effect on September 11. The first call was limited to men between twenty and thirty-four who were unmarried or widowers without children on July 6, 1917. Throughout the country, exemption tribunals were established with power to decide who would be exempt from military service. There were over 1250 boards in Canada, each composed of two men, one appointed by the county judge in the district and one selected by a joint committee of Parliament. There were three tribunals established in this district: No. 2 in Port Alberni, No. 7 in Campbell River, and No. 1 in Parksville.

Robert Blandy, Port Alberni's city clerk, was appointed the local military representative on the Exemption Tribunal. The Tribunal was composed of Arthur E. Waterhouse and Powell Chandler of Parksville. When they held their first session at city hall, there were fifty-two claims for exemption in the Port Alberni section of the district.

Following conscription, the exodus of men in October 1917 from the Alberni district was devastating to the forest industry. Alberni Pacific Lumber Co. lost men from two of their camps of railway workers. Military authorities took twenty of them. More were dismissed when the mill management discovered the Industrial Workers of the World, (I.W.W. or Wobblies) propaganda was being advocated by a number of men from the United States.[76] Scouts were sent to Vancouver to hire more men for the logging camps.

The war effort was costing Canada a lot of money. The answer was "Victory Bonds," which went on sale in 1917. Charles McNaughton was appointed by the Minister of Finance to the Port Alberni Canada Victory Loan Committee. Until this time the war effort had cost Canada $7 million; of this amount, $4 million had been spent in Canada, and another $3 million had been spent on behalf of Great Britain.

Like most other Canadians, residents of the Albernis were doing their best to fight the war as energetically as possible. Never before had government so intervened in the lives of Canadians. All "enemy aliens" were required to register. As the war progressed and the casualty lists grew, hostility towards foreigners increased and eventually led to the decision to strip them of the vote in 1917.

Canadian internal security was of prime importance. The United States did not enter the war until 1917. During the early years of the war, many people of German descent found safe refuge south of the border, but Canada began to tighten its borders and censor the press. All pro-German literature was banned; it could not be printed, distributed, sent through the postal service, or moved across the border from the United States.

Canada's Chief Press Censor in Ottawa, Ernest J. Chambers,[77] had the job of deciding which publications would be permitted in Canada. A list of banned publications was printed periodically in the

Canada Gazette by Deputy Postmaster General R. M. Coulter. Mail and telegraph messages were also censored. Bamfield Pacific Cable Board had instructions to hold certain telegraph messages for a period of time until they were cleared. Special instructions were given for the handling of mail to and from enemy consuls in any country. These communications were diverted to the Postmaster General under cover and unmarked to give no evidence of the diversion.[78] All newspapers in Canada were strictly monitored, and some had plants and machinery seized.

Amid this climate of fear, one man was causing authorities a great deal of consternation. He was Charles Taze Russell, popularly called Pastor Russell, the founder of the International Bible Students Association, which was a forerunner of the Jehovah's Witnesses. The Association was founded in 1879. Russell, whose background was as a Presbyterian and Congregationalist, published books and booklets and six volumes of Studies in the Scriptures, eventually reaching a worldwide audience.[79]

Pastor Russell held Bible-reading sessions throughout Canada. A meeting in Victoria during March 1916 was cancelled by the Mayor of Victoria because of the hostile feelings in the city. One of Russell's publications forbade young men to enlist or have anything to do with military service. Ernest Chambers began receiving protests from individuals and organizations around the country. In July 1916, Pastor Russell was refused entry into Canada. Canadian Immigration authorities had decided he should not be allowed to influence young men against doing their duty. His publications were considered propaganda. "It will be no loss to the country if his sermons and addresses are censored during the period of the war," suggested W. D. Scott, Superintendent of Immigration, to Chambers, in Ottawa.[80]

In September 1917, Chambers recommended to the Secretary of State that action be taken to prohibit the possession within Canada of any publication by the International Bible Students Association (IBSA). A Pastor Russell book entitled *The Finished Mystery* was openly advertised in the *Vancouver Daily Province* in December 1917. "It throws more light than any book yet written on the present war, its real causes and the outcome. All thinking men should have it. An excellent Christmas gift." The 592 page book was priced at sixty cents. "If you tell me that this war is fought for the integrity of international law, I must ask you why it is directed only against Germany and not also against England, which is an equal, although far less terrible, violator of covenants between nations," stated an excerpt from *The Finished Mystery*.

The Secretary of State on February 6, 1918 issued a Warrant banning all publications by the IBSA. Throughout Canada police began making raids, seizing all IBSA literature. Wagonloads of books were seized in Vancouver, Edmonton, Montreal, Toronto, and Ottawa. Russellites, as followers of Pastor Russell were called, were held or arrested. The IBSA protested, claiming the censorship was "an infringement of inalienable rights of all men to full religious freedom."

Many other publications were censored at this time, including *The Liberator*, a paper published by the Industrial Workers of the World (IWW). Another offending magazine, *The Melting Pot*, was also banned. The *Canada Gazette*, with its list of banned publications, was mailed to every newspaper in Canada, including the *Port Alberni News* and the *Alberni Advocate*, although the latter had stopped publishing in 1914. On March 13, 1918 the *Port Alberni News* printed a warning from the Chief of Police to all residents. Anyone possessing literature issued by the IBSA were liable to have it confiscated and themselves called into court. The chief had received instructions to seize all copies of the book *The Finished Mystery* and all copies of the *Bible Students Monthly*. Residents were advised to destroy them or turn them over to police immediately. A list of banned publications was posted throughout town.

The Dominion Intelligence Department hired fire chief Richard Venables as a special constable to search the homes of two Port Alberni men. One was a music teacher, the other a businessman. Why it was decided to search these two homes is unknown. The community was outraged that the privacy of two prominent men had been violated. Businessman Harry L. Mertz, born in Mississippi, was known to be an avid reader. He was the first B.C. Telephone Co. manager in Port Alberni. Mertz operated a stationery and candy store on the east side of Third Avenue near Argyle Street. It was here the telephone exchange was located. The music teacher, whose family wish his name to remain anonymous, was known as a very private man and above reproach.

The Intelligence Department had detailed the circumstances of the visits to the two citizens. Venables found the music teacher had a copy of *The Divine Plan of the Ages*, a publication of the IBSA, while Mertz had in his possession *The Melting Pot*.

The music teacher was represented by lawyer Aubrey T. Sanders in his appearance in court before Magistrate Major George H. Cowan.

He said he did not know the book was in his house. It had been purchased five years before from an agent but he had never read it. He was fined $250 with the option of three months imprisonment.

Mertz, represented by lawyer J. Edward Bird, appeared before Magistrate H. B. W. Garrick. His case was remanded for a week because it was shown the magazine was published by a man whose name was not the same as that appearing in the list of banned publications in the *Canada Gazette*. Garrick sent a telegram asking Chambers to clarify the matter.[81] Chambers replied that *The Melting Pot* publication Garrick referred to was the same as in the *Canada Gazette*, only the address had changed. Garrick waited until verification had arrived before he proceeded with the trial.

Mertz was fined $300 or three months imprisonment. Bird immediately gave notice of appeal. Within an hour of the verdict, Bird was approached by the prosecution with an offer to reduce the amount of the fine provided Mertz would abandon his appeal. Since the appeal was going to cost more than $50, Mertz decided to accept the offer. He was a bit astonished the next day to find out the deal had been accepted. His fine was reduced to $50.[82]

The two cases so enraged John Kendall, he fired off a letter to Port Alberni City Council asking for the resignation of Magistrate Garrick and to have put in his place someone "who will display keener judgment and better foresight."[83] He wrote he had studied the cases of "two of our most reliable and energetic citizens." He was of the opinion the judgment was unconstitutional. Council was used to hearing from Kendall. It dismissed his request by tabling his letter for seven years. Mertz tried to get his fifty dollars refunded, but Council advised him it had no power to refund his fine. If he considered he was badly treated, he should appeal to the courts, he was told.

While the Dominion Intelligence Department had ordered the search and prosecution of the men, it did not feel inclined to pay the expenses of their prosecutions in court. The Port Alberni Police Commission of the city was asked to shoulder the cost. It refused, arguing that since the military authority had started the court proceedings, it should pay the cost.[84]

The Port Alberni men had got off lightly. In other parts of Canada, heavy fines and imprisonment were being imposed. Canada was under a strange condition – war psychosis. The Port Alberni incidents had outraged many residents, as much over the press censorship as the considered "bartering of justice."

Residents packed City Council chambers when the Mertz banned literature case was to be reviewed. In a letter to council, Magistrate Garrick explained that after trying the Mertz case he returned home as usual, having heard nothing about the application for the reduction of the fine. The next morning he was told both sides had agreed on the settlement. He denied any association with the defence in the case. Garrick also appeared before council to defend his honour and face his accusers. City Council remained firm in defence of the magistrate, and dismissed any suggestion of wrongdoing. Harry Mertz was appointed poundkeeper for the City of Port Alberni in March 1926. He died one month later at the age of fifty-two.[85]

The municipal elections of January 1918 went without fanfare. Elected by acclamation to Port Alberni council were Mayor A. D.MacIntyre and Aldermen Edward Exton, Isaac Meyer Lederman, Anthony Watson, George Stawell Pearse, Alexander Bruce Wood, George Henry Proctor. School trustees elected were Percy R. C. Bayne and B. I. Hart. In Alberni, Mayor Harry Hills was elected. Spencer and Best were re-elected to the North Ward; Sid Toy and H. B. Currie to the South Ward; and Henry Blakemore and C. T. Harvey to the West Ward.

Since 1915 strenuous efforts had been made to have the Burde Road (Kinross) completed. The road began with a grant of $5,000, largely through the persistence of former Mayor Burde. Even B.C. Telephone Company, considering the road eventually would be completed, went to considerable expense installing a new toll line through the territory because maintenance was expected to be easier on this road than on the other. An editorial in the *Port Alberni News* called for the squabbling between the towns to cease.

> There can be no reason for this opposition other than pure selfishness. This roadway is the only thing the people of Port Alberni ever asked for from the Provincial government and they are entitled to it. This road is a necessity and in the near future will open a tract of country that is very suitable for small farms.
>
> It is to be hoped that the residents of the Old Town will soon awaken to the fact that anything done for the benefit of Port Alberni will be for the benefit of the whole Alberni Valley. If the people of this West Coast section ever hope to progress they must stand together to do it. Opposition and squabbling over every little matter should cease, for a house divided is sure to meet with disaster.[86]

Conservative MPP Richard Wallis promised to do all in his power to have the Burde Road completed. Despite his and other efforts, the opposition was such that the road was never completed.

With electricity now lighting the town, women began purchasing electric irons. But, because electricity was not turned on during the daytime, their irons were almost useless. About fifty of the women drafted a petition and presented it to the City of Port Alberni council asking for twenty-four hour service. Forty of the women already had electric irons. The city clerk advised council that the electric plant operated an average of thirteen hours a day at an estimated cost for the current year of $5,000. To operate for the full twenty-four hours would require the services of another man, costing at least $1,200 per year, about 13,000 gallons more fuel oil, costing about $1,600, plus another $300 for lubricating oil and repairs, bringing the grand total to $8,100 per year. To make the twenty-four hour service pay would require an increase of at least 60 percent in the consumption of electricity by paying consumers. It was noted that the ironing load in the daytime would to some extent be merely a transfer from the present evening load. The electric irons would have to wait.[87]

Many of the soldiers returning home tried to pick up the pieces of lives disrupted when war was declared. There was a big celebration held when Major Dick Burde, M.C., returned home on leave in August suffering from what was termed "trench fever." He had spent some time in England recovering from German gas and a burst eardrum. A huge crowd gathered in McGrath Hall to honour the Major and other returning veterans. Mayor MacIntyre welcomed them home, noting he regretted they were yet unable to celebrate victory and the end to the war. The audience sang "For They are Jolly Good Fellows."

Burde thanked the audience and appealed for continued support for the men still carrying on the war effort in France. He said Vimy was the worst battle the 102nd had encountered. Eighty percent of the men were casualties.

> I saw fighting at Ypres salient and in the three battles on the Somme. Most of the original officers of the unit were lost on the Somme. These men were nearly all well known on Vancouver Island having gone overseas with Warden's Warriors from Comox.[88]

It was at the battle of Somme that tanks were first used in warfare.

Burde planned to spend his time on leave camping at Sproat or Great Central Lake. Later he planned to join the Canadian Expeditionary force being sent to Siberia. His plans were to change.

Influenza Epidemic

On October 9, 1918 the first hint that Spanish influenza had reached Vancouver Island came when two deaths occurred in Victoria. The provincial capital city began taking drastic steps to stop the spread of the disease. A special order-in-council was passed closing all places of amusement and assembly. Other cities throughout the province were advised of the action and warned to use every effort to stamp out the sickness if a case should develop. Local Boards of Health were empowered close schools, churches, theatres, dance halls, and lodges immediately.

A week later, both Alberni and Port Alberni city councils, acting as Boards of Health, gave the order to close all establishments where people congregated. The city already had one case of influenza. The schools in Alberni were closed, but those in Port Alberni remained open. The regulations particularly affected the moving picture theatre, the two dance halls, and the pool rooms. The churches had voluntarily closed on Sunday. But the moving picture theatre planned to take advantage of the full limit allowed by law.

> Picture shows will be held on Friday and Saturdays and every effort would be made to prevent infection. The theater will be thoroughly fumigated both before and after Friday's performance and liquid antiseptic will be sprinkled throughout the house.[89]

This was a voluntary precautionary measure similar to that being carried out by the large department stores and theatres in Vancouver where over one hundred cases of the plague had surfaced. Surgeon General Blue of the U.S. Public Health Service said the disease had become epidemic. He described the symptoms:

> It is characterized by sudden onset, people are stricken on the street, while at work, in factories, shipyards, offices or elsewhere. First there is a chill, then fever with temperature from 101 to 103, headache, backache, reddening and running of the eyes, pains and aches all over the body and general prostration. Persons so attacked should go to their homes at once, get to bed without delay, and immediately call a physician.[90]

People were warned not to visit homes where the disease was known to exist.

By October 23, the *Port Alberni News* reported there were a large number of influenza cases in the city and district, but most were of the mild ordinary type and not the Spanish variety. Only two actual cases of the "real flu" had materialized. However, one entire family was laid up with the disease after a son returned from Vancouver, spreading it to the family members.

The epidemic was causing considerable inconvenience in the lumber camps, where loggers with the least sign of a cold were treated with the greatest suspicion by fellow workmates. As a result the hospital was full of cases that had been diagnosed by the local health officer as ordinary colds, grippe, and influenza of the common variety.[91]

MPP Richard P. Wallis, forty-eight years of age, was the first with Alberni Valley connections to die of the illness. Wallis died in Moncton, New Brunswick, October 14, a victim of influenza followed by pneumonia. He had been on his way to Newfoundland to attend to some personal business when he was stricken and forced to seek medical attention. Wallis had been a resident of the district since 1890. In January he had been the successful candidate in the district by-election when he defeated John Frank Bledsoe.[92]

By the end of October, the epidemic had become very serious. There were estimated to be well over one hundred cases with new ones occurring every day. The West Coast General Hospital was full, and two emergency hospitals were filled up. Every logging camp in the district was affected by the epidemic, and there was little work being done in the woods. There were an equal number of cases in Alberni. The disease had also hit the Indian Mission. Up to this point the death toll had been small in proportion to the number of cases, but many were in serious condition and not expected to survive.

During the next two weeks, the grim reaper took his toll of Valley residents. Obituaries began appearing on the front page of the *Port Alberni News*. The first victim was Mrs. Sadie Weare, whose husband William was still overseas serving with the Forestry Battalion in France. Some others included Pearl May Dolan, Louie Johnson, Henry Wilson Armstrong, Louie Lorraine, M. W. Jacobs, Alexander James Dowing, and Isabella Telford, wife of the storekeeper at Wallace Fisheries, at Kildonan. Then came the death of William M. Holt, who had managed B.C. Telephone for six years and served as fire chief. Through his efforts the long distance telephone line was brought through via the new Burde (Kinross) Street to the Nanaimo Road as an inducement to have the road completed. As fire chief it was on his recommendation the power fire truck was purchased by the city.[93]

The community became numb from the heavy death toll encountered over the past few years. But there was evidence the flu epidemic was subsiding. There were still many cases, even some serious ones, at the cable station in Bamfield, but by November the illness was generally under control. Although there were nineteen cases of flu at the cable station, only two operators died. They were James Beckerleg, twenty-five years of age, and Harry Townsend Joly, thirty-one years of age. Beckerleg had been married only one year to Miss Guillod, daughter of the former Indian Agent in Alberni.[94]

The hospital discharged the last patient and then closed for two weeks to allow the building to be fumigated. The superintendent, Miss Scott, left for Vancouver to enjoy a well earned rest. At the annual general meeting of the hospital association, Dr. C. T. Hilton referred to the strain on the hospital staff during the Spanish flu epidemic. He said the thanks of the community were due to Miss Scott and Mrs. Eleanor Hodgson. Hodgson had given her services as a nurse free of charge, at a time when the lack of trained nurses had become a serious matter. When the hospital had become filled with influenza patients, Miss Gill, Miss Swanson, and Miss Hill, who had previously been on the hospital staff, went to the assistance of Miss Scott. But one by one they too became ill, and the superintendent was left alone until Mrs. Hodgson volunteered her services.

These were difficult times financially for the hospital which was entirely without funds and owed about $600 for supplies and salaries. There was over $3,000 owed in uncollectible accounts. The Board of Trustees decided to borrow $800 from the Bank of Montreal. The district was canvassed for subscriptions. An appeal was made to the ladies of the Alberni and Port Alberni auxiliaries to arrange to hold a public ball in aid of the hospital in mid-January.[95]

Great War Ends

Burde had no sooner announced he would be a candidate in the forthcoming by-election to replace Wallis, when suddenly came the greatest news of all – peace had been declared. The Germans accepted the terms of the Allies, and the armistice was signed. On November 11, 1918, at 11:00 a.m., all hostilities ceased. The Germans had agreed to leave all invaded territory, to surrender huge quantities of guns and ammunition, to hand over an immense number of railway locomotives and rolling stock, to release all Allied prisoners, and to surrender the German navy.

Both cities went wild with excitement. Every whistle, bell, and noisemaker was turned on, and a civic holiday was proclaimed. Dorrit MacLeod, who was a school student at the time, remembered that special day. The teacher came into the schoolroom and announced: "Children, I have good news for you. Peace has been declared. You can all go home."[96]

Forgotten was the ban placed on all public assemblies for the flu epidemic. A spontaneous automobile parade toured the district in the afternoon; the fourteen mile "Victory Joy Ride" was enjoyed by the large crowd participating. The cars were all decorated for the occasion, and one of them had a scaffold erected at the rear with a hanging effigy of the "most hated man on earth" attached. In the evening a big bonfire was lit opposite the Somass Hotel, and the effigy properly cremated. Major Burde gave what was described as a "thrilling address" to end the day's festivities.

An official celebration held the following week was highlighted by a torchlight procession through the main streets of Port Alberni. In Alberni, the citizens celebrated peace with a huge bonfire on the banks of the Somass River.[97] Dr. C. T. Hilton, medical health officer, declared the danger of contagion from the flu was about over and ordered all restrictions removed.

The Great War had cost 60,661 Canadian lives, nearly 10 percent of the total enlistment.[98] Those who had fought and lived together in the trenches had found a new sense of what it was to be a Canadian. The Victory Loan Campaign wound up its activities in triumph with over $7,000 to spare. The Alberni District had exceeded its quota in the Victory Loan 1918 campaign. The honour flag was received by C. A. McNaughton, chairman of the local committee, but it was now a bit of a white elephant. He did not know what to do with it, now that the war was over.[99] And the City of Port Alberni was to get some war souvenirs – three German machine guns captured by the 102nd Battalion in France. "The commanding officer trusts that this gift will be accepted in the spirit in which it is offered as a tribute and lasting memorial to the citizen soldiers who have so gallantly sacrificed all for the cause of liberty and justice and as an acknowledgment from the soldiers in the field to the fine citizenship at home which has made possible the victory of today."[100]

The Port Alberni Board of Trade reorganized, and within a day of their reorganizing, a resolution was on its way to Ottawa to ask for the completion of the Canadian Northern Pacific Railway.[101] The resolution did not get encouraging results but the Board of Trade did not give up lobbying the dominion government. Instead it prepared another resolution outlining all the reasons why the railway connection should be completed, and it sought the endorsation of every influential public body on the Island.

The January 1919 civic elections saw several women running for office for the first time. The Alberni council was elected by acclamation with Capt. Huff as Mayor. Councillors included Mrs. Thomas Patterson, wife of the magistrate; Mrs. J. A. Croll, whose husband operated a tugboat; Harold Bishop, son of pioneer C. Frederic Bishop; James Hills; A. H. M. Lord; and H. B. Currie. The Port Alberni election had a contest for mayor between Mayor A. D. MacIntyre and Ald. Edward Exton. Exton won by a majority of seventeen votes. Councillors elected were Mrs. Margaret Hill, Antony Watson, George Stawell Pearse, Alex Bruce Wood, B. I. Hart, and Mrs. Hester Hanna, whose husband also operated a tugboat.

Provincially, Major Burde was elected by acclamation in January to replace Wallis. The *Port Alberni News* reported the occasion with shades of Burde's own writing shining through.

Burde was elected by acclamation on Saturday last to represent the Alberni district. Nothing more than formal proceedings, and a quiet time, being expected there were only a few citizens of Alberni and Port Alberni present at the Court House in the former city where the official ceremony took place. In a mild drizzle of rain, Capt. G. A. Huff, returning officer, appeared on the sidewalk in front of the emporium of justice at 12 o'clock and read the proclamation. He announced that he already had one nomination that of Richard John Burde, and if no other nominations were handed to him before 1 p.m. he would declare this candidate elected.

"Might just as well go home now," remarked a well known mariner, who had come fresh from the salt sea breezes, and was standing beside his automobile in which he had proudly escorted the candidate to the scene. The hour wore away without even the faintest indication of a surprise in sight and the returning officer then declared Burde duly elected. Burde will leave tomorrow for Victoria.[102]

Residents were shocked when the news came on January 23, 1919, that Bobby De Beaux had been arrested. The pioneer merchant, who had operated a little store on Argyle Street for a number of years, was arrested by military authorities and taken to Victoria to answer charges of "uttering seditious language." Several times during the Great War De Beaux was suspected of having pro-German feelings and an effort was made to have him interned. When the armistice was declared, attention to his case was temporarily suspended. He admitted having been born in Germany, but claimed to have been naturalized about twenty-five years ago. He was given time to produce proof of his naturalization but failed to satisfy the authorities. The information which led to his arrest surfaced. De Beaux had advised some Indians to be on their guard against returned soldiers as there was a scheme afoot to deprive the natives of their lands for the benefit of the war veterans. He had also suggested violent demonstrations in protest.[103]

De Beaux's business was carried on by I. G. Steeves. The Port Alberni Police Commission was asked to hand over any money received from the business to the Camp Commanding Officer in Vernon, where De Beaux was interned. When questioned by the commission, Police Chief John Richard Edwards told the commission the internment of De Beaux had been at the instigation of military authorities.[104]

De Beaux claimed he had not received a square deal in the internment proceedings and hired a lawyer to look into the charges against him. He believed that after spending thirty-two years in the Alberni district and helping to develop it, he was entitled to more consideration than had been shown by the authorities.[105] De Beaux was deported but returned in June 1921 intent on continuing his life in Alberni.[106]

In Transition – Major Burde, MPP

Major Burde, the Alberni District's newly elected member of the provincial legislature, was the right man at the right time. The community needed a strong voice to attend to the many issues beginning to surface after the war ended. The Prohibition Act was unpopular; returning soldiers required some consideration; and the fishing industry in the Alberni Inlet was almost history, as the fish were fast being depleted by overzealous canneries.

Burde gave his maiden speech in the House in February. It was duly reprinted in its entirety in the *Port Alberni News*. Excerpts were also printed in major Victoria and Vancouver papers. His colourful address captured the spirit of the time. At the outset, Burde advised he would work for the returning soldiers, who wanted action. They did not just want "work sometime" or "beer sometime," they wanted these things now. He told of cases in Victoria where men had waited three months for money from the pay and records office. He did not forget the settlers of the province and said he would be behind the premier in fighting Ottawa for settlers' rights.

The prohibition measure was an absolute farce and an injustice, he said, "being today responsible for new brands of crime as well as much of the industrial unrest. For one thing, it has prostituted the profession of medicine. The House should certainly remodel the bill."[107] Then he lashed out at the Fisheries Department calling it "a standing disgrace to Canada, smelling of fish, but of a rotten brand."

There never was a bigger graft-ring in Canada than there is in the circle where one must wait today for a fishing license. The very fact that an application for a seine net license is made in private to the Chief Inspector of Fisheries, and the public does not know anything about it, must make anyone of the penetrative mind, smell graft. You can sell a fishing license any day in a real estate office for $3,000 or $4,000. Our fisheries are being depleted.

In Alberni, we procured thirty affidavits to prove that there had been almost enough herring wasted by the seine net ringsters to feed Canada for three or four years. The bottom of the harbour is silvery carpeted with dead herring. I am told that the seine net fishermen impound about one hundred and forty tons of herring in each drive. Sixty per cent of them are smothered and dead by the time the other 40 per cent are loaded. The dead fish drop to the bottom of the harbour and thus the waste goes on.

He said the Chief Inspector of Fisheries had admitted to him that hundreds of Japanese working for herring concerns had no right to work in the industry because they were not naturalized.

Somehow or other they produce naturalization papers when called upon to do so. People say the canneries hand out the naturalization certificates to the Japanese whenever they wish to employ them. The Japanese going home to the Orient leave their certificates behind and the Japanese contractors apparently sell them to the newcomers or to the canneries. The Japanese put up tons of immature herring and ship them via Tacoma to Japan, in this way robbing B.C. of one of its most valuable assets.

Burde knew the federal government was about to begin a Royal Commission of inquiry in Port Alberni into the Barkley Sound fisheries. A week before, he had made a motion in the House to have the scope of the inquiry extended to include the entire west coast of Vancouver Island and the whole of the province. He charged the Chief Inspector of Fisheries and his subordinates of misconduct. The House passed his motion unanimously. A message was sent to the Department of the Naval Service, Ottawa, who had been administering federal fisheries during the war years, stating the British Columbia government was behind the request that the scope of the inquiry be extended.[108]

Other representations had been sent to the Department by the Port Alberni Board of Trade, the Great War Veterans, and the Barclay Sound Fisheries Protective Association. As well, copies of affidavits of local fishermen who had witnessed the "wholesale destruction of fish in Barclay Sound" were also forwarded to Ottawa by the Board of

Trade. Most of these affidavits referred to Wallace Fisheries. Only one mentioned Butterfield Mackie Co. Manager F. E. Burke dismissed all the allegations made against Wallace Fisheries.

The Great War had affected the fishing industry. Prior to 1914 there had been little or no demand for canned pink or chum salmon. But with a worldwide food shortage these varieties jumped into prominence, and this increased demand induced those in the canning business to extend their operations into fall fish. It also induced others to participate in the industry. As a consequence, the whole coastline of British Columbia was covered with licenses. To the returned soldiers, entering the fishing industry appeared to be the thing to do, but applications had increased by such a number that those wanting to take up fishing found it difficult to get a license. This led to consideration of a new policy governing the issuing of fishing licenses.

By 1919 there were twenty-nine purse-seine licenses operating in the area from Cape Beale to Sombrio Point. Of these, fifteen were issued to returned soldiers.[109] These men were not in a financial position to supply themselves with boats and nets. Consequently they had to make the best arrangements possible in getting gear to operate their licenses. There was such intensive fishing that practically no salmon reached their spawning beds that year. There were also 150 applications for fishing licenses from returned soldiers that year; only 46 were approved. This created a great deal of dissatisfaction among those who were not successful.

Bringing law and order into fishing on the west coast of Vancouver Island was challenging work. Early patrol officers had a difficult time, for fishermen did not take kindly to rules and regulations governing closed season, restricted areas, and types and size of fishing gear. The contest between the law and its offenders was almost a contest of wits rather than hard-nosed fighting. If he was caught, a fisherman accepted the law. However, if there was doubt or some extenuating circumstances, he might get away with just a stern warning.

By 1919, British Columbia was divided into three districts for more effective control. Each district had its own district supervisor. There were offices in New Westminster (District 1), Prince Rupert (District 2), and Nanaimo (District 3). Headquarters for the chief supervisor was in Vancouver. Edward Taylor was in charge of District 3. The fisheries officer for the Albernis and Barkley Sound area was James Wood.

This was a large area for Wood to patrol, and his duties, like fishing, required a number of skills, including good judgment. If, in the beginning, he lacked experience as a fisheries patrol officer, he made up for it with his knowledge of the area and the people involved. The same could be said for Taylor, who had been a Presbyterian minister in Alberni before becoming district supervisor. Wood was one of the four brothers who started the Barclay Sound Cedar Company.

The local fishermen were skeptical and wary about the ability of the fisheries officers to enforce law and order on the seas. The canneries that now dotted the Alberni Inlet were seen as a threat, and the fishermen suspected the two officers of favouring the cannery interests.

The politicians who governed were also under fire; MP Herbert S. Clements, in particular, was seen as accommodating cannery interests. Stacks of letters mounted between Port Alberni City Council and Clements regarding Fisheries and abolition of seine nets. Clements said he could do nothing. Council suggested he should resign his seat. Allegation followed allegation, until it appeared the whole fishing industry was in chaos.

In the Barkley Sound area, where stock had been reduced by heavy fishing to feed the canneries, feelings were running high against the fisheries officer and his supervisor, as well as against the big canneries. The Barclay Sound Fisheries Protective Association (BSFPA) began a movement for the abolition of seine nets, claiming their use was the reason salmon and herring were being depleted. The movement was supported by the Great War Veteran's Association, Alberni district, Port Alberni City Council, and the Port Alberni Board of Trade. Indian fishermen were also opposed to the use of the seine nets. Some were members of the BSFPA. They said they would press the Department of Indian Affairs for the abolition of the nets.

It was hoped a Royal Commission of Inquiry would clear the air and lay to rest many of the fears and allegations. The fishing inquiry opened Wednesday, February 5, 1919, in the Port Alberni Theatre on First Avenue, with Judge D. M. Eberts, Victoria, from the Court of Appeals, presiding, assisted by Ernest Miller. At the hearing, nine charges and complaints were laid against officials of the Fisheries Department who were suspected of pandering to the interests of Wallace Fisheries and other large canneries in Barkley Sound. Witnesses were called to testify. Arguments were presented by lawyers representing each interest. Throughout the inquiry, the charges were renounced by Taylor and Wood.

Burde helped inflame feelings with his fiery speeches during the hearings. He urged fishermen to "stay with the fight."[110] The inquiry continued in Vancouver, Nanaimo, and Duncan. When B.C.'s Chief Inspector of Fisheries F. H. Cunningham delivered his report for the year he noted the inquiry was a waste of time.

> There is nothing of special interest to report in connection with this district. During the season of 1919 a judicial investigation was held into the actions of the fishery officers in District No. 3. Charges of all kinds were filed against the officers and his Hon Judge Eberts was appointed by the government to investigate the same. All evidence was taken under oath and it is satisfactory to note that not one solitary charge was proven, but it was an unfortunate waste of time and public money. One good feature, however, may have emanated from the investigation in so far as it set at rest in the public mind wild rumours of graft and maladministration of the fisheries in this province generally.[111]

When the fishing season opened in 1920 there was an entirely new policy of open fishing. For years there had been restrictions in the number of licenses that could be issued, a form of conservation to prevent intensive fishing in any one area. The number of applicants for fishing licenses had increased so much that a change of policy had been necessary. The new policy gave every British subject an opportunity to enter the fishing business. The restricted license policy was replaced by a policy of granting unlimited licenses to all British subjects of the white race and Indians.[112] Colonel F. H. Cunningham retired as British Columbia Chief of Fisheries in December 1920.

It was two years before Ottawa reported it had received the Eberts Report. All fisheries officers were exonerated of any wrongdoing. However, the stress and strain of the inquiry took a heavy toll on the health of James Wood. He became ill in 1920, an illness that lasted three years. During this time his eighteen year-old daughter Mary was persuaded by Taylor to continue with her father's Fisheries reports to the department. She did this until her father was able to resume his duties.

By 1920, there were estimated to be 1000 Japanese fishing on the west coast of Vancouver Island,[113] and about 500 who owned and operated fishing boats. Many of these boats operated within the harbours of Ucluelet and Clayoquot and Barkley Sound area. The Japanese fishermen had become so numerous that residents became alarmed at the perceived takeover of this important industry. Headlines such as this one did little to lessen the apprehension:

"Alarming conditions on the west coast. Japanese fishermen swarm in the outer harbours of this district and hold supremacy in the most important industry."[114]

In the early years of British Columbia's fishing industry, young Japanese men in their twenties arrived. They worked for the canneries as fishermen and shore labourers, staying in bunkhouses provided by the company. Drinking and fighting marked those early years. These first immigrants had intended to return to Japan with the money they earned in Canada, but once their families were formed they became permanent settlers, building homes and taking out citizenship. Some of the men sent for their "picture brides," wives chosen on the basis of photographs sent to them from their home village.

Several Japanese centres developed, and one of these was in Ucluelet, at the head of the Alberni Inlet. In the early work gangs the Japanese were resented as unfair competition to white labour. Because they kept together in tight little communities, maintaining their own customs and language, resentment and prejudice against them increased. Their skill as fishermen and willingness to work for low wages made them desirable to the cannery managers but hated by many of the white settlers.

During World War One Japan was an ally; many Japanese residents even volunteered to serve in the army. Rising demand for fish and increased prices bolstered the fishing industry. The Japanese responded. The small fishing communities received an influx of new immigrants.

In addition to Wallace Fisheries at Kildonan, there were now several canneries dotted along the Alberni Inlet. These included Ecoole, Gosse-Millerd Packing Co, Green Cove, and Sarita.[115] A cannery at Nitinat Lake, built by the Lumni Bay Packing Company of Washington State, was bolstering the sagging fortunes of the Nootkans at Clooose and Whyak.[116]

Between 1901 and 1918 the number of canneries licensed for operation had been restricted in British Columbia. After 1918 all restrictions on cannery operations were removed. Any company could open a cannery if it paid the required license fee. This resulted in keen competition along the west coast and the opening of new canneries.

Operating a cannery in a remote location such as the Alberni Inlet was very difficult. With no roads into the various locations and no telephones, getting the workers housed and fed, the fish to the cannery, and the catch processed and sent to market made for a complex operation. The season's supply had to be planned ahead before operations began. The CPR steamers called in regularly during the season, bringing in supplies and taking out the finished product.

When a Japanese cannery was opened at Ritherton Bay, opposite Kildonan, and another opened at Port Albion, the perceived threat of a Japanese takeover of the industry became more real to the people of the Albernis and Barkley Sound. Gradually agitation against the Japanese had increased to such an extent that some white fishermen in Barkley Sound began arming themselves.

The Japanese were not just fishing, they were also branching out into other lines of endeavour. Some were seen as taking trade away from local storekeepers. Their stores were in large boats which catered to customers in and out of port. Some even traded, on the side, in homemade moonshine liquor or imported brands. As there were not enough police to adequately enforce the law, they were able to carry on this traffic with a large degree of impunity.

Some residents of the Albernis thought the Japanese had become quite arrogant in their feeling of security. To the British settler, the situation was becoming truly alarming. The *Port Alberni News* did little to diminish this feeling of hostility towards the Japanese. The Victoria *Colonist* took the *Port Alberni News* to task over its reporting of the Japanese fishermen, stating the Japanese were merely doing what was legal. "The criticism of aliens engaged in our industries should not be allowed to develop into discrimination against the national of any one country."[117]

The *Port Alberni News* was quick to retaliate. It stated that if the *Colonist* choose to adopt the attitude that there should be no discrimination it would find itself

> in discord with a public sentiment that has been proclaimed through all political party channels and has been responsible for the enactment of discriminatory laws and the provision of prohibitive clauses in public contract.
> To place the Japanese, who cannot be assimilated into our national life, on the same ground of desirability as the white foreigner, is to ignore the essentials of nation building. Some of our best and most patriotic citizens are of white foreign extract. Experience has taught us that in most cases, all that is necessary in the process of assimilation can be accomplished in two generations.[118]

In August 1921 a meeting of white and Indian fishermen took place at Dodge Cove. Major Burde, Alberni MLA, and C. Motte, Presbyterian missionary, were there as advisors. The meeting had been called because of the "unsatisfactory conditions of the fishing industry, due to Japanese supremacy, government indifference and difficulties in marketing catches."[119] The delegates at the meeting decided that if the west coast fishing was not to be entirely abandoned to the Japanese, a strong and aggressive organization of white men and Indians must be brought together immediately. Committees were appointed to canvass the whole west coast territory and arrange for a mass meeting of all concerned.

Charles A. McNaughton acted as chairman of the October meeting and introduced the invited speakers Captain Macaulay and H. S. Cowper, of the Asiatic Exclusion League, from Vancouver. Macaulay said people had very little idea of what the Asiatic Exclusion League was trying to do for British Columbia, or of the real menace of the Chinese and Japanese. "Everyone walking the streets of our cities must see something of it, and realize the need of taking steps to remedy it."[120] It was with this in mind that the Asiatic Exclusion League had been formed, the initiative having come from the Soldiers Council in Vancouver.

Macaulay said figures regarding the coming in of Asiatics were astounding. He did not consider the "Hindus" a menace as the number coming to Canada was negligible, only 5000 in twenty years. However, during the same period, until March 21, 1920, approximately 37,000 Chinese and 19,000 Japanese had come to Canada. Other estimates put the figure of Japanese immigration at 60,000, because there was no patrol on the Pacific Coast, where many were reported coming in by the back door route.

The Asiatic Exclusion League proposed to ask the government to stop entirely immigration of the Chinese and Japanese, and to prevent them either owning or leasing land. It suggested a plan for the gradual deportation of those already here. Macaulay stated there were over 3000 fishing licenses held by Japanese people on the Pacific Coast. This figure must have been designed to alarm an audience who already perceived a takeover of an important industry. Cowper said it was not the aim of the League to make mischief, but rather to avert it.[121]

When G. S. Hames of North Vancouver introduced two anti-Asiatic resolutions in the provincial legislature in November 1921, he was intent on ending the Anglo-Japanese alliance formed to protect British interests in China and Korea from Britain's enemy, Russia. One of these resolutions called on the dominion government to take steps by giving the required twelve month notice to end the Anglo-

Japanese treaty, so that Canada could have complete control of Asiatic immigration. The other resolution asked for the amending of the Immigration Act to "totally restrict the immigration of Asiatics into B.C. keeping in view the wishes of the people of B.C. that this province be reserved for people of the European race."[122] Both resolutions passed without a dissenting vote.

Prohibition

Prohibition had been imposed nation-wide as a war policy in October 1917, but the Act, which each provincial legislature had approved, was not repealed at the end of the war as people expected. Outlets for the sale of liquor in Alberni and Port Alberni were still being found, however illegally. In reality, prohibition was the result of a strong temperance movement that had slowly gained strength throughout the 19th century.

The medical profession was not at all happy with the legislation, which allowed them to administer liquor on prescription. The provincial government had established depots in the Government Agent's offices at Cranbrook, Nelson, and Prince Rupert, plus two official stores at Victoria and Nanaimo. Only a legal prescription, signed by a physician, could qualify a person for liquor. A movement that started in Vancouver, the People's Moderation Party, planned to try to have the Prohibition Act repealed and a law substituted that would allow the sale of beer and light wines, but not permit the return of bars.

MPP Burde said in his constituency he had tasted bootlegged whiskey that reminded him of the old Yukon brand, a mixture of tea colouring, wood alcohol, and sewing machine oil. He said it was a shame that fishermen and men in the outposts should have to pay fifteen dollars a bottle for such "hootch," when at the same time, members of the legislature could get from other members prescriptions that permitted them to buy good liquor from the government at two and three dollars a bottle.[123] Burde took aim at the ministerial profession for rallying in favour of prohibition.

> The parsons have been shooting off their mouths on this question just as they did about the rum and cigarettes for the soldiers, but I can tell you that some of the parsons and their sympathizing offices became converted to the rum ration after they saw it served to men who had stood for hours waist deep in mud and water. Parsons who object to the rum ration are too narrow minded to be of use anywhere. And there are not much bigger grafters anywhere than some of the parsons who went to the front.[124]

Prohibition was making distillers out of some of the best wives in the country, he said.

They sneak up on a wild dandelion at night, throw it in a pail of water, throw a yeast cake in with it and in a couple of months offer you what they call dandelion wine. A few quarts of this two per cent beer, just plain bellywash, is harder on a man's stomach than seventeen bottles of real beer. Why can't the workingman get real beer instead of this stuff?[125]

Burde wanted additional police on the west coast of Vancouver Island. Infractions of the Prohibition Act were becoming so serious in the vicinity of Port Alberni that a motor boat patrol was becoming a necessity.[126] On May 15, 1918, the Port Alberni Chief of Police was ordered by the Board of Police Commission to investigate the existence of "blind pigs" in the city. Blind pigs was the name given to places where alcohol was being sold or supplied illegally.

The Beaufort Hotel, then operated by E. Wyatt, was searched twice without notice, and no alcohol was found. The Commission had received complaints that Pineo's Drug Store was selling twelve gallons of alcohol a week. However, this was believed to be the result of the large number of doctor's prescriptions being issued during the influenza epidemic. The drug store was also selling an alcoholic preparation known as "Kennedy's Port Wine," the sale of which was not considered unlawful. However, both Pineo and Wyatt received a warning from the police chief about obeying the law.

The Somass Hotel manager, Mr. Woollett, considered he was not getting a square deal as beer was being sold by other people and he was losing business as a consequence. Customers were asking for beer and refusing "near beer," which was an experiment by the brewers of B.C. to produce a palatable substitute for the original article now banned. Warnings were issued to other hotels in town. Woollett objected to receiving a warning from the Chief of Police.

Alberni Pacific mill management complained to the Police Commission about employees obtaining liquor on Sundays and being unable to work on Mondays.

The Police Commission asked Dr. Hilton to appear before the commission. He stated he had not kept a record of the number of liquor prescriptions he had issued because he was so busy during the influenza epidemic, but he estimated Pineo's Drug Store had sold about forty gallons since the epidemic. Hilton's prescriptions had not exceeded the twenty gallon limit. Many of the prescriptions had been for fishermen. No individual had had as much as two gallons and no one in town had more than six bottles in a year. Usually whiskey, rum, or brandy was specified. No more than three or four prescriptions had been issued for beer, and in some cases Hilton had refused to give a prescription.

The Police Commission asked the Chief of Police to check up on Pineo's liquor account and to take samples of liquor from all suspected places. The Chief was ordered to advise liquor dealers there would be no relaxation of the law for Christmas. Samples were taken from Pineo's store, the Somass Hotel, Mrs. Rowley's Store, and the King Edward Hotel. The government analyst, D. Whittaker, found that only 2.5 percent of the twenty-one samples of near beer were within the limit of the Prohibition Act.

The Prohibition Commissioner for the province, a Mr. Findlay, promised the city assistance in carrying out the Prohibition Act. He promised to send a detective to assist in investigating the illegal sale of liquor.[127] The Chief of Police reported to the Police Commission he had seized four barrels of beer addressed to the King Edward Hotel. The barrels had been hidden under horse rugs in Roseborough's Livery Stable.

The situation was getting so bad that Alderman Hanna asked in council why the Prohibition law was not being enforced in Port Alberni. She had noticed an increase in the number of cases of drunkenness in the city, and she called for an investigation and action. According to Alderman Hanna, conditions were worse than before the Act was passed, especially on Saturday nights. She said women and children were afraid to walk the streets at night because of the number of drunks wandering around, and the boisterous loggers returning to camp could be heard all over the city.

The Mayor asked the Chief of Police about the situation. The Chief said there were some cases of drunkenness but there was nothing he could do about it. He could not arrest a man for the simple offence of being drunk if there was no disorderly conduct connected with it. The Chief did not believe hard liquor was being sold in the city although he was aware that it was being consumed. He claimed it came in from outside the community. Besides, he had no authority outside the city limits, nor could he interfere with tourists or travellers who were lawfully in possession of liquor.

The city clerk was asked to draw up a bylaw that would make drunkenness an offence with or without disorderly conduct. A bylaw was submitted at the next council meeting.[128] When is a man drunk? was the question that vexed city council during that discussion. The draft of the bylaw aptly named "Public Morals Bylaw" was placed before the aldermen. Any person found drunk on any street or highway or public place was guilty of an offence and liable for a fine not exceeding one hundred dollars.

After the draft bylaw was circulated around the council table, Alderman Watson jokingly wondered how anyone could be guilty of being drunk when they had prohibition. Council then tried to define what was meant by being "drunk." How can you tell when a man is drunk if he is not disorderly? Try having him walk a plank or a chalk line, they suggested.

City clerk Robert Blandy said some municipalities had taken advantage of their powers to enact similar bylaws. The draft before council was similar to the Vancouver bylaw. It was suggested the introduction of the bylaw be deferred until after all the citizens had recovered from the effects of the Peace Day celebrations planned for July 19. Council decided it would be better to investigate where the liquor was coming from rather than arresting those who drank it. Mayor Exton said he had spoken to Corporal Taylor of the Northwest Mounted Police and Provincial Constable Wood, and they had told him it was a difficult matter to deal with. The introduction of the bylaw was deferred until after the Peace Day celebration.[129]

The provincial government began to realize prohibition was not working in the province. The problem had been amplified during the influenza epidemic, when doctors were under siege coping with the large number of legitimate prescriptions as well as those for alcohol. After the influenza passed it was difficult for the doctors to get back to the old standard. The situation had become intolerable. The provincial government was now selling more than $150,000 worth of liquor a month, camouflaged as medicine.

In November 1919, B.C.'s Attorney General Farris announced there would be new legislation on prohibition at the next sitting of the legislature in February. "The present prescription evil must be abated," he said. "The remedy should not be by wholesale persecution of the medical profession for a condition forced on them by the legislature and passed without their consent and against their will."[130]

Up the coast and in the interior the number of illicit stills had multiplied. "The number engaged in the business is simply beyond belief. We find them in all kinds of places. Hen houses seem to be a favourite place, also garrets," said the deputy collector of Inland Revenue when visiting Vancouver in December.[131] The bad whiskey industry was alarming the federal government.

In Alberni and Port Alberni former licensed establishments were now selling soft drinks and near beer.[132] Council considered whether the local "morals bylaw" had worked. The bylaw, now in effect, was supposed to put a stop to drinking in the bar rooms and keep the town quiet. However, only one day after the bylaw had been approved the midnight carousing had shifted to the vicinity of city hall. Alderman Watson, speaking tongue in cheek, said, "Don't you know there is prohibition in B.C. There are not any bars any more, only places in hotels where they sell near beer and milk drinks."[133]

The provincial government did change the Prohibition Act in June 1920. A new clause provided two exceptions when a doctor should not prescribe any more than eight ounces for any one person in any one day. Sixteen ounces could be prescribed for a person living five miles away from the nearest drug store vending liquor. A prescription for two quarts could also be issued if the good doctor felt like taking the responsibility of subscribing to a statutory declaration on the back of each prescription.

Again there was a promise of a plebiscite to be put to the people to have the amended Prohibition Act continued or have established government stores where liquor could be sold in sealed packages for household consumption. Doctors were left out of the deal completely.[134]

In June the question of a bylaw for the licensing and regulating of places where near beer could be sold in Alberni and Port Alberni was considered by both councils. Only a few of the Alberni council favoured a bylaw prohibiting the sale of near beer within the muncicipality. The majority favoured a bylaw to license and regulate the hours of opening and closing, and the conduct of the houses where the near beer was for sale. Both councils attempted to make the bylaw the same in both cities.[135]

This sparked the concern of local hotel operators. At the next council meeting when the bylaw was being considered, the Somass, King Edward, and Beaufort Hotels had representatives present to explain how their revenues had gradually diminished. Near beer was expensive to make, almost double the cost of the original beer, and this caused increased prices to the public. The hotel owners asked that a clause increasing the license to one hundred dollars every six months and confining the sale of near beer to hotels operating ten rooms or more be included in the bylaw.

The new Malt Beverages Bylaw, with amended clauses now agreed on, dictated a license fee of two hundred dollars per year, payable six months in advance. Licenses could not be transferred from one establishment to another. Barrooms would be closed from 11:00 p.m. until 6:00 a.m., except Sunday, when they would be closed all day.

Alberni had no restriction on the issuing of licenses. The bylaw sparked more questions at the next council meeting in Port Alberni. Council's solicitor L. A. Hanna wanted to know if council intended to prohibit women from being employed in places where malt beverages were sold. This was something council had not considered. The Chief of Police did not anticipate any danger. "If females are not allowed to serve in the barrooms, will any female be allowed to go in any time she might want a drink of beer?"[136] asked Alderman Pearse. It was unanimously decided that the bylaw should prohibit women from serving near beer.

On October 20, 1920, British Columbians voted again on prohibition. The ballot asked: Which do you prefer – the present Prohibition Act, or an act to provide for Government Control and sale in sealed packages of spirituous and malt liquors? The Alberni district voted 521 for the present Prohibition Act, compared to 1192 for Government Control.[137]

The Liberal government, rather than bring in new legislation, called an election for December, which was fought over the prohibition issue. The Liberals were returned and enacted the Government Liquor Act in 1921.

The first liquor store opened for business in July 1921 with George Dickson as manager and Walter Sharp as his assistant. The goods arrived on the steamship *Princess Maquinna*. The store was located on First Avenue, in the building then partly occupied by the Great War Veterans Association. "All brands of spirituous liquors, wines, beer, ale, and stout, will be carried in stock."[138]

The Chief of Police J. R. Edwards was dismissed after the Police Commission received complaints from the Beaufort Hotel and Pineo's Drug Store about his conduct during prohibition. E. E. McKay was appointed Chief of Police. McKay came with good credentials. He had been with the Cape Mounted Police in South Africa for eleven years, on the Edmonton Police force for two years, with the Provincial Police force at Ladysmith, and, since his return from overseas, with the military police at Esquimalt.

Unfortunately McKay did not last long. He was found the worse for alcohol on several occasions and was fired. He protested, stating there had been no complaints against him from businessmen, and there was no crime in the city. The Commission had had enough with personnel problems and resolved to make an application to have the Royal Canadian Mounted Police (RCMP) take over the policing of the city. The RCMP refused. A new Chief of Police, Robert E. McMinn, was appointed.

Peace Day, July 19, 1919, was one of the biggest and happiest holidays ever celebrated in the history of the Alberni district. It was a typical Alberni Valley summer day; too warm for hard exercises, but nice enough to lay in the sun. The people of both towns rallied early at 9:30 a.m. when the automobile, float, and bicycle parade left from Port Alberni and travelled to Alberni. It was the largest gathering of people ever seen on the streets of the city. There were so many automobiles and children – everyone was out for the day – everything on wheels was decorated, and many in the parade wore character costume.

The procession snaked around three or four blocks of the Old Town and was photographed on Johnston Street. The flag was raised and patriotic speeches were given by Mayor Huff from Alberni, the Rev. Bagshaw, and Rev. Bain. Veterans of the war were in line under the command of Major Burde. Sergeant Major J. B. Watson, one of the first recruits from the Alberni District to sign up with the 67th battalion, had just returned home the week before and was present. A dance held in the Great War Veterans Hall and a display of fireworks on the waterfront concluded the Peace Day activities.[139]

The Albernis entered the age of flight when one Saturday afternoon in May 1920 a Curtiss JN-4 'Jenny' flew into Port Alberni and landed on Lupsi Cupsi field. The visit was sponsored by the Victoria Branch of the Aerial League of Canada.[140] Pilots W. H. Brown and N. A. Goddard took fifty people in flights over the Alberni Valley.[141]

Alberni Attempts Disincorporation

The depression of 1915, the war years, and high unemployment left Alberni, which did not have the industrial tax base of Port Alberni, almost bankrupt by 1919. The situation was so bad no civic election was advertised, and Mayor Huff was elected by acclamation. Some residents questioned the validity of the election because it had not been advertised. Huff went to Victoria and spoke with Attorney-General De Farris about the situation. De Farris said the law was very indefinite and suggested the old council might join in with the council-elect until a Validating Act was passed. Huff proposed to do as little city business as possible until the Act was passed in the provincial House.

During this time, the clerk was instructed to write to the Bank of Commerce suggesting it open a branch in Alberni. The bank wrote back regretting it couldn't open a branch there. The Royal Bank of Canada had closed its doors on November 30, 1918,[142] leaving the community without any banking facility. The bank manager, Arthur G. Freeze, became the district's government agent. Until the community could persuade a bank to open here, residents had to travel to Port Alberni to conduct their banking business.

The city's financial situation was so grim on February 7 that Huff advised ratepayers at a public meeting in Best Hall that their taxes would increase approximately 25 percent to enable a necessary public works program to be carried out. City streets did receive some upgrading when council allocated five hundred dollars. The remainder would have to wait. Then the city clerk resigned after he was refused an increase in salary.[143]

It seemed nothing was going right for Alberni. One bright spot, however, was the Alberni Agricultural and Industrial Association, which wound up its year debt free on all its grounds and buildings. There was even a small credit left over in the bank balance. The fall fair had been a big success.[144]

Huff, termed the "father of Alberni," was now seventy-two years of age. His council survived 1919. An election was held in 1920, and Huff was re-elected as Mayor.[145] Aldermen elected included H. B. Currie, Mrs. A. G. Croll, C. T. Harvey, Miss L. A. Marcon, F. Harold Bishop, and Allan Paul.

While the city's finances may have shrunk, its school enrollment had increased. There were so many pupils in Alberni, the school could not handle them and the school board had to use the Municipal Building as an overflow building. Forty pupils were accommodated there. The municipality needed a new school.

About the same time as West Coast General Hospital was considering closing, the City of Alberni began considering disincorporation. The city was in financial crisis. At an Alberni Board of Trade meeting in May, 1921, Mayor Huff outlined the reasons why the city should disincorporate. The proposition, he said, had met with a favourable response. "It has been said that I am a poor mayor, or that the city has a poor fish for a mayor. If that is the case, the electors have themselves to blame. I was not so anxious to take the job than the people were to have me take it in the last election," said Huff.[146]

There were feelings for and against disincorporation amongst the board members. One said the city had a dwindling population. Another pointed out there was such a large increase of school-age children that a new school was urgently needed. The board decided to appoint a committee to talk to the members of council with the object of having the proposition put before the taxpayers when a statement of the city's water and light distribution systems and other assets could be presented for consideration.

Meanwhile, a petition was circulated towards disincorporation. One hundred and forty-nine residents signed it, representing 90 percent of the ratepayers. At a council meeting on June 27, 1921, council appropriated two hundred dollars towards the expense of circulating the petition in Victoria and Vancouver to gather out-of-town property owners' signatures. A committee was appointed to help in the formation of a company to take over the assets of the community. This committee included Mayor Huff and Aldermen Harold Bishop, Cathcart, and Toy. A special meeting to deal with the city's finances was called by Alderman Bishop for June 29.

At this meeting the grim details of the city's finances came to light. Bishop, chairman of the finance committee, laid the facts on the table. City expenses were $1,325 over what it expected to collect in revenue. The city foreman and constable were asked to take a reduction in salary. The foreman agreed to accept four dollars per day for an eight-hour day with a minimum of eighty dollars per month if he was relieved of the pound and police work. The Police Commission was asked to cancel the appointment of the constable.

The petition for disincorporation, circulated in Victoria, Vancouver, and the Fraser Valley, met with a favourable response. There were now sufficient signatures to give a full majority. The provincial government was asked for permission to disincorporate, and Alberni waited for the government's decision throughout September.

At their October 13 meeting, Alberni council still had not heard from the government. However, permission was given for the mayor to draw from municipal funds enough money to cover his expenses for a trip to Victoria to get a definite answer on disincorporation. A week later, Mayor Huff reported satisfactory negotiations with the government, which was willing to grant disincorporation subject to funds being provided to extinguish the outstanding debt. Huff recommended the transfer to a company of all the assets of the corporation except the fire hall and equipment, the recreation ground and city park, school properties, cemetery property, the old men's home property plus all books and documents of record.

The city's position for disincorporation was outlined. The number of voters in 1921 was 103; the total value of land and improvements was $1,100,315; the value of land owned by the municipality non-voting was $78,590; the total number of names on the petition qualified to vote was 378; the value represented by the names amounted to $603,880: the total debenture debt of the municipality was $70,130; sinking funds on hand was $30,000; the net debt to be assumed by the company taking over the assets was $40,130.[147]

The Alberni Board of Trade asked for a public meeting to discuss disincorporation. However, before this meeting took place, the Alberni Board of Trade president C. Frederic Bishop, (father of Alderman Harold Bishop), and the board's secretary E. M. Whyte sent a telegram to Premier John Oliver, advising against disincorporation. It is not known what the contents of the telegram were, but there were charges made against the honour of the mayor and those associated with the movement to disincorporate.

The public meeting took place October 29. Mayor Huff read a lengthy report in which it was stated that more than the required number of names of property holders had signed the petition asking the government to grant disincorporation. Those signing the petition faced increased taxation the following year. There were many questions asked both by those in sympathy with the petition and those who opposed. The government had signified their willingness to grant the request when full assurance had been given that the indebtedness of the city would be taken care of and the rights of the citizens fully safeguarded. Mayor Huff assured everyone the company would take over the debt. Everyone wanted to know the name of the company, but Huff would not reveal this information.

Always an optimist, former mayor C. Frederic Bishop gave a glowing description of the future prospects of Alberni, indicating the city was anything but defunct. He made a motion, which was seconded by James Thomson and carried, that the government take no action on the petition until a clearer understanding was reached.[148]

On November 2, council, angered by the telegram sent to the Premier, issued a statement to the press.

Be it resolved that this Municipal Council of the City of Alberni, the sworn representatives of the ratepayers and with full knowledge of the facts declare as follows. The Alberni Board of Trade is a minor organization non-official in character with a membership of only a small portion of the

307

resident population, a portion of which membership is not registered on the city's voters list.

The council are persuaded that the communications referred to, do not, however, represent the opinion or wish of the Board of Trade as a body. The movement for the disincorporation of the city was with the knowledge and consent of the council who voted public monies for that purpose. It was signed by over two-thirds of those qualified to sign, representing an interest in property of over three quarters of the whole assessed value in the municipality. The Mayor has acted with the authority of the council. The council entirely repudiates the suggestion that any act has taken place in connection with the proceedings towards disincorporation which can be considered other than honorable and in accordance with the law.[149]

At the November 14 meeting of council the city clerk reported on his recent visit to Vancouver stating that "a sound financial concern"[150] there was prepared to take over the city assets in the event of disincorporation and that negotiations were underway with the provincial government regarding the matter of securities involved. It was not until November 27 that Mayor Huff revealed to his aldermen the name of the interested financial concern. This company was the Royal Financial Corporation Ltd. There was still no word from the government. The following day a letter did arrive from Premier John Oliver. It stated that in view of the opposition, disincorporation could not be carried through at that session of the legislature.

Mayor Huff wrote to the Premier asking for immediate action. The decision could not wait. The Premier replied on December 3, saying the matter had been referred to the Inspector of Municipalities. The Alberni city clerk was instructed to write again to the Premier asking why he was delaying disincorporation and requesting him to supply city council with copies of all the correspondence that he had received from the opposition. This correspondence was received and the letters ordered filed.[151]

When the January civic elections rolled around, Huff was not in the lineup for mayor. Instead, James R. Motion and George (Alex) Spencer both ran for the position, and Motion was successful. The aldermen included some members of the Board of Trade. Elected were E. M. Whyte, George Forrest, L. Hanna, A. J. Pineo, H. B. Currie, and Charles Taylor Jr.

Retrenchment was the note sounded at the first meeting of the new council in January 1922. Alderman Pineo said the city had to dispose of some of its land holdings because of the city's financial condition. He also stated that the Board of Trade was willing to handle the financing of the water. Notice was given for a bylaw to repeal salaries for the mayor and aldermen. The following week the city clerk and foreman's position were terminated. A new city clerk was hired on a part-time basis at a reduced salary. The city health officer agreed to accept a 50 percent cut in his yearly stipend.

Speaking to a special committee on tax lands, Alderman Pineo reported the city was in possession of some valuable lands, both homesites and factories. There were even some subdivisions in the surrounding area where acreage blocks and lots could be grouped together. All it needed was a bit of advertising. Council appropriated thirty dollars for that purpose. Pineo further stated that since the Alberni Board of Trade was organized for the express purpose of assisting the council in the shaping of a vigorous city development policy, he recommended the Board of Trade be invited to meet with council. The two could work together to resolve the community's financial difficulties.[152]

A civic holiday was declared for March 17 as a "cleaning up and improvement day" under the auspices of the Community Club. Forty men and eleven teams were engaged for the "big bee." It was figured the army of workers was large and energetic enough to put the main street of the town into good shape, including the filling of the big hole at the foot of Johnston Road. The women of the community gave a free dinner to all the workers. The meal was served in the old post office building.[153]

This new Alberni council was taking full control. There would be no disincorporation. Alberni would survive. In May 1922 there was a glowing report about Alberni in the *Port Alberni News*. "Mayor Huff had said that 1921 would be a critical year for his community. If it weathered the storm "she might expect to live on forever."[154] Alberni did weather the storm and looked forward to a bright economic future. The resources of the district were being promoted as never before. Negotiations were taking place for the sale of a substantial block of timber in the Valley, which would mean the construction of a large mill catering to the export trade.

In the twin communities, timber had come to mean financial security. There had been a visit from "New York capitalists" looking over the timber areas, and the prospects looked good a pulp mill would be constructed on the Alberni Inlet or in Barkley Sound.

New Challenges

A new era lay ahead for the Albernis. What had started as one small farming settlement had evolved into two communities, each striving for supremacy over the other. With all the forest industry mills located on the waterfront, Port Alberni had a good tax base while Alberni, the original settlement, still struggled.

Those immigrants who had come to the new world with such high hopes stayed to become the pioneer settlers of two new communities. They were still optimistic about the economic future, despite having suffered through one of the worst depressions known to this date. They had survived the Great War, the influenza epidemic, and prohibition. They had witnessed a changing world, while they themselves had changed the lives of the native people of the region, who were now banished to reserves and to a segregated schooling system. The natives' potlatch was banned as was their traditional costume; many had been given new English names; they had been taught a new religion – all this in the name of colonization.

Dick Burde, who came to Alberni to publish a newspaper, had become a leader – first as mayor, then major during the Great War, and now as provincial member in the legislature.

When MP Herbert Clements visited the two cities in August, 1919 it was obvious the fishing inquiry had cost him serious political points. Only a few of his faithful supporters came out to meet him. As far as the twin cities were concerned, the writing was on the wall for Clements. A. W. Neill was waiting in the wings.

The Alberni Land Company still had a vested interest in the community, although municipal taxation was taking a heavy toll of its investment.

New technology in transportation and communications had improved living conditions in the region. The Albernis now had a regular rail service, a regular steamship service to Victoria, electricity, water, telephone, and moving pictures. The Canadian Pacific Railway, through its subsidiary the E & N, was providing a valuable rail service both for passengers and freight, and its future prospects in the Albernis looked good. The community still had not given up on the Canadian Northern Railway, but hopes of ever reviving the impetus to get the line completed between Victoria and Port Alberni were growing dimmer.

Fishing had become an economic force to be reckoned with. The industry had seen changes from sail to steam, from canoe to power

310

boat, from spear fishing to seine and gillnet fishing. Canneries now dotted the Alberni Inlet. Fishermen had successfully challenged the government's authority to impose regulations on the fishing industry. As the twenties began, they were apprehensive about the growing number of Japanese fishermen who excelled in this industry.

The forest industry had also undergone some major changes. No longer were oxen used to get the logs out of the woods; steam engines now performed the job with ease. Fire was still a constant threat. But the industry had taken a strong foothold in Port Alberni. Business and commerce thrived so long as the mills were working.

In the area of politics, the community now had its own electoral representation in Victoria. Women had been given the vote for the first time and had been elected to positions on municipal councils and school boards.

The horse and buggy days were gone, replaced by the bicycle and automobile. Livery stables had been replaced by garages. Horses were put out to pasture. The aeroplane had arrived.

If there was anything that tied the two communities of Alberni and Port Alberni together, it was the sporting events. The great soccer matches, the basketball games, sports events on Dominion Day, and swimming all brought out a friendly rivalry that was difficult to extinquish.

As the twenties began to unfold the optimistic prediction made in the *British Columbia Directory* of 1893 rang true. "Alberni is destined, at no distant date, to become a place of importance and wealth. All it requires to ensure this position is development of its resources and railroad communication with other places." The new lines of communication by road, rail, and sea had ensured development of resources. Still the feeling of isolation persisted. Although located in the middle of Vancouver Island, the twin communities had only one road connection to the outside world. The road to Comox promised to the first settlers had never materialized, and the fight was on to have the one road into the valley extended to the west coast communities of Ucluelet and Tofino, which still could be reached only by sea. If the Alberni Valley communities were to develop further, in line with other Vancouver Island cities, it was clear local politicians would have to remain vigilant and continue to press government for further transportation links.

NOTES

Chapter One

1 Alan D. McMillan and Denis E. St. Claire, *Alberni Prehistory*, Theytus Books, Penticton, for Alberni Valley Museum, 1982. p. 12.

2 Phillip Drucker, *The Central and Northern Nootkan Tribes*, Smithsonian Institution, Bureau of American Ethnology, Bulletin. 144, Government Printing Office, Washington 1951, p. 377.

3 McMillan & St. Claire, p. 13.

4 Gilbert Malcolm Sproat journal, *Scenes and Studies of Savage Life*. Published in England by Smith, Elder and Co. 1868, p. 308.

5 McMillan & St. Claire, p. 16.

6 *Ibid.* p. 22.

7 Helen Ford, *Sproat Lake*, Unpublished manuscript 1956, Alberni District Historical Society Archives, Port Alberni. (ADHSA). Permission to publish granted by Helen Ford, and by Margaret Clutesi, wife of Dr. George Clutesi, now deceased.

8 George Bird, *Tse-Wees-Tah, One man in a boat*, Alberni District Historical Society, (1971) 1972, p. 36.

9 Derek Pethick, *The Nootka Connection*, Douglas & McIntyre, Vancouver, 1980; Pethick, *First Approaches to the Northwest Coast*, Douglas & McIntyre, Vancouver, 1976.

10 *Journades D'Estudois Catalano Americans*, Barcelona: Translation by Mark Fernadez: File L.8.11 ADHSA.

11 Joseph Patraick Sanchez, Thesis 1974. *The Catalonian Volunteers and the Defense of Northern New Spain 1767-1803*, ADHSA.

12 Alberni District Official Bulletin No. 24 published by Legislative Assembly 1908, p. 8, Alberni Valley Museum.

13 Peter C. Newman, *Caesars of the Wilderness*, Viking Press, 1987, p. 305.

14 *Ibid.*, p. 306.

15 *Ibid.*, p. 306.

16 *Ibid.*, p. 308.

17 *Ibid.*, p. 309.

18 *Ibid.*, p. 312.

19 Richard Mayne, *Four Years in British Columbia and Vancouver Island*, John Murray, Albemarie Street, London, England, 1862, p. 460.

20 Ben Hines, *Pick, Pan & Pack: A History of Mining in the Alberni Mining Division*, Booklet by Local Initiatives Program, Alberni Valley Museum, 1976, p. 4.

21 R. Bruce Scott, *Barkley Sound: A History of the Pacific Rim National Park Area*, 1972, p. 49, p. 53.

22 George Nicholson, *Vancouver Island's West Coast 1762-1962*, Morriss Printing Co. Ltd., 1962, p. 76.

23 Adam Grant Horne file, Nanaimo Museum Archives.

24 Adam Grant Horne file L.9.22, ADHSA.

25 Adam Grant Horne file, Nanaimo Museum Archives.

26 Horne file, Carrie Brown Doney, ADHSA.

27 *Ibid.*.

28 Mayne, p. 166.

29 Horne file, ADHSA. Paper given by William Barraclough to the Nanaimo Historical Society on October 23, 1962.

30 *Ibid.*.

31 Emily-Jane Orford, article from *Islander-Times Colonist* July 3, 1988 "J. D. arrived at an opportune time."

32 C. P. Lyons, *Milestones on Vancouver Island*, The Evergreen Press Limited, 1958, Mayne File L5.12 ADHSA.
33 *Ibid.*
34 This was probably Cameron Lake, named after the Hon. David Cameron, Chief Justice of Vancouver Island. He worked for the Hudson's Bay Company in Nanaimo before Sir James Douglas appointed him Chief Justice.
35 Mayne file L5.12.
36 Mayne, p. 167-173. Lyons, see *Milestones*, p. 183.
37 Lyons, see *Milestones*, p. 180-184. Mayne file L5.12 ADHSA.
38 John Hayman, *Robert Brown and the Vancouver Island Exploring Expedition*, U.B.C. Press 1989, p. 108.
39 McMillan & St. Claire, p. 25. Lamb, W. Kaye, article. "Early Lumbering on Vancouver Island," *B.C. Historical Quarterly*, Vol. 2, 1938, p. 100.
40 Sproat, p. 2.
41 *Ibid.*
42 *Ibid.*, p. 2-4.
43 *Ibid*, p. 6.
44 Banfield letters 1860: File Vol I., p. 130. Alberni Valley Museum.
45 Sproat, p. 6, 7.
46 *Ibid.*, p. 7.
47 *Ibid.*, p. 8.
48 McMillan & St. Claire, p. 23.
49 Bird, p. 100. Also Lamb, p. 110-111.
50 Mayne, p. 228-229.
51 Sproat, p. 73.
52 *Alberni Pioneer News,* Feb. 24, 1912. Letter from Cyrus Sears, master of the *Pocahontas*, then a retired resident of Baltimore, MD to Customs Collector Newbury of Victoria.
53 *Ibid.*
54 *Ibid.*
55 *British Colonist*, Victoria, February 5, 1862.
56 Alberni Land Co. file ADHSA.
57 Sproat, p. 278.
58 House of Assembly: Vol. 10, No. 123, p. 3, dated Sat. October 31, 1863. Alberni Valley Museum.
59 *Ibid.*
60 *Ibid.*, Vol. 10, No. 147, p. 3, dated November 28, 1863.
61 Donald MacKay, *Empire of Wood*, Douglas & McIntyre, Vancouver, 1982, p. 6. See also Lamb, p. 107.
62 McMillan & St. Claire, p. 25.
63 MacKay, p. 11.
64 Nicholson, p. 256.
65 Banfield letters 1862: Alberni Valley Museum.
66 McMillan & St. Claire, p. 26.
67 Bird, p. 100.
68 John Hayman, *Robert Brown and the Vancouver Island Exploring Expedition*. All quotations in this section are from this source.
69 F. W. Howay, essay, "The Settlement and Progress of B.C. 1871-1914" from *Historical Essays on B.C.*, edited by J. Friesan & H. K. Ralston, McClelland and Stewart Limited, 1976, p. 23.
70 Craig Brown, *Illustrated History of Canada*, Lester & Orpen Dennys Limited, Toronto, Ontario, 1987, p. 331-2.
71 Robin Fisher, essay, "Joseph Trutch and Indian Land Policy" from *Historical Essays of B.C.*, p. 257. See Howay.
72 *Ibid.*, p. 265.

73 *Ibid.*, p. 272-273.
74 *British Columbia Royal Commission on Indian Affairs 1916*: IV,851.
75 McMillan & St. Claire, p. 25.
76 E. Y. Arima, *The West Coast (Nootka) People*, British Columbia Provincial Museum, 1983, p. 143.
77 Hayman, note page 174 No. 5. Anderson sawmill file 45.7. Annual reports of the Columbia Mission for 1862-1872. ADHSA.
78 Drucker, p. 13.
79 Father Brabant journal. Alberni Valley Museum.
80 Holy Family Catholic Church, "Church in Alberni," Booklet *The Torch* . Vol. 20, No8, p. 10-12. Church file 14.6 ADHSA.
81 *Ibid.*
82 *Ibid.*
83 *Ibid.*
84 *Ibid.*
85 Bird, p. 108.
86 *Port Alberni News*, January 21, 1932.
87 *Place Names of the Alberni Valley*, Alberni District Historical Society, (1978) 1988, p. 82.
88 Charles Taylor file: ADHSA.
89 W. R. H. Prescott Paper on Daniel Clarke dated March 1969. Prescott was the manager of the Royal Bank of Canada Oct. 18, 1907.
90 Mrs. E. Frost Postcard from No. 18 Bedford Place, Seafort, Liverpool, England: Signed Annie Grandy. ADHSA. *Alberni Pioneer News*, Oct. 26, 1907.
91 Information from Lila Mackenzie (nee McKenzie) daughter of Jack McKenzie.
92 *Ibid.*, McKenzie file No. 25.4 ADHSA.
93 Lloyd Hills, file 38.18 ADHSA.
94 Lloyd Hills, article "Ada Prior dead at 97," *Alberni Valley Times*, June 28, 1988.
95 City of Alberni file No. 18.26: C. M. Cathcart booklet *Alberni and Visitors*, published by Stewart M. Read & Co., Vancouver, B.C., date unknown. ADHSA.
96 Huff file ADHSA: Also information from granddaughter Mrs. Belle Sherwood.
97 C. F. Bishop file. Fred Bishop tape recording, ADHSA.
98 Undated newspaper article by Meg Trebett, "Years Ago." ADHSA files. Also information from Dorrit McLeod 1989.
99 Transcript from Susan Morran as given to the author by Lois Abbott, Victoria, October 1988.
100 Kaye Dukowski article July 23, 1978 *Daily Colonist*. Issac Drinkwater file 7.7 ADHSA. Additional articles *Twin Cities Times* October 25, 1967: *Alberni Valley Times* November 15, 1978 and *West Coast Advocate* May 2, 1963.
101 Ford essay.
102 W. Arthur Thompson biography. File No. 8.25. ADHSA.
103 *Ibid.*
104 *Ibid.*
105 George Alexander Spencer file 51.3, ADHSA.
106 *Alberni Valley Times*, December 4, 1968, with reference to *Daily British Colonist*, Victoria, June 28, 1884.
107 *Ibid.*
108 Source Port Alberni Government Agent Joe Stanhope.
109 Bird, p. 77.
110 Reverend A. Dunn, *Presbyterianism in B.C. in the Early Days*, Columbian Company Ltd., New Westminster, B.C., 1905, p. 28. File 47.21 ADHSA.
111 Alfred Carmichael, letter May 1, 1892: File 48.5 ADHSA.
112 Pioneer Parade #62: February 15, 1948 ADHSA.
113 Carmichael file, Alberni Valley Museum.
114 Bird, p. 110.

115 Pioneer Parade #62. "Churches" February 22, 1948 ADHSA.

116 Bird, p.111.

117 *Ibid.*

118 *Alberni Valley Times*, Progress Edition, April 1980.

119 *Ibid.*.

120 Court Records, ADHSA File L.21.6.

121 Walter Stirling file 51.19, ADHSA. All quotations in this section are from this source.

122 Barry Miller, booklet *The E & N Railway*, publication on the 75th anniversary of the railway in Port Alberni.

123 City of Alberni file 18.26. Cathcart brochure. ADHSA.

124 Anderson sawmill file L.7.16.2: ADHSA.

125 *Alberni Valley Times Community Report* 1980.

126 June Lewis-Harrison, *The People of Gabriola*, printed by D. W. Friesen & Sons Ltd., Cloverdale, B.C., 1982, p. 64-67. Also Pioneer Parade September 14, 1947, ADHSA.

127 Peggy Nicholls, paper, Nanooa Historical & Museum Society. ADHSA.

128 *Alberni Valley Times Community Report* 1980.

129 Bird, p. 152.

130 Lyons, see *Milestones*, p. 190-192. Also Mayne file 5.12 ADHSA.

131 George Smith, an autobiography, ADHSA. All quotations in this section are from this source.

132 Crown Lands, *A history of Survey Systems*, Booklet, Ministry of Lands, Parks and Housing, Province of British Columbia, p. 21.

133 George Smith, an autobiography. ADHSA.

134 Bird, p. 102-106.

135 *Ibid.*, p. 104.

136 Margaret Trebett, booklet *Pioneer Women of the Alberni Valley*, Alberni District Museum and Historical Society, 1967.

137 Bird, p. 106.

138 MacMillan Bloedel Ltd. operations in the Alberni Valley file. Alberni Valley Museum.

139 Papermill, Carmichael file, Alberni Valley Museum.

Chapter Two

1 Bird, p. 179. Ford, *Sproat Lake*, p. 16.

2 *British Columbia Directory* 1893, ADHSA.

3 Alfred Carmichael, *Indian Legends of Vancouver Island*. 1922. ADHSA.

4 Carmichael letter to sister Ethel. File 48.51 ADHSA.

5 Bird, p. 36.

6 Carmichael file 48.5, p. 41, ADHSA.

7 *Ibid.*

8 Guillod reports 1881-1903. File No. 980.22a, ADHSA.

9 *Ibid.*

10 *Ibid.*

11 National Archives of Canada. Report on Indian Girls' Home, Alberni, B.C., September 23, 1896.

12 *Alberni Pioneer News*, October 12, 1907.

13 Principal's Report to Department of Indian Affairs March 31, 1909 published in *Alberni Pioneer News*, October 16, 1909.

14 Reverend Chas. Moser, *Reminiscences of The West Coast of Vancouver Island*, 1927, p. 155.

15 Walter Stirling letters. File 51.19 ADHSA.

16 Post Office file 39.3 ADHSA.

17 Bird, p. 158, p. 159.
18 *The Daily Colonist*, June 3, 1979.
19 Bird, p. 161.
20 Post Office file 39.3 ADHSA.
21 Bird, p. 162.
22 Board of Trade minute book, ADHSA.
23 *Ibid.*
24 Bird, p. 156.
25 *Ibid.*, p. 155, p. 156. Meg Trebett "Years Age" article in Spectrum-*Alberni Valley Times*, January 22, 1971.
26 *Ibid.*
27 *Ibid.*, p. 7.
28 Ruth Green, *Personality Ships of British Columbia*, Marine Tapestry Publication Ltd., West Vancouver, B.C., 1969, p. 155-156.
29 *Ibid.*
30 Bird, p. 143.
31 Pioneer Parade, CJAV radio script: Ed Cox: ADHSA.
32 Alberni Band of Hope file, ADHSA.
33 *Ibid.*
34 Bird, p. 12.
35 Erickson file, ADHSA.
36 Frank C. Garrard file, ADHSA.
37 Pioneer Parade #14.
38 Carmichael file 48.5, ADHSA.
39 *Ibid.*
40 *Ibid.*
41 Carmichael file, Alberni Valley Museum.
42 Pioneer Parade #24, ADHSA.
43 *Ibid.*, #25.
44 Guillod report 1883.
45 *Ibid.*
46 Chief Adam Shewish interview with author, September 22, 1989.
47 *Ibid.*
48 Guillod reports 1881-1903: file 980.22a.
49 Pybus file 42.2.1 ADHSA.
50 *Ibid.*
51 Carmichael file 48.5, Alberni Valley Museum.
52 Dr. A. M. Watson file, ADHSA.
53 Dr. Pybus file 42.2.1, ADHSA.
54 Pioneer Parade #25, ADHSA.
55 Newspaper article "Last Rites for Dr. Morgan," May 3, 1934. Also article "The Doctor lived here" undated: Newspaper clipping file, ADHSA.
56 Carmichael file, Alberni Valley Museum.
57 *Ibid.*
58 City of Alberni file No. 18.26. C. M. Cathcart brochure, *Alberni and Visitors*, Stewart M. Read & Co., Vancouver. Date unknown. ADHSA.
59 Farmer's Institute in B.C. file 30.12 ADHSA.
60 *Alberni Pioneer News*, September 21, 1907.
61 Conversation with Dorritt MacLeod 1988.
62 *Alberni Pioneer News*, September 12, 1908.
63 *Alberni Valley Times* Community Report, April 1980, p. 15.
64 Ben Hines, *Pick, Pan and Pack*, 1976.
65 *Ibid.*, p. 13.
66 *Nanaimo Daily Free Press*, July 22, 1896.
67 Hines, p. 39.

68 A. W. Neill file, ADHSA.
69 George Nicholson, *Vancouver Island's West Coast 1762-1962*, p. 322.
70 Alberni Representation Act, S.B.C. 1886, c2: amended Constitution Act, 1871, Alberni Valley Museum.
71 *Electoral History of B.C. 1871-1986*, published by Legislative Library, 1988, p. 67.
72 *Ibid.*
73 *Nanaimo Free Press*, July 21, 1896. Neill scrapbook, ADHSA.
74 Neill Scrapbook. *Daily Columbian*, "More Chinese restriction wanted," July 25, year unknown. ADHSA.
75 Neill Scrapbook.
76 *Ibid.*
77 *Ibid.*
78 *Ibid.*
79 *Ibid.*
80 F. W. Howay, *Historical Essays*, p. 33, p. 34. Also Sam Frketich thesis: "The dash of bitter in the cocktail of Canadian politics." ADHSA.
81 See *Electoral History*, p. 93, p. 95.
82 *Ibid.*, p. 98.
83 Bird, p. 104. Stephen Wells diary. ADHSA.
84 Wells diary. All information in this section from this source.
85 Anderson Sawmill file L.7.16.2, ADHSA.
86 Alberni Land Company file, ADHSA.
87 Pioneer Parade, Early Logging #18.
88 Joe Garner, *Never Chop Your Rope*, Cinnibar Press, Nanaimo, 1988. p. 274.
89 Pioneer Parade. Early Logging #18. ADHSA.
90 Logging and Sawmilling in the Alberni Valley 1908-1928 reference library, p. 3. Article from *Western Lumberman*, Vancouver, B.C., 1911. Alberni Valley Museum.
91 Pioneer Parade. Early logging #18. ADHSA.
92 *Alberni Pioneer News*, August 17, 1907.
93 Donald MacKay, *Empire of Wood*, p. 21.
94 Journal of Edward T. Buxton donated by granddaughter Barbara Sandler, Camp Elizabeth, Maine, USA. Red Cliff Land and Lumber Company Ltd. file, Alberni Valley Museum. All quotations in this section come from this source.
95 *Ibid.*
96 Wood Brothers file 7.11. Barclay Sound Cedar Company article, "Alberni's famed five" by Mary Wood, ADHSA.
97 Mary Wood interview with author April 1988 and September 7, 1990.
98 Bird, p. 157.
99 *Ibid.*, p. 212.
100 R. Bruce Scott, *Breakers Ahead*, 1970, p. 97-111.
101 Donald Graham, *Keepers of the Light*, Harbour Publishing Ltd., 1985, p. 59-63. Also *Seattle Times* article "Nine men owe their lives to this frail woman," January 13, 1907. Interview with Minnie Huff's daughter, Belle Sherwood.
102 B. A. McKelvie, article "British Columbia's Grace Darling," *Islander*, June 30, 1956; Paterson, T. W. article "Minnie Paterson Braved Storm to Fetch Rescuers from *Coloma*," *Islander*, November 20, 1966.
103 *The Colonist*, December 11, 1898.
104 Pioneer Parade #7 shipping, ADHSA.
105 *Alberni Pioneer News*, August 24, 1907.
106 *Ibid.*, September 5, 1908.
107 Progress Edition, *West Coast Advocate*, 1937.
108 *Ibid.*
109 Captain Foote was later drowned in the Islander disaster. Foote obituary, *Port Alberni News*, October 26, 1912.
110 Progress Edition, *West Coast Advocate*, 1937.

111 *Ibid.*
112 *Ibid.*
113 Hines, p. 16.
114 Bird, p. V11.
115 Progress Edition 1937.
116 Conversation with Dorrit MacLeod in May, 1988.
117 *Alberni Pioneer News*, March 4, 1911.
118 Information from Dorrit MacLeod May 1988.
119 *West Coast Advocate*, April 11, 1935.
120 *Alberni Pioneer News*, August 24, 1907.
121 Bird, p. 72.
122 Hines, p. 22.
123 *Ibid.*, p. 22.
124 *Ibid.*, p. 21.
125 Fishing Stations: Box B. Colonist reports, Alberni district 1856-1900, Alberni Valley Museum.
126 McMillan & St. Claire, Alberni Valley Museum.
127 Annual report of the Inspector of Fisheries 1878.
128 *Ibid.*
129 Guillod reports 1882. Alberni Valley Museum.
130 Chief Shewish interview with author September 22, 1989.
131 Guillod reports 1896. Alberni Valley Museum.
132 Annual report of the Inspector of Fisheries 1886.
133 *Ibid.*
134 *Ibid.*
135 Canneries #17: Colonist reports #6. p. 93, Alberni Valley Museum. Pioneer Parade #7 shipping, p. 3, ADHSA.
136 Cicely Lyons, *Salmon: Our Heritage*, B.C. Packers Limited, Mitchell Press, Vancouver, B.C., 1969, p. 130.
137 Canneries #17: Alberni Valley Museum.
138 See Lyons, Salmon p. 207.
139 William Roff lectures file 51.6 ADHSA. All quotations in this section are from this source.

Chapter Three

1 Hines, p. 18.
2 *West Coast Advocate*, September 8, 1938.
3 Margaret Ormsby, *British Columbia: A History*, Macmillan of Canada, Vancouver, 1958, p. 341.
4 Roads file 44.9 ADHSA.
5 *Alberni Pioneer News*, October 2,1909.
6 *Ibid.*, January 25, 1908.
7 *Ibid.*, Februray 15, 1908.
8 Raymond Hull, Gordon Soules, Christine Soules, *Vancouver's Past*, published by Gordon Soules Economic and Marketing Research, Vancouver, B.C. 1974, p. 66.
9 *Alberni Pioneer News*, September 14, 1907.
10 *Ibid.*, February 1, 1908.
11 Bird, p. 171.
12 *Alberni Valley Times*, article "The chalet at Cameron Lake," March 17, 1969.
13 *Ibid.*, March 17, 1969.
14 See Ormsby p. 333.
15 *Ibid.*, p. 337.
16 Edith Dobie, essay, "Party History in B.C. 1903-1933," See *Historical Essays*, p. 70.

17 *Ibid.*
18 S. W. Jackman, *Portraits of the Premiers*, Gray's Publishing Ltd, Sidney, B.C. 1969. Harlan Carey Brewster file 47.28 ADHSA.
19 Dr. A. D. Morgan file, ADHSA.
20 *Alberni Pioneer News*, November 27, 1909.
21 *Ibid.*, September 7, 1907.
22 *Ibid.*, January 11, 1908.
23 *Ibid.*, January 25, 1908.
24 *Ibid.*, editorial.
25 *Ibid.*, February 8, 1908.
26 *Ibid.*, April 11, 1908.
27 *Ibid.*, May 9, 1908.
28 Board of Trade minute book, May 4, 1908.
29 *Alberni Pioneer News*, November 23, 1907.
30 *Ibid.*, June 6, 1908.
31 Vancouver Island Development League file 50.5. ADHSS.
32 Board of Trade minute book, ADHSA.
33 *Ibid.*
34 Leonard Frank file, ADHSA.
35 *Alberni Pioneer News*, May 15, 1909.
36 *Ibid.*, October 23, 1909.
37 *Ibid.*, January 16, 1909.
38 *Twin Cities Times*, Oct. 25, 1967.
39 *Alberni Pioneer News*, July 10, 1908.
40 Stone Brothers file, ADHSA.
41 *Alberni Pioneer News*, Oct. 26, 1907.
42 *Ibid.*, October 26, 1907.
43 *Ibid.*, November 2, 1907. Also *Settling Clayoquot* by Bob Bossin: Sound Heritage Series No. 33, p. 13.
44 Bird, p. 157.
45 *Alberni Pioneer News*, June 10, 1911.
46 *Ibid.*, July 25, 1908.
47 *Ibid.*, October 5, 1907.
48 *Ibid.*, October 19, 1907.
49 *Ibid.*, November 30, 1907.
50 *Ibid.*, September 7, 1910.
51 *Ibid.*, February 12, 1910.
52 See Ford, *Sproat Lake*, p. 22. ADHSA.
53 *Islander*, June 4, 1989, article by Andy Bigg.
54 George Bird, "Christmas recollections," Ed Cox papers file 19.6.72. ADHSA.
55 *Alberni Pioneer News*, February 15, 1908.
56 *Ibid.*, July 16, 1910.
57 *Ibid.*, June 6, 1908.
58 Craig Geiger essay, Dr. Hilton file, ADHSA.
59 Pioneer Parade #24.
60 Agnes Erickson file, ADHSA.
61 *Alberni Pioneer News*, November 9, 1907.
62 W. Arthur Thompson diary. File No. 8.25 ADHSA.
63 Frank C. Garrard memoirs, Garrard file, ADHSA.
64 Bird, p. 131.
65 *Alberni Pioneer News*, November 2, 1907.
66 *Ibid.*, January 7, 1911.
67 *Ibid.*, October 22, November 12, December 17, 1910; January 7, 1911.
68 Pioneer Parade, ADHSA.
69 *Alberni Pioneer News*, January 7, 1911.

70 *Ibid.*, May 21, 1910; Oct. 22, 1910.
71 *Ibid.*, May 27, 1911.
72 *Ibid.*, August 31, 1907.
73 *Ibid.*
74 *Ibid.*, April 4, 1908.
75 Alberni Land Company file, ADHSA.
76 *Ibid.*
77 *Alberni Pioneer News*, March 25, 1911.
78 Information from Dorrit MacLeod 1988.
79 *Alberni Pioneer News*, April 15, 1911.
80 *Ibid.*, March 18, 1911.
81 *Ibid.*, March 25, 1911.
82 *Ibid.*, November 6, 1909.
83 *Ibid.*
84 Board of Trade minute book, February 12, 1910.
85 *Alberni Pioneer News*, February 19, 1910.
86 *Ibid.*, May 7, 1910.
87 *Ibid.*
88 *Ibid.*, July 2, 1910.
89 Alberni Board of Trade minute book, July 23, 1910; *Alberni Pioneer News*, July 30, 1910.
90 *Alberni Pioneer News*, July 30, 1910.
91 Alberni Board of Trade minute book. Notes on special meeting with Dr. Anderson, July 23, 1910. ADHSA.
92 *Ibid.*
93 *Alberni Pioneer News*, November 26, 1910.
94 Alberni Board of Trade minute book, November 6, 1911, ADHSA.
95 *Alberni Pioneer News*, October 14, 1911. All quotations in this section are from this source.
96 *Ibid.*, December 23, 1911.
97 *Ibid.*, December 23, 1911.
98 Alberni Board of Trade minute book, January 2, 1912.
99 George Nicholson article, *Colonist*, November 10, 1953.
100 Alberni Board of Trade minute book, January 2, 1912.
101 *Alberni Pioneer News*, January 6, 1912.
102 Pioneer Parade #32, Frank Bledsoe about his father.
103 Board of Trade minute book, March 25, 1912.
104 *Alberni Valley Times*, *20 Years Together*, anniversary booklet, 1987, p. 10.
105 Victoria *Colonist*, date unknown.
106 *Alberni Pioneer News*, March 25, 1912.
107 Pioneer Parade.
108 *Alberni Pioneer News*, January 6, 1912.
109 *Alberni Advocate*, April 5, 1912.
110 *Ibid.*, April 12, 1912.
111 *Port Alberni News*, May 29, 1912.
112 *Ibid.*, June 12, 1912.
113 Pioneer Parade #9.
114 *Ibid.*
115 *Port Alberni News*, July 24, 1912.
116 "Post planting stressed need for highway" undated newspaper clipping, ADHSA. All quotations in this section are from this source.
117 *Port Alberni News*, May 7, 1912.
118 *Ibid.*, May 11, 1912.
119 City of Port Alberni minute book, City of Port Alberni archives.
120 Alberni Board of Trade minute book, May 20, 1912.

121 *Ibid.*, June 3, 1912.
122 *Ibid.*, June 10, 1912.
123 *Alberni Advocate*, April 5, 1912.
124 *Ibid.*, April 5, 1912.
125 Alberni Board of Trade minute book, July 5, 1912.
126 *Alberni Advocate*, August 2, 1912.
127 *Ibid.*
128 *Ibid.*, August 16, 1912.
129 *Ibid.*, April 26, 1912.
130 *Ibid.*, June 14, 1912.
131 *Ibid.*, August 2, 1912. All quotations in this section are from this source.
132 *Alberni Advocate*, September 20, 1912.
133 *Ibid.*, January 17, 1913.
134 Minute book of the first Alberni Council, City of Port Alberni archives. January 20-April 5, 1913.
135 *Ibid.*

Chapter Four

1 *Alberni Advocate*, August 23, 1912.
2 *Port Alberni News*, October 19, 1912.
3 *Alberni Advocate*, August 20, 1912.
4 *Port Alberni News*, October 19, 1912.
5 *Ibid.*, December 25, 1912. The City of Port Alberni continues to lobby for a road linking the three communities of Cowichan to the south and Comox to the north through Port Alberni. The interior Island route has been named the Link Road.
6 Alberni Board of Trade minute book, August 5, 1912.
7 *Alberni Pioneer News*, February 18, 1911.
8 *Port Alberni News*, November 9, 1912.
9 *Ibid.*, September 18, 1912.
10 *Ibid.*, January 8, 1913.
11 *Ibid.*, February 12, 1913.
12 *Ibid.*, July 23, 1913.
13 *Ibid.*, July 30, 1913.
14 *Ibid.*, July 30, 1913.
15 *Alberni Advocate*, February 20, 1914.
16 *Ibid.*, March 13, 20, 1914.
17 Telephone History: B.C. Telephone Co., October 13, 1988.
18 *Telephone Talk*, "Cut-over at Alberni," B.C. Telephone Co., March 1913: October 13, 1988.
19 *Ibid.*
20 Telephone History: B.C. Telephone Co.
21 *Telephone Talk*, B.C. Telephone Co.
22 *Port Alberni News*, July 19, 1913.
23 Police Commission minute book, May 6, 1912, City hall archives.
24 *Ibid.*, May 9, 1913.
25 Dr. C. T. Hilton file, ADHSA.
26 Dr. Watson file, ADHSA.
27 Pioneer Parade #24.
28 *Ibid.*, #36.
29 Margaret Trebett, *Pioneer Women of the Alberni Valley*, "Kate Dickson."
30 *Alberni Pioneer News*, January 25, 1908.
31 *Ibid.*, February 27, 1909.
32 Alberni Board of Trade minute book, July 23, 1910.

33 *Alberni Pioneer News*, August 6, 1910.
34 Dr. Hilton file ADHSA.
35 *Alberni Advocate*, March 22, 1912.
36 *Ibid.*, August 30, 1912.
37 *Ibid.*, September 13, 1912.
38 *Port Alberni News*, October 16, 1912.
39 *Ibid.*, November 13, 1912.
40 *Alberni Advocate*, December 20, 1912.
41 *Ibid.*, May 9, 1913.
42 *Port Alberni News*, February 19, 1913.
43 *Alberni Advocate*, April 19, 1913.
44 *Port Alberni News*, October 15, 1913.
45 Women's Auxiliary to West Coast General Hospital minute book. File No. 23.1.1: Also West Coast General Hospital Auxiliary booklet, ADHSA.
46 Howitt file L.9.21, ADHSA.
47 Pioneer Parade, "Early Schools," September 22, 1946.
48 Howitt file L.9.21, ADHSA: *Vancouver Province* article August 30, 1935 by Mrs. J. L. Dunn. Also *West Coast Advocate*, June 28, 1934.
49 Pioneer Parade, "Early Schools," September 29, 1949.
50 *Alberni Advocate*, May 9, 1913.
51 *Port Alberni News*, February 5, 1913.
52 *Alberni Advocate*, July 4, 1913.
53 *Port Alberni News*, February 5, 1913.
54 *Ibid.*, October 29, 1913.
55 *Ibid.*, August 20, 1913.
56 *Ibid.*, June 13, 1914.
57 *Alberni Advocate*, February 6, 1914.
58 *Port Alberni News*, May 7, 1913.
59 Pioneer Parade #36.
60 *Port Alberni News*, April 3, 1912.
61 *Ibid.*, March 26, 1913. All quotations in this section come from this source.
62 *Ibid.*, March 29, 1913.
63 *Ibid.*, August 2, 1913.
64 *Ibid.*, February 28, 1914.
65 *Ibid.*, September 18, 1912.
66 *Ibid.*, June 11, 1913.
67 *Ibid.*, August 6, 1913.
68 *Alberni Advocate*, May 3, 1913.
69 *Port Alberni News*, December 25, 1913.
70 Harold E. Warren interview with author, September 25, 1989.
71 *Alberni Advocate*, November 28, 1913.
72 *Ibid.*, October 17, 1913.
73 *Ibid.*, December 26, 1913.
74 *Ibid.*, November 21, 1913; January 16, 1914.
75 Alberni Board of Trade minute book, February 2, 1914 .
76 *Alberni Advocate*, February 6, 1914.
77 *Ibid.*, March 13, 1914.
78 Alberni Board of Trade minute book, May 4, 1914.
79 *Port Alberni News*, May 23, 1914.
80 *Ibid.*
81 *Ibid.*
82 Margaret A. Ormsby, *British Columbia: A History*, p. 370.
83 *Alberni Pioneer News*, September 3, 1910.
84 G. W. Taylor, *Timber, History of the Forest Industry in B.C.*, J. J. Douglas Ltd., Vancouver, 1975, p. 93.

85 *Alberni Pioneer News*, September 3, 1910.
86 *Ibid.*, June 3, 1911.
87 *Western Lumberman*, Vancouver, 1912, p. 70. Alberni Valley Museum reference library.
88 *Port Alberni News*, July 5, 1913.
89 *Western Lumberman*, 1912, p. 38.
90 Forest Industry file, Alberni Valley Museum.
91 *Port Alberni News*, December 20, 1913.
92 *Alberni Advocate*, October 17, 1913.
93 Barry Miller, booklet *2-Spot Steam Ride*, 1986.
94 Donald MacKay, *Empire of Wood*, p. 194.
95 *Port Alberni News*, April 15, 1914.
96 *Ibid.*, April 18, 1914.
97 *Port Alberni News*, August 8, September 2, October 28, 1914.
98 *Ibid.*, May 9, 1914.
99 Alberni Board of Trade minute book, June 5, 1914. ADHSA.
100 Royal Commission on Indian Affairs hearings transcript, May 11, 1914, courtesy Nuu-chah-nulth Tribal Council, Port Alberni. All quotations in this section are from this source.
101 Royal Commission on Indian Affairs, *Indian Reserves in British Columbia, 1916-Summary*, p. 851. Alberni Valley Museum, also BCARS.
102 Box A, File No. 15 D, Royal Commission on Indian Affairs 1916, Alberni Valley Museum.
103 *Alberni Advocate*, August 7, 1914.
104 Leslie F. Hannon, *Canada at War – A record of a fighting people*. The Canadian Illustrated Library, McClelland and Stewart Limited, 1968, p. 30.
105 *Port Alberni News*, August 5, 1914.
106 *Ibid.*, August 5, 1914. *Alberni Advocate*, August 7, 1914.
107 *Alberni Advocate*, August 7, 1914.
108 *Ibid.*, August 14, 1914.
109 *Port Alberni News*, July 8, August 26, August 29, September 2, September 9, 1914.
110 *Ibid.*, November 18, 1914.
111 *Ibid.*
112 *Ibid.*, February 10, February 17, 1915.
113 *Ibid.*, November 25, 1914, September 2, 1914.
114 *Ibid.*, Dec. 23, 1914.
115 *Ibid.*, February 10, 1915.
116 *Alberni Advocate*, April 23, 1915.
117 *Ibid.*, April 9, 1915.
118 *Port Alberni News*, May 26, 1915.
119 *Alberni Adovcate*, May 21, 1915.
120 *Port Alberni News*, April 21, 1915.
121 *Ibid.*, July 28, 1915.
122 Ingrid E. Lave, *Gustav Konstantin Alvo van Alvensleben, The Pioneering Prussian in British Columbia*, German-Canadian Historical Association Inc. and Historical Society of Mecklenburg Upper Canada Inc. 1977 IEL.
123 Taylor. See *Timber*, p. 95.
124 Edward Buxton journal, Alberni Valley Museum. All quotations in this section are from this source.
125 *Port Alberni News*, June 9, 1915.
126 Mary Louise Stacey, "Who was Alvo von Alvensleben," Unpublished manuscript, 1988. BCARS, Add-mss.255, p. 9.
127 *Ibid.*, p. 14, 15.
128 *Port Alberni News*, June 23, 1915.
129 *Ibid.*, June 9, 1915.

130 *Ibid.*, July 7, 1915.
131 Margaret Trebett, article, *Alberni Valley Times*, June 23, 1971: Ruth Roberts, article, *Alberni Valley Times*, April 26, 1974.
132 *Alberni Advocate*, September 3, 1915. All quotations on this incident are from this source.
133 *Ibid.*, September 17, 1915.
134 *Port Alberni News*, November 24, 1915.
135 *Alberni Advocate*, October 8, 1915.
136 See Ormsby, p. 385.
137 *Port Alberni News*, September 1, September 8, 1915.
138 See Ormsby, p. 387.
139 *Port Alberni News*, February 18, 1916.
140 *Ibid.*, June 14, 1916.
141 *Ibid.*, July 12, 1916.
142 *Ibid.*, August 2, 1916.
143 *Ibid.*
144 *Ibid.*, August 16, 1916.
145 *Electoral History of B.C. 1871-1986*, published by Legislative Library, 1988.
146 S. W. Jackman, *Portraits of a Premier*, File 47.28, ADHSA.
147 *Port Alberni News*, February 7, 1917.
148 *Ibid.*, January 17, 1917.
149 *Ibid.*, January 23, 1918. Quotations in next three paragraphs are from this source.
150 *Ibid.*, January 9, 1918, January 23, 1918, January 30, 1918.
151 See Ormsby, p. 395.
152 See *Electoral History*, p. 415.
153 See Ormsby, p. 396.
154 *Alberni Pioneer News*, May 13, 1911.
155 *Port Alberni News*, August 29, 1917.
156 Canneries #17: Interview with Samson Robinson, Kildonan, by Natalie MacFarland, 1981: Alberni Valley Museum.
157 *Ibid.*, MacFarland interview with Pete Gregory & Stan Littleton, June 3, 1981.
158 Margaret McRae file 50.21, ADHSA.
159 MacFarland interview with Gregory and Littleton, June 3, 1981.
160 Canneries #17: Interview July 27, 1981: Alberni Valley Museum.
161 *Port Alberni News*, November 2, 1912.
162 Harold E. Warren interview with author, September 1989.
163 *Port Alberni News*, May 31, 1916.

Chapter Five

1 *Port Alberni News*, November 10, 1915. Statistics from Roll of Honour.
2 *Ibid.*, December 6, 1916.
3 *Ibid.*, August 1, 1917.
4 *Ibid.*, October 24, 1917.
5 *Alberni Advocate*, April 16, 1915.
6 *Ibid.*, October 1915.
7 *Port Alberni News*, November 8, 1916.
8 *Ibid.*, March 7, 1917.
9 *Ibid.*, February 18, 1916.
10 Taylor. See *Timber*, p. 105.
11 *Port Alberni News* November 1, 1916.
12 *Ibid.*, October 18, 1916.
13 *Ibid.*, May 24, 1916.
14 *Ibid.*, May 16, 1917.

[15] *Ibid.*, July 4, 1917.
[16] *Ibid.*, August 29, 1917.
[17] *Ibid.*, November 10, 1915.
[18] *Ibid.*, November 17, 1915.
[19] *Ibid.*, January 21, 1916.
[20] *Ibid.*
[21] *Ibid.*, February 4, 1916.
[22] *Ibid.*, February 11, 1916.
[23] Hines, p. 49.
[24] *Port Alberni News*, March 19, 1916.
[25] *Ibid.*, March 3, 1916.
[26] Hines, p. 48.
[27] *Port Alberni News*, Feb. 25, March 3, March 10, 1916.
[28] Two Spot history file, Alberni Valley Museum.
[29] Fay Flitton (nee Massey) interview with author, January 28, 1989.
[30] *Port Alberni News*, October 4, 1916.
[31] *Ibid.*, October 4, 1916.
[32] *Ibid.*, November 15, 1916.
[33] *Western Lumberman*, Dec. 1916, p. 26. "Logging and sawmilling in the Alberni Valley 1908-1928," compiled by Darryl Muralt of the B.C. Railway Historical Society, 1984.
[34] Port Alberni's Industrial Waterfront Heritage survey, 1984, Alberni Valley Museum.
[35] *Port Alberni News*, December 6, 1916.
[36] *Western Lumberman*, July 1917, p. 28. Alberni Valley Museum.
[37] *Port Alberni News*, February 26, 1919.
[38] *Ibid.*, May 2, 1917.
[39] *Ibid.*, July 11, 1917.
[40] *Western Lumberman*, January 1918, p. 32. Alberni Valley Museum.
[41] *Port Alberni News*, June 6, 1917.
[42] *Ibid.*, July 13, 1921. *Western Lumberman*, August 1921, p. 58.
[43] *Ibid.*, August 13, 1920.
[44] *Ibid.*, June 1918, p. 32.
[45] *Western Lumberman*, October 1918, p. 66.
[46] *Port Alberni News*, October 15, 1919.
[47] *Western Lumberman*, May 1921, p. 30.
[48] Family history courtesy of Peggy Sidey, Tigard, Oregon, USA, daughter of Sam Hoard.
[49] *Ibid.*, A social studies report "Bainbridge" by Mary Wilkie, Division 12, Port Alberni High School.
[50] Kaye Dukowski, article "Bainbridge Mill cut giant timbers," *the Islander*, May 14, 1981.
[51] Denis O'Brien, article "Bainbridge history recalled," *Twin Cities Times*, April 13, 1966. ADHSA.
[52] *Ibid.*
[53] *Ibid.*
[54] Gilbert Renwick, interview with author June 6, 1989.
[55] Bainbridge School file, ADHSA.
[56] *Port Alberni News*, October 27, 1920.
[57] Bainbridge Mill newspaper clipping file ADHSA.
[58] *Western Lumberman*, 1922, p. 40.
[59] Peggy Sidey.
[60] *Port Alberni News*, June 4, 1919.
[61] *Western Lumberman*, December 1919, p. 41.
[62] Donald MacKay, *Empire of Wood*, p. 75.
[63] *Port Alberni News*, April 12, 1916.

64 *Ibid.*, May 9, 1917.
65 *Ibid.*, August 23, 1916.
66 *Ibid.*, September 27, 1916. October 11, 1916.
67 *Ibid.*, January 31, 1917.
68 Cyril Edel Leonoff, *Pioneers, Pedlars & Prayer Shawls, The Jewish Communities in B.C. and the Yukon*, Sono Nis Press, Victoria, B.C., 1978, p. 206. File L.9.13 ADHSA.
69 *Port Alberni News*, February 24, 1915.
70 *Ibid.*, October 19, 1917.
71 *Ibid.*, May 23, 1917.
72 *Ibid.*, May 23, 1917.
73 *Ibid.*, June 6, 1917, July 11, 1917.
74 *Ibid.*, October 27, 1920.
75 Craig Brown, *Illustrated History of Canada*, p. 414, p. 415.
76 *Western Lumberman*, Oct. 1918, p. 58. Alberni Valley Museum.
77 National Archives of Canada: RG 6 E, vol. 492, file 103, part 4a, microfilm reel T-13.
78 *Ibid.*
79 *Encyclopaedia Britannica*, Vol. V111, p. 724.
80 National Archives of Canada: RG 6, vol. 556, file 206-W-1, Pro-German writings 1910-1918, microfilm reel T-58.
81 National Archives of Canada: RG 6, vol. 553, file 206-077-1, Pro-German Writings, 1916, "The Melting Pot," Microfilm T-55.
82 *Port Alberni News*, April 2, 1919.
83 *Ibid.*
84 City of Port Alberni Police Commission minute book, City of Port Alberni archives.
85 *Port Alberni News*, April 28, 1926.
86 *Ibid.*, February 13, 1918.
87 *Ibid.*, May 15, 1918.
88 *Ibid.*, August 21, 1918.
89 *Ibid.*, October 16, 1918.
90 *Ibid.*
91 *Ibid.*, October 16, October 23, October 30, 1918.
92 *Ibid.*, October 16, 1918.
93 *Ibid.*, November 13, 1918.
94 *Ibid.*, November 27, 1918.
95 *Ibid.*, December 18, 1918.
96 Dorrit MacLeod interview.
97 *Port Alberni News*, November 13, 1918.
98 Leslie F. Hannon, *Canada at War–A Record of a Fighting People*, p. 70.
99 *Port Alberni News*, November 20, 1918.
100 *Ibid.*, November 20, 1918.
101 *Ibid.*, December 11, 1918.
102 *Ibid.*, January 15, 1919. January 23, 1919.
103 *Ibid.*, January 23, 1919.
104 Port Alberni Board of Police Commission minute book, City Hall archives, February 11, March 19, March 31, 1919.
105 *Port Alberni News*, May 14, 1919.
106 *Ibid.*, June 6, 1921.
107 *Ibid.*, February 19, 1919. All quotations in this section are from this source.
108 *Ibid.*, February 12, 1919.
109 Department of Fisheries annual report for 1919, Alberni Valley Museum.
110 *Port Alberni News*, February 26, 1919.
111 Annual report of Chief Inspector of Fisheries 1919, Box H, Alberni Valley Museum.

112 Report of Western Fisheries Division B.C. for 1920 by Chief Inspector Lieut. Col. F. H. Cunningham, Box H, Alberni Valley Museum.
113 *Port Alberni News*, June 11, 1919.
114 *Ibid.*, May 19, 1920.
115 Joseph E. Forester and Anne D. Forester, *B.C.'s Commercial Fishing History*, Hancock House Publishers Ltd., 1975, p. 156-159.
116 Interview with Mary Wood, daughter of Fisheries officer James Wood, October 1989.
117 Fisheries research Box A "Canneries" file. Alberni Valley Museum.
118 *Port Alberni News*, May 19, 1920.
119 *Ibid.*, May 26, 1920.
120 *Ibid.*, August 17, 1921.
121 *Ibid.*
122 *Ibid.*, October 19, 1921.
123 *Ibid.*, November 9, 1921.
124 *Ibid.*, February 19, 1919. Burde's maiden speech in the House.
125 *Ibid.*
126 *Ibid.*
127 *Ibid.*, June 11, 1919.
128 Board of Police Commission minute book, Port Alberni City Hall archives.
129 *Port Alberni News*, June 25, 1919.
130 *Ibid.*, July 16, July 23, 1919.
131 *Ibid.*, November 26, 1919.
132 *Ibid.*, December 10, 1919.
133 *Ibid.*, December 18, 1919.
134 *Ibid.*, December 3, 1919.
135 *Ibid.*, May 12, 1920.
136 *Ibid.*, June 9, 1920.
137 *Ibid.*, June 23, June 30, 1920.
138 See *Electoral History of B.C.* p. 417.
139 *Port Alberni News*, July 20, 1921.
140 *Ibid.*, July 23, 1919.
141 *Ibid.*, September 17, 1919.
142 *Ibid.*, June 2, 1920.
143 Royal Bank of Canada archives, Montreal: Kathy Minorgan archivist.
144 City of Alberni minute book 1919, City of Port Alberni archives.
145 *Port Alberni News*, November 19, 1919.
146 *Ibid.*, January 14, 1919.
147 *Ibid.*, May 11, 1921.
148 City of Alberni council minute book, City of Port Alberni archives.
149 *Port Alberni News*, October 26, 1921.
150 *Ibid.*, November 2, 1921.
151 City of Alberni minute book, City of Port Alberni archives.
152 *Ibid.*, November 28, November 30, November 31, 1921.
153 *Ibid.*, January 22, January 30, 1922.
154 *Port Alberni News*, January 18, January 25, March 8, 1922.
155 *Ibid.*, May 31, 1922.

APPENDIX ONE

Government Agents serving the Alberni District 1889-1922

1889-1891: John C. Mollet

1892-1894: George Archibald Smith

No listing for years 1895-1896

1897-1901: Thomas Fletcher

1902-1906: Andrew Lindsay Smith

1907-1913: Herbert Charles Rayson

1914-1916: John Kirkup

1917:   J. E. Hoosan

1918:   J. E. Hoosan and Arthur G. Freeze

1919-1922: Arthur G. Freeze

City Councillors serving Alberni from 1913-1922

1913 – Mayor C. Frederic Bishop
Aldermen: George Forrest, Alan W. Neill, John Grieve, Frank Gibson, James Hills, George A. Spencer

1914 – Mayor George Albert Huff
Aldermen: W. F. Gibson, John Best, James Hill, Clifford M. Pineo, Henry Blakemore, C. T. Harvey

1915 – No election held: All elected by acclamation

1916 – Mayor Alan W. Neill
Aldermen: Henry Blakemore, George A. Spencer, John Best, James Hills, C. T. Harvey

1917 – Mayor Henry Hills
Aldermen: George A. Spencer, Sid H. Toy, Henry Blakemore, H. B. Currie, John Best, C. T. Harvey

1918 – Mayor Henry Hills
Aldermen: George A. Spencer, John Best, Henry Blakemore, C. T. Harvey, Sid Toy, H. B. Currie

1919 – Mayor George Albert Huff
Aldermen: Mrs. T. Paterson, Mrs. J. A. Croll, Harold Bishop, James Hills, A. H. M. Lord, H. B. Currie

1920 – Mayor George Albert Huff
Aldermen: H. B. Currie, Mrs. A. G. Croll, C. T. Harvey, Miss L. A. Marcon, Harold Bishop, Allan Paul

1921 – Mayor George Albert Huff
Aldermen: G. M. Cathcart, Harold Bishop, Sid H. Toy, E. E. Frost, Mrs. J. A. Croll, Miss L. A. Marcon

1922 – Mayor James R. Motion
Aldermen: George Forrest, E. M. Whyte, L. A. Hanna, Albert J. Pineo, H. B. Currie, Charles Taylor Jr.

APPENDIX THREE

City Councillors serving Port Alberni from 1912-1922

1912 – Mayor Arthur Edward Waterhouse
Aldermen: George H. Bird, Frank H. Swayne,
Alexander D. MacIntyre, Joseph A. MacIntyre, Robert M. Ellis,
Alexander D. Cooper

1913 – Mayor Richard Burde
Aldermen: Arthur E. Waterhouse, Alexander D. MacIntyre,
Robert H. Wood, Dr. Caleb T. Hilton, E. Burdett Garrard,
Joseph A. MacIntyre

1914 – Mayor Richard Burde
Aldermen: Antony Watson, Alexander D. MacIntyre,
Robert H. Wood, W. L. Harris, Joseph A. MacIntyre, G. W. Falkner

1915 – Mayor Richard Burde
Aldermen: Edward Exton, Antony Watson,
Archibald Campbell Macfie, R. M. Ellis, W. S. Barton, Robert H. Wood

1916 – Mayor Robert H. Wood
Aldermen: Edward Exton, Antony Watson,
Archibald Campbell Macfie, David Wallace Warnock

1917 – Mayor Alexander D. MacIntyre
Aldermen: Edward Exton, Archibald Macfie, Antony Watson,
Isaac M. Lederman, G. H. Procter, Charles Stewart

1918 – Mayor Alexander D. MacIntyre
Aldermen: Edward Exton, Isaac M. Lederman, Antony Watson,
George Stawell Pearse, Alexander B. Wood, George H. Procter

1919 – Mayor Edward Exton
Aldermen: Mrs. J. L. Hill, Antony Watson, George S. Pearse,
Alexander B. Wood, B. I. Hart, Mrs. Roy Hanna

1920 – Mayor Edward Exton
Aldermen: David Warnock, F. H. Steede, C. Fawcitt, George S. Pearse,
W. Manning, B. I. Hart

1921 – Mayor Alexander D. MacIntyre
Aldermen: George S. Pearse, F. H. Steede, Charles Fawcitt,
Alexander B. Wood, Walter Harris, A. I. Bind

1922 – Mayor Alexander D. MacIntyre
Aldermen: Charles A. McNaughton, Arthur E. Waterhouse,
J. Z. Blower, Archibald Macfie, F. H. Steede, Alexander B. Wood

APPENDIX FOUR

Members who served in the Provincial Legislature 1894-1922

1894	Theodore Davie
1895	George Albert Huff (by-election)
1898	Alan Webster Neill
1900	Alan Webster Neill
1903	William Wallace Burns McInnes
1905	William Manson
1907	Harlan Carey Brewster
1912	John George Corry Wood
1916	Harlan Carey Brewster
1918	Richard Pateman Wallis (by-election)
1918	Richard John Burde (by-election)
1920	Richard John Burde

Members who served in the Federal Parliament 1886-1922

1886   William Wallace Burns McInnes

1900   Ralph Smith

1904   William Sloan

1908   William Sloan

1909   William Templeton (by-election)

1911   Herbert S. Clements

1917   Herbert S. Clements

1921   Alan Webster Neill

Bibliography

Books

Alberni District Historical Society. *Place Names of the Alberni Valley*, (1978) 1988.

Alberni Valley Times booklet. *Twenty Years Together*, 1987.

Arima, E. Y. *The West Coast (Nootka) People*, British Columbia Provincial Museum, 1983.

Bird, George. *Tse-wees-tah, One Man in a Boat*, published by the Alberni District Historical Society, (1971) 1972.

Bossin, Bod. *Settling Clayoquot*, Sound Heritage Series No. 33. 1907.

Bowen, Lynne. *Three Dollar Dreams*, Oolichan Books, Lantzville, B.C., 1987.

Brown, Craig. *Illustrated History of Canada*, Lester & Orpen Dennys Limited, Toronto, Ontario, 1987.

Carmichael, Alfred. *Indian Legends of Vancouver Island*, Musson Book Co. Ltd., Toronto, Ontario, 1922.

Crown Lands. *A history of Survey Systems*, booklet, Ministry of Lands, Parks & Housing, Province of British Columbia, 1981.

Dobie, Edith. "Party History in B.C. 1903-1933," essay from *Historical Essays on B.C.*, edited by J. Friesan & H. K. Ralston, McClelland and Stewart Limited, 1976.

Drucker, Phillip. *The Central and Northern Nootkan Tribes*, Smithsonian Institution, Bureau of American Ethnology, Bulletin 144, Government Printing Office, Washington, 1951.

Dunn, Reverend A. *Presbyterianism in B.C. in the Early Days*, Columbian Company Ltd., New Westminster, B.C., 1905.

Electoral History of B.C. 1871-1986, published by the Legislative Library, 1988.

Encyclopaedia Britannica, Vol VIII, 15th edition, 1974.

Fisher, Robin. "Joseph Trutch and Indian Land Policy," essay from *Historical Essays on B.C.* See Dobie 1976.

Forester, Joseph E. and Anne D. *B.C.'s Commercial Fishing History*, Hancock House Publishers Ltd, 1975.

Garner, Joe. *Never Chop Your Rope*, Cinnibar Press, Nanaimo, 1988.

Graham, Donald. *Keepers of the Light*, Harbour Publishing Ltd., 1985.

Green, Ruth. *Personality Ships of British Columbia*, Marine Tapestry Publication Ltd., West Vancouver, B.C., 1969.

Hannon, Leslie F. *Canada at War – A record of a fighting people. The Canadian Illustrated Library*, McClelland and Stewart Limited, 1968.

Hayman, John. *Robert Brown and the Vancouver Island Exploring Expedition*, U.B.C. Press, 1989.

Hines, Ben. *Pick, Pan & Pack, A history of mining in the Alberni Mining Division*. Booklet by Local initiatives program, Alberni Valley Museum, 1976.

Hayman, John. *Robert Brown and the Vancouver Island Exploring Expedition*, U.B.C. Press, 1989.

Howay, F. W. Essay, "The Settlement and Progress of B.C. 1871-1914" from *Historical Essays on British Columbia*. See Dobie 1976.

Hull, Raymond, Gordon Soules, Christine Soules. *Vancouver Past*," Gordon Soules Economic and Marketing Research, Vancouver, B.C., 1974.

Jackman, S. W. *Portraits of the Premiers*, Gray's Publishing Ltd, Sidney, B.C., 1969.

Leonoff, Cyril Edel. *Pioneers, Pedlars & Prayer Shawls, The Jewish Communities in British Columbia and the Yukon*, Sono Nis Press, Victoria, B.C., 1978.

Kirk, Ruth. *Wisdom of the Elders*, Douglas and McIntyre, Vancouver, B.C., 1988.

Lamb, W. Kaye. *Early Lumbering on Vancouver Island*, B.C. Historical Quarterly, Vol 2, 1938.

Lave, Ingrid E. *Gustav Konstantin Alvo von Alvensleben, The Pioneering Prussian in British Columbia*, German-Canadian

Historical Association Inc. and Historical Society of Mecklenburg Upper Canada Inc., 1977 IEL.

Lewis-Harrison, June. *The People of Gabriola*, Printed by D. W. Friesen & Sons Ltd., Cloverdale, B.C., 1982.

Lipton, Charles. *The Trade Union Movement of Canada 1827-1959*, NC Press Ltd., 1978.

Lyons, Cicely. *Salmon: Our Heritage*, B.C. Packers Limited, Mitchell Press, Vancouver, B.C., 1969.

Lyons, C. P. *Milestones on Vancouver Island*, The Evergreen Press Limited, 1958.

MacKay, Donald. *Empire of Wood*, Douglas & McIntyre, Vancouver, 1982.

McMillan, Alan D. and Denis E. St. Claire. *Alberni Prehistory*, Theytus Books, Penticton, for Alberni Valley Museum, 1982.

Mayne, Richard. *Four Years in British Columbia and Vancouver Island*, John Murray, Albemarle Street, London, England, 1862.

Moser, Chas. *Reminiscences of the West Coast of Vancouver Island*, Acme Press Limited, Victoria, B.C., 1926.

Bergren, Myrtle. *Tough Timber*, Progress Books, Toronto, Ontario, 1966.

Newman, Peter C. *Caesars of the Wilderness*, Viking Press, 1987.

Nicholson, George. *Vancouver Island's West Coast*, Morriss Printing Co. Ltd., 1962.

Olsen, W. H. *Water Over the Wheel*, published by Karl Schutz on behalf of Chemainus-Crofton and District Chamber of Commerce, 1981.

Ormsby, Margaret. *British Columbia: A History*, Macmillan of Canada, Vancouver, B.C., 1958.

Pethick, Derek. *The Nootka Connection*, Douglas & McIntyre, Vancouver, B.C., 1980.

———. *First Approaches to the Northwest Coast*, Douglas & McIntyre, Vancouver, B.C., 1976.

Scott, R. Bruce. *Breakers Ahead*, Review Publishing House, Sidney, B.C., 1970.

———. *Barkley Sound, A History of the Pacific Rim National Park Area*, Sono Nis Press, Victoria, B.C., 1972.

Sproat, Gilbert Malcolm, journal 1868. *Scenes and Studies of Savage Life*, published in England by Smith, Elder and Co.

Stacey, Duncan A. *Sockeye & Tinplate: Technological Change in the Fraser River Canning Industry 1871-1912*, British Columbia Provincial Museum, Victoria, B.C., 1982.

Taylor, G. W. *Timber. History of the Forest Industry in B.C.*, J. J. Douglas Ltd., Vancouver, B.C., 1975.

Trebett, Margaret. Booklet, *Pioneer Women of the Alberni Valley*, Alberni District Museum and Historical Society, 1967.

Young, Charles H. and Helen R. Y. Reid. *The Japanese Canadians*, University of Toronto Press, 1938.

Newspapers and Magazines
Alberni Advocate
Alberni Pioneer News
Alberni Valley Times
British Columbia Historical Quarterly
Daily Colonist, British Colonist, Times Colonist
Daily Columbian, New Westminister
Journades D'Estudois Catalano Americans, Barcelona
Nanaimo Daily Free Press
Port Alberni News
Seattle Times
Telephone Talk
Twin Cities Times
The Province, Vancouver
West Coast Advocate
Western Lumberman

Diaries, Journals, Letters, Notes, Lectures
Banfield letters 1860.
Brabant, Father. Journal.
Buxton, Edward T. Journal.

Carmichael, Alfred. Notes and manuscripts.

Cox, Ed. Papers.

Erickson, William. Notes.

Guillod, Harry. Reports from 1881-1903.

Roff, William. Lectures.

Stirling, Walter. Letters.

Thompson, W. Arthur. Diary.

Wells, Stephen. Diary.

Theses and Manuscripts

Frketich, Sam. "The Dash of Bitter in the Cocktail of Canadian Politics," student essay.

Ford, Helen. *Sproat Lake*, unpublished manuscript.

Miller, Barry. Booklets *The E&N Railway*, 1986; *2-Spot Steam Ride*, 1986.

Stacey, Mary Louise. *Who was Alvo von Alvensleben*, unpublished manuscript, 1988, BCARS, Add-mss.255.

Government Records

Alberni District Official Bulletin No. 24, published by Legislative Assembly 1908.

British Columbia Directory 1893.

INDEX

339

340

342

De Beaux, Bobby, 91, 186, 232, 233,
  289, 290
  exploits, 131-32
  store, 131-32
DeFeaux, A. R., 169
Della Falls, 54, 166
Dent Lumber & Shingle Co., 263, 266,
  269
Dent, Howard A., 263, 265, 266, 268,
  269
dentistry, 99, 160
Derby, Bill, 92
Dick, John, 169
Dinsdale, E., 276
Dominion Government Building, 214-15
Douglas, Sir James, 17-18, 20, 24, 26,
  39-41
Drinkwater family, 53
  Alfred, 89, 167, 169, 170, 220
  Frederick, 54, 167, 170
  George, 54, 89, 112, 168
  Hilton, 140
  Jack, 112
  James, 168
  Joseph, 54, 140, 169, 215
  Susan (Mrs. Andrew Morran), 53
Drinkwater, Della (wife of Joe), 54
Drinkwater, Issac, 53
Duke of York mine, 93, 104, 105, 115,
  140
Dunbar, James, 79-79
Duncan, 201, 218, 294
Dunn, Reverend Alex., 59, 98
Dunsmuir, James, 68, 126, 141
Dunsmuir, Robert, 18, 68, 105, 107, 141
Earle & Magneson, 136
East Indians, 270, 297
  Sikhs, 221-23
Eberts Royal Commission of Inquiry,
  293, 294
Ecoole, 253, 295
Edwards, John Richard, 204, 290, 303
Effingham Island, 36, 96, 133
Electricity, 160-61, 167, 177, 201, 202,
  203, 220
Ellis, Robert McGinley, 187, 261
Emory, D., 120
Erickson William (Bill or Willie), 95,
  167-69
Erickson, Agnes, 82, 88, 89, 95, 167
Esquimalt & Nanaimo Railway (E & N),
  47, 83, 117, 119, 141-46, 153, 159,
  164, 174-75, 179, 193, 196, 200,
  212, 168-70
  break-up dinner 180
  first train 182-84
  land grant, 68
  rail service, 179

See also CPR
Eussen, Father, 43-44, 46
Exemption tribunals, 278-79
Explorers
  Brown, 26-27
  Horne, 20-24
  Mayne, 24-46
  Pemberton, 24
  Richards, 24
  Spanish on west coast, 12-17
Exton, Edward, 245, 261, 276, 289
Faber, Alfred Dennis, 76, 82
Falwell, Ed, 59
Farmer's Institute, 102, 146
Fearman, F. W., 267
Fell, Thornton, 195, 196, 197
Finlayson, Roderick, 20, 22
Fires, 105, 190, 243
  Alberni Residential School, 277-78
  Anderson mill, 35
  Gilroy McKay mill, 267-68
  Wiest logging camp, 264-65
Fish House Point, 47, 136
Fisher, John, 57
Fishing, 11, 36, 51, 66, 120, 132-33,
  136, 139, 214, 310-11
  canneries, 252-55
  guardians, 135
  inquiry, 291-96
  Native concerns, 226-29
  weirs, 133
  whaling, 127
Fitzgerald, Harry, 90, 91, 92, 127, 168
Fleming, Tom, 78
Fletcher, E. H., 88, 90
Fletcher, P., 183
Fletcher, Tom, 59, 66, 69, 107
Florence Group mines, 104
Foote, Captain, 127
Forestry, 262-75
  Bainbridge, 269-74
  conditions, 270, 271
  logging camps, 266, 268
Forfarshire Mines Company, 104
Forrest, George, 54, 61, 63, 129, 130,
  132, 158, 198, 199, 214, 220, 308
Foster, W. W., 191
Fowlie, Hugh, 250
Fox, Captain T. L., 127, 130, 161
Fox, J., 169
Foy, Elsworth, 213
Frank, Bernard, 104, 220, 232, 241, 262
Frank, Leonard, 100, 232
  accusations, 241, 242
  assault trial, 244, 245
  arrest, 276, 277
  Board of Trade, 154, 177, 184, 221
  mining, 104, 262

347

350

351